JAPAN'S QUEST FOR AUTONOMY

JAPAN'S QUEST FOR AUTONOMY

*National Security and
Foreign Policy*

1930-1938

BY JAMES B. CROWLEY

PRINCETON, NEW JERSEY
PRINCETON UNIVERSITY PRESS
1966

TO JOAN

Acknowledgments

READERS in modern Japanese history undoubtedly understand the pitfalls and limitations that distinguish American analyses of Japan's diplomacy. Still, it may not be amiss to mention a few circumstances that have conditioned this presentation. Research on things Japanese imposes formidable linguistic problems; the amount of publicly available primary source material on the 1930's has been limited, and monographic studies of the period are few. However stimulating these types of research challenges may seem, they remain serious impediments to an Occidental historian. Perhaps the only way to offset them, at least partially, is by liberal allocations of research time, an activity admittedly contingent on liberal research grants. In this regard, I have been fortunate indeed.

My major linguistic training and the completion of a doctoral research program in Japan were subsidized by a three-year Foreign Area Training Fellowship from the Ford Foundation. My research in the Department of State archives on documents pertaining to the London Naval Conference, as well as the indexing and typing of the manuscript, was underwritten by two awards from the Stimson Fund of Yale University. The final draft of the book was written at Stanford University during a summer research grant from the Hoover Institute. Without this sustained financial assistance, it would have been impossible to prepare this appraisal of Japanese foreign policy.

Complementing this financial base, many individuals extended countless forms of assistance. To cite only the most obvious examples: General Hayashi Keizo, the former chairman of the Joint Chiefs of Staff, Japan's Self-Defense Forces, opened the door to several interviews with former army officers; Mr. Aritake Shuji, a distinguished political commentator for the *Sankei jiji* newspaper, arranged a series of interviews with former naval officers; Colonel Nishiura Susumu, head of the Historical Section of Japan's Self-Defense Agency, graciously offered a wealth of information on the prewar policies and personnel of the war ministry, plus the use of his office for interview purposes; and Admiral Tomioka Sadatoshi granted access to the records of the naval general staff compiled at the *Shiryō chōsakai,* as well as sharing his personal reflections on naval affairs. Through the good offices of these men, interviews were arranged with Admirals Fukudome Shigeru, Hasegawa Kiyoshi, Hōri Teikichi, and Takagi Sōkichi; Generals Hashimoto Gun, Imai Takeo, Imamura Hitoshi, Inada Seijun, Katakura Chū, Satō Kenryō, and Watchi Takagi; the Honorables Arita Hachirō, Hidaka Shinroku, and Kamimura Shinichi; and Fujinuma Shōhei, chief secretary for the Hirota cabinet. Since I have tried throughout the book to indicate individual obligations, here a simple affirmation is appropriate. These men answered all questions without evasion, and they furnished a background of information which proved essential to an informed reading of the documentary sources.

The contribution of these former officers and officials were supplemented by the suggestions and observations of Professors Ueda Toshio and Eto Shinkichi of Tokyo University and Professors Hosoya Chihiro of Hitotsubashi University. Mr. Hata Ikuhito shared with me his extensive notes, which were based upon interviews with General Araki Sadao, Ikeda Junkyū, Kawabe Torashirō, and Tanaka Shinichi. Without in any degree minimizing the help of these scholars, I remain most deeply obligated to Mr. Kurihara Ken, former chief of the archival division of Japan's Ministry for Foreign Affairs. Mr. Kurihara not only spent several hours each week over a nine-month period answering inquiries about the substance of these archival materials, but became my guide to the voluminous secondary publications on Shōwa Japan. In addition, I wish to express my special appreciation to Professor Kaji Shinzō of Tokyo University and to Mr. Kaji Ryūichi of the newspaper *Asahi* for their vital assistance in launching my research program in Japan.

I am grateful to the Librarian of Sterling Memorial Library,

Acknowledgments

Yale University, and to the Trustees of the Stimson Collection, for permission to quote from the papers and diary of the Honorable Henry L. Stimson. I am also indebted to the Editor, *The Journal of Asian Studies*, for permission to include material originally presented in my articles "Japanese Army Factionalism in the Early 1930's," XXI (May 1962), 309-326; and "A Reconsideration of the Marco Polo Bridge Incident," XXII (May 1963), 277-291. My work in the Department of State archives was enhanced immeasurably by the courtesy and cooperation of Dr. E. Taylor Parks and the staff of the Historical Office of the Department of State.

This study is an elaboration of a doctoral thesis originally written under the supervision of Professor John Whitney Hall. As a *sensei*, friend, and most recently as a senior colleague, he has nurtured my research in so many ways that it is difficult to express my gratitude directly, save to record my constant awareness of and appreciation for his encouragement and stimulation.

If commonplace, it is no less sincere or proper to state that the foregoing individuals and institutions deserve most of the credit for the preparation of this study. Naturally, they share no responsibility for my interpretations. The dedication is an inadequate symbol of esteem and affection for my wife who, despite a nomadic existence, the demands of our children, and the slights of her husband, still retains her gentle sense of humor and charming candor about my notions of Shōwa Japan.

Contents

Preface

BEFORE the stunning military and naval defeats of the Pacific War and the fateful flight of the *Enola Gay*, the history of modern Japan had seemed to confirm the virtues of a nation which, as the Meiji Constitution declared, had been "ruled over and governed by a line of Emperors unbroken for ages eternal." At least, the history of Japan in the nineteenth and twentieth centuries was distinguished by a remarkable series of political, diplomatic, and military achievements. In 1853, when Perry's Black Ships shattered the "closed door" policy of the Tokugawa government, Japan was militarily defenseless and politically fragmented. Yet, by 1890, the Meiji oligarchy had forged a unified national state and the nucleus for a professional army and navy; by 1910, Japan had acquired an extensive empire which embraced Southern Sakhalin, Korea, Taiwan, the Pescadores and Ryūkū Islands, as well as special treaty rights in Manchuria and the treaty ports along the coast of China; and, in the aftermath of the First World War, Japan's preeminent position in East Asia was recognized and confirmed by the Occidental powers at the 1922 Washington Conference. Eleven years later, though, Japan had organized the state of Manchukuo and bolted the League of Nations; by 1938, her national aspirations centered on the creation of a New Order and the destruction of the Nationalist government of China; and by 1941, she intended to displace the colonial empires of the Occidental nations in Southeast Asia with a Co-Prosperity Sphere under the paternalistic direction of the Japanese empire. Although the initial triumphs of the Pacific War succeeded in destroying the colonial empires, the Co-Prosperity Sphere was a brief phenomenon. By 1946, the empire was dismembered, the home islands devastated by incendiary and nuclear bombs, and the sacred soil violated by an army of occupation.

The nature of this defeat was overwhelming, numbering among its victims the efficacy of a religious myth—a belief in the divine qualities of the Imperial institution. Since the dissolution of the Japanese empire was inexorably linked with the outbreak of the Pacific War, the origins of this conflict have understandably absorbed the interest of postwar historians. Indeed, Japanese and American historians have shared two types of generalizations in their appraisals of the Pacific War: (1) Japan's aggressive foreign policy after 1931 was the prime cause of the Pacific conflict; and (2) this policy of aggression was caused by a combination of ultra-nationalism, political assassinations, military conspiracies, and factional disputes within the Imperial army which enabled Japan's military leaders to seize political power and to launch the nation on a program of expansion. Admittedly, one need only mention some of the more memorable domestic and foreign events of the 1930's—the Mukden incident of 1931, the assassinations of 1932, the army rebellion of February 26, 1936, and the Marco Polo Bridge incident of 1937—to convey the pervasive relationship between the behavior of Japan's army officers and the determination of its foreign policy. Still, this book is designed, in part, to show why Japan's foreign policy in the 1930's may not necessarily be adequately or accurately explained in terms of military incidents, political assassinations, and army factionalism. To phrase it more affirmatively, the presentation aims to clarify the substance of Japan's foreign and security policies, as well as the political process by which these policies were formulated and implemented in the period from 1930 to 1938.

Given this task, the book is mainly concerned with two salient aspects of Japanese foreign policy—namely, the changing definitions of national security and national objectives; and the changing policy-making context within the Japanese government. The presentation, therefore, centers on the dynamic relationship between concepts of national security and the formulation and conduct of foreign policy. This orientation inevitably places an emphasis on the attitudes, opinions, and policies which were articulated by those individuals officially responsible for the formulation of the security and foreign policies of the empire—that is, by the ministers of state, the responsible officials of the war, naval, and foreign ministries, and by the senior officers of the two general staffs.

Although this presentation is primarily concerned with the security and foreign policies of the Imperial government in the 1930-1938 period, it is not overtly written as another study of the "origins" or "causes" of the Pacific War. To be sure, the policies of the period were part of a diplomatic and military maelstrom which eventually involved the empire in a losing war. Still, Japan's political and military leaders between 1930 and 1938 did not perceive problems and devise policies in terms of a Pacific War; and all historians are not obligated to appraise those leaders' policies or behavior in the light of subsequent events. Similarly, there is no compulsion to assay the policies and accomplishments of the 1930's by a standard based upon the "successes" of previous eras. The policies of Meiji Japan, self-evidently, yielded the advantages of an empire, whereas those of the Shōwa period reaped the devastation of Hiroshima and Nagasaki. To evaluate the events of the 1930's by the criteria of past achievements or subsequent results in many respects invites a Confucian style of historiography, one which "censures" the policies and leaders of Shōwa Japan and "praises" those of the Meiji era by the technique of contrasting the "statesmen" of earlier decades with the "militarists" of the 1930's.

After offering these observations, it seems appropriate, as part of my prefatory remarks, to indicate briefly the salient suppositions or preconceptions which permeate this appraisal of Japan's foreign and security policies. Essentially, it is my belief that Japan's military and political leaders, throughout the nineteenth and twentieth centuries, consistently and consciously formulated state policies, domestic and foreign, in accordance with two normative standards: the enhancement of national security, and the enhancement of the economic well-being of the state. In the 1870's, these norms were mirrored in the call for "a rich country and a strong army"; and, in the 1930's, they were couched in the phrases "national defense state" and "Co-Prosperity Sphere." Secondly, in the process of creating an empire, Japan acquired a position of political and military hegemony in Northeast Asia, one which prompted Yamagata Aritomo to affirm in the aftermath of the Russo-Japanese War:

> The independence and self-preservation of a country depend, first, upon the defence of its "cordons of sovereignty," and, secondly, upon the defence of its "cordons of interests." ... Now if we wish, as we do, to maintain the integrity of the independence of the country by defending, not only the "cordons of sovereignty" but also the "cordons of interests," we undertake a task which can be accomplished, not by speculative arguments, but only by constant and persevering efforts within the limits allowed by the resources of the land.[1]

Thirdly, the identification of national security and economic prosperity with a hegemonial position in East Asia became an article of faith for the Imperial government that was not compromised until the end of the Pacific War. Fourthly, during the 1930's, the quest for a position of hegemony inspired a cluster of decisions which yielded an increasingly authoritarian government, a new style of imperialism, and a China war. Finally, two hallmarks of post-Perry Japan—an oligarchical form of policy-making, and an aspiration to secure a position of full equality with the Occidental world powers—were also evident during the 1930-1938 period.

Working from these five suppositions, this study offers an explanation of the process by which Japan's political and military leaders became convinced of the need for, and therefore the propriety of, an "autonomous national defense" and a "self-sufficient" economy. More explicitly, it focuses on a host of domestic and foreign concerns which bred three convictions: (1) that the empire's status as a world power, indeed its heg-

[1] Alfred Stead, *Japan by the Japanese* (London, 1904), 84.

emonial position in East Asia, was contingent on an ability to wage war against two strategic enemies—the Soviet Union and the United States; (2) that the ability to confront either of these great powers was not, in Yamagata's words, "within the limits of the resources of the land"; and (3) that in order to rectify this deficiency, it would be necessary to impose a planned economy on Japan and to destroy the Nationalist government of China. To state it simply, the reader is invited to accept a thematic proposition: Japan's foreign and security policies of the 1930-1938 period were designed to realize one cardinal objective, a hegemonial position in East Asia. To the extent that this was a legitimate national aspiration—and it was sanctioned by past policies and past accomplishments— there is no need to deny the political and military leaders of the 1930-1938 period the personal attributes of intelligence, responsibility, and character. On the contrary, they were honorable men, loyal servants of the Throne; they sought what their predecessors had sought, security and prosperity; and, as of 1938, it appeared that their policies were also being blessed by the Shintō gods. If only for this reason, it would be unfair to the responsible leaders of the Imperial government, as well as to the policies they pursued, to view the authoritarianism and imperialism of the 1930's as the consequence of the thoughts and deeds of right-wing ideologues, zealous junior officers, conspiratorial field commanders, and subordinate staff officers who manipulated the ministers of state as if they were Bunraku puppets.

The validity of the preceding remarks cannot be discussed or argued properly in a preface. At best, they should alert the reader to the author's approach to two very complex topics— the relationship between concepts of national security and the formulation of foreign policy, and the changing nature of policy-making in the Japanese government. Neither of these topics can be adequately appraised in regard to the 1930-1938 period without some awareness of the styles of decision-making which prevailed in the preceding years of the twentieth century. Consequently, the following historical synopsis of Japan's foreign and security policies in the opening decades of the century is presented as a prologue to this study of national defense and foreign policy in the 1930's.

JAMES B. CROWLEY

June 1, 1965
Hamden, Connecticut

JAPAN'S QUEST FOR AUTONOMY

Historical Prologue to the 1930's

IN VIEWING the contours of modern Japanese history, one is reminded of a simile of Brooks Adams: history resembles the track of a comet, not the movements of planets. For a span of time. a nation adheres to a steady course; then, as it rounds the sun, it dashes off in a new direction. Throughout the first two decades of this century, the foreign policies of Imperial Japan were fixed on a course of cooperation and accommodation with the Anglo-American maritime powers, only to become comet-like in the next decade, making a sudden thrust into a new path that led eventually to a fatal collision with these Western nations. One witnessed, in effect, the displacement of a diplomacy based upon patterns of collective security by a posture of autonomy, a national defense program that would assure immunization from attack or duress and an ability to pursue whatever political and economic policies were considered essential for the welfare of the Japanese empire. To understand the multiple causes of this transformation, the impetus behind the foreign and security policies of the 1930's, one must consider the bases of Japan's collective security policies in the preceding decades. Otherwise, it is difficult to discern many aspects of the configuration of political, diplomatic, and military problems which inspired the dream of national autonomy, the aspiration which sustained the imperialism and authoritarianism of the 1930's.

At the turn of the century, the diplomacy of East Asia was conditioned by a balance of power noticeably dissimilar from that which governed the European continent. Traditionally and theoretically, Asia had been dominated by one country; yet China, at this time, was militarily impotent, subject to economic, political, and geographical infringements by land and sea powers. In this anomalous situation, the chief roles in the power politics of East Asia were to be played by four actors—Japan, Britain, Russia, and the United States—and, in one fashion or another, their common object was the acquisition of privileged positions in China. When Japan became engaged in this imperialistic diplomacy, it did so with greater intensity than that displayed by the Occidental nations. Unlike the Western sea powers, whose continental aspirations and commitments were casually formed and easily realized, Japan viewed Korea and South Manchuria as an area of prime strategic importance. In order to acquire political hegemony in this region, therefore, Japan fought two major wars; and, although the costs of these conflicts were high, both in material terms and in human lives, the victories in the field created a new pantheon of national heroes and a pervasive sense of nationalism. These accomplishments also sanctified Japanese rights and interests in Korea and Manchuria as matters of national honor.

Unlike Russia, Japan's status as a major power in Asia was not contingent solely on land power, as her islands were still defenseless against the British fleet. Of the major powers, Japan alone was saddled with two sets of strategic concerns: the defense of insular possessions against sea power and the protection of continental interests from a viable land power. Japan's emergence as an Asian power was, moreover, based upon a strategic paradox—namely, Japan became a major actor on the continent at a time when its naval security was absolutely dependent on the good will of the British fleet. Apart from the hazards posed by this fact, the Russo-Japanese War did not assure Japan's position in Korea and South Manchuria. The "open door" policy of the United States, the uncertain dynamics of the European alliance system, and the Far Eastern ambitions of the Russian government presented a specter of future difficulties, future conflicts over the Manchurian problem. Understandably, the protection of Japan's continental interests, as well as the safety of its home islands, depended upon adroit statesmanship guided by the compulsion to avoid any serious clash with the maritime powers.

As a regional power whose influence in East Asia was a composite of its own armament and the friendship of Great

Britain, Japan, in 1906, faced a tangle of diplomatic thickets. The battles of the Russo-Japanese War, symbolized by the bloody siege of Port Arthur and the swift but devastating engagement in the straits of Tsushima, had secured a foothold on the continent. Once this was obtained, the task became one of consolidation, the protection of Japan's position in Korea and South Manchuria. This assignment, reasoned Prince Yamagata, in an October 1906 memorial to the Throne, dictated the need for a comprehensive national defense policy, one that would clarify and confirm the basic strategic principles of Japan's foreign policy and designate the minimal force of strength essential for the realization of Japan's security needs.[1] Acting upon this advice, the Emperor officially requested that a policy guide be prepared by the general staffs, in consultation with the ministers of state. By February 1907, this task was completed and the Saionji cabinet adopted a basic guide to national security. Here, the cardinal strategic concerns of the empire were articulated in a concise form, concerns which were to plague and condition national policies until the holocaust of the Pacific War effected a shattering resolution of the problems created by Japan's dual commitment as a continental and an insular empire.

As defined by both general staffs, the prime security missions of the services were to protect Japan's interests in Korea and South Manchuria and to ensure the safety of Japan's insular possessions, including the home islands. Essential to both aims, as Prince Yamagata had noted in his personal memorial, was the naval alliance with Great Britain; and, by 1907, this prerequisite seemed assured. The European diplomatic context had impelled the British government to prepare an Anglo-Japanese alliance in 1902; and, three years later, this alliance had been broadened to embrace a firm recognition of Japan's special sphere of influence in Korea and Manchuria.

[1] Oyama Adzusa, "Yamagata Aritomo teikoku kokubō hoshinan," *Nihon kokusai seiji gakkai* [NKSG], *Nihon gaikōshi kenkyū: NiShin NichiRō sensō* (Tokyo, 1961), 110.

Although European problems, particularly the Anglo-German naval rivalry, were enforcing the viability of this security pact, both general staffs affirmed, and Japan's naval authorities emphasized, that the ability to wage war against Russia for control of the Liaotung Peninsula, as well as the safety of the home islands, had been derivatives of the Anglo-Japanese alliance. Hence, the key to national defense, to Japan's foreign and security policies, was the protective umbrella of the British fleet. Given this fundamental alliance, the 1907 "National Defense Policy" postulated two distinct security conceptions, both of which were directed at the defense and enhancement of Japan's commercial and political interests in Korea, South Manchuria, and the treaty ports along the coast of China.

In the judgment of Japan's naval leaders, only one naval power posed serious problems. The recent acquisition of the Philippines had given the United States a major colonial possession in the Pacific. Potentially, if they were developed as a naval base, this would compromise the security of Taiwan. Secondly, the "open door" policy raised diplomatic dangers, especially if the United States were to invoke this doctrine as a means to challenge Japan's position in Manchuria and Korea. Aside from these worries, the festering Japanese immigration problem threatened to provoke political turmoil in both countries, thereby accentuating tension between them. Since these three points of conflict were real enough, it is understandable that, as Admiral Fukudome noted, Japan's 1907 naval policy designated "the United States as its sole imaginary enemy."[2] With this axiom, the 1907 "National Defense Policy" advanced two key propositions: first, that Japan should maintain its naval parity with the American fleet; and, secondly, that Japan should construct two new battle fleets, each headed by eight capital warships. This latter stipulation was the well-known "eight-eight" plan and technically it called for the construction of eight battleships, eight heavy cruisers, 27 light cruisers, 177

---

[2] Fukudome Shigeru, *Shikan shinjuwan kōgeki* (Tokyo, 1955), 58-59.

destroyers, and 64 submarines.[3] Lest the empire augment its fleet too rapidly and, in the process, stimulate fears in British naval circles, the 1907 plan judged that the government should, as its immediate goal, authorize twelve capital ships, the so-called "eight-four" program.

This recommendation, it should be noted, did not envision any change in Japan's relative status as a naval power. In 1905, the British introduced the *Dreadnaught*, a name which became the symbol of the new type of battleship, and the *Invincible*, the first battle cruiser. These ships outdated the existing fleets of all the powers, a fact which was appreciated in Japanese naval circles, as well as in the United States, Germany, and France. Consequently, the authorization of the "eight-four" plan did not modify Japan's relative standing as a naval power. Throughout the 1905-1914 period, Japan's battleship ratio vis-a-vis the other nations was as follows:[4]

	United Kingdom	Germany	France	United States	Japan
1905	39	20	12	11	11
1914	39	19	12	10	10

In effect, the naval aspect of the 1907 "National Defense Policy" had two fundamental objectives: maintenance of the Anglo-Japanese alliance, and preservation of Japan's superiority over the American fleet in the Western Pacific.

In the early 1880's, the Meiji oligarchy had concluded that the security of the home islands was contingent on the "independence" of Korea. In particular, they judged that no third country should be permitted to assert its control over the Hermit Kingdom, the "dagger at the heart of Japan."[5] During the Sino-Japanese crisis of 1884, when the Ch'ing government tried to reassert its hegemony over Korea by appointing Yuan Shih-kai as Resident General, the Japanese general staff con-

[3] Kawamura Zenjiro, "Hara Kei naikaku," *Rekishi kyōiku*, VIII (1960), 39.

[4] *Jane's Fighting Ships, 1914* (London, 1914).

[5] Matsushita Yoshio, *Meiji gunsei shiron* (Tokyo, 1956), II, 57-61.

ducted a careful estimate of the situation. It then presented two main conclusions: the security or independence of Korea could be assured only by control of the Liaotung Peninsula; and, given the existing capabilities of the Japanese army and navy, it would not be possible to challenge the Ch'ing forces in the Liaotung region. Under these circumstances, the Japanese government settled this crisis by negotiating the Tientsin Treaty of 1885, the terms of which theoretically precluded any form of interference in the domestic affairs of Korea by China or Japan. Parallel with this treaty, the Meiji oligarchy also resolved to create a military establishment which would, if it seemed necessary, permit Japan to secure the "independence" of Korea by seizing the Liaotung Peninsula.

In harmony with this objective, the Japanese government, between 1885 and 1895, allocated approximately from 28 to 30 per cent of the yearly national budgets to augmenting the military and naval power of the country. The fruits of this expenditure were harvested in the Sino-Japanese War when Japan obtained its cardinal objective, control over the Liaotung Peninsula. As is well known, the 1896 Tripartite intervention of Germany, France, and Russia forced the return of this peninsula to China and shortly afterward Russia moved into Port Arthur. The Korean "security" problem was now no longer a Sino-Japanese affair, and Russia became the prime strategic concern. To counter this threat, the Meiji oligarchy, in 1898, decided to double the size of the Imperial army and navy. Six years later, the government secured a naval alliance with Britain; and, in June 1902, the general staff concluded that "for the long-range planning of our empire," it would be necessary to make "Korea part of the Japanese empire."[6] Convinced of the paramount strategic importance of Korea to the security of the home islands and protected by the Anglo-Japanese alliance, the Imperial government, in 1903, decided to displace the Russians from Liaotung, a decision which precipitated the Russo-Japanese War.

[6] *Ibid.,* I, 271.

Following this conflict, it is not surprising that Japan's army leaders deemed Korea and South Manchuria to be the basic strategic concern of the empire, or that they viewed the continental scene with a proprietary attitude. For twenty years the government had defined its foreign policy in terms of the "independence" of Korea; and Japan had fought two major wars in order to establish its control over Liaotung. Understandably, the general staff, in the 1905-1907 period, pressed for a formal annexation of Korea, a military government in South Manchuria, and the exclusion of American or European investments from both regions. Hence, when Foreign Minister Katō Kōmei, in February 1906, ventured to recommend that Japan should accept the "open door" policy, War Minister Terauchi's adamant opposition forced Katō's resignation after a brief three-month tenure as foreign minister.[7] In additon, the army authorities were most reluctant to set aside the military government which had been established in Liaotung during the war; and it took a special Conference on the Manchurian Problem in March 1906 to end this form of government.[8] Here, Prince Saionji, with the aid of the Genrō—Yamagata, Itō, Matsukata, and Inoue—managed to bring about several decisive administrative changes: the resident military governor (*sōtokufu*) in Liaotung was displaced by a governor general (*totoku*); the South Manchurian Railway was created under the presidency of Gotō Shūmpei; and a consulate general was located at Port Arthur, a post whose occupant was equal in rank to the highest-ranking army officer stationed in South Manchuria. Despite these changes, the first governor general, Field Marshal Ōyama, in November 1906, still argued that "the foreign policy of South Manchuria should be entrusted completely to the governor general."[9] Although Ōyama's views were set aside by the Saionji cabinet, the army

[7] Shinobu Seizaburo, "Taishō gaikōshi no kihon mondai," NKSG, *Nihon gaikōshi kenkyū: Taishō jidai* (Tokyo, 1958), 2.

[8] Imai Seiichi, "Taishōgo ni okeru gunbu no seijiteki chii," *Shisō*, 399 (September 1957), 7.

[9] *Ibid.*

authorities obviously regarded South Manchuria as the army's special province; and the 1907 "National Defense Policy" drafted by the army general staff marked Tsarist Russia as the prime threat to the empire. Anticipating a "war of revenge" by the recently defeated enemy, the general staff calculated that it would be necessary to increase the standing army from 19 to 25 divisions, thereby assuring the empire of an immediate mobilization potential of 50 divisions.[10]

The 1907 "National Defense Policy" had defined one comprehensive objective: the formation of a military establishment that would be capable of protecting Japan's rights and interests in Korea and South Manchuria. Within this postulate, each service had articulated a distinctive mission: the naval policy voiced the need for a fleet of twelve capital ships in order to retain Japan's superiority over the American fleet in the Western Pacific; the army policy claimed the necessity of a 25-division standing army in order to protect Korea and South Manchuria. Both policies were predicated on an awareness of the paramount importance of the Anglo-Japanese alliance, on a recognition that the insular and continental possessions of the empire were ultimately protected by the British fleet. In 1907, however, neither service actually had the "minimal" strength to realize the desired strategic capabilities. The army stood at 19 divisions, not 25; and the navy possessed two new capital warships, not twelve.

1907-1913, NATIONAL DEFENSE AND THE CONSOLIDATION OF THE EMPIRE

The 1907 strategic calculations of the general staffs were not lacking in validity. The fear of a "war of revenge" by the Tsarist government could not be easily discounted; and the world tour of the American fleet of 1906-1907 was, from the viewpoint of Theodore Roosevelt, undertaken to impress upon the Japanese government the power and determination of the American government to exert its influence in Pacific affairs.

[10] Itō Masanori, *Gunbatsu kōbōshi* (Tokyo, 1958), II, 22.

Although the Japanese and American press promptly expressed belief in the imminence of a Japanese-American conflict, in strategic terms Roosevelt's "big stick" naval diplomacy was really a fragile reed. The Anglo-Japanese alliance precluded any Anglo-American accord against Japan; and the Imperial fleet was approximately equal to that of the United States. Given the cruising range of the warships of the period, this parity invested Japan with a commanding superiority in the Western Pacific. Somewhat belatedly, Theodore Roosevelt realized the Philippines were an "Achilles' heel," indefensible against the power of the Japanese fleet. This perception soon reflected itself in a new style of American diplomacy, in the Root-Takahira and Taft-Katsura executive agreements which tacitly confirmed Japan's special position in Korea and South Manchuria. Parallel with this Japanese-American rapprochement, the Russian and Japanese governments negotiated in 1907 and 1909 an entente by which they recognized each other's position in North and South Manchuria. Finally, in 1910, Japan formally annexed Korea, without any objections or reservations on the part of the Western powers.

This favorable diplomatic context did not alter the strategic axioms of the Japanese general staffs. From their standpoint, the softened tone of Roosevelt's policy was the consequence of Japan's naval strength; and they believed Japan's standing army had forced the reluctant acquiescence of the Russian government. However well warranted these opinions may have been, the favorable diplomacy of the postwar period sharply reduced the willingness of the Japanese political parties to underwrite any major expansion of the services. In the past, in 1882 and 1896, the Genrō had only to formulate comprehensive armament programs and the necessary funds were allocated; but, between 1907 and 1911, neither the Diet nor the finance ministry was prepared to champion any significant increase in armament expenditures. This political context affected the services in strikingly dissimilar ways. Since the navy was, after the Russo-Japanese War, literally building a fleet of new ships, it could, by scrapping outdated warships, realize its goal of twelve capital ships without enlarging its budget. The Imperial army, in contrast, could not augment the number of standing divisions unless the Diet authorized increased expenditures. Since this authorization failed to materialize, the army, between 1907 and 1911, remained at nineteen divisions, only one of which was stationed in Korea. To the army authorities this was intolerable, as it provided wholly inadequate forces on the mainland for the defense of Korea and South Manchuria. This frustrating situation bred a conviction in army circles that the government was not abiding by its moral and legal obligations to fulfill the estimates of forces sanctioned by the Throne in 1907, a sentiment which boiled over into a major political crisis.

When Prince Saionji formed his second cabinet in 1911, the army's hope for an armament increase became bleak. The premier imposed a program of fiscal retrenchment, forcing a reduction in the army's existing budget of some six million yen, and in the naval budget, of some eight million yen. The political basis of this reduction was beyond dispute: new budgets were the province of the Diet and Saionji's party commanded a healthy majority in the Diet. In desperation, the army authorities, with the sanction of Prince Yamagata, tried to utilize their control over the war minister's portfolio as a club to beat down Saionji's fiscal policies. On the death of General Ishimoto in May 1912, the army designated General Uehara as the new war minister. Moving directly from his post as chief of the general staff, Uehara confronted the cabinet with an unequivocal demand: the minimal security needs of the empire compelled an increase of the army by two divisions, which were to be stationed in Korea.[11] When Saionji overruled the stipulation, Uehara resigned and the army refused to nominate a new war minister. Because his portfolio was confined to officers on active duty, Uehara's action precipitated the resignation of Prince Saionji. The Genrō, at the insistence of Prince Yamagata, then

11 *Ibid.*, 25-28.

selected General Katsura to organize a new cabinet, one that would presumably effect an increase of the army by two divisions.

The political strategy of the army authorities, abetted by the covert influence of Yamagata, provoked a crisis of the highest order. Were the budget policies of the government, the legal prerogative of the Diet, to be dictated by a clique of army officers? Could the war minister impose his dictates on the other ministers of state? The challenges posed by Uehara's resignation alienated the political parties and the finance and naval ministers, a situation which temporarily at least forged a bond of political unity between two key ministries and the political parties. The results of this new political configuration were promptly displayed. When General Katsura set out to form his cabinet, he discovered the naval authorities were not prepared to provide a naval minister.[10] This public stance revealed an intense resentment of the army's dictatorial methods and, more pointedly, it acted as a blunt warning that the naval authorities could also play the game of cabinet politics according to army rules. In contrast to Prince Saionji, General Katsura did not yield the point, preferring instead to invoke the aid of the Throne and obtain a memorial ordering the appointment of a naval minister. While this maneuver assured the formation of a cabinet, it also intensified the opposition of the majority party in the Diet. Consequently, the Katsura cabinet was unable to enact the desired two-division expansion of the army; and the transparent hostility between the naval ministry and the premier fostered a popular belief that a clique of Chōshū army officers, headed by Yamagata and Katsura, had engineered the downfall of the Saionji government as a means to revive its oligarchical control over governmental policies.

Motivated more by obstinacy than moderation, Katsura retained the premiership for fourteen months. In this interval,

[12] Robert Scalapino, *Democracy and the Party Movement in Prewar Japan* (Berkeley, 1953), 192.

he made no serious overtures to ameliorate the conflict between the war ministry and the finance and naval ministries or to seek an accommodation with the Seiyūkai, the majority party in the Diet. As premier, he pressed for an enlarged army budget, only to see his recommendation vetoed by the Diet. Finally the impasse was vividly revealed in the public arena by Ozaki Yukio. On February 5, 1913, in one of Japan's most memorable parliamentary addresses, often regarded as the symbol of the inception of Taishō democracy, Ozaki censured the Chōshū oligarchs for their wanton violation of responsible cabinet government and the vile technique of concealing partisan interests under the mantle of the Emperor: "They always mouth 'loyalty' and 'patriotism' but what they are actually doing is to hide themselves behind the Throne, and shoot at their political enemies from their secure ambush. The Throne is their rampart. Rescripts are their missiles."[13] The vivid metaphor stirred the Seiyūkai to vote a formal censure of the government; and Katsura rashly retaliated with another Imperial rescript requesting the revocation of the censure. This crude stratagem proved his undoing. Defying the rescript, the Seiyūkai affirmed its lack of confidence in the premier; and, once Katsura's behavior had cast the sanctity of the Throne in jeopardy, Prince Yamagata added his powerful voice to the demand for a new government. The issue was decided. Katsura resigned and Yamagata asked Admiral Yamamoto to organize a cabinet in harmony with the expectations of the Seiyūkai.

With the establishment of the Yamamoto cabinet, the Genrō and the army authorities had, in fact, conceded the imprudence of the army's attempt to bludgeon the government with the regulations governing the service portfolios. The lesson had not been learned easily; and the tactics of Generals Uehara and Katsura had infused the Diet with great confidence. Equally significantly, Ozaki's parliamentary posture had forced the Genrō into a weaker political position. Following the Diet's

13 *Ibid.*, 194.

rejection of the Imperial rescript, even Yamagata understood the necessity for resolving political dissension by negotiations with the leaders of the political parties. Henceforth, as Professor Scalapino has noted, "personal intervention by the Throne in political controversies practically ceased."[14] And, in his opening moves as premier, Admiral Yamamoto assured the Diet that parliamentary appointments would be made in the ministries, that expansion of the army would not be proposed and that the requirements for the service ministries would be broadened to include retired or inactive general officers.[15] These were, to be sure, modest concessions; and if they marked the beginning of the principle of cabinet responsibility to the majority party, they did not usher in an age of party government. Neither the Genrō nor the ministries of state were disposed to accept direction in national policies by the political parties.

In one sense, the first bloom of Taishō democracy had been fostered by a profound conflict within the cabinet—namely, the army's strenuous efforts to impose its fiscal policies. From another perspective, the impasse between the army authorities and the Diet had been caused by two considerations: an international context which discounted the value of the army's estimate of its armament needs; and, within the confines of a fixed military budget, the inability of the service ministers to formulate a common national defense policy which would allocate the available funds according to a schedule of priorities, whether it be an enlargement of the army or a prompt realization of the "eight-four" building program. As war clouds gathered over the European continent, however, the domestic and foreign circumstances which had forestalled the two division expansion of the army slowly dissipated.

1914-1917, EXPANSION VIA THE EUROPEAN WAR

Essentially, the parliamentary and fiscal problems of the 1911-1913 period had been manifested in two distinct

---

[14] *Ibid.*, 196.   [15] *Ibid.*, 202-203.

closely related political issues—the unwillingness of the
ministers of state to propose a budget consonant with the
army's expectations, and the clamoring by a majority party for
a system of cabinet responsibility to the Diet. In these years,
neither the army nor the Seiyūkai had satisfied its prime
ambitions. The two-division expansion had been tabled; and
the premiers nominated by the Genrō—Katsura and Yamamoto
—were not leaders of the Seiyūkai. Owing to a minor scandal
involving some naval officers, the Yamamoto cabinet resigned
in March 1914; and, given no better alternative, Yamagata
resignedly recommended his long-time political adversary,
Ōkuma Shigenobu, as premier. An original member of the
great Meiji oligarchy, Ōkuma had been maneuvered out of
power in the 1880's because of his "liberal" constitutional
opinions. For twenty-five years, he had been relegated to the
outer fringe of power shared by all politicians who lacked
access to the ministries of state. Now, in 1914, although leader
of the minority party—the Doshikai, later the Minseitō he be
came premier. With this lever, Ōkuma, in conjunction with
Katō Kōmei, proposed to separate the Genrō from the ministers of state and to create a harmony of interests between the
cabinet and the Diet. If this objective were attained, it would
resolve the political difficulties which had harassed the government for three years; and it would also bring about a system
of parliamentary responsibility, a style of government which
Ōkuma had advocated at the apex of his power in the Meiji
oligarchy.

The fulfillment of all ambitious political programs depends
on a combination of good luck and clever leadership. In
Ōkuma's case, his success hinged upon two developments:
devising a comprehensive security policy satisfactory to the
ministers of finance, war, and navy; and transforming the Doshikai into the majority party in the Diet. The first requisite was
obtained in July 1914, when Ōkuma created the Council on
National Defense (*bōmukai*);[16] comprised of the ministers

[16] Tatsuji Takeuchi, *War and Diplomacy in the Japanese Empire* (New
York, 1935), 182.

of foreign affairs, war, navy, and finance, and the chiefs of the general staffs, with the premier as chairman. The council, after considering the European situation, quickly agreed on a defense program that advocated the completion of the "eight-four" naval program and an increase of the Korean Army by two divisions. Despite Ōkuma's pleas on behalf of this plan, the majority party, the Seiyūkai, deleted the army's expansion from the budget. Although it was not unanticipated, this was a hazardous move by the Seiyūkai. The European conflagration and Japan's entry into the war against Germany had nullified popular objections to the expansion of the army. Thus, by curtailing the army's budget, the Seiyūkai had taken a dangerous stance for any political party, opposition to a government's wartime policies. The consequences were reaped in the general elections of March 1915 when Ōkuma led the Doshikai to a resounding triumph. The Diet promptly authorized the two divisions and, for the duration of the war, all proposed armament expenditures would be readily endorsed by both political parties.

The war against Germany had fostered an advantageous climate of opinion which enabled Ōkuma to link the paramount interests and views of his ministers with a majority party. To judge by the ballot box, his success was unquestioned. The dangers of adopting particular national policies in order to promote domestic popularity, however, were not minimized by the Genrō, who became extremely apprehensive about another dimension of Ōkuma's leadership. Since the Russo-Japanese War, the foreign and war ministries had been constantly embroiled in heated controversies over Japan's continental policies. The army authorities, especially the general staff, argued that South Manchuria should be treated as the private preserve of the empire; the diplomats, including Katō Kōmei, preferred to encourage foreign investment as a better way to assure American support for Japan's military presence in South Manchuria. Apart from this quarrel, army authorities were divided in their appraisal of the Chinese revolution of 1913. Some officers proposed the launching of an "independence" movement in Inner Mongolia and Manchuria.[17] Others called for extensive aid to the Peking government and the promotion of a central government that would be dependent, militarily and economically, on Japan.[18] Just as the outbreak of the European conflict had enabled the adoption and implementation of a new armament policy, so too it afforded a splendid opportunity for Premier Ōkuma and Foreign Minister Katō to devise a coordinated China policy that would satisfy most groups within the army and foreign ministry.

Technically, the Ōkuma cabinet had declared war against Germany in response to a British request of August 7 for Japanese naval assistance in the Western Pacific. The limited role envisioned for Japan by the British government was, however, supplanted by a resolution to seize the German possessions in Shantung, as well as the German Pacific islands. Though dismayed by the scope of Japanese aspirations, the British government naturally muffled its reservations about Japan's move into Shantung; and the absorption of the European powers prompted General Machida, the attaché in Peking, to recommend an ambitious China policy, one that would presumably solidify Japan's paramount position in North China, Inner Mongolia, and Manchuria.[19] Machida's proposals were enthusiastically approved by the general staff; and, surprisingly, Katō Kōmei added his endorsement. With the sanction of the premier, the foreign and war ministers then formulated an encompassing China policy designed to augment Japan's military position in North China and the provinces opposite Taiwan, and to furnish the legal basis for an extension of Japanese political and commercial influence in the Peking government. This China policy was publicly unveiled as the famous Twenty-one Demands.

The ambitious nature of these demands needs no exposition,

[17] Kurihara Ken, "Daiichiji dainiji ManMō dokuritsu undō," NKSG, *Taishō jidai.*

[18] Imai Seiichi, "Taishōgo ni okeru gunbu no seijiteki chii," *Shisō*, 402 (December 1957).

[19] James Morley, *Japanese Thrust into Siberia* (New York, 1957), 13.

save to note three major consequences brought about by the
Sino-Japanese treaties negotiated in May 1915. They stipulated
that German rights and interests in Shantung were to be
"completely left to the free disposal of Japan"; Japanese existing privileges in South Manchuria and Liaotung were extended
by 99 years; and no military or naval installations were to be
built by any foreign power in Fukien province.[20] The Twenty-
one Demands signified a vaulting imperial ambition which
implicitly threatened the interests of the European powers.
Precisely why the Ōkuma cabinet resorted to this flamboyant
China policy remains unclear. Ōkuma and Katō had not previously been associated with such extremist views. In fact, as
foreign minister in the first Saionji cabinet, Katō had championed the prudence of cooperation with the United States,
including opening Manchuria to American investors. Moreover, the outcome of the European war was undecided and the
hazards of alienating the sea powers were self-evident. Two
considerations suggest the intent of Katō's new definition of
Japan's China policy. Ōkuma and Katō were trying to wrest
control of foreign policy from the hands of the Genrō; and
they were committed to the principle of parliamentary responsibility. Neither of these aspirations was sympathetically
received by the Genrō. Throughout Meiji Japan, even during
the wars with China and Russia when the government had
established a Supreme Command, all basic national policies,
especially in the realm of foreign policy, were decided only
after extensive consultation with the senior statesmen. Consequently, even though Katō's Twenty-one Demands mirrored
the judgment of the cabinet and had the enthusiastic support
of the Doshikai, the Genrō bitterly resented this China policy.
Yamagata, in particular, censured the domestic orientation
underlying Katō's behavior. To confront China with such
demands would, reasoned Yamagata, only alienate the Chinese
people and inhibit the cultivation of friendly Sino-Japanese
relations. More immediately, Yamagata believed the demands

[20] *The Sino-Japanese Negotiations of 1915* (Washington, 1921), 39-63.

would irritate the great sea powers, generating a major diplomatic crisis at the end of the European war.[21]

Behind this acid indictment of Katō was another matter. In formulating Japan's China policy, Katō had deliberately ignored the Genrō. Since his advice was not sought, it seemed clear to Yamagata that Katō and Ōkuma were asserting the autonomy of the cabinet in the act of formulating national policy. This exclusion from policy formulation offended the Genrō; and, when the 1915 treaties unleashed a wave of Chinese resentment and drew polite rebukes from Britain and the United States, Ōkuma found it politically expedient to force Katō's resignation. This gesture did not satisfy the Genrō; and, in October 1916, Ōkuma's ill health forced his own resignation. Katō had, on leaving the cabinet, assumed presidency of the Doshikai; and Ōkuma therefore expected the Genrō to nominate Katō as the next premier, since Katō's party held a clear majority in the Diet. The Genrō, under Yamagata's influence, however, were not prepared to condone Katō's political philosophy; and, by citing his inept handling of the China problem, they rationalized their decision to appoint a "transcendental" cabinet directed by General Terauchi.

The Genrō had vindicated the need for a transcendental cabinet by maintaining that Japan's foreign policies could not be entrusted to politicians who viewed the international scene through the window of domestic popularity. To compromise the role of the Diet and political parties, Terauchi, with Yamagata's backing, publicly insisted that foreign affairs were too complex to be subject to the whim of partisan politics. This rhetoric hardly impressed Katō, nor was it appealing to the leaders of the minority party, Inukai Ki and Hara Kei. Terauchi, however, supplemented his plea for a non-partisan foreign policy with something more tangible, the establishment of the Foreign Policy Deliberative Committee (*gaikō*

---

[21] *Obata Toriyoshi denki* (Tokyo, 1955), 111-116; and Itō Masanori, *Katō Kōmei* (Tokyo, 1929), II, 32-40.

chōsakai).[22] As private citizens, not as official representatives of the political parties, Terauchi requested that Katō, Inukai, and Hara join this committee and advise the cabinet on all foreign policy matters. The intent of the offer was no secret and Katō rebuffed the invitation, insisting it was essential to any viable system of parliamentary responsibility that foreign policy not be divorced from domestic politics. The allure of immediate power proved more appealing to Inukai and Hara, who joined the *gaikō chōsakai*. If their decision undermined the authority of the Diet in foreign affairs, it nevertheless gave the Foreign Policy Deliberative Committee a vital role in decision-making. Henceforth, from 1916 to 1922, this committee, not the venerable Genrō, reviewed and guided all foreign-policy decisions of the cabinet.[23]

Once a government is politically committed to a foreign policy, it is nearly impossible to cast it aside completely, especially if its enunciation has immediate repercussions in domestic and international politics. Certainly, the Terauchi cabinet could not undo the effects of the Twenty-one Demands; but it could seek the promotion of Japanese interests by sincere cooperation with the Western powers. Thus, internally the Terauchi government espoused the slogan originally articulated by some Japanese industrialists—"Japanese brains and American money"—as the most beneficial commercial policy for China; and, diplomatically, it offered to cooperate with the International Corporation, a group dominated by American investors, in a conservation and canal project in the Huai River valley.[24] There was, however, no compulsion to rewrite the special advantages obtained in the 1915 treaties. On the contrary, the German submarine campaign dissipated British disapproval of the Shantung expedition when the Japanese government offered the use of its destroyers in the Medi-

---

[22] *Obata Toriyoshi denki,* 202-210, is the best appraisal of the *gaikō chōsakai.*

[23] Morley, *Japanese Thrust,* 26.

[24] Burton Beers, *Vain Endeavor: Robert Lansing's Attempt to End the American-Japanese Rivalry* (Durham, 1962), 79-81.

terranean in return for recognition of Japan's seizure of German possessions in the North Pacific. As the British government phrased its policy in February 1917, it would "with pleasure . . . support Japan's claims in regard to the disposal of Germany's rights in Shantung and possessions in the islands north of the equator . . . it being understood that the Japanese Government will in the eventual peace settlement treat in the same spirit Great Britain's claim to the German islands south of the equator."[25] Comparable agreements were negotiated with the Russian, French, and Italian governments.

Only the American government resisted this inclination to solicit Japanese cooperation at the expense of the Chinese government. In order to assuage American fears, the Terauchi government despatched Viscount Ishii to the United States with a proposed *modus vivendi*: the United States would not challenge Japan's position in Manchuria; Japan would permit American investment in this region. The overture was rebuffed by President Wilson; and Secretary of State Lansing and Viscount Ishii muffled the disagreement with a joint statement combining the divergent views of both governments. This famous Lansing-Ishii note of November 2, 1917, affirmed the "open door" principle and respect for Chinese "integrity," and it agreed that "Japan has special interests in China, particularly in the part to which her possessions are contiguous."[26] Armed with this Janus-headed declaration and the series of secret agreements with the European powers, the Terauchi government looked forward to the end of the war, confident that it had built a solid foundation for the recognition of Japan's claims to Shantung and the German islands.

1918-1921, A NASCENT JAPANESE-AMERICAN CONFRONTATION

The expectations of the Terauchi cabinet were not un-

[25] Russell Fifield, *Woodrow Wilson and the Far East* (New York, 1952), 54.

[26] *Ibid.*, 84.

warranted, as long as Japan's ambitions and attitudes were confined to a confirmation of the secret treaties and the 1915 treaties with China. The Bolshevik revolution, however, added a new element to Japan's diplomacy which severely aggravated Japanese-American relations. The ministers of state reacted to the Russian civil war as they had to the outbreak of the European war in 1914: War Minister Oshima called for a Sino-Japanese military alliance and Foreign Minister Motono emphasized the need for military operations that would enable Japan to seize North Sakhalin and establish its "predominant position in the Orient."[27] Unlike 1914, however, the cabinet needed the concurrence of the *gaikō chōsakai*; and this body, dominated by Hara Kei and Makino Shinken, insisted that no action be taken unless the United States gave its approval.[28] Despite the complaints of the general staffs and the service ministers, Prince Yamagata neither questioned Hara's judgment nor tried to subvert the authority of the *gaikō chōsakai*. Ironically, the contention between the council and the cabinet was resolved when the American government proposed a joint military intervention in Siberia.

The decision to move into Siberia demonstrated the marginal authority of the Genrō; and it highlighted the tendency of the ministers to espouse an expansionist continental policy. Once the government obtained lukewarm approval of the Siberian intervention, it pushed ahead with excessive vigor. Instead of a modest expeditionary force, an army was despatched which spread like a great fan throughout North Manchuria, Kamchatka, and Northern Sakhalin. Manifestly, this was no program to protect foreign nationals or the beleaguered Czech troops, and the American government viewed the intervention as a crude brand of Japanese imperialism. Sensitive to this displeasure, Hara demanded greater restraint, questioning Terauchi's interpretation of the views of the

[27] Morley, *Japanese Thrust*, 50.
[28] *Ibid., loc.cit.*; and Hosoya Chihiro, *Shibeiya shuppei no shiteki kenkyū* (Tokyo, 1955).

gaikō chōsakai. Since Hara's party, the Seiyūkai, ruled the Diet, his strictures could not be totally ignored; and the Genrō sympathized with his demand for greater attention to the implications of the intervention for Japanese-American relations. Moreover, in contrast to Katō Kōmei, Hara utilized his position in the Seiyūkai to buttress his influence in the council, without at the same time insisting that foreign policies should be decided by a cabinet responsible to the dominant political party. In short, he won the confidence and respect, if not the friendship, of the Genrō; and, in September 1918, Hara received the Imperial mandate to organize a new cabinet.

Although the new premier could not disavow the nature of the Siberian intervention, he was determined to control future operations. Since no Supreme Command had been created, Hara reasoned that the cabinet must assume direct responsibility for such vital matters as the scope and timing of operations. The army general staff challenged this claim by protesting Hara's judgment that the army must not advance beyond Khabarovosk. After a brief dispute, the issue was decided in favor of the premier: the conduct of all operations was invested in the general staff; the determination of objectives would be the responsibility of the war minister.[29] On this administrative accord, Hara wryly commented: "There should be a reform of the army, not within it."[30] Despite the tenor of his private estimate of the army, Hara had won a vital political struggle. Under this administrative agreement between the war minister and the chief of the general staff, the opinion of the cabinet, as reflected in the orders of the war minister, was to take precedence over the views of the general staff, even in the midst of hostilities. This approach was not new, as it had been employed in the Sino and Russo-Japanese wars; but, in those conflicts, the Meiji oligarchs had ruled the cabinet and the highest command positions in the army. Without the dual

[29] Imai Seiichi, *Shisō*, 399 (September 1957), 18-19.
[30] *Ibid.*

civilian-military roles of the Genrō, Hara had reaffirmed the primacy of the war minister and the cabinet in the determination of operational objectives, an achievement that contributed immensely to the development of Taishō democracy in the ensuing decade.

Hara's dispute with the general staff was not his gravest problem. Despite his personal approach to the Siberian intervention and his earnest desire for friendly relations with the United States, as premier, Hara was necessarily committed to confirmation of the wartime treaties and agreements with China and the European powers. His task proved particularly difficult at the Paris Peace Conference, in view of the personal attitude and diplomacy of President Wilson. In fact, on every major Pacific problem—Shantung, the German islands, and the meaning of the "open door" policy—the Japanese delegation encountered sharp opposition from Wilson; and, when the Senate failed to ratify the Versailles Treaty, all of these problems persisted, thereby becoming a rash of canker sores irritating relations between the two countries.

From the Japanese vantage point, this friction with the United States was a very serious matter. During the war, the American navy had expanded enormously, transforming the United States into a great naval power. Given the obvious sentiments underlying Wilsonian diplomacy, this caused portentous security problems for Japan. In 1914, Japan had approximate parity with the United States, and its basic naval policies called for the maintenance of this naval equality. This was easier to recommend than to implement; but, on the basis of the battle of Jutland, Japan's naval authorities, in harmony with the conclusions of their Anglo-American counterparts, judged that an attacking force needed at least a 40 per cent superiority to assure victory. To Japan, this meant that superiority over the American fleet in the Western Pacific could be guaranteed by a 70 per cent ratio. Even with this new calculation, to secure this ratio in the face of America's wartime expansion necessitated a huge program of naval armaments. The spiraling dimension of this 10:7 naval policy is readily conveyed by a glance at Japan's naval budgets from 1914 to 1921:[31]

1914	83,260,000 yen	*1918*	215,903,000 yen
1915	84,376,000 yen	*1919*	316,419,000 yen
1916	116,625,000 yen	*1920*	403,201,000 yen
1917	166,243,500 yen	*1921*	483,589,000 yen

However heavy the burden created by this expenditure, the naval general staff adamantly and correctly emphasized that a failure to obtain a 10:7 ratio would fatally compromise the naval security of the empire and force Japan to defer to an American definition of Japan's proper continental policies.

By 1921, Japan was caught in the whirlpool of an imminent armament race with the world's richest and most industrialized nation. Domestically, the Hara cabinet defined its main mission as the expansion of the nation's industrial capacity and the "fulfillment of national defense."[32] The latter goal presented many hurdles. Japan's continental policies, in 1915 and 1918, had generated widespread apprehension and resentment in the United States; the defeat of Germany had destroyed the prewar alliance system, a primary impetus for the Anglo-Japanese alliance; and the United States had proclaimed its determination to undertake a mammoth postwar naval program involving ten battleships, six battle cruisers, and 100 submarines. Although desperately anxious for an accommodation with the United States that would end an obvious armament race, the Japanese government, in 1920, demonstrated its grim determination to maintain supremacy over the American fleet in the Western Pacific by announcing it would construct a fleet of sixteen capital warships.

WASHINGTON CONFERENCE TREATY SYSTEM

Despite the public affirmations of the cabinet and the force

[31] Fujiwara Akira, *Gunjishi* (Tokyo, 1961), 137.
[32] Kawamura, "Hara Kei naikaku," 36-38.

of the argument in favor of a 10:7 ratio with the American fleet, Japan's political and naval leaders were deeply distressed by this armament race. Naval Minister Katō Tomosaburō was particularly concerned about its repercussions on the Anglo-Japanese alliance. Before her wartime naval construction, Japan had not been in any position to offer a potential threat to British interests in the Pacific area or to the Commonwealth countries. By 1920, however, the Japanese fleet was approaching a 60 per cent ratio vis-à-vis the British fleet, a ratio which theoretically would equalize the operational capabilities of both fleets in the Southwest Pacific. Consequently, if Japan were to enlarge her fleet in order to retain a 70 per cent ratio with the projected American fleet, this would force Great Britain to join the armament race in order to safeguard the security of Australia and New Zealand. Furthermore, although the British government was publicly committed to its traditional policy of world-wide naval supremacy, it was patently clear that Great Britain did not regard the United States as a serious threat to British interests. Under these circumstances, Naval Minister Katō believed that an unrestrained armament race with the United States would ultimately precipitate an Anglo-American alliance, one which would completely shatter the security of the empire and of the home islands. Primarily because of this worry, the Japanese naval ministry was prepared, in 1922, to seek some type of diplomatic and naval accommodation with the United States which would, in one fashion or another, confirm Japan's existing superiority in the Western Pacific.

At the opening session of the Washington Conference, on November 12, 1921, the American secretary of state, Charles Hughes, astounded the delegates with a dramatic and comprehensive naval limitations proposal.[33] Essentially the American plan advanced four main principles—the United States, Great Britain, and Japan should (1) abandon their projected

[33] *Conference on the Limitations of Armaments* (Washington, 1922) has a complete record of the plenary sessions.

construction programs; (2) limit their naval power by scrapping overage warships; (3) accept a balanced ratio of naval power; and (4) limit the number of auxiliary warships according to the tonnage of warships. If adopted, this plan would give the United States eighteen battleships (500,650 tons) ; Great Britain, twenty battleships (604,500 tons) ; and Japan, ten battleships (299,700 tons). Since this, in effect, would establish a 10:6 ratio between Japan and the United States, the American proposal was bitterly assailed by Admiral Tōgō and the naval general staff. The chief member of the Japanese delegation, Naval Minister Katō, however, judged that Japan could accept a 10:6 ratio in capital warships, if the United States would agree to forgo future fortifications of its insular possessions in the Western Pacific. In turn, Secretary Hughes was prepared to meet this stipulation, if Japan would agree to respect the principles of the "open door" and the "territorial integrity of China."

The competing diplomatic and naval objectives of the Japanese and American delegations were harmonized by the negotiation of three separate but interrelated treaties.[34] The Five Power Treaty established a 10:6 ratio in capital warships between the Anglo-American fleets and the Imperial navy; and it precluded the construction of any new naval fortifications in the Western Pacific. The Four Power Treaty committed Great Britain, France, Japan, and the United States to respect the insular possessions of each power in the Pacific. And, in the Nine Power Treaty, the major nations of the world, including Japan, agreed, under Article I of the Treaty, to abide by the following principles:

I. To respect the sovereignty, the independence and the territorial and administrative integrity of China;

[34] Among the many accounts of the Washington Conference, the following seem most pertinent: A. W. Griswold, *The Far Eastern Policy of the United States* (New York, 1938); Raymond L. Buell, *The Washington Conference* (New York, 1922); and Asada Sadao, "Japan's Special Interests and the Washington Conference, 1921-1922," *American Historical Review*, LXVII (October 1961). In Japanese, Somura Hoshin, "Washington kaigi ichi kosatsu," NKSG, *Taishō jidai*, 117-129.

II. To provide the fullest and most unembarrassed opportunity to China to develop and maintain herself as an effective and stable government;

III. To use their influence for the purpose of equal opportunity for the commerce and industry of all nations through the territory of China;

IV. To refrain from taking advantage of conditions in China in order to seek special rights or privileges which would abridge the rights of subjects or citizens of friendly states and from countenancing action inimical to the security of such states.[35]

In addition to this pledge, Japan soon restored the former German-leased territory in Shantung to China, withdrew from North Sakhalin and Eastern Siberia, and allowed an international consortium to participate in the development of Manchuria and Inner Mongolia.

Subsequently, the Japanese and American governments would differ appreciably in their approach to Japanese rights and interests in Manchuria. At the Washington Conference, though, neither the American nor the Japanese delegation viewed the Nine Power Treaty as entailing any modification of Japan's existing rights in Manchuria. What Secretary Hughes sought and obtained was a commitment by Japan to the 1915 *status quo* on the continent, an affirmation which he believed would allow China the "fullest and most unembarrassed opportunity" to develop a stable government. Essentially, the success of the Washington Conference could be attributed to the willingness of all the major powers to accept the existing military and naval *status quo* as the basis of their diplomatic negotiations. And, like most major diplomatic accomplishments, the treaties negotiated at the Washington Conference may be evaluated in a variety of ways. In terms of Japanese diplomacy, they attained the major strategic objective of the Imperial government: naval hegemony in the Western Pacific

[35] *Report of the American Delegation on the Conference on the Limitation of Armament* (Washington, 1922), 1116.

—and, simultaneously, they forced Japan to adopt a new diplomatic approach to her continental interests. After 1922, Japan no longer could rely upon the security of the Anglo-Japanese alliance, nor could it pursue politically expansionist policies in China or Manchuria. Instead, Japan's diplomacy after 1922 was based on the principle of cooperation with the Anglo-American nations; and, implicit in this approach was the conviction that it afforded the best means of protecting the empire and Japan's existing treaty rights on the continent.

After 1922, there appeared within Japan an approach to foreign and security policies which placed primary importance on an adherence to the Washington Conference treaties. This was reflected in the desire and ability of the government to curtail military expenditures from 49 per cent of the national budget in 1921 to 30 per cent in 1923.[36] Although this caused some concern in both services, the reduction was publicly justified by Premier (Admiral) Katō Tomosaburō on the grounds that Japan's national defense was a composite of agricultural, financial, and industrial capabilities, plus friendly relations with the Anglo-American nations.[37] This emphasis on armament reduction and cooperation with the Western powers forced War Minister Ugaki, in 1924, to reduce the standing army by deactivating four divisions.[38] Without discounting the significance of these steps, the ability of either service to carry out its prime strategic mission was not appreciably affected by the reduced budgets and cutback in the strength of the army. The Four and Five Power Treaties did guarantee Japan's naval security; and, paradoxically, the naval policy of the American government after 1922 greatly augmented Japan's hegemony in the Western Pacific. In particular, between 1922 and 1930, Japan built a new fleet of heavy cruisers and submarines, while American shipyards were relatively dormant. In the process, since Japan acquired an

[36] Takeuchi, *War and Diplomacy*, 29.
[37] Matsushita, *Meiji gunsei*, II, 300.
[38] Matsushita Yoshio, *Nihon gunji hattatsushi* (Tokyo, 1937), 200.

absolute superiority over the American fleet in these categories of warship, it is understandable why Japan's naval leaders viewed the Washington Conference with some satisfaction. From a naval perspective, a system of international control over naval armaments had proved to be a most effective way to safeguard the empire.

The position of the Imperial army did not coincide exactly with that of the navy. After the 1924 reduction in the army, Japan possessed a force of seventeen divisions. Although this was a modest establishment, it was, in the early 1920's, sufficient for the security of Korea and for the protection of Japanese rights in South Manchuria. With the development of the Chinese Nationalist movement and the gradual strengthening of the Soviet army in the maritime provinces, however, the army's main mission—the protection of Japan's privileged position in Manchuria—became more complex. Neither of these problems, from the viewpoint of the army general staff, could be handled by reliance on a program of armament restrictions and a policy of cooperation with the United States. Given Japan's increasing naval strength vis-à-vis the United States, the army authorities discounted the risk of serious diplomatic tensions with the American government, if Japan were forced to act unilaterally in defense of her treaty rights in Manchuria. This appraisal prevailed within the Tanaka cabinet, most evidently at the 1927 Eastern Conference. Here, the entire cabinet, in conjunction with the senior officers of the army general staff and the Kwantung Army, formulated a China policy which conceded the probability of a "unified China." In view of this contingency, the assembled officials concluded that Japan, in cooperation with the powers, should adhere to three directives: (1) an endorsement of "legitimate" Chinese aspirations; (2) a willingness to implement "decisive" actions whenever Japanese lives or property were placed in jeopardy; and (3) a commitment to a "vigorous" course of action designed to dissipate all anti-Japanese movements on the mainland. More crucially, the Tanaka policy marked

Mongolia and Manchuria as regions of prime importance to the security of the empire. "If disturbances should spread to Manchuria and Mongolia and menace Japan's special position and interests in these regions, the Imperial government must be prepared to combat this menace, regardless of where the danger may originate."[39] Obviously the Tanaka cabinet had, in 1927, resolved to forestall the Kuomintang in Manchuria.

In 1928, the determination to block the northern advance of the Chinese Nationalists was revealed in the Tsinan intervention and in the assassination of Marshal Chang Tso-lin.[40] Although this forceful Tanaka policy was received with some favor within Japanese political circles, it also inspired the opposition party, the Minseitō, to level a strong indictment of this unilateral intervention on the mainland. In particular, the official foreign-policy spokesman for the Minseitō, Baron Shidehara, castigated the "positive" China policy of the Tanaka cabinet as having been motivated by partisan domestic ambitions. If a desire to curry popular support by a belligerent foreign policy were "allowed to dominate and control the conduct of foreign relations," admonished Shidehara, "we cannot but be apprehensive of the future of our country and of the peace of the world."[41] Despite this censure, the views of Shidehara and Tanaka did not offer a clear-cut choice between a peaceful and a positive China policy. Neither Tanaka nor Shidehara advocated the sacrifice of Japan's treaty rights in deference to the wishes of the Kuomintang. The essential distinction centered on a more complex problem—namely, whether Japan's rights and interests on the mainland could be sufficiently protected by a China policy which relied on Japanese political and economic pressure and a policy of cooperation with the Anglo-

[39] Japanese Foreign Ministry, *Nihon gaikō nenpyō narabini shuyō bunsho* (Tokyo, 1954), II, 101-102, gives the text of this policy decision.

[40] Usui Katsumi, "Cho Sakurin bakushi no shinso," *Himerareta shōwashi* (Tokyo, 1956), 26-39; Ashida Hitoshi, *Dainiji sekai taisen gaikōshi* (Tokyo, 1959), 40-41; and Akira Iriye, "Chang Hseuh-liang and the Japanese," *Journal of Asian Studies*, xx, 1 (November 1960), 37-41.

[41] Takeuchi, *War and Diplomacy*, 256.

American nations; or whether Japan must be prepared to act unilaterally in defense of her continental interests whenever they seemed to be threatened by the Nationalist government.[42] This posed a question over which honest men could and did differ.

In the fall of 1928, the Minseitō party, the proponents of Shidehara diplomacy, came to power. Thereafter, the Hamaguchi government based its foreign and armament policies on the premise that Japan's national interests would be served best by a cautious continental policy. Without overtly challenging Shidehara's emphasis on friendly relations with the Occidental sea powers, however, the leaders of the Seiyūkai and the army general staff continuously voiced the demand that the government should be willing to protect Japanese interests in Manchuria, regardless of the views and attitudes of the Anglo-American nations. And, in many respects, the political viability of Shidehara diplomacy after 1928 was dependent on a belief that friendship with the United States, a program of armament limitations, and the safety of Japan's continental interests could be harmonized into a creditable foreign policy.

By 1929, the Seiyūkai, as well as many nationalistic societies and organizations, was openly questioning the utility of a China policy which precluded the use of force. In this context, the diplomacy of Shidehara was dubbed "weak-kneed," too deferential to the wishes of the United States. The only sensible way to prevent irresponsible Chinese actions in Manchuria, argued Shidehara's critics, was to proclaim a positive China policy which would clearly indicate a willingness to act whenever Japanese lives or property were endangered by the behavior of Chinese business, political, student, or military organizations. The cogency of this viewpoint and the difficulties unleashed by the great depression did not, however,

---

[42] Usui Katsumi, "Shidehara gaikō oboegaki," *Nihon rekishi* (December 1958); and his "Tanaka gaikō ni tsuite no oboegaki," *Nihon gaikōshi kenkyū: Shōwa jidai* (Tokyo, 1960).

compromise Shidehara's conviction that Japan's national interests were still rooted in the security system created at the Washington Conference. The leaders of the Minseitō and the naval authorities espoused a cautious or "weak-kneed" China policy because they were unwilling to endanger the security and economic advantages gained through friendly relations with the Anglo-American sea powers by a program of unilateral action in defense of the Japanese position in South Manchuria.

The desire of the Hamaguchi government to avoid any major Sino-Japanese conflict which might adversely affect Japan's relations with the Anglo-American nations was based on a belief that a harmony of interests had been created by the Washington Conference treaties. This notion was disabused in 1930, not, as Shidehara had feared, by a Sino-Japanese dispute over Manchuria, but by an international conference devoted to the promotion of two commendable objectives: the reduction of naval armaments, and the preclusion of the use of force in the settlement of international disputes. It seems appropriate, therefore, to review the 1930 London Naval Conference in order to show how it yielded an armament agreement which challenged the principle of Japanese naval hegemony in the Western Pacific; and, in the process, how it generated a host of controversies which seriously compromised the viability of Shidehara diplomacy.

CHAPTER I

The London Naval Treaty Controversy

"The age when strength of force determines everything has already passed."
Admiral Takarabe, Naval Minister, 1930

"Justice is only superficial courtesy among nations
and the ultimate resort is military power alone."
Minister Kaneko, Privy Council, 1930

IN 1922, at the Washington Conference, Japan, Great Britain, and the United States negotiated a series of treaties on the basis of the existing fleets and the Pacific island fortifications of each nation. From the standpoint of Japan, the most immediate task centered on the continuance of its naval superiority over the United States in the Western Pacific. Japan's naval leaders wished, above all, to prevent any Anglo-American détente which might unite the two greatest naval powers against Imperial Japan. This potential danger had been attenuated, in 1921, by the existence of the Anglo-Japanese alliance, and by the traditional policies of Great Britain, which were based on the belief that friendly relations with Japan would best guarantee British interests in China, as well as the security of the Commonwealth nations. In addition, the postwar American demand for naval parity had been bitterly resented in British naval circles; and President Wilson's championing of the cause of the Chinese government at the Paris Peace Conference had been viewed skeptically in Whitehall. The diplomatic interests and attitudes shared by the British and Japanese delegations, plus the desire of the American government to avoid a naval armament race, in large part produced the Four, Five, and Nine Power agreements at the Washington Conference, treaties which assured Japan's naval hegemony in the Western Pacific in exchange for a public commitment to respect the integrity of China.

Throughout the 1920's, Japan faithfully adhered to the terms of the Washington Conference treaties. In this context, the fundamental cleavage between American and Japanese naval policy did not cause any serious diplomatic difficulties. Nevertheless, American naval policy after 1922 continued to seek two fundamental objectives: absolute parity with Great Britain, and a 10:6 ratio with the Japanese fleet. The former goal did not directly affect the Imperial government; but the latter conflicted with the premise of Japanese naval superiority in the Western Pacific. From the perspective of the American Naval Board, the Washington Conference treaties had established, in principle, both objectives. Technically, however, parity with Great Britain and the 10:6 ratio with Japan were applicable only to capital warships; and throughout the Washington Conference the Japanese delegation had insisted that any comprehensive armament control over other categories of warships, particularly heavy cruisers, would have to be in terms of a 10:7 ratio. Moreover, because of an inability to determine the relative worth of heavy versus light cruisers, the British and American delegations simply could not agree on what would constitute parity in these categories. In view of Britain's world-wide empire and numerous port facilities, the British delegation at the Washington Conference favored a large number of light cruisers; the American delegation, conscious of the United States' necessity to defend two coastlines and lack of comparable world-wide port facilities, preferred a large number of heavy cruisers. The inability of the two delegations to agree upon the number of American heavy cruisers which would be equivalent to the British fleet of light cruisers, and the Japanese insistence on a 10:7 ratio with the United States in heavy cruisers, frustrated all efforts at a comprehensive system of armament control. Consequently, although the Washington Conference established parity in capital warships between Britain and the United States, as well as a 10:6 ratio between Japan and the United States in this category of ships, the American fleet did not, in 1922, nor throughout the

1920's, actually obtain either goal. Quite the contrary. Following the Washington Conference, the American fleet was not refurbished by any significant amount of new naval construction, whereas both Britain and Japan built several new cruisers, submarines, and destroyers.

Despite the discrepancy between the existing strength of the American fleet and the basic objectives underlying American naval policy, the success of the Washington Conference inspired the hope that control over all naval armaments could be attained and the belief that it should be. Public confidence in the efficacy of disarmament agreements, and a conviction that the armament race prior to the outbreak of the First World War had been a major cause of that conflagration, decisively structured the policies of the Western nations during the 1920's. These sentiments were most dramatically embodied in the famous Kellogg-Briand Pact, which bound the signators to abandon war "as an instrument of national policy" and to settle "all disputes or conflicts of whatever nature or of whatever origin" by diplomatic means.[1] Less dramatically, the major naval powers pursued the quest for armament limitation in a series of meetings in Geneva, Switzerland. These talks, however, were frustrated by the contentions between the British and American delegations: the Americans sought a quota of 23 heavy cruisers; and the British rejected the proposal as a demand for superiority, not parity.[2] The inability of the two delegations to find an acceptable mathematical formula to adjudicate the claims of both parties finally induced the United States Congress to authorize the construction of the fleet of 23 heavy cruisers deemed necessary by the American Naval Board.

Although Britain and Japan both possessed a commanding

[1] Recent studies of the disarmament problem include Robert Ferrell, *Peace in Their Time* (New Haven, 1952); L. Ethan Ellis, *Frank B. Kellogg and American Foreign Relations, 1925-1929* (New Brunswick, N.J., 1961); Gerald Wheeler, *Prelude to Pearl Harbor* (Columbia, Mo., 1963); and Alexander de Conde, ed., *Isolation and Security* (Durham, 1957).

[2] Elting Morrison, *Turmoil and Tradition* (Boston, 1960), 318-320.

superiority in this category of warship, the projected American construction program inevitably contained the risk of unleashing a retaliatory naval expansion program by the other two powers. Mainly because of the calamitous effects of the great depression, however, neither Japan nor Great Britain viewed the prospect of an increased military budget with approval; and the same consideration, of course, dictated a conciliatory attitude by the American government. In the spring of 1929, the first overture for another try at a comprehensive naval agreement emanated from Great Britain.

THE PARITY DISPUTE

Since the earlier Geneva talks had foundered on Anglo-American technical disputes, the British prime minister, Ramsay MacDonald, on May 27, 1929, proposed that the two countries initiate direct conversations in order to arrive at a "yardstick" acceptable to both parties.[3] When the American secretary of state, Henry Stimson, responded favorably on the 24th of June, MacDonald explored the matter with Ambassador Matsudaira, who expressed the willingness of the Japanese government to participate in a new naval limitation agreement. Specifically, Matsudaira recommended two steps to be taken prior to the convening of any naval conference: a preliminary adjustment of the parity issue between Britain and the United States; and a Japanese-American discussion of Japan's minimal strategic needs.[4] With this encouragement, Prime Minister MacDonald proposed, on July 9, that Britain and the United States should jointly announce a desire for a comprehensive reduction in naval armaments and the realization of parity between the fleets of the two countries.[5] In addition, MacDonald thought this public plea for disarmament should be linked with the principles underlying the Kellogg-Briand Pact.

---

[3] United States Department of State, Archives: London Naval Conference, Record Group 43, Box 53, Item 64, "Telegrams on Subject of Naval Disarmament," London Cable #130. [Hereafter cited as USDS, Archives, LNC.]

[4] *Ibid.*, London Cable #181.   [5] *Ibid.*, London Cable #179.

More precisely, the British prime minister suggested that England and the United States should (1) prepare a yardstick to determine parity; (2) apply this yardstick in their discussions; (3) keep Japan, France, and Italy fully informed of the Anglo-American talks; and (4) when the parity issue was resolved, call an international conference to discuss the problems of naval limitations.

The American secretary of state, on July 11, concurred with MacDonald's proposals, adding that the two countries should first formulate a basic policy guide before undertaking any technical discussion of the parity issue.[6] Ten days later, however, Secretary Stimson advised MacDonald that the crux of the problem would be the cruiser question: how many heavy cruisers would Great Britain be prepared to grant?[7] Before responding to this query, the British prime minister sounded out the British Admiralty and the Japanese ambassador. In his formal reply of August 8, MacDonald recommended that the Anglo-American discussions should proceed in a "give and take" spirit.[8] Continually citing his personal "indifference" to the projected building program of the United States, Mac-Donald reminded the American secretary of state that Japan's naval policy was pegged to a 10:7 ratio in heavy cruisers with that of the American fleet.[9] Only in this indirect way, Mac-Donald insisted, did American policy affect his approach to the cruiser issue. If the United States were to demand a quota of more than 18 heavy cruisers, reasoned the British prime minister, Japan would wish to increase her strength beyond her existing 12 heavy cruisers; and, noted MacDonald, if the United States were to insist on a quota of 23 heavy cruisers, even at a 10:6 ratio, Japan would obtain 14 heavy cruisers. Inasmuch as Great Britain currently possessed 15 heavy cruisers, an increase in Japanese strength to 14 cruisers would compromise British security in the South Pacific. For this

---

[6] *Ibid.*, Washington Cable #174.   [7] *Ibid.*, Washington Cable #182.
[8] *Ibid.*, London Cable #228.
[9] *Ibid.*, London Cable #254, August 31, 1929.

reason alone, stressed the British prime minister, the "dominions would reject any agreement of this sort."[10] Hence, MacDonald hoped that the American government would settle for a quota of 18 heavy cruisers, in the expectation that Japan would be satisfied with her existing fleet of 12 heavy cruisers. In that event, he concluded, the United States could still build a new fleet of heavy cruisers, and Japan and Great Britain could avoid the necessity of any new construction in this category of warship.

When the opinions and suggestions of the British prime minister failed to evoke any evident spirit of "give and take," MacDonald sensed that the major difficulty was a deep-rooted suspicion of Britain's ulterior motives in requesting a quota of 18 heavy cruisers for the United States. Unless he could convince the leaders of the American government that Britain sincerely was prepared to grant naval parity, there would be slight chance of an Anglo-American accord. On the 18th of September, MacDonald discussed the situation thoroughly with Ambassador Matsudaira and concluded that the Japanese government would, in fact, accept an armament limitations agreement which imposed a quota of 18 heavy cruisers for the United States, 15 for Great Britain, and 12 for Japan.[11] A week later MacDonald sent off his third personal letter to Washington. After professing his acceptance of parity between the Anglo-American fleets—"take it with both hands heaped and running down"—MacDonald added the caution that the parity principle should not be "an attempt to clothe unreality in the garb of mathematical reality."[12] By this, the British prime minister wished to convey the necessity of adjusting the cruiser question in terms of the existing fleets and of the traditional policy of the Japanese government.

During his October good-will visit to the United States, MacDonald studiously avoided any public discussion of the cruiser problem. Instead, at every opportunity, the British

---

10 *Ibid.*   11 *Ibid.*, London Cable #332.
12 *Ibid.*, London Cable #281.

leader emphasized the historic bonds of friendship between England and the United States and he vigorously called for a joint Anglo-American effort to champion the principles of the Kellogg-Briand Pact by a general reduction of naval armament. The parity issue, MacDonald claimed, was a dead issue: "What is all this bother about parity? Take it, without reserve, heaped up and flowing over."[13] In the more reserved confines of diplomatic negotiations, however, this public profession failed to surmount the difficulties impeding a specific agreement. The United States authorities repeatedly pressed for a quota of 21 heavy cruisers, a figure which the American Naval Board judged to be the equivalent of Britain's large fleet of light cruisers. Their British counterparts countered with the necessity to consider the third great naval power— Imperial Japan—in the discussion of the parity quotas. Britain simply could not allow Japan to increase her number of heavy cruisers; and Japan would never agree to a quota of 21 heavy cruisers for the United States. "Either therefore the United States must come down to eighteen 8″ ships," stipulated a spokesman for the British Foreign Office on October 10, "or Great Britain and Japan must build further 8″ cruisers."[14]

Despite this stalemate between the two delegations over the cruiser question, President Hoover and Prime Minister MacDonald engaged in a friendly discourse at Rapidan and easily agreed that the two countries should seek a comprehensive control over naval armaments.[15] In their joint communiqué, the two leaders praised the Kellogg-Briand Pact and they committed both governments to an effort to work together in the arduous task of reaching a comprehensive system of naval armament controls. Thus, without reaching a specific accord between the two governments, MacDonald's trip to the United

[13] Robert Ferrell, *American Diplomacy in the Great Depression* (New Haven, 1957), 85.
[14] Henry L. Stimson, Correspondence with Japan, Sterling Memorial Library, Yale University, New Haven, IF 0667 (October 6, 1929). [Hereafter cited as Stimson, *Correspondence*.]
[15] On the Rapidan meeting, consult Ferrell, *American Diplomacy*, 80-84.

States had nevertheless dissipated one major obstacle to a resolution to the parity question. It had, in the judgment of a recent appraisal, "left behind an atmosphere of friendship for Englishmen such as Americans had not known for a long time."[16] In so doing, the British prime minister inaugurated a new era in Anglo-American naval policies. Henceforth, the parity issue no longer acted as the divisive element in Anglo-American naval conversations. The only remaining point of serious friction was the extent to which the American cruiser policy should be modified to satisfy the political expectations and strategic concerns of the Japanese government. The implications of this new situation slowly manifested themselves at the London Naval Conference, to the dismay and disadvantage of the Hamaguchi government.

THE RATIO DISPUTE

After his Rapidan conversations with President Hoover, the British prime minister extended formal invitations to the major powers to attend a conference on naval armament limitation. The Hamaguchi cabinet received this invitation with a sense of confident expectation. The platform of the Minseitō listed fiscal austerity and armament reduction as two essential objectives of the Hamaguchi government; and the foreign policy of Baron Shidehara stressed the benefits of a moderate China policy and of cooperation with the Anglo-American nations. The Japanese government was, moreover, in the enviable position of being able to propose an absolute reduction in the size of the Imperial navy, without risking the security of the empire. This possibility was afforded by the non-fortification clauses of the Four and Five Power Treaties, and by the existing ratio between the American and Japanese fleets. Throughout the 1920's, Japan had constructed a number of new cruisers, submarines, and destroyers, thereby obtaining a commanding naval superiority over the United States in the

16 *Ibid.*, 84.

Western Pacific.[17] By the end of 1929, Japan would possess twelve heavy cruisers and the United States one—the *Salt Lake City.* If, as Admiral Yarnell noted in 1930, "it is the ships that are built or under construction that count in any naval conference," the Japanese government obviously would hold a strong hand in the forthcoming disarmament negotiations.[18] Still, neither the Hamaguchi cabinet nor the naval general staff entertained any hope of perpetuating the advantages it had acquired through the lack of any American naval construction during the 1920's. Japan's naval policy in 1930, as in 1922, sought one objective: supremacy over the American fleet in Japanese home waters. Paradoxically, this goal could be attained even by a reduction of the Japanese fleet; and the Hamaguchi government therefore anticipated no major diplomatic difficulty when it accepted MacDonald's invitation to attend the 1930 London Naval Conference.

In order to demonstrate the earnest desire of the Japanese government for a real reduction in naval armaments, as well as to indicate the basic unity among all important political and naval groups in Japan, the entire Hamaguchi cabinet, the leaders of the opposition party, the Seiyūkai, and the leading members of the Privy Council attended an October 10 briefing session on national defense policies at the official residence of the naval minister. Following this conference, Premier Hamaguchi advised the press of the government's intention to seek a 10:7 ratio with the United States in the heavy-cruiser category.[19] This ratio, the premier indicated, was indispensable to the security of the empire. From the viewpoint of the Hamaguchi government, the demand for a 10:7 ratio seemed reasonable. It revealed the defensive nature of Japan's naval strategy; and it demonstrated a willingness to allow the

---

[17] USDS, Archives, LNC, Record Group 43, Box 46, Item 161, "Background of the London Naval Conference."

[18] *London Naval Treaty of 1930: Hearings Before the Committee on Naval Affairs, United States Senate* (Washington, 1930), 182.

[19] Tatsuji Takeuchi, *War and Diplomacy in the Japanese Empire* (Chicago, 1935), 283-284.

United States to overcome its existing inferiority in heavy cruisers without the necessity of resorting to an armament race. "Our claim to a definite amount of naval strength [10:7]," Premier Hamaguchi informed the Diet on January 21, 1930, "is based upon the practical necessity to make our defenses secure against foreign invasion. We offer no menace to any nation, we submit to menace from none. On that fundamental principle, it is our desire to seek a naval agreement satisfactory to all the parties concerned."[20]

The determination of the Imperial government to press for a 10:7 ratio obviously conflicted with the assumption of the American Naval Board that the 10:6 ratio which had been established for capital warships at the Washington Conference should be applied to all categories of warships. Thus, throughout October and November, whenever Ambassador Debuchi requested a preliminary discussion of the cruiser question between the American and Japanese delegations to the London Conference, he was constantly put off by the American secretary of state.[21] At last, on November 12, Secretary Stimson met with the Japanese ambassador and, during the meeting, he dismissed the 10:7 ratio as a legitimate claim. "If you will refer to the records of the [Washington] conference," advised Stimson, "you will find that the original formula proposed by this government covered not only capital ships . . . but also all auxiliary combatant craft, and especially covered cruisers."[22] Three days later, without mentioning the original formula proposed by the Japanese delegation at the Washington Conference, Foreign Minister Shidehara simply replied that no such agreement had actually been incorporated into the negotiations in 1922. The Japanese foreign minister thought that, instead of considering the original American proposals at the Washington Conference, the cruiser problem should best be dealt with in the light of "actual conditions."[23] For under-

20 *Ibid.*, 289-290.
21 Stimson, *Correspondence*, October 23, 1929.
22 *Ibid.*, November 12, 1929.
23 *Ibid.*, December 2, 1929.

standable reasons, Secretary Stimson neither desired nor intended to discuss the cruiser question in terms of the existing fleets.

Frustrated in its initial effort to reach a preliminary Japanese-American understanding, the Hamaguchi government had its delegation to the London Conference stop in Washington in hopes of pursuing the cruiser problem. On December 19 and 27, the Japanese and American delegations reviewed their general approaches to the London Conference.[24] The head of the Japanese delegation, Wakatsuki Reijirō, professed the willingness of his government to reduce its cruiser and submarine tonnage and to declare submarine warfare against commerce illegal, if the United States would accept a 10:7 ratio in heavy cruisers. In response, the American secretary of state talked at some length on the unusual problems posed by the necessity of the United States to defend two coastlines and on the "great concessions" which the American government had made at the time of the Washington Conference. Following this discourse, Stimson notified the Japanese delegation that, unless it would approve the principle of a 10:6 ratio, the American navy would be expanded until this goal was achieved. Since neither government wanted an armament race, the secretary concluded with the suggestion that instead of discussing the cruiser problem in terms of a fixed mathematical ratio, the Japanese government be content with its *de facto* naval supremacy.

The American delegation to the London Conference had, by focusing on one aspect of the Washington Conference, come to believe that the 10:6 ratio had been established in principle at the Washington Conference. The treaties negotiated in 1922, however, had not been confined to naval matters; and they had recognized Japan's naval hegemony in the Western Pacific.

[24] USDS, Archives, LNC, 500 A15 A3/594, "Minutes of Conversations Between Heads of Japanese and U.S. Delegations to London Conference," December 19, 1929; and "Draft Minutes of Informal Conversations Between American and Japanese Delegates to the London Naval Conference," December 17, 1929.

The contention of the Japanese government that a 70 per cent ratio would maintain this security, while a 60 per cent ratio would compromise the defense of the empire, was, moreover, recognized by all American naval experts as a professionally sound judgment. Every ranking American naval officer who subsequently testified on the Three Power Treaty which was negotiated at the London Naval Conference, for example, granted two propositions: (1) a 10:7 ratio would guarantee the security of the Hawaiian Islands; (2) this ratio would not permit the American navy to wage offensive operations in Japanese waters.[25] "I estimate," testified Rear Admiral Pringle, the chief of the Naval War College, "that with the five to five to three ratio, we would have a chance of conducting a successful campaign, but the minute this ratio began to be altered in favor of the Japanese, our chances are reduced thereby and become less than what you would possibly call an even chance."[26] It was natural and proper for American naval officers to seek a ratio which would, in the event of war with Japan, enable the American fleet to carry the war to Japan's home islands. Whether the policy of the American government vis-à-vis an international conference ostensibly seeking an effective system of international control over naval armaments should have been governed by this perspective is another matter. In any event, the ratio dispute—10:6 or 10:7—was not an abstract mathematical quibble. It affected the basis of the Washington Conference Treaty Order: an acknowledgment of Japan's supremacy in the Western Pacific. If it were legitimate for the Hamaguchi government to seek a confirmation of this supremacy in 1930, the insistence on a 10:7 ratio in heavy cruisers was neither unreasonable nor surprising.

ANGLO-AMERICAN UNITY

In view of the existing strength of the American fleet, the

[25] See testimony of Admirals Pratt, Pringle, Yarnell, Bristol, Hepburn, and Coontz, *London Naval Treaty of 1930*.
[26] *Ibid.*, 162.

twin desires for parity with Great Britain and for a 10:6 ratio with Japan placed the American delegation in an awkward bargaining position at the London Naval Conference. In effect, it was asking both Japan and Britain to accept a moratorium on naval construction while the United States engaged in a major program of expansion. The only way to compel the Japanese delegation to amend its policy hinged upon some type of Anglo-American accord. Yet, when the American delegation left the United States, its basic policy guide still called for a quota of 21 heavy cruisers, a figure which the British had already vetoed. On January 19, 1930, Secretary Stimson and Prime Minister MacDonald explored the major issue involved in any three-power discussions among Japan, Great Britain and the United States. Emphasizing that the United States Senate would never accept a treaty which granted Japan a 70 per cent ratio, the American secretary of state predicted that a united stand by the American and British delegations would settle the matter, because Japan would not relish the prospect of an Anglo-American two-power treaty "which might enable Great Britain and the United States to build fully two to one against her."[27] As for parity, Secretary Stimson reasoned that the admirals could never agree on a suitable yardstick and the only solution would be an agreement reached by the "responsible statesmen."[28] The British prime minister concurred with both propositions, adding that if the United States would accept a quota of 18 heavy cruisers, "he could make almost an' settlement in 6 inch cruisers."[29]

Regardless of MacDonald's assurances, within a few days spokesman for the British Foreign Office advised Senator Ree of the American delegation that "absolutely no progress" h; been made on the 10:7 ratio problem in discussions with t' Japanese delegation, despite the assumption that the Unit

[27] USDS, Archives, LNC, 500 A15 A3/621, Stimson Cable #4, Janu 19, 1930.
[28] Henry L. Stimson Diary, Sterling Memorial Library, Yale Univer New Haven, February 3, 1930. [Hereafter cited as Stimson, *Diary*.]
[29] *Ibid.*

States would accept a quota of 18 cruisers.[30] Confronted by this information, the American delegation was compelled to reconsider its initial policy. In the course of the discussion, Admiral Pratt admitted that the desired goal of 21 heavy cruisers would actually mean superiority, not parity with the British fleet. Once this statement was articulated, the American delegation, as Stimson informed President Hoover, on February 4, readily agreed that the 21-cruiser program could be "insisted on only with great danger to the Conference's success."[31] The President "heartily approved" this decision; and Secretary Stimson soon reached a tentative solution of the parity question with the British prime minister. By February 12, both men agreed "that Great Britain and the United States would continue to pursue identical lines with reference to Japan, in view of the very strong feelings of Australia of the necessity for keeping [the] Japanese big cruiser figures down."[32]

This Anglo-American unity was revealed to the Japanese delegation on February 17, at the first round-table discussion held by the three delegations.[33] After outlining the tentative solution of the parity question. Secretary Stimson expressed his unhappiness at the unwillingness of the Japanese delegation to modify its policies, particularly since the United States had agreed to accept a quota of 18 heavy cruisers. Unmoved by the personal feelings of the American secretary of state, the head of the Japanese delegation, Wakatsuki Reijirō, reiterated the conviction of his government that a 70 per cent ratio was essential to the security of the Japanese empire. Without challenging the validity of this opinion, the British prime minister called Wakatsuki's attention to the anxiety which any increase in Japan's fleet of heavy cruisers

[30] USDS, Archives, LNC, Record Group 43, Box 52, Item 163, "Informal Meeting of American Delegation," January 24, 1930.

[31] Stimson, *Diary*, February 5, 1930, includes a paraphrase of Stimson's cable to Acting Secretary of State Cotton.

[32] *Ibid.*, February 12, 1930.

[33] USDS, Archives, LNC, Record Group 43, Box E161 (unlabeled and not officially indexed or filed), "Notes of Meeting of Heads of the Japanese, English and American Delegations," February 17, 1930.

would generate in Australia and New Zealand. MacDonald then reminded the Japanese delegation of the necessity to approach the cruiser problem in terms of a three-power agreement, not simply as one between the United States and Imperial Japan. After discounting any concern with the policies and strength of the British fleet, Wakatsuki continued to direct the thrust of his presentation at the American delegation. Neither he nor the Japanese people could understand why Japan should not be given a 70 per cent ratio, unless the United States actually harbored the idea of ultimately engaging in a war with the Japanese empire. "As long as America held that ten percent advantage," concluded Wakatsuki, "it was possible for her to attack. So, when America insisted on seventy percent instead of sixty percent, the idea would exist that they were trying to keep that possibility, and the Japanese people could not accept that."[34] After dryly noting that both Japan and the United States had "something to ponder over," the British prime minister promptly adjourned the meeting.[35]

This session did not undermine Secretary Stimson's expectations that eventually Japan would amend its policy. From all that he had heard, Stimson believed that Wakatsuki was the "kind of man" who would be willing to make a politically unpopular decision.[36] Moreover, the secretary of state interpreted Wakatsuki's categorical statement that he could never sign a treaty which did not embody a 70 per cent ratio as being no more than a "gesture."[37] The main difficulty, Stimson reasoned, was the forthcoming general election in Japan. Since the Hamaguchi cabinet had unwisely made the 10:7

[34] *Ibid.*, 13.

[35] Rowan Butler, ed., *Documents on British Foreign Policy, 1919-1930*, Second Series, I (London, 1956), 233, attributes this quote to Mr. Henderson of the British delegation.

[36] Stimson, *Diary*, February 17, 1930, includes a copy of Stimson's letter to Hoover.

[37] *Ibid.* In a postscript Stimson advised Hoover that Wakatsuki had indicated "he could not sign a treaty which did not contain it [a 10:7 ratio]; but he said it in such a way . . . that he produced on Reed, Robinson and myself, who were present, the conviction that it was a gesture pending the [Japanese general] elections."

ratio a public issue, it could not amend this policy in the midst of a political campaign. Stimson believed that, once the elections were over, the Japanese delegation would assume a more moderate approach to the cruiser question. With this assumption, Stimson temporarily set aside any further discussion of the Japanese problem, concentrating his efforts on winding up the parity issue with Great Britain.

The parity matter was by February 23 informally settled and Stimson and MacDonald devised a joint strategy vis-à-vis the Japanese delegation.[38] Both statesmen agreed on the necessity to avoid any confrontation over the cruiser question until the Japanese general elections were completed; and both men assumed that the threat of an Anglo-American naval pact would compel a more conciliatory attitude on the part of the Japanese delegation. This conclusion was not unwarranted. Premier Hamaguchi, Foreign Minister Shidehara, and Wakatsuki Reijirō previously had been articulate spokesmen for a system of international armament control and of friendly relations with the Anglo-American nations; and certainly an Anglo-American treaty directed against Japan would unquestionably pose a grave threat to Japan's security. Nevertheless, there was much less willingness in Tokyo to discount the commitment of the Hamaguchi government to the 10:7 ratio.

The American ambassador to Japan, William Castle, appreciated the fact that the ratio dispute was prompted less by technical considerations than by an apprehension that one day Japan and the United States might conflict over a matter affecting the mainland. To abate this suspicion, Ambassador Castle, on his own initiative, assured Foreign Minister Shidehara that he could "conceive of no circumstance in which America would go to war over China."[39] When Shidehara requested some type of public assurance to this effect, however, Castle was promptly advised to avoid any statement which

[38] USDS, Archives, LNC, 500 A15 A3/702, Stimson Cable #80, February 23, 1930.
[39] *Ibid.*, 500 A15 A3/661, Tokyo (Castle) Cable #14, January 31, 1930.

might bracket Japanese and American policy vis-à-vis China.[40] Instead, the ambassador was ordered to confine any further remarks to the terms of the Nine Power Treaty and the Kellogg-Briand Pact.

Despite this rebuke, Ambassador Castle sensed that Shidehara diplomacy was itself contingent upon the maintenance of the Washington Treaty Order, and that any compromise of the 10:7 ratio would have serious repercussions on Japan's foreign and domestic policies. Thus, although he too stressed the personal integrity of the Japanese leaders, their friendship for the Anglo-American nations, and their earnest desire for reduction in naval armaments, Castle repeatedly emphasized that the demand for a 70 per cent ratio was "a political doctrine" in Japan, the *"sine qua non* of the Japanese program."[41] This judgment, plus the ambassador's apparent sympathy with the policies of the Hamaguchi government, understandably vexed the American secretary of state, if only because Castle might inadvertently lead the Japanese government to anticipate a change in American naval policy. Thus, on February 28, Stimson ordered the acting secretary of state, Joseph Cotton, "not to repeat to Tokyo any details regarding negotiations, unless I expressly express it."[42] This step was taken because Stimson understood only too well the practical difficulties he faced at London. He simply could not risk having his strategy at the London Conference unwittingly compromised by the American ambassador in Tokyo.

REED-MATSUDAIRA COMPROMISE

The diplomacy of the American delegation at the London Conference considered two alternative solutions to the cruiser problem: either the Imperial delegation would relax its posture, once the Japanese general elections were completed;

---

[40] *Ibid.*, 500 A15 A3/662, Washington (Cotton) Cable #25, February 1, 1930.
[41] *Ibid.*, 500 A15 A3/689, Tokyo (Castle) Cable #27, February 14, 1930.
[42] *Ibid.*, Record Group 43, Box 53, Item 164, Stimson Cable #48, February 8, 1930.

or, failing this, the American delegation would have to bring
about the change by diplomatic pressure. The latter option,
in turn, would depend upon two considerations: (1) convincing
the Japanese delegation that the United States would under
no circumstances accept a 10:7 ratio, thus inducing the responsible leaders of the Japanese government to negotiate a
three-power pact granting this ratio; or (2) as a last resort,
confronting the Japanese with the threat of an Anglo-American
naval pact in order to convince the political and naval leaders
of the Japanese government that the alternative to a three-
power treaty would compromise Japan's naval security more
decisively than the imposition of a 10:7 ratio in heavy cruisers.

Stimson's belief in the salutary effects of the general election
in Japan was short-lived. On February 25, Ambassador
Matsudaira again presented the original Japanese proposal;
and, since this was unacceptable to Senator Reed of the American delegation, the joint talks were tabled for several days.
During this interval, Saito Hiroshi of the Japanese delegation
informed Mr. Craige of the British Foreign Office that the
Japanese-American impasse could be resolved in a diplomatic
fashion: Japan would accept a quota of 18 cruisers for the
United States, if the American government would defer construction of the last three cruisers until 1935.[43] An agreement
of this sort, ventured the Japanese diplomat, would satisfy the
American desire for a formal enunciation of the 10:6 ratio;
and it would also assure Japan's wish for a *de facto* 10:7 ratio
until 1936, at which time the two nations could reconsider
their positions at the next conference on naval limitations.

Saito's proposition received a cool reception from the American delegation, at least until Secretary Stimson was notified of
a growing dissatisfaction with his handling of the negotiations
at London. On March 5, President Hoover pointedly observed
that, even if the United States were to grant the cruiser ratio
desired by Japan, the Imperial navy "still would be greatly inferior to the American fleet and no national anxiety need be

[43] Stimson, *Diary*, February 21, 1930.

caused by it."[44] The next day, Acting Secretary of State Cotton also informed Stimson that Senators Borah and Swanson preferred a concession in the cruiser matter to any political agreement with any country, because neither senator feared "Japan as an immediate potential enemy with trade conditions and fleets as they are."[45] Subject to this pressure, Secretary Stimson promptly reported, "We are making progress in our negotiations with Japan"; he added that "better results" could be obtained than those suggested by the March 5 reflections of President Hoover.[46] After this statement, on March 8, the American delegation elected to follow the compromise outlined by Saito Hiroshi, with a slight variation. If Japan would sanction a quota of 18 cruisers for the United States, Senator Reed conceded the United States would defer construction of the last three cruisers until 1934, 1935, and 1936.[47] Since this plan would give the American government a stronger bargaining position in 1936 than that contained in Saito's original plan, Ambassador Matsudaira countered with a modest amendment to Reed's proposal—namely, he would accept the latest American proposal if Japan were permitted to spread an additional 20,000 tons of naval construction over other categories of warships. This concession, noted Matsudaira, would furnish Japan with a combined fleet tonnage slightly "in excess of seventy percent during the life of the treaty."[48] Although Senator Reed responded favorably to Matsudaira's suggestion, it was vigorously challenged by the American naval advisors. In this context, Secretary Stimson decided to play his

[44] USDS, Archives, LNC, Record Group 43, Box 53, Item 164, Washington (Cotton) Cable #178, March 5, 1930.

[45] *Ibid.*, 500 A15 A3/741a, Washington (Cotton) Cable #181, March 6, 1930.

[46] Stimson, *Diary*, March 8, 1930, includes a paraphrase of Stimson's cable to Cotton.

[47] USDS, Archives, LNC, 500 A15 A3/733, Stimson Cable #107, March 3, 1930. On March 7, Shidehara noted that an "agreement would be simple," if the United States would postpone the last three cruisers until 1935. *Ibid.*, 500 A15 A3/741, Tokyo (Castle) Cable #39, March 7, 1930.

[48] *Ibid.*, 500 A15 A3/743, Stimson Cable #122, March 8, 1930.

diplomatic trump, the threat of an Anglo-American accord directed against Japan.

At the secretary's request, the heads of the three delegations —Stimson, MacDonald, and Wakatsuki—met in Stimson's private suite at the Ritz Hotel on March 12 for the purpose of reviewing the proposed three-power naval treaty. Foregoing the usual amenities, Stimson directly informed Wakatsuki that Senator Reed's proposal of March 8 represented the maximum concession the United States was prepared to make on the cruiser dispute.[49] Any further wrangling on this subject, he warned, would completely rupture the tri-power negotiations. In this eventuality, continued Stimson with the silent concurrence of the British prime minister, Great Britain and the United States were fully prepared to negotiate a two-power agreement.[50] On this note, the secretary terminated the meeting with the hope that Wakatsuki understood the gravity of the situation, as well as the benefits which Japan would share in a three-power treaty.

The next morning, March 13, Senator Reed presented the "final" American proposal to Ambassador Matsudaira. Essentially it contained the following ratio stipulations:[51]

	U.S.	*Japan*	*Percentage*
Large cruisers	180,000	108,400	60.2
Small cruisers	143,500	100,450	70.0
Destroyers	150,000	105,500	70.3
Submarines	52,700	52,700	100.0
	526,200	367,050	69.75

The plan called for a 10:6 ratio in heavy cruisers; but the United States also agreed that it would not begin construction of the final three cruisers until 1934, 1935, and 1936. Thus, in

[49] Stimson, *Diary*, March 12, 1930.
[50] *Ibid.*
[51] Aritake Shuji, *Okada Keisuke denki* (Tokyo, 1956), 32-33. Also, USDS, Archives, LNC, 500 A15 A3/750, Stimson Cable #134, March 13, 1930.

terms of the fleets-in-being, Japan would possess a *de facto* 10:7 ratio at least until the 1936 conference on naval limitations.

The final proposal of March 13, subsequently known as the Reed-Matsudaira Compromise, has been interpreted in many ways. To some, especially to the American Naval Board, the commitments governing the last three heavy cruisers constituted a real and unnecessary concession. From another perspective, the stipulation seemed less crucial. Under the Reed-Matsudaira Compromise, Japan could not build a single heavy cruiser and she could construct only 50,768 tons of new shipping. Under the same accord, the United States could construct 14 heavy cruisers between 1930 and 1936, lay the keels for three additional cruisers in these years, and carry out a building program totaling some 346,811 tons of new shipping.[52] This 7:1 imbalance in naval construction was, in fact, inherent in any naval treaty. An acceptance of a principle of a 10:7 ratio by the American delegation, for example, would have produced a comparable amount of allotted naval construction. This fact was not lost on Secretary Stimson, who reminded Cotton that the American delegation was in the "position of asking a nation greatly superior to us in existing young ships . . . to stop active construction and to accept a position of inferiority to our potential program."[53] For this reason, Stimson viewed the Reed-Matsudaira Compromise with pride; and, for similar reasons, the plan posed a major crisis for the Hamaguchi cabinet.

The unwillingness of the American government to grant a 70 per cent ratio at a time when Japan possessed a fleet far in excess of this figure unavoidably invited the suspicion that the United States actually wished to compromise Japan's naval

[52] After reviewing these statistical facts, Walter Lippmann judged: "Japan is now going to take what amounts to a naval holiday." "The London Naval Conference: An American View," *Foreign Affairs*, VIII, 4 (July 1930), 509.

[53] USDS, Archives, LNC, 500 A15 A3/755, Stimson Cable #136, March 14, 1930.

security in the Western Pacific. The Hamaguchi government was placed, therefore, in the position of having to choose between two distressing alternatives—to withdraw from the conference, or to modify its basic national defense policy. On March 14, Foreign Minister Shidehara fired one question at the Japanese delegation: was it possible to obtain further concessions? The dreaded reply came the following morning. In remarkably precise language, Ambassador Matsudaira advised that it was absolutely impossible to obtain a 10:7 ratio. The American secretary of state, on March 12, had shattered any hopes in this direction. "In these circumstances," concluded Matsudaira, "I urge the government to give earnest consideration to the full import of the Stimson-Wakatsuki and the Reed-Matsudaira talks and, one way or another, to amend the instructions to the Japanese delegation."[54] The resolution of this problem was to consume sixteen days.

REVISED JAPANESE INSTRUCTIONS

When Ambassador Matsudaira notified the government that Japan could not obtain a clearly defined 10:7 ratio, the naval general staff promptly tried to preclude any reconsideration of the original instructions to the Japanese delegation.[55] During the morning of March 15, the chief and vice-chief of the general staff, Admiral Katō Kanji and Vice-Admiral Suetsugu, conferred with the commanding officer of the home fleet, Admiral Kobayashi, and the vice-naval minister, Vice-Admiral Yamanashi. Here Katō, Suetsugu, and Kobayashi reiterated the strategic significance of the 10:7 ratio and soon formulated their response to the Reed-Matsudaira plan: the

[54] Aritake, *Okada Keisuke*, 36, reproduces Matsudaira's cable. Secretary Stimson also advised Ambassador Castle: "Please impress on Shidehara that we have gone to the limit to accommodate Japan. . . . We can go no farther." USDS, Archives, LNC, 500 A15 A3/749, Stimson Cable #133, March 13, 1930.

[55] Without sharing responsibility for any opinions or judgments, I am indebted to Rear Admiral Hōri Teikichi for his detailed recollections of the events in Tokyo between March 12 and April 15, 1930. At that time, as chief of the Bureau of Naval Affairs, Hōri was a major actor in this drama.

Imperial navy simply could not permit the Hamaguchi cabinet to endanger national security by accepting an armament limitation agreement which would not meet the nation's minimum security needs—namely, a 10:7 ratio in heavy cruisers with the United States.

For his part, however, Vice-Naval Minister Yamanashi failed to join this harmonious chorus, lest he introduce a discordant note. Finally Suetsugu pressed the matter directly by inquiring: "Don't you also believe that it is necessary to cable the Japanese delegation that the policy of the Imperial navy is unalterable?"[56] After vaguely referring to the necessity to include fiscal and diplomatic conisderations in national defense policy, Yamanashi stated he would need at least a week before making up his mind.

Directly after this meeting, Yamanashi conferred with Foreign Minister Shidehara and reviewed the strong feeling of the general staff. Baron Shidehara countered with the importance of international cooperation and the desire of the government to reduce military expenditures, indicating in the process that Premier Hamaguchi was determined, at least, to reconsider the original instructions to the Japanese delegagation. When Yamanashi returned to the naval ministry, he was plagued by an awareness of the antithetical approaches being taken within the general staff and the foreign ministry. In effect, Yamanashi was in the position of having to oppose either his chief of staff or the premier. The former course of action undoubtedly would precipitate violent internal turmoil within naval circles; the latter would provoke a political crisis, possibly bringing about the downfall of the government. Of necessity, this situation dictated great caution and astute political maneuvering.

In order to appreciate the complexity of Yamanashi's position, it is necessary to observe that he was the vice-naval minister, junior in rank and position to the chief of the

---

[56] Aritake, *Okada Keisuke*, 36-38.

naval general staff, Admiral Katō. The naval minister, Admiral Takarabe, was in London, the senior naval member of the London delegation. During Takarabe's absence, Premier Hamaguchi technically had assumed the portfolio of naval minister, a situation which led some observers to attribute great authority to the premier in naval matters.[57] In fact, although Hamaguchi was legally the naval minister, he exercised no real control over the naval ministry. Throughout Takarabe's absence, Hamaguchi never set foot in the naval ministry; and, at all cabinet meetings, Vice-Naval Minister Yamanashi acted as the official spokesman for the navy. No one, least of all the politically astute premier, assumed it would be possible to obtain an Imperial sanction for a cabinet decision affecting the naval security of the empire, unless the responsible officers in the naval ministry concurred with that decision. This fact in no way minimizes the decisive leadership of the premier in the crisis generated by the Reed-Matsudaira agreement. Hamaguchi's commitment to the twin goals of disarmament and cooperation with the Anglo-American nations prompted a willingness to override the objections of the naval general staff. Still, this could not be realized without the active support of the staff of the naval ministry. Obviously, in this quest, much depended upon Vice-Admiral Yamanashi.

Following his initial conversations with the foreign minister and the naval general staff, Yamanashi ordered his subordinates to evaluate carefully the terms of the Reed-Matsudaira agreement in order to ascertain whether it could be accepted without fatally compromising the security of the empire. While this assignment was being carried out under the direction of the chief of the Bureau of Naval Affairs, Rear Admiral Hōri Teikichi, the vice-naval minister solicited the assistance of the secretary of the Supreme War Council, Admiral Okada Keisuke.[58] Both Yamanashi and Okada interpreted the silence of the naval minister, Admiral Takarabe, as a tacit accept-

[57] Hugh Borton, *Japan's Modern Century* (New York, 1955), 315-316.
[58] Aritake, *Okada Keisuke*, 52.

ance of the Reed-Matsudaira agreement. Accordingly, they based their initial actions on the premise that the naval ministry should cooperate with the foreign ministry in an effort to negotiate a three-power treaty. Both men also appreciated the concern felt by the naval general staff; but, in their judgment, this opposition had to be neutralized. To this end, Okada discreetly marshaled the support of Admiral Saitō, the governor general of Korea, Prince (Admiral) Fushimi, Prince Saionji, the senior statesman of Japan, and the Lord Keeper of the Privy Seal, Count Makino. On March 24, Okada formally convened a session of the Supreme War Council in order to adjudicate formally between the viewpoints expressed by the naval ministry and the general staff.[59]

Since the Supreme War Council had been rigged in advance, Katō presented his brief with an evident awareness of its futility. Except for Fleet Admiral Tōgō, who eight years earlier had fought a losing battle against the acceptance of the Washington Conference treaties, the councilors affirmed their unequivocal support of the approach espoused by Vice-Naval Minister Yamanashi. Three days later, Naval Minister Takarabe formally cabled his support of the decision to accept the Reed-Matsudaira agreement. In effect, the London delegation, the naval ministry, the Supreme War Council, and the Emperor's personal advisors had sanctioned a revision of Japan's naval policy, a consensus which allowed the government to draft a new set of instructions.

The nature of this backstage maneuvering to muffle the complaints of the naval general staff went undetected in London, where the heads of the Anglo-American delegations misconstrued the significance of a press interview given by Admiral Suetsugu, the vice-chief of the general staff. On March 18, Suetsugu revealed the gist of the Reed-Matsudaira accord; and, after characterizing it as "the latest American proposal," he added, "The Japanese navy by no means accepts such a

[59] *Ibid.*, 53.

proposal."[60] Although this view of the Reed-Matsudaira agreement was prominently reported in the popular press, the British and American ambassadors both evaluated the interview as a calculated but ineffectual effort to embarrass the cabinet; and, accordingly, they expressed their confidence in the ability of Hamaguchi and Shidehara to secure cabinet approval of the Reed-Matsudaira agreement.[61] This analysis, however, was discounted in London, where Suetsugu's remarks gained ominous overtones.

In deference to the official request of the Japanese delegation, Secretary Stimson and Prime Minister MacDonald had avoided any public discussion of the Reed-Matsudaira accord. Consequently, after learning of Suetsugu's remarks, they were apprehensive that Wakatsuki might not have conveyed fully the import of the March 12 conversation to his government. After reviewing the situation and "methods for stirring them up," Stimson and MacDonald sent representations to Premier Hamaguchi.[62] On March 19, Ambassador Castle was advised that the Reed-Matsudaira agreement represented "the fullest concession to which we or the British can go and, if not accepted by Japan, then Great Britain and ourselves see no course open but to make a two-power treaty covering only auxiliary categories. . . . We suggest that all this should be impressed directly upon Hamaguchi."[63] Although he did not fully understand the nature of the controversy raging within the Japanese government, the American ambassador re-

[60] USDS, Archives, LNC, 500 A15 A3/761, Tokyo (Castle) Cable #48, March 18, 1930; Aritake, *Okada Keisuke*, 83-84.

[61] Butler, *Documents on British Foreign Policy*, I, 258-261; United States Department of State, *Foreign Relations of the United States 1930*, I, 66. Castle, on March 21, did not distrust Shidehara's "willingness to take responsibility. He realizes that this is a test of his statesmanship." USDS, Archives, LNC, 500 A15 A3/768.

[62] Stimson, *Diary*, March 19, 1930.

[63] USDS, Archives, LNC, Record Group 47, Box 53, Item 164, Stimson Cable #38, March 19, 1930. A slightly different version was presented to Foreign Minister Shidehara. See *Checklist of Archives in the Japanese Ministry of Foreign Affairs, Tokyo, Japan, 1868-1945* (Washington, 1954), Reel S114, S2.12.03, 549-51. For MacDonald's instructions to the British ambassador, see Butler, *Documents on British Foreign Policy*, I, 261-262.

garded this type of action as most unwise. This feeling was confirmed when Castle, on his own authority, discussed the substance of Stimson's cable with Japanese Foreign Minister Baron Shidehara.

The American ambassador promptly advised Stimson that neither he nor the Japanese foreign minister favored any type of direct representation to Hamaguchi, let alone one which could be interpreted as a form of coercion.[64] Secretary Stimson then reassured Castle that he too "was anxious to take no step that can be misconstrued by the opponents of the agreement."[65] Stimson allowed Castle to exercise his personal discretion in the matter, adding that if Shidehara thought it would be helpful, any message to Hamaguchi should emphasize that the three-power treaty would contribute handsomely to the "peace of the entire world."[66] Despite this belated change in tone, the initial Anglo-American representation to the Japanese foreign ministry could easily have been utilized by Admiral Katō as specific evidence that the premier was acting under duress, that the United States was not really committed to the principle of cooperation with the Japanese empire. Later, in reviewing these developments, Ambassador Castle privately, and Hugh Byas of the *New York Times* publicly, concluded that if the Anglo-American representations of March 19 had been revealed at that time, they "might have defeated the government's patient efforts to obtain an agreement."[67] This had not occurred because Baron Shidehara had pocketed the representations of MacDonald and Stimson for several days, thereby keeping the exchange a careful secret from the naval general staff.

Following the March 25 decision of the Supreme War Council, Baron Shidehara and Admiral Yamanashi drafted a

---

[64] USDS, Archives, LNC, 500 A15 A3/775, Tokyo (Castle) Cable #7, March 23, 1930.
[65] *Ibid.*, 500 A15 A3/776, Stimson Cable #155, March 23, 1930.
[66] *Ibid.*
[67] *Ibid.*, 500 A15 A3/669, Castle Report #144, May 26, 1930; and *New York Times*, April 2, 1930, 1.

new set of instructions for the London delegation, one allowing the acceptance of the Reed-Matsudaira agreement. In a last-minute bid for internal harmony, Premier Hamaguchi, on March 30, held an informal conference at his official residence. Attending were Admirals Katō, Yamanashi, and Okada, the foreign minister, Baron Shidehara, and the premier.[68] Here, Shidehara and Yamanashi reviewed in detail the revised instructions; and Hamaguchi affirmed his intent to have the cabinet ratify the instructions the following afternoon. Although these words were meant to reassure Admiral Katō and to emphasize the prudence of accepting the government's decision gracefully, the chief of staff responded with an adroit countermove, a request that he be invited to participate in the cabinet discussion of the proposed treaty on naval limitations. At this point, Hamaguchi discarded his moderating tone with a curt retort: if the general staff was willing to endorse the new instructions to the London delegation, Katō's presence in the cabinet would be superfluous; if this were not the case, Katō's presence would in no way affect the cabinet's willingness to approve the policy recommendation drafted by the naval and foreign ministry.

With this acrimonious exchange, Katō's position became desperate. Convinced that the new instructions would compromise the security of the empire, Admiral Katō believed he should, somehow, frustrate the acceptance of the Reed-Matsudaira agreement. Shortly before this conference with the premier, Katō had confronted Admiral Okada with a request that the Supreme War Councilor convene a special meeting of the Board of Fleet Admirals.[69] As there was only one member of this Board, Fleet Admiral Tōgō, Okada greeted the proposal coolly. Katō then vainly pressed for another session of the Supreme War Council. In effect, every legal outlet, save one, had been blocked. As chief of the naval general staff, Katō legally could report directly to the Throne on

[68] Aritake, *Okada Keisuke*, 69-78, reviews this meeting in detail.
[69] *Ibid.*, 58-59.

matters affecting the "right of supreme command."

As early as March 28, Katō had hinted to Okada that he might invoke this "supreme command" privilege in order to express the objections of the general staff to the Reed-Matsudaira agreement.[70] At that time, Okada cautioned against such a step, if only because the Supreme War Council, the naval ministry, the premier, the foreign minister, and the naval minister had already expressed their acceptance of the agreement. A direct report to the Throne, reasoned Okada, would merely involve the navy in political affairs, thereby violating a traditional axiom of the officer corps. Nevertheless, around 10:30 a.m. on April Fool's Day, Katō suddenly demanded an immediate audience with the Emperor, citing his legal rights under Article 11 of the Meiji Constitution. Technically the requested audience could not be denied; but, after checking with Admiral Okada, the Grand Chamberlain, Admiral Suzuki, discovered that the Emperor's calendar was completely full. Katō's audience, therefore, was scheduled for the following morning—a maneuver which would enable the premier to obtain Imperial sanction for the revised instructions to the London delegation before Katō could present a personal memorial. It was hoped this fact would dampen the ardor of the commanding officer of the general staff; and, in addition, Okada reminded Admiral Suetsugu, the vice-chief of the general staff, that Katō should be careful not "to make a mistake in the presence of the Emperor."[71] This was a backhanded warning that Katō should not claim too much authority by virtue of the "right of supreme command." Instead, Okada suggested that the chief of the general staff could, if he felt so strongly opposed to the revised instructions, submit his resignation directly to the Throne.

Despite Katō's request for an Imperial audience during the morning of April 1, the afternoon cabinet session was conducted without evident discord.[72] After reviewing the

[70] *Ibid.*, 59.   [71] *Ibid.*, 83.   [72] *Ibid.*, 78-81.

objections raised by the naval general staff, Vice-Naval Minister Yamanashi reviewed in some detail the reasons why the naval ministry agreed to a revision of the original instructions governing the London delegation. Essentially, Yamanashi stressed three ideas: (1) the Reed-Matsudaira agreement did compromise the principle of a 10:7 ratio; (2) this deficiency could be minimized by a skillful adaptation of technological improvements and by an increase in the size of the naval air force; and (3) Japan would, in fact, retain a *de facto* 10:7 ratio until the 1936 naval conference, when the government could again press for acceptance of the desired ratio. Following this presentation, Hamaguchi declared:

> From the specialized viewpoint of the Imperial navy, the opinion expressed by the Vice-Naval Minister is correct. If one did not hold it in proper esteem but spoke from the standpoint which had been stated initially at a previous cabinet meeting, the government could not accept it. Still, as far as the navy is concerned, even though the new in-structions contain regrettable features, it prefers to act in unison with the government. . . . I believe that you also will wish to decide in accordance with the revised instructions.[73]

Hamaguchi was not disappointed. The cabinet unanimously approved the revised instructions. Late that afternoon, the Imperial sanction was obtained, and the new instructions were then cabled to the London delegation.

TRI-POWER TREATY

The following morning, Wakatsuki Reijirō informed the Anglo-American delegations that his government had accepted the terms of the Reed-Matsudaira Compromise. While doing so, Wakatsuki called attention to the fears of his government, emphasizing in particular that although this decision might assure a three-power agreement, ultimately it might not

[73] *Ibid.*, 80.

strengthen the cause of friendly relations among the powers. Since a treaty of this type would decrease the relative strength of the Imperial fleet, affirmed Wakatsuki, it would necessarily provoke a great deal of uneasiness within Japan concerning the security of her empire. "In such eventuality . . . suspicions and misunderstandings in international relations will only be deepened. This is what the Japanese government views with the most serious concern."[74] This apprehension, however, was not equally shared by the Anglo-American delegates; and, following Wakatsuki's address, the three delegations resumed their technical negotiations. By April 10, a three-power agreement embodying the initial objectives of the American policy— parity with Great Britain and the denial of the principle of a 10:7 ratio to Imperial Japan—was completed.[75]

Once the three-power treaty was concluded, Secretary Stimson appreciated the wisdom of moderation, informing Cotton that the United States should be "careful not to claim so much advantage for ourselves as to hurt ratification in Japan and embarrass MacDonald."[76] Although Stimson correctly estimated the advantages obtained by this treaty, subsequently the American Navy League and the American Naval Board were to express their bitter resentment of the restrictions governing the construction of the last three heavy cruisers.[77] In their judgment, the American government had not obtained an iron-clad 10:6 ratio, and the Japanese government had secured naval hegemony in the Western Pacific at least until the next naval conference. This was, of course, true, as was the fact that the Japanese navy had had this strategic advantage since 1905. It was also true, as Admiral Yar-

[74] *Checklist of Archives*, Reel S114, S2.12.03, 698. Also USDS, Archives, LNC, Record Group 43, Box E161, "Translation of a telegram received by the Japanese Delegation from the Japanese Minister for Foreign Affairs, on Tuesday, April 1st, 1930."

[75] Morrison, *Turmoil*, 334-336.

[76] USDS, Archives, LNC, 500 A15 A3/841, Stimson Cable #228, April 15, 1930.

[77] Council on Foreign Relations, *Survey of American Foreign Relations, 1931* (New Haven, 1931), 403-405.

nell remarked, that the security of the American possessions in the Western Pacific was, in 1930, still contingent on the cultivation of friendly relations and understandings with a potentially hostile enemy.[78]

In some British circles the London Treaty also came under severe censure, mainly on the grounds that a granting of parity to the United States marked the demise of British imperial greatness. Winston Churchill, for one, abused the three-power agreement on the grounds that it would make Great Britain "an inferior sea power."[79] Since articulate naval groups in England and the United States promptly criticized the London Naval Treaty, one might regard a similar manifestation within Japan to be of a comparable nature, dictated by a narrow or technical professional consideration. This, however, would constitute a false equation. The London Treaty, in fact, did not render England a second-class naval power, nor did it endanger the safety of the United States or its insular possessions in the Pacific. It did, however, require a basic modification of Japan's traditional naval policy. To overlook this is to deny the statesmanship involved in the decision of the Hamaguchi cabinet and the Japanese naval ministry to accept the Reed-Matsudaira agreement. Equally important, it obscures the fact that the opposition to the London Naval Treaty was based in part upon the valid contention that this treaty had compromised the principle of Japanese naval hegemony in Japan's own waters.

RIGHT OF SUPREME COMMAND CONTROVERSY

While the head of the Japanese delegation was expressing apprehension in London about possible domestic repercussions of the three-power treaty, Admiral Katō was presenting his memorial to the Throne.[80] Ignoring the earlier hints

[78] *London Naval Treaty of 1930*, 182-183.
[79] *Survey of American Foreign Relations*, 395; and Morrison, *Turmoil*, 317.
[80] Aoki Tokuzō, *Taiheiyō sensō zenshi* (Tokyo, 1953), I, 16-17 and 33-35.

of Admiral Okada, the naval chief of staff offered no resignation but expressed his personal dissatisfaction with the revised instructions. Admiral Katō argued, in particular, as follows: (1) the Reed-Matsudaira plan would adversely affect the security of the empire; (2) this proposal, therefore, was a matter which came within the scope of the "right of supreme command" defined by Article 11 of the Meiji Constitution; (3) the head of the naval general staff bore personal responsibility for exercising this "right of supreme command"; (4) the government should respect the professional opinion of the general staff in such a situation; and (5) by ignoring the views of the chief of the general staff, the cabinet had violated Article 11 of the Meiji Constitution. Later that afternoon, the vice-chief of the general staff, Admiral Suetsugu, held another informal press conference in downtown Tokyo where he reviewed the substance of Katō's memorial to the Throne. In so doing, Suetsugu doubly violated the previously accepted canons of proper behavior for an Imperial naval officer: he revealed the substance of a memorial to the Throne, the most sacred of governmental documents; and he granted an interview that was a manifest intrusion into politics designed to embarrass the government.

Suetsugu's latest dialogue with members of the fourth estate soon inspired a number of newspaper articles and editorials which championed the reservations expressed by the general staff vis-à-vis the proposed London Naval Treaty.[81] In this situation, at the April 9 cabinet meeting, Premier Hamaguchi informed Vice-Naval Minister Yamanashi he was determined to support the ratification of the London Treaty, even if this were to entail a constitutional crisis over the meaning of Article 11 of the Meiji Constitution.[82] Once again, the vice-naval minister was caught between the antithetical policies of the premier and the general staff. This time, the naval ministry approached the crisis as essentially a legal one. Was

---

[81] *Checklist of Archives*, S Series 612, S2.12.00-8, 1-270.
[82] Hōri Teikichi interview.

Katō's interpretation of "right of supreme command" correct? Should the navy seek clarification of Article 11 of the Meiji Constitution by means of a formal constitutional ruling by the Privy Council?

Yamanashi entrusted both questions to the head of the legal department of the naval ministry, Vice-Admiral Yamada. In the judgment of Yamada's staff, the chief of the general staff could not, on his own authority, interpret the scope of Article 11; and the ministry's legal experts felt that it would be in the best interests of the service not to wage a constitutional battle over the "right of supreme command."[83] In addition, the legal department recommended that Suetsugu resign his commission because of his improper behavior during this controversy. The officials in the naval ministry, in effect, believed that Suetsugu's resignation, plus the avoidance of a formal legal controversy over Article 11, would quash the entire issue. To this end, on April 10, Admiral Okada discreetly inquired about the health of the vice-chief of the naval general staff; and, when this indirect method proved futile, Admiral Yamada directly informed Suetsugu of his "moral" responsibility to resign his commission. The criteria of good health and proper morals apparently differed as between the naval ministry and the general staff and, supported by his superior, Suetsugu refused to submit the requested resignation. In so doing, it became evident that Katō and Suetsugu were determined to ignore the pleas of their colleagues, who wanted to keep the navy out of a major political dispute; and, more crucially, that they were looking to the forthcoming Diet session as a means of waging their battle against the treaty in a public forum.

Technically, the ratification of the London Treaty was not a legal concern of the Diet. Under the Meiji Constitution, only the Privy Council could review treaties, and then strictly on procedural grounds. Still, if sufficient political opposition were generated, the cabinet would be compelled at least to reconsider the treaty. In order to blunt public criticism, the

83 Aritake, *Okada Keisuke*, 88-90.

cabinet opened the Diet session with a ringing defense of the London Naval Treaty.[84] It would, declared Shidehara, enable the government to reduce naval expenditures while guaranteeing that the security of the nation would be "adequately assured for the duration of the treaty." Noting that the government had taken "fully into consideration the views of naval experts," Shidehara reaffirmed the intention of the government to ratify the London Treaty.

The opening speech by a non-cabinet member was by Inukai Ki, a prominent leader of the opposition party, the Seiyūkai.[85] Inukai's text was Article 11 of the Meiji Constitution; his charge, the government had violated the "right of supreme command" by overruling the views of the naval general staff. This line of criticism was raised by all the leaders of the Seiyūkai, along with a persistent demand that the government reveal the substance of Katō's memorial to the Throne. Hamaguchi, however, replied in each instance that the Diet had no authority to discuss the legality of the treaty. "So far as the Diet is concerned," Shidehara informed Inukai, "the government accepts full responsibility for the national safety."[86] Two days later, Representative Uchida Shinya, who previously had been parliamentary vice-naval minister in the Tanaka cabinet, queried the premier as to who was responsible for the determination of national security. Once again, Premier Hamaguchi brusquely shrugged the matter aside. "In proceeding to conclude the treaty, the government thoroughly explored the views of the naval authorities; but it is not necessary to remind you that the extent to which such views were considered is not a matter to which I should have to make any reply."[87]

---

[84] For recapitulations of Shidehara's address, see Takeuchi, *War and Diplomacy*, 305-307; and *Japan Advertiser*, April 26, 1930.

[85] *Ibid.*

[86] USDS, Archives, LNC, 500 A15 A3/909, Tokyo (Castle) Report, May 5, 1930.

[87] *Ibid., loc.cit.* Hamaguchi added: "The chief of the naval general staff participates in planning the logistical estimates of national defense. His responsibilities, however, do not extend into the whole realm of

Despite this parliamentary posture, the "right of supreme command" issue quickly assumed major political proportions. Virtually every major newspaper went on record in favor of some type of constitutional clarification of Article 11 of the Meiji Constitution.[88] Neither the cabinet nor the naval ministry, however, wanted this type of action; and the premier successfully frustrated all interpellations from the Diet floor about the constitutional implications of the "right of supreme command." Hamaguchi could do this because, as "acting" naval minister, he served as the formal spokesman for the navy throughout the special session of the Diet. So long as Naval Minister Takarabe remained absent from Japan, the critics of the treaty could not penetrate the parliamentary defense of the wily premier; and to forestall the possibility of a direct question's being asked of a naval officer, Admiral Yamanashi cabled the naval minister of the delicate political context and of the government's desire to avoid a constitutional discussion of the London Treaty.[89] Admiral Takarabe understood the message: while en route to Japan he became sufficiently ill as to find it necessary to recuperate at the residence of Admiral Saitō, the governor general of Korea, until the special Diet session terminated.

By refusing to concede any legal grounds on which the Diet could challenge the cabinet's actions in negotiating the London Treaty, and by avoiding any constitutional discussion of Article 11 of the Meiji Constitution, Premier Hamaguchi managed to frustrate his parliamentary critics of the three-power treaty. This was a clever but hazardous political strategy. The minority party, the Seiyūkai, the Reservist Organization, the popular press, as well as countless patriotic clubs and nationalistic societies, had rallied to the defense of Katō's interpretation of the "right of supreme command." Moreover, the vice-

national defense." Matsushita Yoshio, *Meiji gunsei shiron* (Tokyo, 1956), II, 300.

[88] Takeuchi, *War and Diplomacy*, 310-313.
[89] Hōri Teikichi interview.

chairman of the Privy Council, Baron Hiranuma, reassured Katō that he would do his best to insert the "supreme command" question into the Privy Council's hearing on the London Naval Treaty.[90] This was no idle threat; and if Baron Hiranuma could realize this ambition, the ratification of the treaty would become extremely doubtful. This possibility, plus the apparent lack of popular enthusiasm for the treaty, once again highlighted the importance of the senior naval officers and the staff of the naval ministry. Just as the Reed-Matsudaira Compromise had been accepted because of the role of Admirals Okada, Yamanashi, and Takarabe, so too the ultimate ratification of the London Treaty would depend upon these men.

In many respects, the ratification process depended upon the attitude of the naval minister. Would Takarabe support the treaty, now that the "right of supreme command" had been advanced and in the face of the strident opposition of the navy general staff? The Naval Reserve Organization hoped not, and to this end it passed a resolution calling for Takarabe's resignation. To make their views known directly to Takarabe, members of the Reservist Organization, along with a number of similarly motivated individuals, assembled in Yokohama in order to present their petitions personally to the naval minister. Alerted to this welcoming committee, Takarabe, on May 18, quietly disembarked at Shimonoseki; but a youthful patriot spotted the naval minister and gratuitously presented him with a dagger in hope that Takarabe would atone for his treacherous behavior in London by employing it in the time-honored rite of disembowelment.[91] Unmoved by the youth's high motives, the naval minister continued his trip to Tokyo; and after arriving in the capital, Takarabe proceeded directly to a private conference with the chief of the general staff. The long-anticipated showdown between the two senior officers on active duty materialized in a fateful three-hour confrontation:

[90] Aritake, *Okada Keisuke*, 106.
[91] Takeuchi, *War and Diplomacy*, 313.

Katō reiterated his opinion that the London Naval Treaty had compromised national security, and he defended the substance and style of presentation of his memorial; Takarabe expressed his support for the treaty and questioned the legality and propriety of Katō's memorial.[92] Following this exchange, the naval minister, after conferences with his staff and Councilor Okada, resolved that the matter should be decided by another session of the Supreme War Council.

While making the necessary preparations, Okada also appealed to the leaders of the Seiyūkai to drop the "right of supreme command" controversy. On May 25, however, Kuhara Fusanosuke expressed his party's deep concern about the national crisis caused by the London Treaty, and indicated that out of patriotic duty, the Seiyūkai must consider the grave constitutional issues raised in the special session of the Diet.[93] Although the leaders of a major political party apparently felt no qualms about supporting the principle of the "independence" of the supreme command, the naval ministry and the Supreme War Council manifested less devotion to the alleged sacredness of the "right." At the May 29 meeting of the Supreme War Council, Vice-Admiral Hōri read the official opinion of the ministry's legal staff. Essentially, Hōri stressed the necessity to keep navy policy beyond the scope of party politics and to avoid a formal constitutional interpretation of Article 11 of the Meiji Constitution. These two objectives could be obtained, concluded Hōri, if the Supreme War Council were to rule that "the chief of the naval staff and the naval minister should concur on a common policy of national defense."[94]

Following this lead, the Supreme War Council resolved that, as far as the cabinet was concerned, the opinions of the naval ministry could be regarded as reflecting the views of the navy. Consequently, it rejected Katō's basic legal contention, ruling

[92] Aritake, *Okada Keisuke*, 111-112.
[93] *Ibid.*, 117-118.
[94] *Ibid.*, 125. Also Hōri Teikichi interview.

that the premier could inform the Privy Council that the revised instructions of April 1 had not conflicted with the professional advice of the Imperial navy. This semantic compromise would prevent the Privy Council from probing into the
behavior or views of the members of the general staff during
the negotiation of the London Treaty; and, as a *quid pro quo*,
the Supreme War Council thought the premier should not
claim any authority over the "right of supreme command," nor
should he base the ratification of the treaty on any constitutional grounds. As far as the Supreme War Council was
concerned, the treaty had been accepted by the naval ministry
and this fact alone gave it legal force.

This decision of the Supreme War Council was explained
fully at the May 30 cabinet meeting when Hamaguchi and
Takarabe reached a mutual agreement: throughout the Privy
Council hearings, the government would not justify its behavior on any constitutional arguments and the naval minister
would not challenge the premier's contention that the London
Treaty had not conflicted with the opinions of the Imperial
navy.[95] This arrangement would guarantee the ratification
of the treaty and it would leave the question of the "right of
supreme command" to the give and take of cabinet politics. In
effect, the immediate objectives of the naval ministry and of
the premier were well served by this accord. Underlying this
solution to the "right of supreme command" controversy, as
well as to the matter of acceptance of the Reed-Matsudaira
accord, were the strong political leadership of the premier and
the moderate policies of the Supreme War Council and the
naval ministry. Hamaguchi had on April 9 declared his
willingness to wage a constitutional battle, if this were
necessary to curb the behavior of the general staff. Despite this
warning, the premier had carefully avoided any constitutional
defense of his policy throughout the Diet session. This political strategy enabled the Supreme War Council to cooperate
with the Hamaguchi cabinet without in any way having to

[95] *Ibid.,* 126-127.

accept formally the premise that the premier could legally override the opinions of the general staff on matters affecting national security. Whether or not the development of a responsible parliamentary cabinet system would have been better served by a more forthright constitutional discussion of the powers of the premier must remain a moot question. Undoubtedly, Hamaguchi's policies and political maneuvering had provided the framework for an effective compromise which ultimately ensured the ratification of the London Naval Treaty.

Although the Supreme War Council had resolved the main political problems posed by Katō's memorial, it had not settled the matter of internal naval discord. Most officers believed the London Treaty had endangered the security of the empire; and, for this reason, they viewed the conduct of Admiral Yamanashi quite critically. While the majority of them also sympathized with the indignation and professional judgment of Admiral Katō, the overt attempts of Admiral Suetsugu to drag the navy into the political arena by means of press conferences also provoked a great deal of criticism. In this context, Admiral Okada hoped the joint resignations of Suetsugu and Yamanashi would expiate the "mistakes" of both officers, thereby bringing about greater harmony within central headquarters. This solution was outlined to Admiral Katō on June 6 by Naval Minister Takarabe. In addition, however, Takarabe proceeded to dispose of Katō's memorial in an unusually blunt manner:

> Your memorial to the Emperor cannot be supported because it was a belated petition. This fact, in my opinion, is of paramount importance. Moreover, when I consider the substance of your memorial, I find three basic objections. First of all, your constitutional explanation contains several dubious elements. Even if I did not question these and, for the moment, set aside the manner of your explanation, the navy,

by itself, has no right to interpret the constitution and to determine the extent of the right of reporting to the Throne. Secondly, your memorial not only has been referred to as an "arbitrary report to the Throne" but also as a willful act. Of course I don't subscribe to this viewpoint. Although there are unquestionably many points of criticism which could be directed against the procedure of the government in this matter, I am absolutely opposed to your "arbitrary memorial to the Emperor." Thirdly, there is your proposition of a "transgression" upon the right of supreme command. Is this not an act which criticized something which the Emperor once approved? I must deem this point quite serious.[96]

This censure by the naval minister proved too much for Katō. On June 10, approximately two hours after Suetsugu and Yamanashi formally resigned their commissions, Katō utilized the opportunity of reporting to the Emperor on the forthcoming maneuvers of the home fleet to renew his opposition to the London Treaty. In addition, the chief of staff asked to be relieved of his command.

This unorthodox method of resignation occasioned a minor crisis in the Imperial household. Later that afternoon, Admiral Takarabe formally requested that the Emperor elevate the chief of the naval general staff to the Supreme War Council. The next morning, Admiral Katō became a councilor, and Admiral Taniguchi was appointed the chief of the naval general staff. By timing his latest protests to coincide with the resignations of Suetsugu and Yamanashi, Katō nullified the purpose behind these resignations—namely, soothing the acrimonious feelings generated by the London Naval Treaty. In the process, he also dramatized the isolation of the naval minister. Admiral Taniguchi and the new vice-chief of staff, Vice-Admiral Nagano, echoed the views of their predecessors; and the new vice-naval minister, Vice-Admiral

[96] *Ibid.*, 133-134.

Kobayashi, had been one of Yamanashi's most caustic critics during the discussions of the Reed-Matsudaira proposal. Furthermore, as a member of the Supreme War Council, Katō could and did continue his abusive indictment of Takarabe's leadership. Whoever was responsible for the assignments of Taniguchi, Kobayashi, and Nagano in central headquarters had, in effect, sealed the fate of the naval minister. By July 4, Admiral Taniguchi felt sufficiently secure in his new position to notify Admiral Okada that the resignation of the naval minister was essential for the welfare of the Imperial navy.[97] The next day, Admirals Takarabe, Okada, Taniguchi, and Katō discussed this problem and Takarabe agreed to tender his resignation as soon as the treaty was officially ratified. When his critics pressed for an immediate resignation, Okada reminded them that the Supreme War Council had ruled against any move which might embarrass the cabinet's handling of the ratification of the treaty. Takarabe was, therefore, allowed to retain his portfolio, at least until the treaty was ratified by the Privy Council. From that moment on, however, Hamaguchi could no longer rely on the ability of Takarabe to moderate or control policies of the naval general staff.

The significance of this personnel change was soon apparent. Although it was unable to challenge the legality of the London Treaty because of the ruling of the Supreme War Council, the general staff soon demanded the approval of a supplemental naval budget. When the cabinet had met on April 1 to consider the revision of instructions to the London delegation, Vice-Admiral Yamanashi had noted that the security of the empire could be guaranteed by an enlarged naval air force and by building up to the full limits authorized for each category of warship governed by the treaty. Normally, the actual budget allocation would have been determined by negotiations among the finance minister, the naval minister, and the premier. On July 21, however, the chief of staff, Admiral Taniguchi, recommended a budget to the Supreme War Council that

[97] *Ibid.*, 149-150.

would "offset" the dangers created by the London Treaty. Although this budget had been prepared exclusively by the naval general staff, the Supreme War Council unanimously endorsed it.[98] This action was not legally binding on the cabinet, and the principle that the general staff could set the naval budget by itself was fraught with potential political implications. Nevertheless, Premier Hamaguchi readily capitulated by verbally agreeing to authorize the supplemental naval budget, adding that it would be formally approved following the official ratification of the treaty by the Privy Council.

This fiscal triumph of the naval general staff was buttressed by another maneuver designed to curtail the authority of the premier at the 1936 disarmament conference. On July 22, the Supreme War Council presented an "official reply to the Throne" on the problems raised by the three-power treaty.[99] Without explicitly commenting on the "right of supreme command," the councilors advanced four propositions: (1) the fundamental policy of naval supremacy in Japanese waters established in 1922 had been ignored at the London Conference; (2) the London Treaty had created "deficiencies in our naval position"; (3) this would necessitate an expansion of the navy to the authorized limits imposed by this naval treaty; and (4) at the forthcoming naval conference in 1936, the national defense policy established in 1922 should be rigidly followed. "For this reason, we believe that the empire should renew its efforts, upon expiration of the [London] treaty, for the completion of its national defense through whatever policy it considers to be best."[100]

After the submission of this memorial to the Throne, the government formally submitted the three-power treaty to the scrutiny of the Privy Council. During the ensuing two months, Baron Hiranuma valiantly strove to raise the "right of supreme command" issue. Each time Premier Hamaguchi blandly re-

[98] *Ibid.*, 162-164.
[99] *Ibid.*, 167-168, is the Japanese text of this report.
[100] *Ibid.*

sponded that the London Treaty had been negotiated with the approval of the Imperial navy; and on each occasion the naval minister assured the Privy Council of the veracity of this statement. Finally, on October 1, the Privy Council formally approved the treaty; and, the next day, the Imperial seal officially sanctioned the three-power agreement. Despite this successful outcome, the notion that the government had endangered the security of the empire was not easily dispelled. On November 14, while Hamaguchi was preparing to board a train in Tokyo station, a patriotic youth stepped from the crowd of well-wishers and shot the premier because he thought that, among other things, Hamaguchi had violated the "right of supreme command" in negotiating the London Naval Treaty. So began the series of violent attacks on the legally appointed leaders of Japan which would characterize the political history of that country during the early 1930's.

Some Reflections on the Controversy

The political ramifications of the London Naval Treaty confirmed only too well the original fears of the Hamaguchi cabinet that the Reed-Matsudaira agreement would generate serious political problems within Japan. The dimensions of the controversy were cogently and appropriately summarized by Secretary Stimson in his testimony before the Foreign Relations Committee:

> When you consider that Japan had been having a very active popular campaign in her own country on behalf of a ten to seven ratio, joined in by all the prominent Japanese newspapers, and when you consider that she had as well a very active naval party that was conducting that work; and when you consider that her admiralty, under the Japanese constitution, is treated as a favorite class, not subordinate to the Cabinet but having direct access to the Emperor, you will see the task she had before her. . . . [The] Japanese delegation and the Japanese government which confirmed the action of

the Japanese delegation, had a harder problem and solved it with a greater faith in the pacific relations of the three great powers than any other nation at the Conference.[101]

Only within the context described by Stimson can one fairly evaluate the cooperation of Hamaguchi, Shidehara, Takarabe, Yamanashi, and Okada, as well as the behavior of the Seiyūkai politicians, the members of the naval general staff, and Baron Hiranuma.

In retrospect, the Hamaguchi government had, in negotiating and ratifying the London Treaty, been obliged (1) to overcome the opposition of the general staff to the Reed-Matsudaira plan; (2) to frustrate the interpellations of the Seiyūkai in the Diet; (3) to ignore the popular demand for a constitutional clarification of Article 11; and (4) to structure the Privy Council session so that it could not pass beyond a strictly procedural review. Each of these political feats had been possible only because of the oligarchical nature of policy-making within the Japanese government. Equally important, the cumulative effect of these steps had resulted in decisive changes at the highest level of the government—in the context of cabinet politics and in the composition of the leadership of the Imperial navy.

In the context of cabinet politics, the July 23 memorial of the Supreme War Council signified a sharp reaction to the authority of the premier to determine disarmament policies affecting the nation's defense. In terms of the officer corps, every ranking officer who supported the three-power treaty—Takarabe, Yamanashi, Hōri, and Yamada—had been cashiered because they had, in the opinion of most naval officers, failed to support the basic strategic policy devised by the general staff. The fate of this handful of men greatly diminished the prospect that the naval ministry would, in any future conference, defer to the leadership of the premier, if he were to adopt a policy

101 *Treaty on the Limitations of Naval Armaments: Hearings before the Committee on Foreign Relations, United States Senate* (Washington, 1930), 26.

at odds with the basic security requirements established by the naval general staff. Thus, even though Hamaguchi had apparently vindicated the principle of civilian leadership in negotiating the London Naval Treaty, in fact the influence of the general staff on national defense matters was greatly augmented by the controversy.

This change in naval personnel and naval policy was paralleled by a popular enthusiasm for the "right of supreme command," a development which further weakened the principle of strong civilian leadership. Indeed, throughout the Diet session and the hearings of the Privy Council, prominent political leaders openly asserted that the government had violated Article 11 of the Constitution, thereby placing an alleged bulwark of parliamentary government, the political parties, at the head of the queue supporting the "right of supreme command." In particular, the Seiyūkai platform now included two prominent planks: the maintenance of Japan's privileged position in Manchuria, and a foreign policy which discounted the necessity of cooperation with the Anglo-American nations in defense of Japan's continental interests or in the cause of naval armament agreements.

Without endorsing the outlook of the Seiyūkai, it is by no means easy to censure its viewpoint or its policies. Deprived of any degree of responsibility in foreign policy matters, the Diet had proved to be a breeding ground for a host of politicians who approached foreign and security problems in terms of partisan domestic advantages. Moreover, the Hamaguchi cabinet had negotiated a treaty which could legitimately be challenged because it compromised the fundamental security policy adopted at the time of the Washington Conference. By avoiding a public justification of its actions, the Hamaguchi government implicitly denied the right of the Diet to participate in foreign affairs.

Here resides one of the more ironic aspects of the entire controversy: the adherents of Shidehara diplomacy, the symbol of cooperation with the Western powers and of a moderate

China policy, had, in deference to the demands of the American delegation, negotiated a treaty which caused pervasive political unrest in Japan. The problems plaguing the proponents of Shidehara diplomacy in the dispute over the London Naval Treaty were sympathetically and perceptively evaluated by Ambassador Castle. Offering his diagnosis of the controversy, Castle observed in May 1930:

> Opinion is virtually unanimous among Japanese that the only possibility of war occurring between the United States and Japan lies in the present state of China. . . . Until China has a stabilized government and is prepared to give serious considerations to the vested rights of foreign powers in China, it is felt that the possibilities of serious trouble arising between Japan and China must be at all times guarded against. . . . There is no doubt whatever that if China should attempt to wrest the South Manchurian Railway from Japan, Japanese opinion would force the Government to resist the attempt by all means at its command. In such an event, it is likely the Chinese would appeal for sympathy to the United States. So long as the Treaty to Outlaw War has not been seriously tested and found to be capable of restraining a third nation from participating in a quarrel of this nature, the Japanese feel no assurance that the United States would not be obliged by an inflamed American public to take the part of China.[102]

Castle's premonition of things to come, especially the shift in public opinion and cabinet politics which was rapidly weakening the basis of Shidehara diplomacy, was soon confirmed by the development of the Mukden crisis in September 1931.

[102] USDS, Archives, LNC, 500 A15 A3/969, Castle Report #144, May 26, 1930.

CHAPTER II

The Crisis at Mukden

"In bringing about a general understanding within
Japan and abroad of the necessity to use force in
Manchuria, efforts should be made to obtain prac-
tical results, at least by the spring of 1932."
Policy Directive of Army Central Headquarters,
August 1931

"Yes, let it be done on my responsibility."
General Honjō, Kwantung Army,
September 18, 1931

THE negotiation and ratification of the London Naval Treaty
had been accomplished over the vigorous objections of the
naval general staff, and despite articulate opposition within
the Privy Council and the Diet. Within a year, however, the
Japanese premier and foreign minister were to discover their
control over foreign policy had been corroded to the degree
that the pretext of a Chinese bombing of the South Manchurian Railway was sufficient to unleash a meticulously planned
series of military operations which soon brought South Manchuria under the control of the Kwantung Army.

To understand the political and military motivations and
circumstances which precipitated the famous Mukden incident of September 18, 1931, it is necessary to consider the
manner in which the fiscal and foreign policies of the Minseitō
cabinets, especially the adherence to a program of armament
limitation and a moderate China policy, influenced the behavior of a number of groups within the officer corps of the
Japanese army. More particularly, attention must be given to
the process by which a virulent anti-Japanese movement in
China and Manchuria, the growing capabilities of the Soviet
Maritime Army, and the political turmoil provoked by the
London Naval Treaty generated in the officer corps a pervasive
disaffection toward the policies of Baron Shidehara.

These sentiments of discontent were reflected in three distinctive ways—the organization of the Sakurakai, the Cherry Society, in the fall of 1930; the abortive *coup d'état* of March 1931; and the political and strategic plans devised by the war ministry, the general staff, and the Kwantung Army in the spring and summer of 1931. Each of these signs of dissatisfaction was, in turn, affected by factionalism among the army's senior officers and by passionate controversies arising from new strategic doctrines based upon evaluations of the First World War. Factional disputes, new concepts of warfare, new estimates of the significance of Manchuria, and the security problems posed by Chinese nationalism and the Soviet army undammed in army circles a torrent of discontent with the government's foreign and fiscal policies, and ultimately impelled the Mukden incident in September 1931. Since the determination to seek a forceful solution of the Manchurian problem was caused by multiple concerns, it seems desirable to begin this account of the origins of the Mukden incident with a brief description of the salient traits of the Japanese officer corps.

TRAITS OF THE OFFICER CORPS

After the establishment of a comprehensive educational system in the 1880's, the professional officer corps of the Japanese army was soon monopolized by graduates of the Military Academy.[1] Theoretically, admission to the academy was by competitive exams; and, once admitted, cadets were taught basic tactical skills, the command and administrative system of the army, and, above all, the ethics of the warrior, the cult of *bushidō*. The avenue of advancement to the positions of high-

[1] My understanding of the nature of the officer corps is, in many respects, based upon interviews with Colonel Nishiura Susumu, General Imamura Hitoshi, General Satō Kenryō, General Inada Seijun, Mr. Mitarai Tatsuo, the official biographer of General Minami Jirō, and Mr. Hata Ikuhito. The literature on the Imperial army is voluminous; but of greatest value are the following: Matsushita Yoshio, *Meiji gunsei shiron*, 2 vols. (Tokyo, 1956), and his *Nihon gunsei to seiji* (Tokyo, 1960); Hata Ikuhito, *Gun fuashizumu undōshi* (Tokyo, 1962); Itō Masanori, *Gunbatsu kōbōshi*, 3 vols. (Tokyo, 1957-1958); Iwabuchi Tatsuo, *Gunbatsu no keifu* (Tokyo, 1948); and Fujiwara Akira, *Gunjishi* (Tokyo, 1961).

est command, however, was through the War College. Since this college was specifically designed to train a select group of officers, its curriculum included courses on strategic and logistical planning, the principles of command and administration, and foreign-language specialization. Admission to the War College was contingent on a superior record at the academy, the recommendations of commanding officers, and passing a stiff entrance examination. Although the competition was keen, the rewards were golden. Graduates of the college were virtually assured eventual promotion to a divisional command; a sterling record at the college paved the way for assignment in central headquarters. Indeed, the general staff and the war ministry maintained separate personnel divisions which, each year, selected a limited number of graduates from the War College for immediate or subsequent assignment to their headquarters.

This educational system and pattern of personnel selection slowly invested the officer corps with two general characteristics: it created a professional cleavage in career patterns between graduates of the academy and of the War College; and, among those trained at the War College, there emerged a small elite group destined for careers in central headquarters. Subsequently, the significance of each of these bifurcations will be outlined in some detail; but, at this point, two preliminary observations should be offered. First, the role of younger officers from the Military Academy was of vital importance in the assassinations of 1932 and the famous rebellion of February 26, 1936; and, when considering these events, attention will be given to the behavior and points of view of this younger group. Secondly, the selection of officers from the War College by the separate personnel departments of the war ministry and the general staff tended to yield career patterns oriented toward one of the main branches of central headquarters.[2] In effect, this created two groups of officers with

[2] In English, A. Frank Reel's *The Case of General Yamashita* (Chicago, 1949), 59-60, expresses the same observation.

differing professional experiences and perspectives. While this point should not be overemphasized, it is apparent that extended duty in the war ministry would cultivate a keen awareness of the political and economic factors limiting army policies and planning; and protracted assignments in the general staff would nourish a style of reasoning based on strategic and intelligence estimates. More precisely, as will become evident in the subsequent narrative, the staffs of the war ministry and the general staff in 1931 approached the subjects of armament limitation and the Manchurian problem in different terms.

Apart from the inherent tendency of the army's educational system to produce a limited number of officers marked for promotion to the highest command and staff positions, the nature of army politics was influenced by two further interrelated traits. One centered on the traditionally preeminent position held by officers from the Chōshū and Satsuma regions; the other stemmed from the controversies caused by appraisals of the nature and significance of the First World War. Throughout the Meiji era and the early Taishō period, the highest positions in the army had been saturated with regional politics, the so-called *han-batsu*. In particular, between 1880 and 1924, a Chōshū clique prevailed in the war ministry, and the general staff was dominated by Satsuma officers. By the end of the First World War, however, most War College graduates were not from either domain; and this fact produced a great deal of criticism of *han-batsu*. In order to attenuate this anxiety, General Tanaka Giichi, the doyen of the Chōshū clique, purposely selected Ugaki Issei in 1924 for the position of war minister.[3] Born in Okayama prefecture, Ugaki had been an outstanding honor student at the War College and he had been carefully groomed for this appointment. Because he was the protégé of General Tanaka, many of Ugaki's contemporaries—Generals Mutō Nobuyshi, Araki Sadao, Hata Shinroku, Mazaki Jinzaburō, Yanagawa Heisuke, and Yamaoka

[3] Takamiya Tahei, *Gunkoku taiheiki* (Tokyo, 1951), 12-13.

Jukō—regarded Ugaki's appointment with skepticism and envy. Although this hostility was originally inspired by the expectation that Ugaki would continue to favor Chōshū officers, it was soon compounded by a resentment of the policies which the new war minister pursued.

Following the Saigō Rebellion of 1877, the leaders of the Imperial army had based their planning on three guiding axioms: the desirability of training a professional officer corps, the maintenance of a large standing army, and the organization of an active reserve army which could be mobilized quickly. In the triumphs of the Sino-Japanese and Russo-Japanese wars, the validity of these axioms was confirmed.[4] Victory in battle had depended upon the mobilization capabilities of the army and on a professional officer corps committed to the principles of attack *à l'outrance*. Accordingly, all ranks in the officer corps placed the utmost importance on the cultivation of an aggressive combat spirit, of a willingness constantly to seek out and engage the enemy in direct combat. This philosophy, in turn, produced within military circles a distinctive amalgam of myth and ideology: the army was regarded as the personal servant of the Throne; the Imperial institution was symbolically invested with divine qualities; and all soldiers were inculcated with the doctrine that the noblest of duties was to die in battle for the Emperor. Whether or not the original leaders of the Imperial army actually believed in the divinity of the Emperor, their profession of this belief unquestionably created a remarkable combat ideology.

Over the years, therefore, the indoctrination of the officer corps with the code of the warrior occasioned among many senior officers and most junior officers a mystical belief in the divine qualities of the Imperial institution, as well as in the corollary, the unique obligation of the soldier to render absolute loyalty to the Throne. With the development of Taishō democracy in the 1920's, these convictions slowly acquired a

---

[4] Fujiwara, *Gunjishi*, 110-114.

peculiar potency within the army.[5] In particular, most officers considered the political climate of the 1920's as one which debilitated the intense patriotism of Japan's Imperial subjects—thereby, in effect, fatally undermining the combat effectiveness of the army. Since the army's educational program canonized the unique "spiritual powers" of the Japanese state, implicitly it censured the prevailing notions of parliamentary democracy, armament limitations, and pacifistic approaches to international politics. In the process, the professional officer developed a profound antipathy toward the political scene where, it seemed, politicians and businessmen voiced the principles of European liberalism and workers were beguiled by socialism and communism. Within this configuration of ideas and sentiments, most officers viewed the army as the last bastion of "traditional" values, the true repository of the nation's unique political, social, and ethical ideals. Thus, when War Minister Ugaki set out to reorganize the army in the mid-1920's, many officers were fearful that the "Emperor's most trusted servant" was also being subverted by alien doctrines.

After the Russo-Japanese War, the army general staff had estimated that the security of the empire was contingent on the maintenance of a 25-division standing army.[6] Following the Siberian intervention in 1921, this estimate was scaled down to 21 active divisions as the minimal requirement consistent with national security needs.[7] At that time, the standing army totaled 18 divisions and, despite the professional opinion of the general staff, the Katō cabinet, in 1924, adopted a program of fiscal austerity which precluded any increase in total military expenditures. Confronted by this policy, the new war minister, Ugaki Issei, proceeded to deactivate the 14th, 15th, 17th, and 18th divisions, to demobilize 38,000 men, and

[5] *Ibid.*, 143-148. Also Fujiwara Akira, "Taishōgo ni okeru gunbu no seijiteki chii," *Shisō*, 399 (September 1957), 3-21, and 402 (December 1957), 106-122.

[6] See Prologue, 10.

[7] Itō, *Gunbatsu*, II, 107-109; Nakamura Kikuo, *Shōwashi* (Tokyo, 1958), 16-18.

to put some 6,000 cavalry horses out to pasture.[8] In so doing, Ugaki was able to divert the resulting fiscal savings into
a program which established a regiment of tanks, two regiments for the army air corps, an anti-aircraft regiment, a
battalion of field artillery, and a number of new technical
schools for the signal corps.[9] The popular press labeled
these steps a "disarmament program"; but, in fact, Ugaki had
initiated a rationalization of the Imperial army.

Behind this emphasis on tanks, airplanes, and communications was a concept of military strategy based upon appraisals
of the First World War. In particular, Lt. Colonel Nagata
Tetsuzan, who had studied at the War College of the Imperial
German Army, prepared a number of careful evaluations of
the European war which drove home the point that any future
war would necessitate the "total mobilization" of the economic, political, and military resources of the nation.[10] Victory in this viewpoint would ultimately depend upon the
industrial capabilities of the country, the ability and determination to wage a "total war." War Minister Ugaki concurred with this evaluation and, in 1927, he created the
Bureau of Equipment and Supplies under General Matsumoto
Naosuke. Included within this bureau was a mobilization
department commanded by Nagata Tetsuzan.

Drawing on his earlier staff studies, Colonel Nagata soon
drafted a "general plan of mobilization"—the first planning
of this type in the history of the army.[11] Shortly afterward,
Nagata's staff also formulated the concept of a "national
defense state."[12] Each of these terms—"general mobilization"
and "national defense state"—would serve during the 1930's
as a rationale for the increasing economic and political
overtones in military plans and policies. Whether this fact
merits the conclusion that Nagata's views marked the inception

8 Matsushita Yoshio, *Nihon gunji hattatsushi* (Tokyo, 1937), 200.
9 Mitarai Tatsuo, *Minami Jirō denki* (Tokyo, 1957), 183.
10 Interviews with General Satō and Colonel Nishiura.
11 *Ibid.*   12 *Ibid.*

of Japanese "fascism" and were the primary cause of the expanding political power of the military in the 1930's is a moot question.[13] It would, perhaps, be more appropriate to suggest that Nagata's ideas and Ugaki's support of the "total war" doctrine contained potential political and economic implications, the first of which were discernible as early as 1929.

At that time, General Ugaki, with the cooperation of the minister of education, instituted the "school military training program" and established the "young men's training schools."[14] These innovations were, in many respects, comparable in importance to the Reservist Organization which had been created by General Tanaka as one means by which the army could exert political pressure without legally disobeying the Imperial rescript which precluded military personnel on active duty from engaging in political activities. Unquestionably, the inclusion of vocational training and military drill in the public educational system had wide sociological consequences; but, as yet, these are difficult to gauge. Still, it is clear these incursions into the realm of public education were inspired by the desire of the war ministry to build a technologically oriented military establishment.

The emphasis on equipment, education, and economic planning as essential ingredients in the conduct of a future war may well have been professionally sound. This tenet, nevertheless, clashed with the axiom that the army should remain loyal to its great combat traditions, relying on a large body of infantry inspired by the "spiritual power" of the Japanese civilization. Logically, there was no irreconcilable conflict between a stress on "mass tactics," the way of the warrior, and the development of a mechanized army. In view of the budget restrictions imposed by the cabinet, however, War Minister Ugaki had to choose between a reduction in the number of active divisions or a postponement of the rationalization program. When Ugaki opted for the latter, he generated a

[13] This theme is forcefully developed in Fujiwara's *Gunjishi*, 148-151.
[14] *Ibid.*, 151-152.

bitter resentment within the officer corps, one best personified by the behavior of Colonel Kobayashi Junichiro.

Resigning his commission in protest against Ugaki's "disarmament policy," Kobayashi readily secured an outlet for his views through the Reservist Organization and numerous ultra-nationalistic societies. Kobayashi's pamphlet, *The Reformation of the Japanese Army*, became, in 1928, a bestseller within military circles and nationalistic societies. In it, Kobayashi articulated the traditional canons of the Imperial army—namely, that the Imperial Way (*kōdō*), the "spiritual power" of Japanese civilization (*seishin-shugi*), and the "soul of the Japanese state" (*yamato damashii*) constituted the eternal foundations of the Imperial army.[15] To relegate these to an inferior position would, in Kobayashi's estimation, eventually produce an excessive reliance upon "materialism," thereby corrupting the martial spirit of the army. This rhetoric encountered an enthusiastic reception among younger officers, the Reservist Organization, and nationalistic societies. Within these groups, War Minister Ugaki was soon regarded as a "political general," too deferential to the desires and views of politicians and industrial magnates.

Parallel with this indictment of Ugaki's policies and personality, General Araki Sadao and other senior officers publicly expounded the wonders of Kōdō, and the glorious achievements and traditions of the Imperial army. At first glance, one might conclude that Araki was also opposed to the rationalization program being devised by the staff of army central headquarters. Araki, however, was no simpleton. As the ranking student in his class in the War College, he had had an outstanding career in the general staff.[16] From 1929 to August 1931, he was chief of the operations division; and he and his staff fully appreciated the importance of the plans being devised in the war ministry. Furthermore, in 1931-1932, when Araki became war minister, he extended his professional support

15 Mitarai, *Minami Jirō*, 181-182.
16 Interviews with Generals Katō and Imamura and Colonel Nishiura.

to those colonels who were most passionately committed to
the ideas of total war—e.g. Colonels Nagata Tetsuzan, Suzuki
Teiichi, Tōjō Hideki, Umezu Yoshijirō and Yamashita
Tomoyuki.[17] Although it is impossible to determine the
extent to which Araki's public posture as an exponent of the
Imperial Way was prompted by a shrewd sense of army politics
or by sincere convictions, two conclusions seem warranted:
General Araki resented Ugaki's leadership; and his public
performance earned him the admiration of most professional
officers, especially among the recent graduates of the Military
Academy.

<h2 style="text-align:center">ARMY BUDGET PROBLEMS</h2>

In spite of his professional critics, War Minister Ugaki remained in his post throughout the duration of the Wakatsuki
and the Hamaguchi cabinets. As war minister, Ugaki was
obliged either to work out a military budget that would meet
the dictates of the fiscal policies of the government or else
resign in protest. As early as January 1929, Premier Hamaguchi
advised Ugaki of his wish to implement a further reduction
in total military expenditures. In response, Ugaki created, in
August 1929, a Research Committee on Army Administration,
and he charged this body, under the command of Colonel
Nagata, with the task of preparing a policy guide that would
meet the premier's demand for a reduction in expenditures
and yet enable the army to increase its combat effectiveness.[18] While Nagata's investigating committee was engaged
in this task, the context of cabinet politics and of public attitudes toward the disarmament issue was appreciably altered by
the London Naval Treaty controversy. Most noticeably, the
Supreme War Council had, in July 1930, officially advised the
Throne that the cabinet, in the forthcoming 1936 conference
on naval limitations, must adhere to the minimal "national
defense" requirements postulated by the naval authorities; and

---

[17] See Chapter IV, 203.
[18] Mitarai, *Minami Jirō*, 183-184.

the premier had been compelled to authorize a supplemental naval budget which had been prepared exclusively by the general staff.[19] These developments, plus the assassination attempt on Hamaguchi, encouraged the assumption that the premier would not be prone to risk a similar crisis with the army authorities. Thus, in early February 1931, the Research Committee on Army Administration completed its assignment with a policy guide containing five basic principles: (1) the number of active divisions should not be reduced, but a manpower cutback equivalent to two divisions could be effected by maintaining all divisions at less than full strength and by a curtailment in the length of active duty required of conscripts in non-specialized branches of the army; (2) the savings produced by these steps should be utilized for the mechanization of the army, especially the development of the army air corps; (3) the army stationed in Korea should be increased to three divisions; (4) the above three points could be realized within the existing army budget; and (5) since the mechanization program could not be postponed without endangering national security, any reduction in the existing budget would be impossible.[20] These recommendations were endorsed by General Ugaki and submitted to the cabinet for its consideration.

Whatever the expectation of the Research Committee on Army Administration might have been, Premier Hamaguchi, although still suffering from the severe wounds inflicted by his assailant on November 14, adamantly insisted on an absolute reduction in army expenditures. While the inevitable political crisis was brewing, he suffered a serious relapse brought on by the extensive interpellations from the Diet floor by the leaders of the opposition party.[21] Physically unable to exercise his duties, Hamaguchi resigned the premiership in April, and the

[19] Chapter I, 76-77.

[20] Mitarai, *Minami Jirō*, 184-185.

[21] In English, A. Morgan Young, *Imperial Japan, 1926-1938* (New York, 1938), 60-62, is a vivid account of the circumstances behind Hamaguchi's resignation.

Imperial mandate passed to the senior statesman of the Minseitō, Wakatsuki Reijirō.

In the process of changing cabinets, Ugaki escaped the dilemma of trying to devise a budget that would satisfy both the wishes of the cabinet and the desires of his staff. Pleading ill health, he resisted Prince Saionji's personal entreaties to remain in office; and General Shirakawa, who had been war minister in the Tanaka cabinet of 1925-1927, also refused to accept the portfolio, unless the government would modify its armament policy. When this assurance was not forthcoming from Wakatsuki, the appointment as war minister went, by default, to General Minami Jirō of the Supreme War Council.[22] Before describing the difficulties which Minami encountered in drafting a new budget, however, it is necessary to review briefly the activities of the Sakurakai, the Cherry Society, and the *coup d'état* escapade of March 1931.

THE MARCH INCIDENT

In the midst of the controversies surrounding the London Naval Treaty, a number of officers in army central headquarters met in informal groups to ventilate their anxieties.[23] Encouraged by the existence of a common concern about the foreign and fiscal policies of the Hamaguchi cabinet, Lt. Colonel Nemoto Hiroshi, along with Lt. Colonels Hashimoto Kingorō, Sakata Yoshirō, and Azuchi Kuchio, founded the Cherry Society so that all officers below the rank of colonel could meet on an organized basis to consider the major issues confronting the nation. Membership in the Sakurakai swelled to approximately one hundred men and it included officers from the war ministry, the inspectorate general of military education, the military police, the War College, and the general staff. Almost half of the membership, however, and virtually

[22] Mitarai, *Minami Jirō*, 171-174.

[23] My comprehension of the Sakurakai is derived from two main sources: interviews with Generals Inada Seijun and Wachi Takagi; also Hata Ikuhito, "Sakurakai shuisho," *Rekishi kyōiku*, VI, 2 (1958), 81-89, and his "Rikugun no hanbatsu 'sakurakai,'" *Jiyū*, III, 3 (1960), 88-101.

all of its leadership came from the army general staff. According to the recollections of one participant, the original meetings invariably degenerated into rambling discussions about the desirability of a Shōwa restoration—i.e., a reorganization of the government under the leadership of the army.[24] Although the specific means to attain this restoration remained ill-defined, these discussions explored the economic, social, and political problems caused by the great depression. In addition, Colonel Hashimoto, who had recently returned from an assignment in Turkey, invoked the Young Turk Movement as a specific illustration of how army officers could renovate a country.[25]

Once these officers became interested in a Shōwa restoration, the discussions often focused on Kita Ikki's *Outline for the Reconstruction of Japan*.[26] Kita's volume was a fascinating mixture of state socialism and naïve faith in the unique qualities of the Japanese nation. In his eyes, the political and economic inequalities of contemporary Japan had been produced by the selfish actions and interests of a few privileged groups—the *zaibatsu*, the court nobility, and the political parties. Only the military, argued Kita, had remained loyal to traditional values—in particular, to a belief that the Japanese race was really one large family in which the interests of all should be protected by paternalistic policies of the government. Thus, Kita's *Outline* called for a National Reconstruction cabinet, headed by the military, to smash the privileges of the ruling cliques and to limit the wealth of the industrial combines. In this fashion, reasoned Kita, the country would be renovated; the economic well-being of all Japanese, but especially of the farmers and workers, would be

[24] Wachi Takagi interview.

[25] Nezu Masashi, *Dai nihon teikoku no hōkai* (Tokyo, 1961), 106-108.

[26] Kita Ikki, *Nihon kaizō hōan taikō* (Tokyo, 1924). The literature on Kita's doctrines and their influence on Shōwa Japan is overwhelming in quantitative terms. A cogent résumé of the major interpretations of Kita's influence is Ishii Kinichiro, "Kita Ikki to seinen shōkō," *Shisō*, 404, 2 (February 1958), 59-74. In English, Ryasaka Tsunoda, et al., *Sources of Japanese Tradition* (New York, 1958), 775-784.

protected. Once this was accomplished, Japan could carry on its great civilizing mission throughout all Asia.

Considering the idealistic appraisal of the Imperial army articulated by Kita, it is not surprising that his writings became a favorite topic of conversation within the Sakurakai, or that they inspired some political discussions with revolutionary overtones. Indeed, the combination of Kita's *Outline* and the Cherry Society has been commonly identified as the catalyst of two major political events of 1931: the March *coup d'état* and the Mukden incident of September.[27] In this perspective, the staff officers involved in the Sakurakai first tried to overthrow the government by a military coup in order to renovate the nation along the lines drafted by Kita Ikki. When this plan failed, the revolutionary officers instigated the Mukden affair in order to renovate Manchuria, and, in this indirect manner, to effect a comparable style of reform within Japan. Although this evaluation flourished in the atmosphere created by the revelations of the Tokyo Military Tribunal, it had been articulated as early as October 1931 by Baron Harada, the private secretary of Prince Saionji: "Because the plan by elements of the army to storm the Imperial Diet during the March 20 session had failed, the Manchurian incident was started to give vent to their emotions."[28] Despite the general currency of this interpretation, it seems necessary to interject a cautious note and to appraise the March incident and the Cherry Society without assuming they were a primary cause of the Mukden incident.

The Cherry Society, as noted, included a large number of younger staff officers from the Tokyo area, a majority of whom came from the general staff. The organizers of the Sakurakai

[27] In English, Richard Storry, *The Double Patriots* (London, 1957), 85-86. In Japanese, Eguchi Bokuro, *et al.*, *Taiheiyō sensōshi* (Tokyo, 1953), I, 125-128.

[28] International Military Tribunal Far East [IMTFE], *Saionji-Harada Memoirs*, October 2, 1931. The Japanese text of this diary is *Saionji-kō to seikyoku* (Tokyo, 1950-1952), 8 vols. [Hereafter cited as Saionji-Harada, *Memoirs*.]

and of the March incident were, in particular, members of the intelligence division of the army general staff. Since the primary mission of this division focused on manipulating, assisting, advising, and undermining the various warlord cliques in North China and Manchuria, it was staffed mainly by officers who specialized in Chinese affairs, the so-called *Shina-han*, or China group.[29] In 1930-1931, Colonel Shigefugi Chiaki was the commanding officer of the seventh department (China) of the intelligence division; his staff included Nemoto Hiroshi, Mutō Akira, Watchi Takagi, and Sakai Takashi; and the commanding officer of the intelligence division was General Tatekawa. Another important department of this division was the special service section assigned to the Kwantung Army; and, in 1931, this was under the direction of the "Lawrence of Asia," General Doihara Kenji. In common with most officers, the army's China experts believed that the Nationalist government of China responded only to the threat or the actual employment of force; and they were, of course, acutely aware of the military weaknesses of Marshal Chang Hsueh-liang in Manchuria and of the efforts of the Kuomintang to establish itself in the three eastern provinces. Convinced that the army should and could impede the development of the Chinese Nationalist movement in Manchuria, these China experts viewed Shidehara diplomacy with open contempt and increasing concern. Considering their accustomed, if not always skillful, role in the game of warlord politics, their dismay at the China policy of Baron Shidehara, and the physical incapacitation of Premier Hamaguchi, it is not surprising that an exercise in domestic political intrigue would, in 1930, strike some intelligence experts of the Imperial army as a feasible enterprise.

Actually, the idea of a military coup had flourished briefly in some army circles in 1927, especially among members of the

---

[29] Information on the "China group" was secured in interviews with Generals Wachi, Katakura Chū, and Imai Takeo.

Imperial Flag Society.[30] A leading participant in this society had been Shigefuji Chiaki. In 1930, Shigefuji was, as noted, head of the China department in the general staff; and, moreover, his chief assistant, Nemoto Hiroshi, had been a driving force behind the formation of the Sakurakai. Exactly when and by whom some type of military coup in the fall of 1930 was first proposed remains obscure; but the available evidence indicates that Colonels Nemoto and Hashimoto Kingorō of the intelligence division broached the idea at a meeting of the Cherry Society in early December.[31] Apparently the discussion remained quite abstract, a natural condition since the officers could not but be aware that they were treading on very sensitive and perhaps illegal ground. While little is known about the specific activities of Nemoto and Hashimoto during December and January, it seems clear their revolutionary ideas were channeled through Colonel Shigefuji to General Tatekawa, the commanding officer of the intelligence division.

In late January, War Minister Ugaki held one of his frequent conferences on the impending internal reorganization of the army with Major General Koiso Kuniaki, the chief of the Bureau of Military Affairs, Major General Tatekawa, Vice-War Minister Sugiyama Gen, and Lt. General Ninomiya Harushige, the vice-chief of the general staff.[32] At this time, the nebulous slogan "national reconstruction" was current in every ultra-nationalistic society in Japan, and most officers readily endorsed this abstract concept. Thus, it was not unusual when General Tatekawa, at this meeting, mentioned the views of one Ōkawa Shūmei, an ardent rabble-rouser, and raised the vague possibility of some type of army action to assist in the "renovation of Japan." General Ugaki apparently professed sympathy with those seeking to improve the evil state of affairs in Japan and asked Tatekawa whether he had any

30 Storry, *Double Patriots*, 45.

31 The main sources, apart from those already cited, on the Sakurakai and the March incident are IMTFE, *Exhibits 183, 2177,* and *2188*; and IMTFE, *Document 3166.*

32 Takamiya, *Gunkoku taiheiki*, 79-80; and IMTFE, *Document 3166.*

specific program in mind. The director of army intelligence, however, professed ignorance of such a program, but agreed to inform General Ugaki if any scheme were called to his attention. After this conference, General Ninomiya also asked Tatekawa to keep him informed of the details of any political plan involving the use of the Japanese Imperial army.

The interest of War Minister Ugaki and the specific probe by General Ninomiya should not be taken as direct support of a *coup d'état*. Ugaki's career had not been characterized by any radical political inclinations; and his rapport with party politicians, Prince Saionji, and the Emperor's advisors obviated the necessity of his taking any radical political action. Furthermore, General Ninomiya, the ranking general on active duty from the Chōshū group of senior officers, had always criticized the excessive political aspirations of General Ugaki.[33] For different reasons, therefore, neither Ninomiya nor Ugaki could be regarded as a potentially sincere supporter of a *coup d'état* designed to bring War Minister Ugaki to power. The astute Colonel Nemoto appreciated this fact and he advised his fellow conspirators to prepare two separate *coup d'état* plans: a moderate, innocuous program of reform designed to test the intentions of the war minister; the other, a *bona fide* plan of rebellion.

The specific planning of the *coup d'état* occurred during the evening of February 7, 1931, at the residence of Colonel Shigefuji, who by virtue of his rank technically was not a member of the Sakurakai.[34] Assisting Shigefuji were Lt. Colonels Sakata, Hashimoto, and Nemoto, and Captain Tanaka Kiyoshi. These officers eventually settled on a seven-point program of action: (1) a large political rally scheduled to be held at Hibiya Park in Tokyo would act as the prelude of the *coup d'état*; (2) the actual coup would occur the day the proposed Labor Law was to be debated in the Diet; (3) some

[33] Maejima Shōzō, *Nihon fuashizumu to gikai* (Kyoto, 1956), 239-40.
[34] Aoki Tokuzō, *Taiheiyō sensō zenshi* (Tokyo, 1953), is an excellent digest of the material presented at the Tokyo Tribunal.

10,000 demonstrators, led by Dr. Ōkawa Shūmei, would march on the Diet; (4) ostensibly to control this mob, the army would throw a cordon of soldiers around the Diet; (5) the commanding officer of the First Division, General Mazaki Jinsaburō, would escort General Tatekawa or General Koiso to the Diet, where they would request the resignation of the cabinet; (6) a group of officers would visit the residence of the premier and persuade Hamaguchi to resign; and (7) the army would send a representative to Prince Saionji requesting the appointment of General Ugaki as the next prime minister.[35]

Whether General Tatekawa ever conveyed the details of this plan to General Ugaki remains uncertain. During February, however, the conspirators managed to smuggle thirty bombs into the hands of one Shimizu Gionosuke; and the glib Ōkawa Shūmei charmed some 200,000 yen from Marquis Tokugawa Yoshichika.[36] At the same time, Generals Koiso and Tatekawa intensified their personal propaganda campaign with Ugaki and finally badgered the war minister into a meeting with Ōkawa on February 11, 1931. Again, the details of this conversation remain obscure. Ugaki claims he rebuffed Ōkawa's request for bombs, withheld any assurance that the army would not crush a mass disturbance in Tokyo, and disclaimed any aspiration of becoming prime minister; Ōkawa recollected strong attacks by Ugaki on the Hamaguchi cabinet and on the evils of the political parties.[37] There is, of course, no logical contradiction between these summaries. One point is certain. General Ugaki, on February 11, did not lend his support to any scheme of Ōkawa. This is evident in a letter from Ōkawa to Ugaki dated March 6, 1931, in which the professional patriot proclaimed: "The time is just ahead for a great mission to descend upon you. *Please cherish self-respect, make up your mind to be the head of a group accomplishing a*

[35] Maejima, *Nihon fuashizumu*, 240.

[36] Saionji-Harada, *Memoirs*, July 30, 1930. Also Storry, *Double Patriots*, 60-61.

[37] Ugaki Issei, *Ugaki Issei nikki* (Tokyo, 1953), 157-158.

great work, and do not be induced by such common people as men of the political parties to become their leader."[38]

At the Tokyo Military Tribunal, General Ugaki testified that this letter from Ōkawa startled him into an awareness that his talks with General Sugiyama, Koiso, and Tatekawa were not part of an "ordinary plot."[39] Consequently, he immediately ordered General Koiso to cancel any conspiratory plans, thereby bringing about the collapse of the entire intrigue. Unquestionably, General Ugaki forced the senior officers involved to abandon the plot; but his explanation of the reason for his action is too ingenuous. Perhaps a desire to curry favor within the officer corps led Ugaki to condone indirectly the conspiratorial suggestions of Generals Sugiyama, Koiso, and Tatekawa. Regardless of the reason, his willingness to discuss even vaguely any scheme involving the use of troops of the Imperial army involved a grave breach of army discipline and behavior. Indeed, any act utilizing the army without the sanction of the Emperor bordered on the ultimate of crimes— disloyalty to the Throne. Hence, even if General Ugaki had not been directly informed of the precise nature of the *coup d'état*, his political talks with the senior officers involved in the conspiracy, as well as with Ōkawa, must be deemed as diverging from the "ordinary" canons of behavior of a Japanese war minister.

Mention must be made of another factor, besides Ōkawa's letter, which played a vital role in aborting the March incident. The seven-point program outlined at Shigefuji's residence on February 7 had quickly degenerated into an open secret within the war ministry and general staff. Those officers in the war ministry who were vitally concerned with the disarmament question and the army's budget abhorred any risky venture which might rebound and adversely affect the refurbishment program being developed in central head-

---

[38] IMTFE, *Proceedings*, 1610-1613. (Italics not in original letter.) The Japanese text of this letter is reprinted in *Ugaki nikki*, 158-159.
[39] IMTFE, *Proceedings*, 1627.

quarters. Consequently, these officers, headed by General Hayashi Katsura, the chief of the Bureau of Equipment and Supplies, Colonels Nagata Tetsuzan, Imamura Hitoshi, Nakamura Kotaro, Okamura Neiji, and Lt. Colonel Suzuki Teiichi, strongly opposed the proposed *coup d'état*, which might easily fail and cause irreparable damage to the prestige and policy of the army.[40] This criticism, as well as Ōkawa's open invitation to become involved in some type of conspiracy, unquestionably prompted Ugaki's direct order to quash any intrigue involving the participation of Japanese army officers.

The March incident had no immediately discernible effects on military planning or on domestic politics. It did, however, reveal the willingness of a handful of officers to entertain the possibility of a military coup. Moreover, since the revolutionary plan devised by Colonels Shigefuji, Nemoto, Hashimoto, and Sakai had been at least condoned by Generals Koiso and Sugiyama and covertly encouraged by General Takekawa, the March incident should not be regarded as an instance of junior staff officers' manipulating their superiors. As Ugaki's actions clearly demonstrated, a specific negative response by a senior officer could and did readily terminate the intrigue. Moreover, on closer scrutiny, the March incident would appear to have been the brain child of the intelligence division of the general staff, not of the Cherry Society. The political discussions in the Cherry Society certainly gave expression to the profound dissatisfaction with the government's foreign and fiscal policies which prevailed in army central headquarters; but the willingness to implement a political coup in order to rectify the deficiencies attributed to the Hamaguchi government was confined to the army's experts in political manipulation on the continent, the intelligence specialists of the general staff.

Without discounting the significance of either phenomenon in terms of their corrosive effects on military discipline, neither

---

[40] Hata, "Sakurakai shui-sho," *op.cit.*, 86; and Maejima, *Nihon fuashizumu*, 240.

the Cherry Society nor the March incident was directly responsible for the Mukden crisis of September. During the
spring and summer of 1931, the questions of arms limitations
and the Manchurian problem became major political issues
in regard to which the attitudes and policies of the army
authorities in central headquarters, as well as those on the
staff of the Kwantung Army, conflicted with the official policies
and aspirations of the Wakatsuki cabinet. From this clash
emerged the Mukden conspiracy.

MANCHURIAN AND DISARMAMENT CONTROVERSIES

When the second Wakatsuki cabinet took office in April
1931, the most pressing problems confronting the government
were the preparation of the national budget, the forthcoming
Geneva Conference on Armament Limitations, the protection
of Japanese treaty rights in Manchuria, and the general context
of Sino-Japanese relations.[41] At the beginning of 1931,
Foreign Minister Shidehara had publicly outlined the principles underlying the government's foreign policy: cooperation
with the Anglo-American nations and a determination to reach
a peaceful settlement of all Sino-Japanese problems. Viewing
the policies of the Nationalist government as one following
a "trail once blazed by Japan in her struggle to emerge from a
position of international inequality," Shidehara projected the
vision of eventual abrogation of all unequal treaties affecting
the mainland.[42] First, however, advised the Japanese foreign minister, China must effect "constructive reforms" in
her government and adopt a foreign policy which recognized
the complementary needs of China and Japan. In effect, Shidehara was suggesting some type of new confirmation of Japanese rights in southern Manchuria, especially in terms of the
South Manchurian Railway.

[41] Mitarai, *Minami Jirō,* 172-174.
[42] Rowan Butler, ed., *Documents on British Foreign Policy, 1919-1939,*
Second Series, VIII (London, 1960), 462-463, is a fine summary of Shidehara's speech.

Technically, under a 1905 protocol, China was barred from building any railway lines parallel to the South Manchurian Railway or from constructing any lines which might endanger the commercial traffic along it. In view of the great depression and Japan's extensive investments and special interests in South Manchuria, not even Baron Shidehara entertained the notion, in 1931, of allowing the Nationalist government to construct a competitive railway system in Manchuria which would compromise the economic position of the Japanese in this region. Indeed, in the spring of 1931, Mr. Kimura of the Japanese foreign ministry was assigned to the South Manchurian Railway and given the specific task of working out a local settlement which would allow the Japanese to construct a double-track railroad from Seishin in Korea to Kirin in North Manchuria.[43] The projected advantages of this construction were twofold: it would allow the Japanese army to despatch troops quickly to Chientao or Kirin, in the event of any emergencies; and it would hasten the channeling of Korean immigrants into Chientao and Kirin districts. On both counts, the proposed railway construction met with slight approval in Chinese circles.

When Kimura's negotiations proved ineffectual, Viscount Uchida, a former Japanese foreign minister, was appointed president of the South Manchurian Railway in the hope that he could convey more forcefully the determination of the Japanese government. The foreign ministry also openly declared that Japan would no longer underwrite Chinese railway construction in any part of Manchuria and that the Japanese government was prepared, if necessary, to invoke the 1905 Sino-Japanese protocol in order to prevent any independent Chinese railway construction.[44] "The essence of the whole question," judged a British diplomat, "is how far there is room for both Chinese and Japanese in South Manchuria and whether the amazing economic development of the three provinces is likely to continue sufficiently rapidly to justify the

43 *Ibid.*, 648-650.   44 *Ibid.*

construction of Chinese railway lines and ports on economic grounds without injuring the South Manchurian Railway or the Japanese port of Darien."[45] In response to this problem and the public warnings of the Japanese foreign ministry, Marshal Chang Hsueh-liang and General Kao Chi-i, the representative of the Nationalist government in Manchuria, agreed to participate in "technical talks" concerning these railway matters with Uchida and Kimura. The negotiations were scheduled to commence in late May or early June; but, on the eve of the conference, both Marshal Chang and General Kao were "taken ill" while in Nanking, thereby suspending the railway negotiations.[46] Shortly afterward, this pending problem was fused into a series of crises created by the outbreak of a general anti-Japanese movement on the mainland.

As part of its efforts to consolidate Japan's position in South Manchuria, the Japanese government encouraged both Korean and Japanese farmers to settle in Chientao and Kirin. This was done mainly by granting individual loans to Koreans and Japanese so they could purchase land from indigent Manchurian and Chinese farmers. Few Japanese responded to this policy, but thousands of Koreans emigrated across the border; and, as might be expected, this incursion produced some unrest in Manchuria, with periodic outbursts of violence. In early June, a number of Chinese peasants attempted to eject an entire Korean community from the Wanpaoshan region. Although the Japanese police managed to intervene promptly and prevent any fatal casualties, the Wanpaoshan incident triggered a number of attacks on Chinese property and lives throughout Korea. In retaliation, the Chinese Chamber of Commerce in Shanghai initiated a boycott of Japanese goods as an overt protest against these Korean outrages.

Underlying the Wanpaoshan affair and the Shanghai boycott was a pervasive anti-Japanese movement: in Manchuria it assumed the indirect form of an attack upon Koreans; in Shanghai, a more direct pattern of economic protest. In this

45 *Ibid.*, 647.   46 *Ibid.*, 650.

context, a Young Men's Federation of Manchuria was organized under the auspices of the South Manchurian Railway. These young men soon urged the Japanese government to create a central administration for South Manchuria which would prove more responsive to the views of the resident Japanese "public opinion" and effectively terminate the anti-Japanese propaganda being carried out by the Nationalist government in Manchuria.[47] These semi-official demands were complemented by the statements of the lame-duck president of the South Manchurian Railway, Baron Okura, who publicly warned that the recent Chinese activities had strained Sino-Japanese relations to the "snapping point."[48] Okura's estimate was seconded by the British military attaché in Peking, who noted on July 13 that "unless the protagonists speedily altered their viewpoints, something in the nature of a serious explosion will surely occur."[49]

Clearly, by midsummer, the China policy of Baron Shidehara was encountering serious obstacles. The spokesmen for the minority party, the Seiyūkai, renewed their attacks on the government's foreign policy, citing the Shanghai boycott as one consequence of Shidehara's public assurance that Japan would not resort to force in its negotiations with China. In the face of open Chinese attacks on Japanese property and Korean subjects, wondered the Seiyūkai politicians, how long was the government prepared to endure these insults supinely? Identical questions, of course, were manifest in army circles. Before we review the latter subject, particularly the way in which it contributed to the Mukden incident, it is necessary to consider another aspect of the government's foreign policy —namely, the forthcoming Geneva Conference.

In the spring of 1931, the most evident source of conflict between the policies of the army and of the government stemmed from the determination of the cabinet to participate in the 1932 Geneva Conference on Armament Limitations. Premier Wakatsuki was fully cognizant of the recommendations of the

---

[47] *Ibid.*, 636-638.   [48] *Ibid.*, 637.   [49] *Ibid.*, 639.

army that its budget not be trimmed; and his recent role in the London Naval Conference had instilled in him a keen appreciation of the potential political power possessed by the military if it were to make the Geneva Conference a question of the "right of supreme command." In order to avoid a crisis of this type, Wakatsuki introduced a procedural innovation in the formulation of the government's disarmament policies. Convening a special liaison conference with the highest officials of both services on June 18, the premier and foreign minister discussed the general principles governing the cabinet's approach to the Geneva Conference.[50] In response to the suggestions of Wakatsuki and Shidehara, the spokesman for the army, War Minister Minami, agreed that a statesman, not a professional officer, should head the Japanese delegation. In addition, Minami conceded that the chief delegate should possess complete authority to speak for the entire Geneva delegation throughout the negotiations. The war minister insisted, however, the government's policy should be determined before the opening of the conference, and that the delegation "must adhere to the original instructions of the government and not take into consideration the opinions of other delegations."[51] Regardless of the diplomatic limitations inherent in this stricture, it seemed a prudent way to avoid another crisis comparable to that caused by the London Naval Treaty, and Premier Wakatsuki accepted Minami's stipulation. The central issue then became that of drafting the specific policy to govern the delegation to the Geneva Conference.

The responsibility for preparing this policy devolved on three men: War Minister Minami, Foreign Minister Shidehara, and Premier Wakatsuki. In view of the public and private views of his colleagues, Minami faced a formidable challenge in his quest to avoid any reduction in the total army budget. To prevent the premier from seeking the assistance of the

---

[50] Mitarai, *Minami Jirō,* 178.
[51] *Ibid.,* 179.

Supreme War Council in case of a major disagreement between the army and the cabinet, as Hamaguchi had done the year previously, the war minister committed the Supreme War Council in advance to the army's basic policy.[52] Meeting with the inspector general of military education, General Mutō and the chief of staff, General Kanaya, on May 31, Minami readily obtained their unqualified endorsement of the five-point program which had been prepared under the direction of Colonel Nagata. The following morning, prior to the initial cabinet discussion of the forthcoming Geneva Conference, Minami conferred with the Supreme War Council and obtained its approval of the five-point program. Both steps were designed to preclude any possible ambiguities about the army's point of view and to forestall any type of internal dissension which might enable the premier to compromise this policy either during the drafting of the initial instructions to the Japanese delegation or as a consequence of the negotiations at Geneva.

In this game of cabinet politics, General Minami's strategy of circumscribing the authority of the premier and foreign minister was strengthened immeasurably by the incidents in Korea, Manchuria, and Shanghai which broke out in the summer of 1931. The climax of these "insults" was the murder of Captain Nakamura by some troops of Marshal Chang Hsueh-ling's army.[53] By August, the Seiyūkai leaders were espousing the familiar charges of the ultra-nationalistic societies: the Imperial army had been insulted; Japanese property rights and lives were being jeopardized; and the responsibility for these indignities resided in the "weak-kneed" diplomacy of Baron Shidehara.[54] Seeking to capitalize upon this public concern with the Manchurian problem as another way of compelling the government to abandon its commitment to reduction in total military expenditures,

[52] *Ibid.*, 185-186.
[53] Takeuchi, *War and Diplomacy*, 346-348, reviews the Nakamura affair.
[54] Mitarai, *Minami Jirō*, 222-224.

General Minami, on August 4, delivered a most unusual address at the annual conference of the divisional commanders of the army. Subsequently this talk has been viewed as an implicit warning that the army was planning to execute a forceful move in Manchuria—namely, the Mukden incident.[55] A more restricted reading of Minami's text, however, suggests that it was a calculated move to exert pressure on the cabinet to amend its fiscal policies by means of a public disclosure of the army's armament recommendations well in advance of a formal cabinet decision on these issues.

The bulk of Minami's talk contained no references to Manchuria.[56] Rather the war minister reviewed the process by which the army had formulated its armament policies, the budget, and the proposed internal reorganization of the army—namely, (1) the investigations of the Research Committee on Army Administration; (2) the consensus reached at the May 31st meeting of the war minister, the inspector general of education, and the chief of staff; and (3) the July 1st meeting of the Supreme War Council. More specifically, Minami's address emphasized five themes: (1) the necessity to perfect the organization and equipment of the Imperial army; (2) the impossibility of postponing armament expenditures; (3) the general nature of the proposed reforms in military administration; (4) the proposed policy for the 1932 Geneva Conference; and (5) the Manchurian-Mongolian problem. On the last question, the war minister reasoned as follows: (1) Mongolia and Manchuria were vitally connected to Japan's "national defense," as well as to the political and economic welfare of the empire; (2) recently, conditions in this region had not followed the course best-suited to the interests of Japan; (3) the fundamental cause of this adverse development was an anti-foreign sentiment which had been carefully cultivated in adjacent countries; and (4) since this anti-Japanese movement was not a temporary phenomenon, it posed a grave

[55] Storry, *Double Patriots*, 68-69.
[56] The full text is reprinted in Mitarai, *Minami Jirō*, 217-218.

question which Japan must eventually resolve. "Accordingly," Minami concluded, "those who must render service in military affairs this fall have the obligation to pursue their training and arduous education diligently. It is to be expected that they will be completely prepared to exercise their duty."[57]

This public address was a manifest intrusion into domestic politics, and, as the war ministry anticipated, it drew widespread attention in the popular press. After criticizing Minami's speech, the Tokyo *Asahi*, in its lead editorial on August 8, observed: "The relationship between the government and the army recently has been aggravated. The cause of this situation is the anachronism of the military's being ignorant of the national situation. Although disarmament is a world-wide tendency which is supported by public opinion, there is no doubt that the military is openly disregarding public opinion and defying the government."[58] At best, this conclusion was only partially correct. No doubt the main current of international diplomacy and public opinion in Western nations was in harmony with the disarmament movement; but, in Japan, many groups, not just the military, deemed it hazardous to follow this stream in view of the delicate situation in Manchuria. In order to channel these fears into an effective political pressure, other army leaders followed Minami's intrusion into the public realm. The chief of the general staff, General Kanaya, on August 12, openly censured the disarmament movement in Japan; and, on September 1, General Suzuki Soroku, the president of the Reservist Organization, announced the adamant opposition of his group to any cutback in military expenditures. "If we lack adequate armaments," reasoned General Suzuki, "then an international crisis occurs and peace is disturbed."[59]

One cannot dismiss this point of view as merely the expression of an irresponsible or ultra-nationalistic group. Nor

[57] *Ibid.*, 218.
[58] *Asahi shinbun*, August 8, 1931.
[59] *Japan Weekly Chronicle*, September 10, 1931, 310.

can one discount the favorable political circumstances supporting an active propaganda campaign against the basic axioms
of Shidehara diplomacy. Essentially, Shidehara's main support
came from conservative elements—the advisors of the Emperor,
the senior statesmen, Prince Saionji, and major industrial
leaders, such as Dan Takuma of the Mitsui *zaibatsu*. Furthermore, the foreign ministry itself contained a powerful current
of thought flowing against that of Baron Shidehara. At the
famous 1927 conference on East Asia called by Prime Minister Tanaka, the China hands of the *gaimushō*, including
Tani Masayuki, Mori Kaku, and Yoshida Shigeru, had set
forth the premise of Japan's rightful leadership in Manchuria
and throughout East Asia.[60] The proposals of these diplomats
were governed by the nineteenth-century concepts of balance
of power and spheres of influences; and, although they advocated the use of force only as a last resort, they never
doubted that Japan's future lay in the political leadership
of an East Asia power bloc. This vision, not the new rules
of diplomacy established by Occidental and satiated powers
in the League of Nations, attracted many devotees in the ranks
of the foreign ministry; and, by 1931, Foreign Minister Shidehara lacked firm support for his Manchurian policy within
his own ministry.

MILITARY VIEWS OF MANCHURIA

Within the Imperial army, of course, faith in the use of
military power as the best method to protect the property and
lives of Japanese nationals on the continent had never faltered.
Indeed, the special position which the army attached to
Manchuria had expressed itself as early as 1927. At that time,
General Tanaka despatched troops to Shantung for the
ostensible purpose of protecting "Japanese lives and property,"
but with the transparent objective of preventing the army of
Chiang Kai-shek from advancing into Manchuria. The Im-

[60] See Introduction, 31-32. Also Morishima Morito, *Imbō, ansatsu guntō* (Tokyo, 1950), 74; Shigemitsu Mamoru, *Shōwa no dōran* (Tokyo, 1952),
51; and Mitarai, *Minami Jirō*, 227-230 and 240-241.

perial army preferred the certain impotence of a warlord in Manchuria to a potentially more independent authority stemming from Nanking. Four years after the Shantung expedition, Manchuria still remained independent of the Kuomintang government, ruled by the Chinese warlord Chang Hsueh-liang. In the intervening years, however, the five-year economic programs of the Soviet Union had greatly augmented the strength of the Red Army in the maritime provinces. A vastly improved Red Army on the borders of Manchuria in turn inspired legitimate concerns in the Japanese general staff. Moreover, Generals Araka Sadao and Hata Shunroku, who headed the operations division of the general staff from 1927 to 1931, loathed communism with an intensity born of their devotion to the Imperial institution. On emotional and professional grounds, these officers constantly urged some type of military action in Manchuria that would secure a strategic advantage vis-à-vis the Soviet army in the maritime provinces.[61] By 1931, the operations division was convinced of the historical inevitability of a Soviet-Japanese conflict, and consequently these officers favored a program of direct military action in Manchuria as essential to Japanese interests in the area.

In addition to the strategic challenges imposed by the Soviet army, the Chinese nationalistic movement had compromised Japan's ability to manipulate Chinese political affairs in North China and Manchuria by the time-honored tactics of playing one warlord faction against another. When the assassination of Chang Tso-lin in 1928 failed to blunt the nationalist movement in Manchuria, the intelligence division of the army general staff concluded that the Japanese army should expel all Chinese nationalist groups from Manchuria in conjunction with the fostering of a Manchurian-Mongolian independence movement.[62] This dual policy, the army's China experts reasoned, would curtail the influence of the Kuomintang and

---

[61] Mitarai, *Minami Jirō*, 162-164; Takamiya, *Gunkoku taiheiki*, 47.
[62] Interview with General Wachi.

enable the army to extend its influence into the strategic region of Inner Mongolia. Consequently, by the summer of 1931, the major branches of the general staff—the operations and intelligence divisions—were prone, for complementary reasons, to sanction a display of force in order to confirm Japan's preeminent position in Manchuria.

The consensus within the general staff in favor of some type of action in Manchuria was buttressed by the sentiments prevailing in the war ministry. Here, the concepts of "total war," "general mobilization," and "internal army reorganization" were set forth as the means by which Japan could be molded into a first-class military power. Inherently, this viewpoint contained the premise that Japan was not yet capable of waging a "total war."[63] Since the ability to wage this type of war was contingent upon a powerful industrial complex and a highly mechanized army, the war ministry, in the spring of 1931, had recommended a program of internal reorganization, a rationalization of the army, and avoidance of any curtailment of total military expenditures. Underlying the planning of the war ministry, moreover, was a desire for complete access to the natural resources of Manchuria. These resources, when combined with the industrial complex in Japan, would, reasoned Nagata's committee, enable Japan to wage "total war" against the Soviet Union. In short, although the war ministry favored some type of military action that would guarantee actual control over Manchuria, these staff officers preferred that this be done as part of a comprehensive diplomatic, economic, and military program and not as an independent act of the army.

In order to provide the army with a long-term policy vis-à-vis Manchuria, War Minister Minami and the chief of the general staff, General Kanaya, ordered Colonels Nagata and Imamura, in July 1931, to draft a policy guide for central headquarters.[64] This assignment was completed by early

[63] Interview with General Imamura.
[64] *Ibid.*

August and Imamura and Nagata submitted the "Basic Principles of a Plan to Settle the Manchurian Problem," which specified that (1) the anti-Japanese movement in Manchuria was creating a serious problem; (2) the general staff should prepare a plan of operations to govern any situation requiring the use of force in Manchuria; (3) the military, for the present, should rely upon the efforts of the foreign ministry to combat the anti-Japanese forces on the mainland; (4) the general staff, the war ministry, and the foreign ministry should formulate a fundamental policy for Manchuria; and (5) the Western powers and the Japanese people should be educated to an awareness of the true conditions existing in Manchuria. "In bringing about a general understanding within Japan and abroad of the necessity to use force in Manchuria," the policy guide concluded, "efforts should be made to obtain practical results, at least, by the spring of 1932."[65]

These basic principles were far more than an exercise in abstract military planning. Implicitly they challenged the basic tenets of the government's foreign policy and they called for a concentrated propaganda campaign designed to undermine the Wakatsuki cabinet. Moreover, Colonel Nagata helped to organize the Breakfast Club—a group which included a number of important officials in the finance ministry, home ministry, and House of Peers—as an innovation specifically designed to bring about the necessary liaison between the army and other branches of the government.[66] By this indirect means, Nagata was seeking support for the army's long-term objective: the introduction of some type of planned economy in conjunction with the seizure of Manchuria. Shigemitsu Mamoru, whose views were not very dissimilar from those of Nagata, noted some twenty years after the Mukden incident: "If the Manchurian affair had ended with Manchou-

---

[65] The text of these "Basic Principles" is included in Mitarai, *Minami Jirō*, 242-243.

[66] *Ibid.*, 244. Also Chitoshi Yanaga, *Japan Since Perry* (New York, 1949), 520.

kuo it should not have been impossible to settle it internationally. Or if it had been initiated in plan by a united nation, a settlement might have equally been planned and carried out."[67] Although each of these contingencies would have been met by the plans which had been developed in the war ministry, this advantage was not appreciated by the staff of the Kwantung Army or by the intelligence and operations divisions of the general staff.

CRYSTALLIZATION OF THE MUKDEN CRISIS

Prior to the 1930 controversy over the London Naval Conference, the army had worked within the framework of deference to the leadership of the civilian ministers, at least in the realms of fiscal and diplomatic policies. Resentment of cabinet policies had existed within the army; but this was usually expressed in indictments of the "political orientation" of War Minister Ugaki. Between 1930 and 1931, however, many indications appeared that this deference was being compromised—e.g., the Sakurakai, the March incident, the views of the intelligence and operations divisions of the general staff, and the planning and recommendations of the war ministry. Parallel with this increasingly political orientation of army planning and attitudes in central headquarters, the staff of the Kwantung Army also initiated comprehensive studies of the problems posed by the Soviet army, the growth of Chinese nationalism, and the protection of Japanese rights in Manchuria.

Somewhat isolated from the domestic political context in Japan, the Kwantung staff was mainly influenced by the specific situation in Manchuria. In particular, Colonels Itagaki and Ishiwara developed very careful estimates of the capabilities of the Chinese troops in Manchuria and drafted a systematic detailed plan of operations which would enable the Kwantung Army to seize control of Manchuria.[68] These esti-

[67] Shigemitsu Mamoru, *Japan and Her Destiny* (New York, 1958), 117.
[68] Nezu, *Dai nihon teikoku*, 109-112; and Nihon kokusai seiji gakkai [NKSG], *Taiheiyō sensō e no michi* (Tokyo, 1963), I, 366-374.

mates, as subsequent events dramatically revealed, were professionally sound. Nevertheless, until the spring of 1931, the mission of the Kwantung Army had been defined strictly in terms of protecting Japanese property and nationals in South Manchuria. Itagaki and Ishiwara, in effect, had added a new strategic orientation to the staff planning of the Kwantung Army: the premise that the Japanese army should extend its control throughout Manchuria. Once this goal was postulated, a related effort was made to have this viewpoint serve as the guiding axiom of strategic planning for the Kwantung Army. The process by which Ishiwara and Itagaki converted their senior officers—General Honjō, the commanding officer of the Kwantung Army, and General Miyake, the chief of staff—as well as the army general staff itself to a similar point of view constitutes a fascinating illustration of how strictly military judgments and concerns can produce an incident with far-ranging diplomatic and political consequences, few of which are seriously considered or even recognized at the time.

The operational plans devised by Ishiwara and Itagaki in the summer of 1931 certainly constituted one of the important contributing factors to the Mukden incident. Ishiwara and Itagaki, however, were not the "manipulators" of the Imperial army, men who engineered the Mukden affair by "ruling from below."[69] They were, after all, the responsible operational officers assigned by the general staff to the Kwantung Army; and, under a time-honored principle of command authority —the *dokudan-senkō*—the staff of field armies possessed complete freedom in the area of operational planning.[70] The operations division of the general staff, of course, always determined strategic objectives and it had to amend, approve, or reject the plans drafted by its staff officers assigned to field commanders. Furthermore, as noted, the "basic principles"

[69] For a different viewpoint, Yale Maxon, *Control of Japanese Foreign Policy* (Berkeley, 1957), 100-101.

[70] I am indebted to Colonel Nishiura and General Imamura for calling my attention to the *dokudan-senkō* principle. Also NKSG, *Taiheiyō sensō e no michi* (Tokyo, 1962), II, 13-16.

articulated in the policy guide prepared by Colonels Nagata and Imamura in August 1931 called for a set of operational plans for Manchuria. Given the general context of Sino-Japanese relations, as well as the evident unrest in central headquarters in regard to the cabinet's foreign and fiscal policies, it is comprehensible why the staff of the Kwantung Army might make a liberal interpretation of the discretionary authority sanctioned by the *dokudan-senkō* principle. The central question haunting Ishiwara and Itagaki, in the summer of 1931, was whether the two senior officers of the Kwantung Army—Generals Honjō and Miyake—and the operations division of the general staff would approve implementation of their plans in the event of a political or military incident.

Until August 1931, the operations division of the general staff had been commanded by General Araki Sadao. Although Araki regarded the Soviet Union as the primary strategic threat to Japan and viewed the diplomacy of Baron Shidehara with transparent disdain, he had no sympathy for political intrigues by army officers. Since he neither condoned nor encouraged the type of operational planning being devised by Itagaki and Ishiwara, as long as he remained on the general staff many of his subordinates may have personally dreamed of a military conquest of Manchuria, but they never submitted any specific plans to this end—least of all one which contained the possibility of deliberately creating an incident that would conflict openly with the official foreign policy of the Japanese government.

This type of control over operational planning loosened appreciably in 1931, in conjunction with the annual August personnel changes within the Imperial army. At this time, General Tatekawa became chief of the operations division, along with a flock of new assistants—Colonels Tōjō, Imamura, and Kawabe Torashirō and Major Mutō Akira. Only Kawabe had been promoted from within the operations division. Mutō was transferred from the intelligence division of the general staff, Imamura from the war ministry, and Tōjō from the

Imperial Guard Division. In mid-August, as part of the normal orientation of senior field staff officers by the general staff, Lt. Colonel Ishiwara was called to Tokyo; and, at this time, he revealed the gist of the elaborate operational planning which had been prepared by the Kwantung staff, along with the suggestion that it should be implemented in the event of any major incident affecting Japanese property or lives in Manchuria.[71] Although both aspects of his presentation were fraught with grave administrative political consequences, neither General Tatekawa nor his staff expressed any serious disapproval. Fortified by this tacit endorsement, Ishiwara and Itagaki then revealed the details of their planning to their new commanding officer, General Honjō. Although Honjō was unaware that this plan contained the possibility of deliberately provoking an incident, as Ishiwara later recalled, he "greatly heartened" his staff by approving the operational plan in the event of any major crisis.[72] By late August, therefore, Ishiwara and Itagaki had drafted a specific set of operational plans which envisioned bringing all Manchuria under the control of the Kwantung Army; it had been informally submitted to the operations division of the general staff; and the commanding general of the Kwantung Army had expressed his specific approval of the operational plans.

Concurrently with these significant developments, Sino-Japanese relations had been irritated by a rash of incidents which broke out in July and August, in particular by the Nakamura incident. Within the domestic political arena, the Seiyūkai and countless nationalistic societies articulated their conviction that Chinese xenophobia could not be controlled unless the Imperial army were allowed to deliver retaliatory punishments whenever such events as the murder of Captain Nakamura occurred. This point of view was not altered by the public remarks of Colonel Doihara, the chief of the special service section of the Kwantung Army, who one week before

[71] Interview with General Imamura.
[72] IMTFE, *Proceedings*, 22155.

the Mukden incident cryptically advised the press, "there is no telling what might happen to Manchuria."[73] This bombastic statement contained more substance than Doihara realized, for, during his absence, the staff of the Kwantung Army decided to provoke an incident at Mukden, in the hope that this would sanction the new contingency plans for the seizure of Manchuria.

By mid-September, the outstanding source of friction in Sino-Japanese relations was the unresolved Nakamura incident. Colonel Doihara was the army's representative in the negotiations with Marshal Chang Hsueh-liang's army to settle this matter. Despite his reputation as the army's most adroit intelligence operator in Manchuria, Doihara could not effect the type of settlement originally desired by central headquarters—namely, one that ensured that Marshal Chang (1) accepted personal responsibility for the shooting of Captain Nakamura, (2) apologized for this crime, and (3) promised that a similar event would not occur again. Since the army failed to achieve an adequate settlement of the Nakamura case, the incident gradually became a source of political controversy in Japan.[74] Finally, Premier Wakatsuki and Foreign Minister Shidehara demanded that General Minami bring the matter to a prompt and diplomatic close. Yielding to this pressure, the war ministry had Doihara recalled to Tokyo for a careful review of the situation; and, overruling the recommendations of the intelligence division, the chief of the general staff, General Kanaya, ordered Doihara to negotiate an agreement that would not affix any personal responsibility for the Nakamura incident on Marshal Chang Hseuh-liang.

Once this decision had been made, the intelligence division cabled Doihara's new orders to the special service section in Port Arthur.[75] Major Hanaya passed on this information

[73] Takeuchi, *War and Diplomacy*, 348.

[74] *Ibid.*, 346-348.

[75] Hanaya Tadashi, "Manshū jiken wa ko shite keikaku" [The Planning of the Manchurian Incident], *Himerareta shōwashi* (Tokyo, 1956), 45. Hanaya was, in September 1931, Doihara's chief assistant at Mukden.

to Colonels Ishiwara and Itagaki, who were understandably dismayed by the prospect of a peaceful resolution of the Nakamura incident. Since the existing political environment seemed ripe for some type of military action in Manchuria, Ishiwara and Itagaki proposed that the Kwantung Army act prior to Doihara's return. The chief of staff of the Kwantung Army, General Miyake, however, was unmoved by their assurances that central headquarters would extend *post facto* approval of their plan. Without specific authorization from Tokyo, Miyake refused to sanction any movement by the Kwantung Army that might produce important diplomatic problems for the government. Moreover, Miyake personally questioned whether Generals Tatekawa and Koiso were actually in favor of some type of incident. To settle this matter once and for all, Miyake cabled central headquarters, on September 14, that since "the present situation was becoming very delicate," he wished to engage in "extensive personal talks" with Generals Koiso and Tatekawa.[76] Apparently Miyake anticipated that this cable would terminate the proposed intrigue, as it seemed highly unlikely these responsible senior officers would, in fact, condone an independent act by the Kwantung Army.

Miyake's cable alerted everyone in Tokyo to the tense situation in Mukden. After reviewing the problem, War Minister Minami and the chief of the general staff, General Kanaya, decided to send General Tatekawa to Port Arthur with specific orders advising General Honjō to exercise "prudence and patience" in these difficult circumstances.[77] Tatekawa left Tokyo on September 17 and his departure was used by War Minister Minami to allay the fears of Foreign Minister Shidehara, who was apprehensive lest an incident be provoked by

---

Hashimoto Kingorō once claimed that he communicated this message directly to Colonel Itagaki. Nakano Masao, ed., *Hashimoto taisha shuki* (Tokyo, 1963), 123-125.

[76] Mitarai, *Minami Jirō*, 255.

[77] *Ibid.*, 256.

the Kwantung Army.[78] By all the canons of correct military behavior, Tatekawa's mission should have prevented the Mukden incident. Prior to his departure, however, Tatekawa conferred with his former assistant, Colonel Shigefuji, the chief of the China section of the general staff; and, late in the afternoon of September 15, Shigefuji cabled a secret message to Major Hanaya at the Mukden Special Service Agency.[79] In it, Shigefuji outlined the official purpose of Tatekawa's visit and indicated that Tatekawa would not actually arrive in Port Arthur until the 19th because he was proceeding to Honjō's headquarters via Korea and Mukden.

Major Hanaya understood the message: the Kwantung Army had forty-eight hours in which to act before General Tatekawa would officially confer with Generals Honjō and Miyake. The complicity of the general staff in this matter also extended to the operations division, which simply advised Miyake that Tatekawa would arrive at Port Arthur on the 19th to discuss the Manchurian situation. Since no one bothered to inform Miyake about Shigefuji's cable, the chief of staff of the Kwantung Army alerted Honjō to Tatekawa's forthcoming visit and he allowed Major Hanaya and Colonel Itagaki to meet Tatekawa upon the latter's arrival in Mukden. When General Tatekawa reached Mukden, the three conspirators chatted ostentatiously, observing the social amenities but carefully avoiding any discussion of Tatekawa's particular mission.[80] After this brief meeting, Tatekawa was taken to a convenient geisha house where he passed an enjoyable evening that was disturbed only by the occasional rumble of distant artillery and rifle fire.

Around 11:00 p.m., a mysterious bomb explosion occurred on the outskirts of Mukden, along the main line of the South Manchurian Railway and adjacent to the most effective com-

[78] Storry, *Double Patriots*, 75-76.
[79] Hanaya, "Manshū jiken," 45.
[80] IMTFE, *Proceedings*, 30261.

pany of Chinese troops within the city.[81] Although the bomb was not powerful enough to cause any delay in rail traffic, a company of Japanese troops on night patrol close to the explosion managed, in the darkness and confusion, to provoke a skirmish with their Chinese counterparts. Colonel Hirata, the regimental commanding officer in Mukden, promptly reported this incident to the senior staff officer in the area, Colonel Itagaki. On his own authority, Itagaki authorized a full-scale attack against the North Barracks of the Chinese army, as well as the capture of the entire walled city. Morishima Morito, the Japanese consul, arrived at the Special Service Agency in Mukden at 11:00 p.m. and protested this course of action; but, when Major Hanaya unsheathed his sword, the diplomat left in silent resignation.[82]

General Honjō had retired before news of the Mukden events reached Port Arthur. Consequently Miyake immediately summoned a staff meeting to discuss the problem, after which they proceeded *en masse* to Honjō's residence. Here, Lt. Colonel Ishiwara reviewed the contingency plans of the Kwantung Army and stressed the urgent need for their prompt implementation. Despite the silent protest of General Miyake, the commanding officer of the Kwantung Army meditated a few minutes and declared, "Yes, let it be done on my responsibility."[83] The Manchurian incident had begun.

[81] The details of the Mukden bombing are reviewed by League of Nations, *Appeal by the Chinese Government, Report of the Commission of Enquiry* (Geneva, 1932), Chapter IV. More recently by Richard Storry, "The Mukden Incident," *Far Eastern Affairs* (St. Anthony's Papers, No. 2), 1-12.

[82] Morishima, *Imbō*, 52.

[83] IMTFE, *Proceedings*, 22119.

CHAPTER III

Withdrawal from the League of Nations

> "The Japanese people are locked in their own territory by treaties. As long as the Nine Power Treaty and the Anti-War [Kellogg-Briand] Pact are construed in their present sense, Japan cannot expand in the Far East. If we are to progress, we must break down this fence of treaties."
>
> Mori Kaku, 1932

As NEWS of the Mukden events flowed into central headquarters, the offices and corridors of army central headquarters rippled with premature activity.[1] By 5:00 a.m., General Umezu had summoned an emergency meeting of all departmental and section heads to formulate a policy recommendation for the chief of the general staff, General Kanaya. Here, Colonel Imamura, the acting head of the operations division in the absence of General Tatekawa, articulated what proved to be the final consensus: the Kwantung Army should implement its contingency plan to secure control over South Manchuria. Simultaneously with this resolution, Vice-War Minister Sugiyama convened a similar meeting of his departmental and section chiefs; but, pending a clarification of the military and diplomatic issues involved in the incident, these officers preferred a posture of temporary inaction. In order to draft a joint policy recommendation for the war minister, the department heads of the general staff and the war ministry assembled

[1] The initial responses described in this paragraph are based upon Tateno Nobuyuki, Shōwa gunbatsu (Tokyo, 1963), 95-98; Mitarai Tatsuo, Minami Jirō denki (Tokyo, 1957), 249-250; Imamura Hitoshi, Kōzoku to kashikan (Tokyo, 1960), 176-203; and Nihon kokusai seiji gakkai [NKSG], Taiheiyo sensō e no michi (Tokyo, 1962), II, 3-6. For an excellent reappraisal of the Mukden problem, see Sadako N. Ogata, Defiance in Manchuria (Berkeley, 1964), a study which appeared after the writing of this chapter. Although Mrs. Ogata evaluates the Manchurian crisis somewhat differently and includes invaluable details on the Kwantung army, she does not, I think, compromise the main themes of this interpretation. Still, the reader should form his own opinion by a firsthand reading of her incisive study.

at 7:30 a.m. in General Sugiyama's office; and, within minutes, the discrepancy in their initial reactions was resolved by the adoption of an ambivalent evaluation: since the Imperial army did not favor a localization of the Mukden incident, unless this were the prelude to a comprehensive solution of the Manchurian problem, whatever emergency operations were considered necessary by the Kwantung Army should be approved by the general staff. In effect, prior to any cabinet discussion of the incident, the army authorities had ruled in favor of an aggressive diplomatic and military approach to the Manchurian question.

Although War Minister Minami understood the purpose of this suggested policy, he could not dictate its adoption to the cabinet. Instead, at the 8:00 a.m. cabinet meeting, Minami justified the actions of the Kwantung Army in terms of alleged threats to Japanese lives and property.[2] This argument was dismissed by Foreign Minister Shidehara and Finance Minister Inoue as a fatuous contention. The only things in jeopardy at Mukden, countered the civilian ministers, were the foreign and fiscal policies of the government. Confronted by this opposition, Minami reluctantly concurred with the premier's ruling that the crisis should be settled promptly; and, with some anguish, the war minister assured his colleagues the general staff would not sanction any additional operations in South Manchuria.[3] Once this policy had been decided, Premier Wakatsuki officially notified the Throne that the government would seek a peaceful solution of the Mukden incident.

MODIFICATION OF THE CABINET POLICY

The statements of the war minister in the cabinet, in conjunction with the premier's report to the Throne, should have produced an immediate compliance with the official policy of the government. To this end, at 6:00 p.m. General Minami

[2] Tateno, *Shōwa gunbatsu*; Mitarai, *Minami Jirō*, Imamura, *Kōzoku*; and NKSG, *Taiheiyō*. . . .

[3] Wakatsuki Reijirō, *Kofūan kaiko-roku* (Tokyo, 1950), 375-376.

cabled the gist of the cabinet's "localization" decision to General Honjō, the commanding officer of the Kwantung Army.[4] Parallel with this message, however, the head of the operations division of the general staff, Colonel Imamura, also advised Honjō that the viewpoint of the cabinet was not necessarily binding for the army, because the Manchurian crisis involved the "right of supreme command."[5] Shortly afterward, General Kanaya, the chief of the general staff, issued a cryptic directive: the Kwantung Army was to advance beyond the limits of Mukden by "several miles"; and, under the discretionary authority entrusted to field commanders on the *dokudan-senkō* principle, General Honjō could "undertake limited operations without waiting for direct orders from the chief of the general staff."[6] By invoking the "right of supreme command" and sanctioning a liberal construction of the *dokudan-senkō* prerogative, the general staff patently invited Honjō to implement Ishiwara's contingency plan for the seizure of South Manchuria.

The contention that the general staff could, by itself, invoke the "right of supreme command" and allow the Kwantung Army to define the limits of its operations in South Manchuria raised several thorny problems. The Manchurian issue had been simmering for many months and public sentiment was not adverse to a more militant stance in defense of Japanese lives and property rights in South Manchuria. Indeed, on September 17, the British ambassador in Tokyo, Sir Francis Lindley, estimated that public criticism of the foreign minister's handling of the Wanpaoshan affair, the latest Chinese boycotts, and the Nakamura incident had intensified to the degree that "the fat was in the fire, leaving the Shidehara policy very near the melting point."[7] More crucially, with-

[4] Mitarai, *Minami Jirō*, 251.

[5] Imamura interview.

[6] Hanaya Tadashi, "Manshū jiken wa kō shite keikaku," *Himerareta shōwashi* (Tokyo, 1956), 48.

[7] Rowan Butler, ed., *Documents on British Foreign Policy, 1919-1930*, Second Series, VIII (London, 1960), 655. [Hereafter cited as Butler, DBFP.]

out the direct intervention of the Throne, the cabinet could not legally countermand the orders of the general staff; and the convening of a special session of the Privy Council in order to attain a formal constitutional ruling against the general staff would only provoke a protracted political crisis, possibly resulting in the overthrow of the government. While the premier considered these limited political options, the commanding officer of the Korean Army, General Hayashi Senjurō, despatched some of his troops into South Manchuria.[8] Hayashi had acted in response to a request of the Kwantung Army and with the encouragement of the operations division of the general staff; but, once his troops passed the Korean border, the legal posture of the general staff was automatically compromised. Even in wartime, the "right of supreme command" did not permit a field commander to send troops beyond his command jurisdiction without first obtaining the sanction of the Emperor. Thus, to Baron Shidehara and Finance Minister Inoue, General Hayashi's dash across the Korean border presented the government with an incontestable legal basis on which to challenge the army's interpretation of the "right of supreme command." If the government merely refused to appropriate the funds for Hayashi's actions, insisted Inoue and Shidehara, the army would be compelled either to halt its operations in Manchuria or else to defend Hayashi's transgression of the Imperial prerogatives before the Privy Council and the Supreme War Council.

The strategy outlined by the foreign and financial ministers was legally sound but politically fragile. In order to dissuade the premier from this course of action, the Big Three of the army—War Minister Minami, the chief of the general staff, General Kanaya, and the inspector general of military education, General Araki Sadao—affirmed they would defend Hayashi's behavior in any public discussion of the "right of supreme command"; and, at the September 23 cabinet

[8] NKSG, *Taiheiyō sensō e no michi*, II, 9-24, reviews this problem in detail.

session, Minami agreed that the Kwantung Army would be restrained by the general staff if the government promised to negotiate a comprehensive settlement of the Manchurian problem.[9] The war minister, in effect, was asking the cabinet to accept the policy initially suggested by the department heads of the war ministry and the general staff. Neither Foreign Minister Shidehara nor Finance Minister Inoue was inclined to accept this approach to the Mukden crisis, preferring, if necessary, the imposition of the original cabinet policy on the army by a formal censure of General Hayashi. Premier Wakatsuki, however, elected to follow the "compromise" offered by General Minami—namely, the government would not legally contest the "right of supreme command" prerogative; the general staff would preclude further operations by the Kwantung Army; and the government would use the Mukden incident to reach a new treaty with the Nationalist government, guaranteeing Japanese rights and interests in Manchuria. Thus, as Wakatsuki later recalled, after the cabinet meeting of September 23, "I went directly to the palace and reported to the Emperor that the government would defray the expenses of the Korean troops."[10]

The decision of the premier not to challenge General Hayashi's actions was undoubtedly induced by a belief that the army and the Japanese public would accept nothing less than a reconfirmation of Japan's treaty rights in Manchuria. The enthusiastic response within Japan to the Mukden incident constituted a viable political influence which, in the judgment of Sir Francis Lindley, forced the cabinet to "form a solid front." The ambassador added: "Any action they may take to defend her [Japan's] interests in Manchuria will receive unanimous public support."[11] After September 23, the central problem confronting the Wakatsuki cabinet was whether it could resolve the Manchurian problem with the concurrence of the Western powers. During the subsequent

[9] *Ibid.*, 32-34; Mitarai, *Minami Jirō*, 260-262.
[10] Wakatsuki, *Kofūan*, 377.   [11] Butler, *DBFP*, viii, 684.

ten weeks, Baron Shidehara devoted his considerable diplomatic talents to the task of negotiating a direct settlement of the incident with the Chinese Nationalist government, one which would confirm what most Japanese and all army officers considered a self-evident proposition: Manchuria was a special region in which Japanese rights were paramount.

The political necessity to settle the Mukden incident in a manner which would require a Chinese government to recognize, by treaty, Japan's special position in Manchuria was not fully appreciated outside the home islands of the Japanese empire. In the United States, Secretary Stimson elected "to watch" the situation, confident that Shidehara would reassert his leadership and restore the *status quo ante* in Manchuria.[12] In Paris, meeting in response to an appeal of the Chinese government, the Council of the League of Nations requested the Japanese government to withdraw its army to the positions held before September 19, and to accept a team of neutral observers to investigate the incident at Mukden.[13] On this optimistic note, the Council promptly adjourned until October 14, when it proposed to reconsider the problem. The American secretary of state and the Council had acted on the assumption that Japan's commitments to the Covenant of the League and the Kellogg-Briand Pact would serve as the basis of any diplomatic settlement. The Wakatsuki cabinet, however, was proceeding on the primacy of Japan's existing treaty rights and a determination to have the Chinese government reconfirm these legal privileges. Moreover, although the general staff had, on September 23, vetoed additional offensive operations in Manchuria, it was not prepared to defer to the wishes of the Council—that is, to order the withdrawal of the Kwantung Army to its original positions. Indeed, the operations division under General Tatekawa urged a clean sweep of Chinese troops from all of Manchuria.[14] This

[12] Robert Ferrell, *American Diplomacy in the Great Depression* (New Haven, 1957), 130-134.

[13] Butler, *DBFP*, VIII, 676-677.

[14] NKSG, *Taiheiyō sensō e no michi*, II, 41-45.

type of resolute action, ventured Tatekawa's staff, would confront the League, China, and the Soviet Union with a *fait accompli*, the most certain way to ensure Japanese control in Manchuria.

The advantages of an immediate advance into North Manchuria seemed incontestable, at least to the architects of the Mukden affair—the operations officers in the Kwantung Army and the general staff. The war ministry staff, however, could not casually disregard the fear of the foreign and naval ministries that a seizure of Manchuria might well unite the great sea powers and the Soviet Union against the empire, thereby precipitating a humiliating tripartite intervention comparable to that of 1895, when the powers had forced Japan to surrender its position in Manchuria. Nor could General Minami dismiss Baron Shidehara's argument that the self-evident superiority of the Kwantung Army in Manchuria would bring the Chinese government to the conference table. If Japan could negotiate a new treaty governing Manchuria, reasoned Shidehara, it would not necessarily be placed in the position of violating the Nine Power Treaty and its position in the League would not be compromised. Although openly skeptical of the projected benefits to be reaped by reliance on diplomacy, General Kanaya agreed not to sanction any offensive operations in Manchuria, pending the outcome of the forthcoming session of the Council of the League of Nations.[15]

Although General Kanaya directly ordered the Kwantung Army to refrain from further offensive operations, General Tatekawa and Colonel Imamura of the operations division continually reminded Honjō's staff that the Kwantung Army could act in "self-defense," especially whenever Chinese "bandits" posed a security problem.[16] With this prompting, the Kwantung staff detected some bandits in the area of the Chinchow railway junction; and, on October 18, an aerial bombardment of Chinchow was executed. Since Chinchow

[15] *Ibid.*, 45-46.   [16] Imamura interview.

was some two hundred miles north of the South Manchurian Railway zone, Shidehara's assurances to the Council that the army would refrain from further aggressive actions appeared meaningless. Amid the hostility generated by the Chinchow bombing, Ambassador Yoshizawa notified the Council that any withdrawal of Japanese troops to the railway zone was now contingent on a "satisfactory assurance regarding the protection of the South Manchurian Railway."[17] In this situation, the Council had to decide whether to approach the crisis in terms of the Kellogg-Briand Pact, as argued by the Chinese delegate, or in terms of the special rights which Japan had acquired between 1905 and 1916. This choice was especially explosive, thought Mr. Pratt of the British delegation, because "the one thing on which both civil and military are united in Japan is that they will not allow the League of Nations to intervene between them and China."[18]

In hopes of skirting the issue, M. Briand, the French representative on the Council, urged the Chinese to agree to formal negotiations with the Japanese government, providing such talks were begun in conjunction with a Japanese troop withdrawal observed by officials of the League of Nations. Dr. Sze, the Chinese spokesman at the Council, rebuffed this entreaty on the grounds that his government had publicly affirmed that "evacuation is a precondition of direct negotiations."[19] The Wakatsuki government was equally unrelenting on this point. Baron Shidehara, on October 19, assured Sir Francis Lindley he could never secure a withdrawal of the Kwantung Army before the inception of formal Sino-Japanese negotiations. "Nor," added Shidehara, "could any Japanese government remain in office which agreed to evacuate by a date fixed in advance."[20] Four days later, Ambassador Yoshizawa informed the Council that Japan would require the fulfillment of five principles as the prerequisites to any Sino-

---

[17] Butler, *DBFP*, VIII, 684.
[18] *Ibid.*, 758.   [19] *Ibid.*, 787.   [20] *Ibid.*, 791.

Japanese settlement of the Manchurian issue—namely, (1) mutual repudiation of aggression, (2) respect for the territorial integrity of China, (3) suppression of Chinese boycotts, (4) protection of Japanese interests in Manchuria, and (5) confirmation of Japan's railway rights in Manchuria.[21] Despite the polite terminology, in fact, Yoshizawa's principles would commit China to a recognition of all existing protocols and treaties affecting Manchuria as the precondition for a withdrawal of the Kwantung Army to the railway zone in South Manchuria. Since the Council ruled this would be equivalent to the use of force in the settlement of the Mukden incident, it considered Yoshizawa's principles inappropriate.[22] Confronted by the antithetical policies of the Chinese and Japanese delegates, the Council sought temporary refuge in a resolution calling for the withdrawal of Japanese troops by November 16, at which time the Council would meet again to review the Manchurian problem.[23]

Since the Council members were thinking mainly in terms of the Kellogg-Briand Pact, they were not especially responsive to the political situation within Japan, or to the perils of fixing a specific date for the withdrawal of the Kwantung Army. Certainly the Council was neither willing nor able to enforce this ruling; and Shidehara had already revealed that the Japanese government could not accomplish this feat, unless the Chinese government furnished tangible evidence of its willingness to negotiate a new treaty confirming Japan's special rights and interests in Manchuria. Following the October 24 resolution of the Council, Shidehara's position became most precarious. The Kwantung Army favored an advance to Tsitsihar and Chinchow, in conjunction with the formation of "local" Manchurian governments; and, while the war ministry and the general staff debated the merits of this policy as opposed to Shidehara's diplomatic maneuvers, a group of staff officers dreamed of launching a military *coup d'état* that would

21 *Ibid.*, 791.   22 *Ibid., loc.cit.*   23 *Ibid.*, 809-810.

bring the government under the complete control of the army.[24]

THE OCTOBER INCIDENT

Although the Kwantung Army had, by late September, secured control of South Manchuria, the Big Three of the army had also endorsed the cabinet's wish to seek a diplomatic settlement of the Manchurian problem in cooperation with the Council of the League of Nations. This latter policy visibly annoyed General Tatekawa, who feared that "his offspring"— the Mukden incident—was unnecessarily being placed in an incubator.[25] The paternalistic anxieties of the chief of the operations division were sympathetically shared by his subordinates; and a dozen younger staff officers, led by Colonels Hashimoto Kingorō and Nemoto Hiroshi, formed a special group within the Sakurakai with the self-appointed task of drafting a program of action which would allow a less cautious handling of the Manchurian crisis.[26] After conferring with several professional patriots, including Nishida Zei, Kita Ikki, and Ōkawa Shūmei, these officers concluded the Manchurian situation had created a momentous opportunity for the renovation of the empire in terms of Kita's *Outline of the Reconstruction of Japan*. To accomplish this transformation, the army would have to seize control of all Manchuria, organize an independent regime there, and, in Japan, replace the party system of cabinets with a government headed by military personnel. By October 10, Hashimoto and Nemoto had formulated a projected program of action: (1) the operations division of the general staff was to allow the Kwantung Army, under the "right of supreme command," to implement whatever action it considered essential for national security, including,

---

[24] The October incident has been appraised in many ways, of which the following seem most creditable: Hata Ikuhito, *Gun fuashizumu* (Tokyo, 1962), 41-45; Aoki Tokuzō, *Taiheiyō sensō zenshi* (Tokyo, 1953), I, 170-178; and Tateno Nobuyuki, *Shōwa gunbatsu* (Tokyo, 1963), 111-126.

[25] Tateno, *Shōwa gunbatsu*, 112.

[26] Hata, *Gun fuashizumu*, 32-33.

if necessary, the conquest of North Manchuria and the creation of a "Manchurian" government; (2) the cabinet and the Emperor's advisors would be informed that the army was unwilling to tolerate the spineless and inept diplomatic and fiscal policies of the Wakatsuki cabinet; and (3) Prince Saionji would be directed to nominate a cabinet composed of General Araki as premier and war minister, Admiral Kobayashi as naval minister, General Tatekawa as foreign minister, Ōkawa Shūmei as finance minister, Colonel Hashimoto as home minister, and Colonel Nemoto as chief of the military police.[27]

The simplicity and naïveté of this planning were most impressive, and it is hard to believe that anyone, apart from the conspirators, could seriously have imagined a cabinet composed of Araki, Tatekawa, Ōkawa, Hashimoto, and Kobayashi. Still, the sentiments underlying this program of action accurately mirrored the general staff's dissatisfaction with the foreign policy of Baron Shidehara; and Nemoto and Hashimoto knew the Kwantung Army had recently requested permission to organize local Manchurian civil administrations in South Manchuria. More particularly, the exponents of this program were not discouraged by their exploratory conversations with Generals Tatekawa and Araki.[28] Although neither of these senior officers was apparently concerned by their call for a renovation of the government, the behavior of Hashimoto and Nemoto soon caused a violent whiplash within central headquarters. On October 15, Vice-War Minister Sugiyama and the vice-chief of the general staff, General Ninomiya, pointedly informed General Tatekawa that any type of political incident involving the Imperial army would be "a foolish action which must be prevented."[29] Concurrently with this reprimand, Colonel Tōjō Hideki of Tatekawa's staff circulated a memorandum revealing the gist of the revolutionary outline prepared by Nemoto and Hashimoto. General Sugiyama im-

[27] Aoki, *Taiheiyō sensō*, I, 173-175.
[28] Hata, *Gun fuashizumu*, 36-38.
[29] Tateno, *Shōwa gunbatsu*, 114.

mediately summoned the key staff officers in central head-
quarters—Generals Koiso, Nakamura, Ninomiya, Umezu, and
Tatekawa and Colonels Nagata, Okamura, Imamura, and
Tōjō—to his office for a discussion of Tōjō's memorandum.[30]
Here, Colonel Nagata acted as the spokesman for the war
ministry's staff; and, in this role, Nagata vigorously challenged
the propriety and sagacity of the program outlined by Colonels
Hashimoto and Nemoto. If the army were to intervene openly
in politics by sanctioning a political coup and the creation of a
Manchurian government, reasoned Nagata, the long-term consequences would not be beneficial to the security of the empire.
Domestically, this program would generate a tumultuous
political situation which would preclude the possibility of any
stable government; and, internationally, it would prevent an
adequate diplomatic settlement of the Manchurian problem.
Furthermore, insisted Nagata, this type of behavior would have
calamitous effects on army discipline. No one present effectively
questioned the cogency of Nagata's brief, and even Colonel
Imamura, who had diligently sabotaged the cabinet's efforts
to localize the Mukden incident, endorsed Nagata's viewpoint.
Accordingly, these army authorities reaffirmed what was, in
most military circles, an article of faith: the war minister and
the chief of staff were responsible for every action of the army.

Since General Minami and Kanaya had agreed to the cabinet's approach to the Manchurian question, this resolution
was an euphemistic way of censuring General Tatekawa, as
well as presumably terminating the conspiracy set in motion
by Colonels Hashimoto and Nemoto. On October 16, however,
Nemoto invited the inspector general of military education,
General Araki, to a party at a second-rate geisha house in
downtown Tokyo.[31] That evening, after several cups of sake,
Colonel Hashimoto directly notified Araki of the Wakatsuki cabinet's manifest inability to solve the problems caused

[30] *Ibid.*, 115-116. Also Imamura Hitoshi, "Manshū hi o fuku goro,"
Himerareta shōwashi, 66.
[31] Eguchi Bokuro, *et al.*, *Taiheiyō sensōshi* (Tokyo, 1953), I, 149.

by the great depression. Above all, insisted Hashimoto, the government was insensitive to the marvelous potentialities inherent in a Japanese-sponsored government in Manchuria. The only solution, pressed the revolutionary spokesman, was a resolute course of action by the army—that is, General Araki should assume control of the government and, with the help of Tatekawa, Nemoto, and Hashimoto, renovate the nation.[32] Araki graciously attributed this political vision to too much rice wine and responded with a sober admonishment: no officer of the Imperial army could participate in any political conspiracy against the government and still remain loyal to the Throne.[33]

The behavior of General Araki in this episode was no doubt proper and, superficially at least, above reproach. Still, Araki had been apprised of the revolutionary views of Nemoto before accepting the latter's invitation to a social gathering; and he was not ignorant of the resolution adopted by the departmental and section chiefs on October 15. His presence at the clandestine geisha-house meeting, therefore, provoked great concern lest Hashimoto and Nemoto interpret his sociability as an implicit approval of their revolutionary plans. On October 17, Vice-War Minister Sugiyama conducted another review of the problem with the departmental heads of the general staff and the war ministry and this time the authorities decided in favor of three specific steps: (1) to inform the military police of the conspiracy; (2) to reassign the conspirators from central headquarters; and (3) to order the dissolution of the Cherry Society.[34] This first recommendation was implemented the next morning when the military police placed Hashimoto, Nemoto, Tanaka Kiyoshi, Watchi Takagi, and seven other staff officers in protective custody, pending a complete investigation of

[32] Saionji-Harada, *Memoirs*, October 29, 1931.

[33] Reputedly Araki replied, "The army officers of Japan are the so-called Kusunosuki Sword, which should always be polished; but it should not be drawn indiscriminately from its scabbard." *Ibid.*

[34] Tateno, *Shōwa gunbatsu*, 118-120.

their political behavior.[35] And, by the end of December, the last two stipulations were realized—the Sakurakai was disbanded and the proponents of the October *coup d'état* were transferred from central headquarters.

This *machiai*, or geisha house, conspiracy of Colonels Nemoto and Hashimoto has been viewed by most postwar historians as a momentous step in the advance of the fascist movement of the 1930's.[36] In this perspective, the October incident symbolized the willingness of army officers to work with ultra-nationalistic groups; and, even though it failed in 1931, the army authorities were later to utilize assassinations and the threat of military coups as part of their systematic assault on the policies of the civilian ministers of state. A more reserved appraisal suggests that the October incident was not representative of the mainstream of army thought or policies. This abortive coup, in fact, precipitated a sequence of events which tightened internal discipline and, at least temporarily, curtailed political proclivities among staff officers in central headquarters. Whether or not the October incident symbolized the subsequent development of a fascist movement in the army is a question not readily answered. In the course of this presentation, however, the process by which army views were impressed on national policy will be portrayed in terms suggesting that those officers who sought political power via *coups d'état* or by close associationship with the major ultra-nationalistic organizations were not particularly influential in the determination of national policy. The October incident may have revealed a radical facet of the staff of central headquarters, but it was not necessarily representative of a fascistic movement which eventually prevailed in the officer corps.

[35] *Ibid.*, 122. Also Watchi Takagi interview.

[36] E.g., Maruyama Masao, *Gendai seiji no shisō to kōdō* (Tokyo, 1957), I, 25-83, "Nihon fuashizumu no shisō to undō"; and Fujiwara Akira, *Gunjishi* (Tokyo, 1961), 171-176. Hata Ikuhito, *Gun fuashizumu*, offers a judicious refinement of Professor Maruyama's essay on the ideology of Japanese fascism and the October incident. In English, Maruyama Masao, *Thought and Behavior in Modern Japanese Politics* (New York, 1963).

DOWNFALL OF THE WAKATSUKI CABINET

In the aftermath of the October incident, the army authorities had vetoed any political *coup d'état* by army officers, as well as the possibility of permitting the Kwantung Army to act independently in Manchuria. Still, most staff officers in central headquarters concurred with the views of Ōkawa Shūmei—namely, if the civilian leaders of the government continued to "dilly-dally, as they were doing, all would end in vain, although the lid for the solution of the Manchurian Incident had been thrown open."[37] In this context, Colonel Nagata and his staff favored a patient and circumspect approach to the Manchurian problem, confident that Foreign Minister Shidehara would not obtain a new treaty confirming Japan's special position in Manchuria. The government, in this eventuality, would either resign or accept the necessity to create a new government in Manchuria. The advantages of this policy, reasoned Nagata, resided in the continuity of responsible government, with the cabinet assuming official responsibility for the nation's policy vis-à-vis Manchuria.[38] The operations division of the general staff, however, still preferred an ostensible adherence to the policies of the foreign minister, while ordering the Kwantung Army to implement a new civil administration in Manchuria. Because all forms of Chinese administration had been shattered in North and South Manchuria, Tatekawa's staff argued, it was inevitable that the Kwantung Army create a matrix of new civil administrations in South Manchuria. War Minister Minami eventually yielded to the latter viewpoint; and, on November 15, the day before the Council of the League was scheduled to review the Manchurian situation, Minami informed General Honjō that he should not "participate in a Manchurian independence movement, . . . but neither should you ignore the general trend for independence."[39] In this ambiguous style, General Minami

---

[37] Storry, *Double Patriots*, 87.
[38] Interview with General Imamura.
[39] Mitarai, *Minami Jirō*, 285.

paid verbal homage to the foreign policy of the government and covertly condoned the creation of a "Manchurian" government.

Prior to this new phase of army policy, public opposition to the policies of Baron Shidehara had assumed dramatic proportions. The Seiyūkai berated the "spineless" posture of the government; and, as early as September 30, Baron Hiranuma in the Privy Council called for an immediate solution of the Manchurian question.[40] Such complaints and demands were not surprising, as the same groups had been vocal defenders of the "right of supreme command" during the London Naval Treaty controversy. For the first time, however, the cabinet was subject to an open assault on the leadership of Shidehara by a dissident wing of the Minseitō. In early October, the home minister, Adachi Kenzō, announced a personal "boycott" of all cabinet meetings in protest to the policies of Baron Shidehara.[41] Adachi did not resign his portfolio; and, since a formal request for his resignation would technically dissolve the cabinet, the premier found it politically advantageous to tolerate the maverick behavior of his home minister. Nevertheless, the prospect of facing any general elections without the apparatus of the home ministry at the party's full disposal, when combined with the evident popular resentment of Shidehara policies, stimulated great unrest within the Minseitō. Hoping to capitalize on these fears, Adachi and Kuhara Fusanosuke of the Seiyūkai proposed the formation of a "coalition" government.[42] Although this scheme was rebuffed by Prince Saionji, Adachi and Kuhara won some support among the Emperor's closest advisors. Saionji, for example, was sufficiently dismayed with the attitude of the Lord Keeper of the Privy Seal as to admonish Count Makino with an allegorical recollection of how Ōkubo Toshimichi, Makino's grandfather, had served his

---

[40] *Ibid.*, 272-273.

[41] A. Morgan Young, *Imperial Japan*, 114-115, provides a vivid sketch of Adachi's behavior.

[42] Maejima Shōzō, *Nihon fuashizumu to gikai*, 274.

country to great advantage by opposing a scheme to invade Korea in the early years of the Meiji government.[43]

The coalition intrigue of Kuhara and Adachi, the public boycott of the home minister, and the outcries of the Seiyūkai and the Hiranuma faction in the Privy Council were not the only signs of political dissatisfaction with the Wakatsuki government. Even the proletarian parties rallied to the defense of the Kwantung Army. In particular, the Social Democratic Party (*shakai minshūtō*), under the leadership of Akamatsu Katsumaro, adopted "A Decision Concerning the Problem of Manchuria and Mongolia."[44] After blaming Chinese warlords and selfish Japanese capitalists for the difficulties in this region, the party's resolution eulogized the lofty ideals underlining the policy of the Imperial army. The only just solution to the Manchurian problem, concluded the Social Democrats, would be the creation of a socialistic system in Manchuria, one that would benefit "both Chinese and Japanese living in Manchuria."[45] In this fashion, Japan's special rights in Manchuria would contribute to the development of socialism within Japan.

Apparently, all the "minority" political groups in Japan— the Adachi wing of the Minseitō, the Kuhara element of the Seiyūkai, the Hiranuma faction in the Privy Council, and the major proletarian party—were anxious to ride the political tiger of an "independent" Manchuria, certain that their interests would be well served with the demise of Shidehara diplomacy. Given this climate of opinion and the policy of the Imperial army, an informed observer might have considered Shidehara's faith in his ability to effect some sort of diplomatic settlement of the Mukden incident somewhat misplaced. By mid-November, Japan had not acceded to the Council's resolution calling for a withdrawal of the Kwantung Army by November 16; the Chinese government had revealed no incli-

[43] Saionji-Harada, *Memoirs,* October 24, 1931.
[44] Maejima, *Nihon fuashizumu,* 272.
[45] *Ibid.*

nation to enter into direct negotiations; all forms of Chinese civil administration in South Manchuria had been destroyed by the Kwantung Army; and the possibility of the Imperial army's organizing a Manchurian government could not be discounted. Shidehara's one hope centered on the Council of the League of Nations. Without its support, estimated the Japanese foreign minister, China would have to negotiate a treaty acceptable to the Imperial government.

From the vantage point of the Japanese foreign ministry, either one of two resolutions by the Council would be satisfactory. The Council could simply express regret over its inability to contribute to a diplomatic solution of the Manchurian incident and drop the matter; or, it could reverse its earlier policy and support Japan's claim that formal negotiations between China and Japan should precede any modification in the deployment of the Kwantung Army. If the Council became convinced that Japan would not modify its position, reasoned Shidehara, either of the alternatives might be realized. This evaluation was not an illusion prompted by the foreign minister's travails in Japan. By early November, at least some members of the Council appreciated the dimensions of the Manchurian problem, as well as the fact that the Council's efforts in Paris were slowly corroding public confidence in the efficacy of the League. "If the Manchurian situation is one which League authority cannot clear up, it is a pity," declared Sir John Simon, the British foreign minister. "But it would be much better, I think, for the League to face this fact, if it is a fact, and to tell Japan . . . it is not possible owing to Japanese opposition to reach a unanimous and effective conclusion."[46] Though this would hardly be a satisfying solution to the crisis, Sir John considered it superior to pretending that the League could control the situation in Manchuria. Unless Japan were prepared to utilize the offices of the Council to resolve the matter, he concluded, further discussion of the Manchurian problem by the Council would be pointless.

[46] *DBFP*, VIII, 921.

The Chinese proposition that "evacuation is a precondition of direct negotiation" and the Japanese incantation of Yoshizawa's five principles had, in fact, placed the Council in an impossible situation. The daily recitation of these antithetical standpoints was leading nowhere, except, as Sir John said, to an undermining of public confidence in the effectiveness of the League. Baron Shidehara had anticipated the attitude of the British foreign minister in this context, as well as the corollary that this would lead the Western powers to a gradual, if reluctant, deference to the wishes of the Imperial government. Shidehara's strategy, however, was compromised on November 17 when Ambassador Matsudaira submitted a "personal suggestion" to the British and French representatives on the Council.[47] The Japanese government, suggested Matsudaira, might consider the appointment of a commission to investigate the entire scope of Sino-Japanese relations, if China would agree to negotiate a direct settlement of the current Manchurian crisis on the basis of Yoshizawa's principles. After discussing the proposal, Sir Eric Drummond, on behalf of the Council, wondered whether Japan would consider the appointment of a commission as "a separate concrete proposal."[48] In the process, Sir Eric also observed that any commission formed by the League would require several months to complete its report, during which time the Council would take no further action in terms of the present Manchurian issue. To Ambassador Matsudaira, this response seemed most satisfactory: by proposing a commission of inquiry, Japan's position vis-à-vis the Council would be enhanced; and, while the commission fulfilled its assignment, Japan could pressure the Nationalist government into a settlement of the Manchurian matter. Hence, the ambassador urged Baron Shidehara to sanction the course of action outlined by Sir Eric Drummond.

Ambassador Matsudaira had attempted to break the stalemate at the Council mainly because of his sensitivity to the attitudes and policies of the Western powers. Of much greater

[47] *Ibid.*, 926.   [48] *Ibid.*, 924.

concern to the general staff were the railways in North Manchuria and the remnants of Marshal Chang Hsueh-liang's army. By seizing the railroads and ejecting these Chinese forces, Japan would acquire viable control over Manchuria and augment its strategic position in relation to the Soviet Maritime Army. Throughout October and November, the operations division therefore recommended an advance to Tsitsihar and Chinchow. Each time the war minister raised these issues in the cabinet, Baron Shidehara countered with his own definition of Japan's security needs—namely, that the government should use diplomacy, along with the *status quo* in Manchuria, to obtain a settlement confirming Japan's special position in the area. Any further advance northward, insisted the foreign minister, would only damage Japan's position at the Council, alienate the United States, provoke a serious crisis with the Soviet Union, and preclude fruitful diplomatic relations with the Nanking government. Such consequences, reasoned Shidehara, outweighed whatever immediate advantages might be gained by an advance to Chinchow.

The war minister and the chief of the general staff deferred to this estimate; and, between October 16 and November 19, the operational proposals of the Kwantung Army were repeatedly overruled. Despite the restraining authority of General Kanaya, the army was reminded by General Tatekawa of its right to act in "self-defense" whenever Chinese troops presented a security threat.[49] Perhaps by accident, but more likely by design, while the cabinet was debating the merits and risks involved in Ambassador Matsudaira's latest recommendation, the Kwantung Army detected an ominous grouping of Chinese forces at Tsitsihar. In the absence of any contrary orders from the operations division of the general staff, General Honjō sanctioned an advance to Tsitsihar.[50] This action convinced the American secretary of state that the situation in Manchuria was now "in the hands of virtually mad dogs" and he promptly

[49] Imamura interview.
[50] NKSG, *Taiheiyō sensō e no michi*, II, 75.

fired off a strong verbal blast, reminding the Japanese foreign minister of his earlier assurances that the Kwantung Army would not move into North Manchuria.[51] This personal censure no doubt impressed the secretary's feelings on the foreign minister; but Shidehara was more concerned with the situation in Paris. Matsudaira had opened a possible avenue to a diplomatic settlement of the Manchurian incident which could only be pursued by the cessation of operations in Manchuria.

At the November 18th cabinet meeting, after citing the specific assurances of the war minister that the general staff would not permit an advance to Tsitsihar, Shidehara demanded the prompt recall of the Kwantung Army.[52] General Minami, however, preferred first to review the government's policy towards the Council. In particular, Minami feared the proposed commission of inquiry might claim the authority to oversee and control the movements of the Imperial army. A commission invested with this power would, in the opinion of the army authorities, constitute a violation of the "right of supreme command." After the premier and foreign minister unequivocally reassured the war minister that the government would never accept a commission thus empowered, Minami declared that the general staff would countermand Honjō's recent orders and recall the Kwantung Army from Tsitsihar.[53] Since similar promises had been made in the past, Baron Shidehara requested a more specific guarantee of cooperation from the general staff. Thus, after the cabinet meeting, Minami and Shidehara conferred personally with General Kanaya, and the foreign minister obtained a firm commitment from the chief of the general staff to cancel the Tsitsihar operation.

Once Baron Shidehara was satisfied the army would adhere to the cabinet's policy, he authorized Matsudaira to propose the appointment of a commission of inquiry by the Council.

51 Stimson, *Diary*, November 19, 1931.
52 On this cabinet meeting and decision, see NKSG, *Taiheiyō sensō e no michi*, II, 77-81; *Mitarai, Minami Jirō*, 293-300.
53 *Ibid.*

With the clear understanding that any commission would not intervene in negotiations between China and Japan or seek to control the movements of the Imperial army, Matsudaira advised M. Briand on November 20 that his government was prepared to request a commission of inquiry to study the diplomatic maze of Sino-Japanese relations.[54] Within twenty-four hours of Matsudaira's statement, the Kwantung Army reluctantly withdrew from the Tsitsihar region. This latter development was greeted with some satisfaction by Secretary Stimson, who attributed it to "the stiff tone which I have taken to Shidehara."[55] So encouraged, Stimson called in the Japanese ambassador and alerted Debuchi to the imperative necessity for meticulous control of the Kwantung Army. In particular, warned the secretary, if the Japanese army were to move on Chinchow, "nobody would trust Japan again."[56]

The sentiments of the American secretary of state were shared by the Nationalist government. Consequently, when Japan formally proposed a committee of inquiry, the Chinese delegate in Paris insisted that any commission formed by the Council should be combined with a declaration calling for the withdrawal of the Japanese army to the South Manchurian Railway zone.[57] Otherwise, reasoned Dr. Sze, the Chinese government would never enter into direct negotiations of the incident with the Japanese government. By this time, however, the Anglo-French representatives were unwilling to endorse Sze's recommendation; and, despite the moral support of the American secretary of state, the Chinese realized they could expect no tangible form of assistance from the United States. In this context, on November 23, Wellington Koo advised the French and British ministers in Nanking of his government's willingness, pending a formal diplomatic settlement of the Manchurian problem, to withdraw all Chinese troops "from Chinchow to Shanhaikuan," if Japan would guarantee to

54 *DBFP*, VIII, 937.
55 Stimson, *Diary*, November 21, 1931.
56 *Ibid.*, November 22, 1931.
57 *DBFP*, VIII, 941-942.

leave this demilitarized zone under Chinese civil administration.[58]

Once this proposal was confirmed, Baron Shidehara notified Generals Minami and Kanaya that his diplomacy had attained the essential objective desired by the army—the removal of all Chinese troops from North Manchuria. On this optimistic note, the foreign minister reiterated the importance of a coordinated foreign policy, especially the preclusion of any incidents in the Chinchow locale. If the Chinese actually implemented their withdrawal, General Kanaya stipulated he would prevent any attack on Chinchow. In view of the strong convictions of the American secretary of state on this matter, Shidehara then called in Ambassador Cameron Forbes; and, after reviewing the recent developments, Shidehara asked that Stimson be appraised, "in strictest confidence," of the resolution of the war minister, the foreign minister, and the chief of the general staff to prevent any attack on Chinchow.[59] Stimson concluded that this assurance had been the consequence of his forceful stance with the Japanese ambassador; and, equally significantly, the secretary of state interpreted Shidehara's private message as a binding commitment on the part of the Imperial government.[60] Since Stimson was apparently ignorant of the Chinese proposal which had produced Shidehara's confidential statement, he did not affix a comparable degree of moral responsibility on the Chinese government to execute faithfully its proposed evacuation of Chinese troops from Chinchow.

Wellington Koo's original proposal of November 23 had contained two main stipulations: a withdrawal of Chinese troops from Chinchow to Shanhaikuan; and the continuance of Chinese civil administration in the demilitarized zone. On November 25, however, Dr. Sze requested the Council to send a contingent of "neutral troops" to the Chinchow region. In response, the Council proposed the despatch of a team of neutral

58 *Ibid.*, 955.

59 Stimson, *Diary*, November 28, 1931, reviews the secretary's interpretation of Forbes' cable.

60 Stimson, *Diary*, November 21, 1931.

observers, "with a view to the possibility of establishing between Chinese and Japanese troops a neutral zone, or any
similar arrangement for avoiding a clash."[61] This latest
recommendation unleashed new disagreement between Baron
Shidehara and General Minami; and, in the midst of this
controversy, the American secretary of state was mistakenly informed that the Kwantung Army had attacked Chinchow.
Considering the recent remarks of the Japanese foreign
minister, Stimson felt "like kicking the whole thing over and
publishing the whole record."[62] In order to obtain a public
disclosure of Japan's duplicity, the secretary arranged a press
conference on November 27; and, when the Chinchow matter
was raised by a reporter, Secretary Stimson responded:

> I merely read to them my telegram of inquiry and Tokyo's
> direct assurance that there would be no such expedition.
> I told them that in the light of this direct assurance from the
> Foreign Minister, the Minister of War, and the Chief of
> Staff of the Japanese Government, I could hardly credit
> the present dispatches.[63]

Because Shidehara had given this statement "in confidence,"
and the Kwantung Army had not actually attacked Chinchow,
Ambassador Forbes was understandably vexed by the secretary's public remarks.[64] In an unusual gesture of protest,
Ambassador Forbes directly questioned the propriety of the
press conference, stressing, in particular, the embarrassment
Stimson's statement had caused in his personal relations with
the Japanese foreign minister.[65] Confronted by this blunt
criticism, Stimson retorted that his public observations had, in
any case, performed one valuable purpose: "It got the [Japa-

[61] *DBFP*, VIII, 960.
[62] Stimson, *Diary*, November 26, 1931.
[63] *Ibid.*, November 27, 1931.
[64] *Ibid.*, November 28, 1931. Stimson's diary notes that Forbes did not
specifically indicate this assurance had been in confidence.
[65] *Ibid.*, November 28, 1931.

nese] army nailed up to their promise not to go to Chinchow. Now they won't dare to go."[66]

The implications of Stimson's press conference were somewhat differently interpreted in Tokyo. The popular press termed Stimson's remarks both presumptuous and arrogant, but the major criticisms were leveled at Baron Shidehara. Accusations of "treason" and "betrayal of military secrets" were hurled at the foreign minister in a reckless fashion. Long-conditioned to such intemperate outbursts, Shidehara stoically discounted them as a temporary inconvenience. Still, as Shidehara remarked to the British ambassador, Sir Francis Lindley, he was apprehensive lest the Chinese government take Stimson's declaration at face value. If China believed the American government capable of controlling the Imperial army, this might, worried Shidehara, "stiffen her attitude as regards the evacuation of Chinchow."[67] Although it is difficult to determine whether Stimson's interview with the press should be credited with this influence, Shidehara's fear that the Chinese might reverse their promise to evacuate Chinchow soon materialized into a real problem.

On November 27, parallel with Secretary Stimson's discussion of Japanese duplicity, Baron Shidehara officially advised the French ambassador that his government had accepted the Chinese proposal to evacute its troops from Chinchow to Shanhaikuan and that, in return, the Kwantung Army would not advance to Chinchow.[68] One week later, M. Briand formally informed the Council that the Chinese plan for a demilitarized zone in Chinchow had been accepted by the Japanese government, subject to two amendments: (1) that Chinese troops would be withdrawn behind the Great Wall; and (2) that Chinese national officials and local Japanese representatives would immediately negotiate the precise limits of the zone and the number of Chinese police to be stationed in the Chinchow-Shanhaikuan district.[69] Dr. Sze, in response,

[66] *Ibid.*
[68] *Ibid.*, 990.

[67] *DBFP*, VIII, 1007.
[69] *Ibid.*, 979.

offered two counter-propositions—namely, (1) his government would need to know the limits of the zone before it would formally engage in any negotiations; and (2) it wanted the agreement to be supervised by a team of neutral observers.[70] Neither of these demands seemed to present insurmountable obstacles; and M. Briand undertook the task of working out a suitable compromise with the Japanese delegate. His efforts, however, were nullified by an abrupt switch in the Chinese approach to the Chinchow problem.

The British minister in Nanking, on December 4, reported that Wellington Koo's initial plan for a demilitarized zone had been "conditional and tentative," not a formal offer to evacuate Chinese troops from Chinchow to Shanhaikuan.[71] Two days later, in Paris, Dr. Sze notified the Council that his government no longer favored a demilitarized area in the Chinchow district. The Chinese forces in this area, added the Chinese delegate ingenuously, would not advance beyond Chinchow toward the Imperial army, but any Japanese move in the direction of Chinchow would be met by "appropriate measures of self-defense."[72] This diplomatic stance was supported by mass student demonstrations in Nanking against any "withdrawal of Chinese troops from Chinese soil," a public protest which one British diplomat thought reminiscent of the great student movement of the First World War.[73]

This new attitude in Nanking represented an acute crisis for the Japanese foreign minister. Shidehara promptly informed the British and French ambassadors of Japan's willingness to support a commission of inquiry by the League, but, added the foreign minister, this could be done only if the Chinese abided by the November 23rd proposal—namely, to withdraw all Chinese troops "from Chinchow to Shanhaikuan."[74] By December 10, the American secretary of state also realized that Wellington Koo had made this offer; and he assured Ambassador Debuchi that the American government would

[70] *Ibid.*, 980.   [71] *Ibid.*, 983.   [72] *Ibid.*, 990.
[73] *Ibid.*, 992.   [74] *Ibid.*, 998.

do everything possible to obliterate the "misunderstanding" which caused the Japanese government to believe it "had been tricked" into withdrawing to the Liao River.[75] At the same time, Secretary Stimson indicated that any Japanese attack on Chinchow would still constitute an act of aggression. Unfortunately, the Chinese cancellation of its offer to demilitarize Chinchow was not viewed in Tokyo as a misunderstanding, nor was the Wakatsuki cabinet able, politically speaking, to consider the Chinchow matter in terms of the Kellogg-Briand Pact.

From the inception of the Mukden incident, the army authorities had insisted the Nationalist government would never negotiate directly with Japan. By "playing barbarian against barbarian," argued the general staff, China would try to check Japan's interests and rights in Manchuria by relying on the cooperation of the Anglo-American nations and the League of Nations. Despite the credibility of this viewpoint, the cabinet had, with the September 23 decision, based its policy on the premise that it could compel the Chinese government to negotiate a treaty confirming all the treaty rights and privileges which Japan had acquired in the first two decades of the twentieth century. When Shidehara cited the Chinese proposal of November 23 as tangible evidence of the viability of his diplomacy, the general staff had not been impressed, believing the Chinese offer had been prompted only by the imminent probability of a Japanese move on Chinchow. Consequently, when the Nationalist government rescinded its projected withdrawal of Chinese troops, War Minister Minami and General Kanaya demanded that the foreign minister face the realities of the situation: the government must conduct its foreign policy on the assumption that Japanese interests in Manchuria were more vital to the welfare of the empire than the principles of the Kellogg-Briand Pact.

Confronted by the army's insistence on a forceful ejection of all Chinese troops from North Manchuria, the political

---

[75] Stimson, *Diary*, December 10, 1931.

maneuvers of Home Minister Adachi, Baron Hiranuma, and the Seiyūkai, and the popular enthusiasm for a more resolute solution of the Manchurian crisis, Shidehara finally capitulated. On December 12, the Wakatsuki cabinet resigned, conceding its inability to fuse two strands of Japan's foreign policy—cooperation with the Western powers, and consolidation and extension of her special position in Manchuria.

THE SELECTION OF INUKAI KI

Although the party of Shidehara diplomacy commanded a majority of seats in the Diet, the resignation of Wakatsuki yielded a confident prediction among Japanese political pundits: either the dissident Adachi wing of the Minseitō would formally fuse with the Seiyūkai in support of a Seiyūkai cabinet, or it would generate enough support for a coalition government. Either way, it seemed manifest that the new government would seek to unify the nation behind a forceful Manchurian policy. The actual selection of the premier, however, still resided with the Senior Statesman, Prince Saionji. Since he was anxious to maintain the principle of party cabinets, the primacy of the premier in the determination of national policy, and a cautious foreign policy, Saionji was not favorably disposed toward the views and groups represented by Adachi Kenzō or Kuhara Fusanosuke. The Senior Statesman was in a peculiarly delicate political quandary. The leaders of the opposition party naturally urged the appointment of the Seiyūkai's titular head, Suzuki Kisaburō, as premier, a recommendation which was enthusiastically seconded by Count Itō Myoji and Baron Hiranuma of the Privy Council. The responsible Minseitō leaders—Wakatsuki, Shidehara, Inoue Junnosuke, and Izawa Takeo of the Privy Council—counseled against this action, stressing their unwillingness to cooperate with a Suzuki cabinet which would, in their opinion, pursue an overly ambitious and ill-considered foreign policy. In this political maze, Saionji's search for a premier who would effectively champion the principle of civil leadership and resolutely contest the army's efforts to dictate foreign policy was almost comparable to Diogenes' quest for an honest man.

The immediate objective, as far as the Emperor's personal advisors were concerned, was the selection of a premier who would sincerely endeavor to restrain the army in Manchuria and continue the nation's commitment to a policy of cooperation with the Western powers. After carefully canvassing the personal views of all the major figures within the Seiyūkai, as well as the sentiments of the movers and shakers in the Minseitō, Prince Saionji engineered a subtle compromise which would meet the public demands for a Seiyūkai government and satisfy the private concerns of the Minseitō: the nomination of Inukai Ki as premier and the organization of a Seiyūkai cabinet.[76] Inukai had acted as one of the Seiyūkai's leading spokesmen during the "right of supreme command" controversy in 1930; and he had berated the "weak-kneed" diplomacy of Baron Shidehara. Throughout the Manchurian controversy, however, Inukai had not aligned himself with the army's interpretation of the "right of supreme command," nor had he joined the chorus singing the praises of an "independent" Manchuria. In his private discussions with the Senior Statesman, moreover, Inukai expressed concern about the current trend in Japanese politics which increased the power and prestige of the military and invited potentially serious conflict with the Occidental nations. Once Saionji, the leaders of the Minseitō, and the Imperial household were convinced of the integrity of these reflections, Saionji again conferred with Inukai and indicated that the mandate to form a cabinet would be forthcoming. In the process, Saionji emphasized the necessity for a prudent foreign policy; and, in an unprecedented move, the Senior Statesman imparted the personal sentiments of the Emperor: "The meddling of the army in domestic and foreign affairs is something which, for the welfare of the nation, must be viewed with apprehension. Be mindful of my anxiety. Please convey its full report to Inukai." Although it is im-

[76] Saionji-Harada, *Memoirs*, December 24, 1931.

possible to ascertain the full impact produced by the Emperor's personal plea, Inukai was visibly moved by Saionji's confidence, and he promised the Senior Statesman that the responsibilities of the premiership would be exercised with complete dedication to the wishes of the Throne.[77] These were not idle professions of intent; and, until his assassination on May 5, 1932, Inukai steadfastly ignored the advice of his party's leaders by adhering to a set of policies which circumscribed the plans and aspirations of the army authorities. Inukai's commitment to this stance, in fact, contributed directly to his unfortunate political destiny.

The Imperial household and the Senior Statesman had bypassed the president of the Seiyūkai, Suzuki Kisaburō, because of their desire to restrain the army's influence on foreign policy. Still, regardless of the personal wishes of the Emperor, neither Saionji nor the household ministers were prepared to sanction any direct intervention of the Throne in the determination of cabinet policies. In 1913, Premier Katsura had obtained an Imperial command ordering the naval authorities to furnish a minister for his cabinet. In so doing, Katsura provoked a public parliamentary attack on the partisan nature of this Imperial order, a debate which implicitly questioned the sanctity of the Imperial institution. After this controversy, the Emperor's advisors concluded that the Throne should never again be implicated in an effort to resolve a bitter political dispute, because even if it temporarily assisted the premier, doing so would, in the long run, only corrode public confidence in the Imperial institution. Consequently, during the London Naval Treaty controversy and the Mukden crisis, neither Hamaguchi nor Wakatsuki advocated trying to settle the "right of supreme command" issue by requesting the direct intervention of the Emperor. In December 1931, Inukai appreciated only too well the validity of this political axiom.[78]

[77] *Ibid.*

[78] Inukai's son, however, testified that his father intended to secure an Imperial edict in order to control the army. IMTFE, *Proceedings*, 1545.

In other words, Saionji's injunction to respect the personal wishes of the Emperor did not mean the new premier could, if necessary, invoke the aid of the Throne in any effort to restrain the army.

The authority of Inukai was, politically speaking, circumscribed by several paramount considerations. The leaders of his party—Suzuki Kisaburō, Mori Kaku, and Kuhara Fusanosuke—were espousing a Manchurian policy which could have been written by the intelligence division of the general staff; the Minseitō leaders had already confessed their impotence vis-à-vis the army's actions in Manchuria; and, while Saionji was arranging the selection of Inukai as premier, the army authorities had implemented a program designed to meet any wily moves of the Senior Statesman. In mid-December, the Big Three of the army—Araki, Minami, and Kanaya—concluded that the war minister in the new government should adhere to three demands: (1) the Kwantung Army should be reinforced in order to achieve prompt and complete control over North Manchuria; (2) the army should cultivate a Manchurian "independence movement" in the area under its administrative control; and (3) the Kwantung Army should, if feasible, move into Jehol province and acquire command of the Shanhaikuan pass.[79] Along with this resolution, the Supreme War Council ruled that General Minami should resign his portfolio because of his close association with the efforts of Baron Shidehara to effect a diplomatic settlement of the Mukden crisis. This rejection of Minami was also prompted by a desire to select a war minister who would promote unity within central headquarters.[80] In particular, the Supreme War Council wished to alleviate the unrest provoked by the doctrine of "total war" and to instill confidence throughout all ranks that the army's approach to the Manchurian problem would be vigorously championed in the new government.

[79] Mitarai, *Minami Jirō*, 285-286; and NKSG, *Taiheiyō sensō e no michi*, II, 102-105.

[80] Mitarai, *Minami Jirō*, 317-320; Tateno, *Shōwa gunbatsu*, 134-136.

With these criteria, the councilors selected Araki Sadao for the post of war minister. As inspector general of military education, Araki's eloquent speeches on the Imperial Way had won the admiration of the field officers; and his previous assignments in the general staff had earned him the respect of most staff officers. Above all, since Araki was the protégé of Generals Mutō and Uehara, his selection would obliterate the Chōshū stamp on the post of war minister. In order to augment further the army's voice in matters affecting Manchuria, His Imperial Highness Prince (General) Kanin was made titular head of the general staff. In effect, when Inukai assumed office, he was confronted by a formidable combination of army policies and individuals: an Imperial prince commanded the general staff, thereby subtly enhancing the army's proprietary claims on the "right of supreme command"; the army's ranking officers had adopted a policy pegged to the conquest of Manchuria and the promotion of a Manchurian independence movement; and a fiery exponent of the Imperial Way was his war minister.

In view of these circumstances, Inukai's promise to exercise firm control in the determination of national policy was truly an act of political courage. As an astute politician, however, he was not prepared to wage this battle over the Chinchow matter. The resignation of Shidehara had, in effect, signified the impossibility of preventing the seizure of North Manchuria. Thus, on December 24, the war minister's request for a reinforcement of the Kwantung Army was readily approved by the cabinet.[81] Unlike the army authorities, however, the premier had not abandoned hope of negotiating a settlement with the Nationalist government which would still preserve the fiction of Chinese sovereignty over Manchuria. This realization of his aspiration was contingent upon two questionable propositions—the willingness of the Japanese army to accept even an amenable Chinese administration in Manchuria; and

[81] IMTFE, *Proceedings,* 28139-40; and *Exhibit 188.*

the willingness of the Western powers to cooperate with Japan in an effort to win Chinese approval of a new political arrangement for Manchuria.

THE SEIZURE OF CHINCHOW

With the opening of the new year, the Kwantung Army advanced on Chinchow. This move was not unanticipated; and in the United States some influential commentators had even voiced a tolerant attitude toward the extension of Japanese control in Manchuria. On December 10, Walter Lippmann expressed a belief that the Japanese were employing force in Manchuria "to set up local Chinese governments which are dependent upon Japan. The procedure is a familiar one . . . [for example] in Nicaragua, Haiti, and elsewhere. The Japanese army is, in a word, carrying out not a 'war' but an 'intervention.' "[82] More pointedly, the *New York Herald Tribune,* on December 22, claimed that the Chinese had originally proposed to the American ambassador in England, Charles Dawes, the evacuation of Chinchow. Since this offer had not been honored, concluded the editorial, the United States could not insist that Japan abide by its commitment not to attack Chinchow. These second thoughts were not shared by the secretary of state, who, no doubt correctly, failed to see much in common between his earlier role in Nicaragua and the actions of the Kwantung Army in Manchuria. Perhaps less disinterestedly, Stimson viewed the *Tribune*'s observations as "a really treasonable editorial, for it attempted to nullify my own work toward Japan."[83] Before being stung by the *Tribune,* Stimson had planned to say nothing more about the Chinchow matter, preferring to let the Japanese "go their own sweet way and then lambast them if they do go to Chinchow."[84] Fearful that the Japanese government might interpret the *Tribune*'s observations as reflecting a change in attitude in govern-

[82] Walter Lippmann, *Interpretations, 1931-1932* (New York, 1932), 196.
[83] Stimson, *Diary,* December 22, 1931.
[84] *Ibid.*

mental circles, Stimson sent one more note warning the Japanese government that any attack on Chinchow would be an act of aggression. Consequently, when the Japanese army ignored this warning in the opening week of the new year, the secretary regarded this as a personal insult and a gross violation of the Nine Power Treaty.

It was manifest, by January 5, that the Imperial army was extending its control throughout North Manchuria. Only a joint and forceful statement by the Anglo-American nations would, in Stimson's estimation, compel the Japanese government to abandon this irresponsible and illegal action. Advising the British foreign minister of his opinion, Stimson suggested that both nations promptly condemn the Chinchow attack as a clear violation of the Nine Power Treaty.[85] When this appeal was not answered immediately, the secretary of state decided to act independently; and, without discussing his plans with President Hoover, he announced his famous démarche of January 7, 1931.[86] In this public statement, Stimson reviewed the Washington Conference treaties and the Kellogg-Briand Pact and affirmed that the United States "does not intend to recognize any situation, treaty, or agreement which may be brought about by means contrary to the covenants and obligations of the Pact of Paris of August 27th, 1928, to which Treaty both China and Japan, as well as the United States, are parties."[87] The secretary of state no doubt believed his "non-recognition" doctrine would be seconded by the British foreign minister. The following day, however, Stimson learned that the British government did not "think it was opportune at this time" to participate in any Anglo-French démarche against the Japanese actions in Manchuria.[88]

[85] *Ibid.*, January 5, 1932.
[86] The sparse degree of communication and consultation between Hoover and Stimson has prompted the conclusion that there were in fact two doctrines. Richard N. Current, "The Stimson Doctrine and the Hoover Doctrine," *American Historical Review*, LIX (1953-54), 513-542.
[87] Ferrell, *American Diplomacy*, 157.
[88] Stimson, *Diary*, January 7, 1932.

"Rightly or wrongly," remarked Sir John Pratt many years later, "we attached little importance to the démarche. Non-recognition was a peculiarly American technique, . . . wholly out of harmony with the British tradition in international affairs."[89] Equally important, the British foreign office considered the Anglo-Chinese trade and British investments in Shanghai to be more relevant to its interests in China than the events in Manchuria. Reflecting the official Whitehall attitude, the London *Times*, on January 11 belittled Stimson's recent invocation of the Nine Power Treaty with the observation that the sovereignty of China was a legal phantom: "It did not exist in 1922, and it does not exist today."[90] This wholly negative response to his statement dismayed the secretary of state because, without the firm support of Great Britain, the viability of the "non-recognition" policy was fatally compromised. Indeed, on January 9, the Japanese government brusquely dismissed the relevance of the Nine Power Treaty in its official reply to Stimson's démarche—"the present unsettled and distracted state of China is not what was in the contemplation of the high contracting powers at the time of the Treaty of Washington."[91] In view of the official responses of Japan and Great Britain, plus the League's discreet silence over the Chinchow issue, the immediate results of the "non-recognition" doctrine were hollow indeed. Whatever satisfaction the secretary of state could salvage from his statement of January 7 was of a highly personal nature. "It takes a good deal of courage," judged Stimson, "to keep up the necessary firm front not to compromise the rights of one's government during a period of general depression and discouragement. . . . I don't propose to have some of my successors find that we yielded to it during this time."[92]

Underlying Stimson's démarche and his anger at the British

[89] Sir John Pratt, *War and Politics in China* (London, 1943), 226.
[90] Ferrell, *American Diplomacy*, 159.
[91] *Ibid.*, 161.
[92] Stimson, *Diary*, January 7, 1932.

attitude was a basic conviction which had governed his
diplomacy at the London Naval Conference: the Japanese
government would always yield to any demand leveled jointly
and forcibly by the Anglo-American nations. This assumption
had been vindicated at London; and a fear of an Anglo-
American détente had enabled Shidehara to remain in power
for several weeks after the Mukden incident. The efficacy of this
approach in 1932, however, was diminished by three considerations: the British were clearly not prepared to challenge
Japan's policy in Manchuria openly; the American fleet, by
itself, could not act as an effective deterrent; and the Japanese
government was committed to a continental policy which
would not be altered simply out of consideration for cordial
relations with the United States. Stimson's forceful tone in
London had worked mainly because the Hamaguchi cabinet,
including the naval minister, had been predisposed to a
reduction of naval expenditures and a desire for friendly
relations with the United States. Neither of these factors was
equally operative in January 1932. With the capture of Chinchow, the Inukai government regarded the expulsion of all
nationalist forces from Manchuria as an accomplished and
irrevocable fact. The only unsettled question was the type of
political arrangement to be organized in Manchuria.

In mid-December, the senior officers of the Japanese army
had included among their basic resolutions the promotion of
an independence movement in Manchuria and the acquisition
of the Shanhaikuan pass. Neither of these recommendations
was formally approved by the cabinet on December 23, although, as noted, Inukai had agreed to the seizure of Chinchow. Since no one at that time articulated the doctrine of
"residual sovereignty," Inukai hoped to settle the Manchurian
problem through a treaty with the Nationalist government
which would grant a high degree of autonomy to Manchuria,
yet retain the principle of Chinese sovereignty. If this type of
accommodation could be realized, reasoned the premier, the
Occidental powers would not be confronted with a flagrant

violation of the Nine Power Treaty; the Japanese government could exercise its control over Manchuria through a compliant Chinese political organization; and the Nationalist government could salvage some satisfaction from the fact that the principle of Chinese sovereignty was being confirmed by a new treaty. Despite the cogency of this viewpoint, War Minister Araki had slight interest in Inukai's diplomatic strategy; and the Kwantung Army was ordered to assemble capable Manchus and create local administrative units in North Manchuria. Thus, Inukai, of necessity, pursued his quest for a new treaty with Nanking in a quiet and indirect manner.

In late January, Inukai sent a personal representative to Shanghai and Nanking to discuss informally his proposed solution to the Manchurian question with prominent Nationalist officials.[93] Encouraged by the Chinese responses, Inukai appealed to Field Marshal Uehara for assistance in this matter.

> Although the end of the Manchurian incident is at hand, if the situation develops towards the formation of an independent country, we shall have serious trouble with the Nine Power Treaty nations. For this reason, I am actively trying to achieve our national purpose in Manchuria within the existing forms of political power. I hope to settle the incident as quickly as possible; and, on this occasion, I would like to improve our relations with China. Since I have been in contact with important circles in North and Central China, I may have a greater advantage in diplomatic negotiations than the ordinary army officer. If I can continue with my purpose, the Manchurian problem will become a smaller matter.[94]

This appeal to the venerable field marshal illustrated the tenuous control of the premier on national policy affecting Manchuria; but it was not an unreasonable attempt. If any

[93] IMTFE, *Proceedings*, 1547-1584.
[94] The text of this letter is available in Maejima, *Nihon fuashizumu*, 308.

senior officer could have exerted significant influence on the war minister, it would have been Field Marshal Uehara. As the army's ranking non-Chōshū officer, Uehara had been Araki's sponsor during the years when clan politics had determined promotions and appointment to central headquarters. There is no evidence, however, suggesting that Uehara endorsed the views of Inukai; and, by the end of February, the premier had abandoned his private diplomacy. In large measure, this was caused by policy of the army authorities in Tokyo and the creation of local Manchurian administrations, under the guise of military government, by the Kwantung Army. Still, the army's policy of an "independent" Manchuria received a powerful impetus from two developments—the Shanghai incident of 1932 and a pattern of political intrigues and assassinations which had one common purpose, the removal of Inukai from the premiership.

THE SHANGHAI INCIDENT

Throughout the 1920's, the Nationalist party of China was characterized by a passionate anti-foreign ideology. Originally, this xenophobia was indiscriminate, being directed at Occidentals and Orientals alike. In the summer of 1931, however, this hatred of foreigners was mainly focused on the Japanese, as demonstrated by the boycotts of Japanese goods which mushroomed in all the treaty ports. The effectiveness of the boycotts increased in proportion to the increasing antipathy produced by the Mukden incident; and the most severe or effective boycotts occurred in Shanghai, the major focus of foreign investment in China. The animosities engendered by this boycott movement against Japanese goods, plus the related indictment of all foreigners and imperialists, prompted the Municipal Council of the Shanghai international settlement, on January 28, 1932, to proclaim a state of emergency.[95]

---

[95] Three excellent and contending summaries of the Shanghai crisis are Robert Ferrell, *American Diplomacy in the Great Depression* (New Haven, 1957), 170-178; Reginald Bassett, *Democracy and Foreign Policy*

Parallel with the efforts of the Shanghai Council to reach a peaceful termination of the boycott, the commandant of all Japanese forces in the international port, Admiral Shiozawa, notified the mayor of Shanghai, General Wu Teh-chen, that all the local boycott societies would have to close by January 29. As the deadline approached, the treaty powers quietly deployed their troops in accordance with a prearranged plan for the mutual defense of the international settlement; and, on the afternoon of January 28, General Wu yielded to Shiozawa's ultimatum with a promise to terminate the boycott as quickly as possible. Since General Wu had not actually implemented his promise, the Japanese commandant ordered his marines to secure the Japanese sector of the international settlement.[96] Around midnight, a company of Japanese marines crossed into the Chinese district of Chapei, where it encountered some troops of the 19th Chinese Route Army. The confrontation resulted in a brief quarrel, during which some shots were exchanged. Although there were no serious injuries, Admiral Shiozawa interpreted this incident as a calculated "insult" to the Japanese empire and, in retaliation, he ordered an aerial bombardment of the Chapei district "to punish" the intransigent Chinese troops. This indiscriminate use of air power against a small contingent of Chinese soldiers dispersed among a congested civilian population generated a profound sense of shock and indignation in England and the United States.[97] More crucially, it inspired the Chinese forces with a determination to eject the Japanese from Shanghai.

During the immediate prelude to this outburst of hostilities, the American secretary of state concluded that the Japanese

---

(London, 1952), 65-211; and Payson Treat, "Shanghai: January 28, 1932," *Pacific Historical Review*, IX (1940), 337-343.

[96] Hallet Abend, *My Life in China* (New York, 1945), 186-187, judges that Shiozawa ignored General Wu's acceptance of the ultimatum.

[97] George McReynolds and Eleanor Tupper, *Japan in American Public Opinion* (New York, 1937), concludes that this episode, not the Mukden affair, generated a pervasive anti-Japanese feeling in the United States. Bassett makes a similar judgment vis-à-vis British public opinion in *Democracy*, 65.

government would use the Shanghai crisis as an excuse to declare war on China. Stimson believed that once a formal state of belligerency existed, the Japanese would impose a blockade of Shanghai. As this would "play hob with both our interests and the much larger ones of Britain," the secretary proposed to Sir John Simon, the British foreign minister, that the two countries issue a joint note advising the Japanese government not to send any of its troops to Shanghai, because the Anglo-American nations would guarantee the safety of the international settlement.[98] In addition, Stimson suggested that this note be combined with a joint reinforcement of the Anglo-American naval squadrons at Shanghai. The next morning, at a cabinet meeting on January 26, the secretary of state outlined this plan of action, adding that these two steps should also be supported by a strong verbal indictment of Japanese actions in Manchuria. The secretary of war, Patrick Hurley, sharply dissented by citing the inability of the United States to execute any forceful policy in the area of Shanghai. Hurley's sentiments, noted Stimson, were "forcibly and emphatically" endorsed by President Hoover, who commented on "the folly of getting into a war with Japan on this subject."[99] After this rebuke, the President complimented Stimson on his note of January 7, and suggested that the secretary should adopt a similar position in the current situation, this being "the safe course for us to follow now rather than by getting into a war in China."[100] Stimson, however, was not deterred by this advice and he argued that his recommendations would not involve the government in any war. The United States was a great nation, insisted the secretary, and Japan would never risk a confrontation over Shanghai. All that was needed to settle the matter, judged Stimson, was a willingness to emulate Theodore Roosevelt's maxim, "Speak softly but carry a big stick."[101] The secretary of war, however, was not impressed by

[98] Stimson, *Diary*, January 25, 1932.
[99] *Ibid.*, January 26, 1932.
[100] *Ibid.*   [101] *Ibid.*

Stimson's slogan or by his policy recommendations. Since the army and navy could not bring any significant military force to bear in Shanghai, Hurley believed the United States should indeed speak softly because it had no big stick to wield in the Western Pacific. When Hoover again seconded the remarks of the secretary of war, Stimson was obviously dismayed by the President's lack of "the slightest element of even the faintest kind of bluff."[102] Nevertheless, the secretary of state also realized he could not impress his views on the cabinet.

Following the Chapei bombing, the Hoover cabinet met again to review the Shanghai matter. This time the secretary of state pursued a different strategy with his colleagues, requesting that "there should be no talk or action by anyone which would indicate that we were not going to use any weapon that we might have, whether it be the fleet or the boycott."[103] A few hours after obtaining this commitment from the cabinet, the British government proposed that England and the United States should try to settle the Shanghai crisis by creating a neutral zone in Shanghai, in conjunction with the joint reinforcement of the Anglo-American garrisons in the international settlement.[104] President Hoover concurred with this plan; and, on January 31, Stimson advised the British foreign minister that the United States would send two heavy cruisers to Shanghai. Independent of this Anglo-American decision, the Inukai cabinet had resolved to seek the assistance of the United States in an effort to quiet the Shanghai waters. On February 1, Ambassador Debuchi informed Stimson of his government's wish to use the "good offices" of the American government in order to reach a diplomatic settlement of the Shanghai incident.[105] The overture convinced the secretary of state the Japanese government knew that "it is up against it. It has got the bear by the tail and it can't let go and it is try-

102 *Ibid.*
103 *Ibid.*, January 29, 1932.
104 *Ibid.*, January 31, 1932.
105 *Ibid.*, February 1, 1932.

ing to get help to get out of the situation, without losing too much face."[106]

With this estimate of the situation, Stimson believed he could link the settlement of the Shanghai crisis to the Manchurian problem. To this end, he formulated a five-point program which he submitted to the Japanese government—namely, (1) prompt cessation of violence in Shanghai; (2) no mobilization of troops by Japan; (3) withdrawal of Sino-Japanese forces from all points of contact in Shanghai; (4) formation of a neutral zone to be policed by the Western powers, and (5) settlement "of all outstanding controversies between the two nations in the spirit of the Pact of Paris and the Resolution of the League of Nations; . . . without prior demand or reservations and with the aid of neutral observers or participants."[107] Although the British foreign minister demurred over the fifth point, Stimson ordered Ambassador Forbes to present the five proposals to the Japanese foreign minister as the only basis on which the United States would participate in a resolution of the Shanghai crisis.[108] On February 3, Ambassador Debuchi reviewed the proposals with Stimson, indicating that his government could accept the first four. However, Debuchi stressed Japan's unwillingness to have "a third party take part in negotiations over Manchuria"; and he wondered whether Stimson really "ought to dictate to us as to the fifth point."[109] In response, the secretary restated his firm commitment to all five stipulations and added three further observations: (1) the United States was determined to defend the Shanghai settlement; (2) this could not be done if Japan were to use Shanghai as a base for operations; and (3) all aggressive actions by Japanese forces in Shanghai must terminate immediately.[110] Despite this tone, Debuchi rejected Stimson's fifth proposal and he expressed grave reservations about the appropriateness of the third and fourth points.

106 *Ibid.*
107 United States Department of State, *Foreign Relations of the United States, 1931* (Washington, 1946), VI, 174.
108 *Ibid.*, 175.　　　109 *Ibid.*, 178.　　　110 *Ibid.*, 178-179.

When Stimson advised the British foreign minister of Debuchi's response, Sir John urged the secretary to "spin out" his discussions with Japan.[111] Since Stimson preferred to cut the talks "off short," Simon, on February 6, suggested that the League of Nations might assume the role of working with Japan in an effort to negotiate a diplomatic settlement of the crisis.[112] The same day, however, Ambassador Forbes cabled Stimson that the Japanese government was prepared to propose a truce and the creation of a neutral zone in Shanghai; and that it had accepted "the essentials" of the first four points outlined by the secretary on the 3rd of February.[113] This favorable news, however, was quickly negated by the resumption of fighting in Shanghai on February 7, hostilities which the American secretary likened to the German invasion of Belgium. Clearly, judged Stimson, the major powers should convene a Nine Power Conference; and, if the Japanese refused to cooperate with this body, the powers should impose an embargo on the Japanese empire. Whether or not Stimson spelled out his ideas to President Hoover is uncertain; but, on February 8, the President agreed that Stimson should sound out the British attitude toward a Nine Power Conference.[114] However, Sir John Simon promptly indicated that Great Britain was not willing to invoke the Nine Power Treaty against Japan, let alone support an embargo against Imperial Japan. Instead, on February 15, the British foreign minister informed Stimson that the Council of the League of Nations had decided to endorse the secretary's non-recognition doctrine, but without the inclusion of any sharp references to recent events in Manchuria or Shanghai.[115]

The British spokesman, no doubt, believed Stimson would be pleased with the Council's belated support of his démarche of January 7. By mid-February, though, the secretary of state was so vexed with Britain's "soft and pudgy" attitude that he was casting about for some new way in which to vent his ada-

---

111 Stimson, *Diary*, February 5, 1932.
112 *Ibid.*, February 6, 1932.   113 *Ibid.*
114 *Ibid.*, February 8, 1932.   115 *Ibid.*, February 15, 1932.

mant opposition to Japanese aggression on the mainland of China.[116] In this mood, Stimson hit upon the idea of a public letter to Senator Borah, the ranking member of the Foreign Relations Committee.[117] Here, in a document which Stimson subsequently considered his most important public pronouncement, the secretary passed far beyond his non-recognition posture.[118] After reviewing the various safeguards provided by the Washington Conference treaties, Stimson observed: "The willingness of the American government to surrender its then commanding lead in battleship construction and to leave its position at Guam and in the Philippines without further fortifications was predicated upon, among other things, the self-denying covenants contained in the Nine Power Treaty."[119]

By openly implying that the United States no longer felt obliged to abide by the non-fortification agreements established at the Washington Conference, the Borah letter unleashed a minor "war scare" in Japan. The Japanese press cited this slightly veiled warning, along with the secretary's démarche of January 7 and the despatch of American naval forces to Shanghai, as proof of the irreconcilable national objectives of Japan and the United States.[120] In this context, the Inukai cabinet discarded the idea of utilizing the "good offices" of the American government; and Japan's naval leaders concluded that the Washington Conference treaties could no longer be viewed as an adequate guarantee of the empire's naval security. In this sense, as will be described, Stimson's forceful posture was to have far-reaching consequences. At present, one should note that by mid-February the League of Nations was committed to the non-recognition doctrine in its approach to the Man-

[116] *Ibid.*

[117] *Ibid.*, February 21, 1932.

[118] Borah's letter is reprinted in Ferrell, *American Diplomacy*, 188-193. For Stimson's evaluation of it, see Henry Stimson and McGeorge Bundy, *On Active Duty in Peace and War* (New York, 1948), 246.

[119] *Ibid.*, 191.

[120] The major Japanese sources on the Shanghai crisis are Aoki Tokuzō, *Taiheiyō sensō zenshi* (Tokyo, 1952), I, 252-316; and NKSG, *Taiheiyō sensō e no michi*, II, 116-149.

churian issue; and the American secretary of state had publicly questioned the efficacy of the existing naval treaties.

Many contemporary observers considered the Shanghai
incident as part of a grand design of the Japanese government
to impose its control over North and Central China, a sentiment embodied in the appearance and popularity of the
spurious Tanaka Memorial. Actually, surprise and consternation were the dominant reactions in Tokyo official circles to
the hostilities provoked by Admiral Shiozawa.[121] At all costs,
the foreign and naval ministries wished to avoid any action
which might be construed as a threat to British interests in
Shanghai, lest this precipitate an Anglo-American accord
directed against Japan. The cardinal concerns in army central
headquarters were the creation of a new government in Manchuria and the implementation of a rationalization program.
Even the army's China experts saw no value in a Shanghai
campaign. The main objective in China, in their judgment,
was the inhibition of a united Nationalist party under the
leadership of Chiang Kai-shek. In 1931, Shanghai was under
the control of Wang Ching-wei, one of Chiang's strongest rivals
and one of the few prominent Nationalist leaders lacking in
Japanophobe tendencies. To shatter his army or political prestige would, in effect, only promote the fortunes of Chiang Kai-
shek. This composite of diplomatic, strategic, and political
considerations had yielded a decision to utilize the "good
offices" of the United States in hopes of settling the Shanghai
incident quickly.

From the point of view of the Inukai cabinet, this solici-
tation of American assistance had been interpreted in a most
unfortunate manner. In particular, two demands of Stimson
seemed completely unacceptable—namely, his condemnation
of Japan's position in Manchuria and his stipulation that
the Western powers should assume complete responsibility for
the defense of Japanese rights and interests in Shanghai. In
lieu of deferring to these proposals, the cabinet decided to

121 *Ibid.*, 126-127.

resolve the Shanghai incident by compelling the Chinese to accept a settlement which would embrace the main desires of the Western governments—that is, to restore the political *status quo ante* in Shanghai and to impose a neutral zone around all foreign settlements.[122] This policy would presumably indicate Japan's lack of territorial or new imperial aspirations in Shanghai and dramatize Japan's ability and determination to protect her rights in China in the face of any Chinese military or economic threat. A quick, decisive military victory in Shanghai, if followed by a moderate diplomatic settlement, would, reasoned the Inukai cabinet, enhance Japan's policies in East Asia. It would also remind the Chinese government and the Western nations that Japan was not willing to accept any outside intervention in matters affecting Sino-Japanese relations, whether in terms of Manchuria or of Shanghai; and it would demonstrate that the Japanese government had no intention of challenging Western treaty rights or investments in Central China.

Once this policy had been formulated, the Japanese general staff revealed its contempt for the 19th Route Army by estimating that a single division and one mixed brigade of the Imperial army could secure control over Shanghai.[123] When this calculation proved excessively optimistic, the government despatched two more divisions and placed the army's senior officer on active duty, General Shirokawa of the Supreme War Council, in command of the newly created Shanghai Expeditionary Army. This enlarged force, as General MacArthur advised Secretary Stimson, was not capable of conducting any major operations beyond the immediate environs of Shanghai.[124] It was, however, adequate for the specific objectives of the Shanghai campaign: to obtain a commanding control over Shanghai and to impose a truce on the Chinese forces. By May 5, General Shirokawa had routed the

[122] Kiyozawa Kiyoshi, *Nihon gaikōshi* (Tokyo, 1942), II, 472.
[123] NKSG, *Taiheiyō senso e no michi*, II, 129-130.
[124] Stimson, *Diary*, February 15, 1932.

Chinese forces and Admiral Shiozawa negotiated an armistice which created a neutral zone around the international settlement.[125] Although the Japanese government had originally hoped this solution would be received favorably, the dynamics of the crisis had adversely affected Japanese relations with the Western nations. Indeed, on March 12, the Inukai cabinet authorized the formation of a Manchurian government under Pu Yi in response to the Council's resolution to investigate the Manchurian problem in terms of the non-recognition policy.[126] These antithetical policies adopted in the midst of the Shanghai incident ultimately culminated in an irreconcilable confrontation between the League of Nations and the Japanese government. Before describing this phase of Japan's foreign policy, however, it is necessary to consider some important domestic events which resulted in the demise of party cabinets and the assassination of Inukai Ki.

Signs of Political Unrest

In terms of the diplomatic reactions of the powers, as well as its effects on Japanese public opinion, the Shanghai incident completely destroyed Inukai's hope of settling the Manchurian problem without provoking a major cleavage between Japan and the Anglo-American nations. No premier, following the rancor generated by the Shanghai hostilities, could anticipate support for a policy which would confirm the "principle" of Chinese sovereignty in Manchuria; and the adoption of the non-recognition resolution of the League precluded the possibility of any effective rapport with this international organization. Another less discernible but equally effective pressure compromising the policy favored by Inukai materialized in conjunction with the Shanghai crisis. In mid-January, Mori Kaku, the chief secretary of the Inukai cabinet and one of

[125] NKSG, *Taiheiyō sensō e no michi*, II, 144-146, reviews the settlement.

[126] Gaimushō, *Nihon gaikō nenpyō narabini shuyō busho, 1840-1945* (Tokyo, 1955), II, "ManMō modai shori hōshin yoko," March 12, 1932, 205.

the most influential leaders of the Seiyūkai, urged the appointment of a special committee to investigate the diplomatic and political problems caused by the army's actions in Manchuria.[127] This committee, reasoned Mori, should devise a basic policy which would promote greater unity in the cabinet and enable the premier to bring the army under more effective political control. Superficially, this was a reasonable suggestion; but Mori thought the committee should be headed by Count Itō Miyoji, Suzuki Kisaburō, or Baron Hiranuma. Since each of these men was an avowed supporter of the army's activities in Manchuria, there was an evident inconsistency between Mori's professed objective and the projected composition of the committee. Inukai, therefore, tabled the proposal.

Throughout January and February, the leaders of the Seiyūkai focused their prime attention on the general elections to be held on February 20. The Minseitō, hampered by the unpopularity of Shidehara diplomacy and the effective slogan "Minseitō depression—Seiyūkai boom," suffered an impressive defeat at the polls. The Seiyūkai captured 301 seats in the Diet to the Minseitō's 147.[128] Despite this victory, the leadership of the premier was not solidified. Directly after the elections, Mori Kaku conspired to bring about the downfall of the Inukai cabinet. Sensitive to the discontent in military circles with the premier's attitude toward Manchuria and conscious that the extremist policies of Kuhara Fusanosuke and Adachi Kenzō had previously alienated the financial supporters of both parties, Mori first moved against the Kuhara faction of the Seiyūkai. On March 27, Mori secured the appointment of Yamaguchi Giichi as the party's secretary general in place of the incumbent Yamazaki Tasunosuke, who represented the Kuhara faction.[129] After this maneuver, Mori tried to cultivate the conservative leadership of the Minseitō. In early April, Mori

[127] Saionji-Harada, *Memoirs*, February 16, 1932.
[128] Maejima, *Nihon fuashizumu*, 289-290. In this election, the Minseitō lost 99 seats (from 246 to 147); the Seiyūkai gained 130 seats (from 171 to 301).
[129] *Ibid.*, 305-306.

conferred with Izawa Takeo, the most influential Minseitō member of the House of Peers. "Japan," argued Mori, "is now in a stage of rapid change. If we remain indifferent to this, no one knows what sort of evil events may occur at any moment. In order to prevent such happenings, we must establish a 'whole nation' government. Consequently the cooperation of the Seiyūkai and the Minseitō is desirable."[130] Specifically, Mori recommended that Izawa support a new cabinet to be headed by Baron Hiranuma and Suzuki Kisaburō. This overture by the chief secretary to the Inukai cabinet, however, elicited a polite refusal; and it soon proved to be a gross miscalculation. Following Inukai's violent death on May 15, Izawa was to use this premature campaign for a "whole nation" cabinet in support of the candidacy of Admiral Saitō Makoto for the premiership.

The covert maneuver of Mori Kaku against the Inukai cabinet was complemented by other manifestations of dissatisfaction with the current government. Directly after Inukai's personal letter to Field Marshal Uehara, War Minister Araki solicited the help of Prince Konoe Fumimaro in an effort to replace the Inukai cabinet by one more receptive to the army's approach to the Manchurian problem.[131] Fortunately for the premier, Araki's advocacy of a "whole nation" cabinet which would presumably unite the nation behind the deeds of the Imperial army was not combined with the intrigues of Mori Kaku. In part, this was due to the personal character of the war minister, who regarded all professional politicians with disdain; but, more crucially, Mori's activities were calculated to promote the fortunes of Baron Hiranuma. Although a distinguished defender of the "right of supreme command," Hiranuma was closely associated with the Katō-Suetsugu faction of naval officers, as well as being a political rival of Prince Konoe. If only for these reasons, General Araki viewed the candidacy of Hiranuma with concern; and Prince Konoe

---

130 *Ibid.*, 307.
131 Saionji-Harada, *Memoirs*, February 23, 1932.

was not personally enthusiastic about a "whole nation" government to be headed by Baron Hiranuma. Even though these multiple complaints against Inukai's leadership did not unite into an effective political movement, they did signify a pervasive discontent which flourished within the Katō-Suetsugu group of naval officers, the war ministry, and the Seiyūkai.

Apart from these quiet indictments of the Inukai government, a vigorous public censure of the cabinet and of the political influence of the Emperor's advisors materialized with the creation of the Japan Production Party (*Dai nihon seisantō*). This new party was a combination of the Radical Political Party (*Kyūshin aikokutō*) and the Japan Nationalist Party (*Nippon kokumintō*); and, in January, its platform articulated an imposing list of political objectives: (1) removal of all statesmen lacking "national ideals" (*kokka kannen*); (2) abolition of *zaibatsu* control over the economy, as well as the "parasitic insects" of the *zaibatsu*—the Seiyūkai and the Minseitō; (3) adoption of a positive foreign policy based upon Japanese values (*Dai nihon shugi*); (4) promotion of an independent Manchuria and Mongolia; (5) transfer of the invested rights in Manchuria and Mongolia to the Japanese people; (6) assumption of leadership in the economic development of China; (7) expulsion of the Occidental powers from Asia; (8) building of a new Asia under the benevolent guidance of Japan; and (9) enrichment of Japan's national defense.[132] Although this platform failed to garner many votes in the February elections, it may be regarded as an accurate gauge of the direction of political currents in Japan. Within four years, the Seiyūkai platform would be a carbon copy of that advanced by the Japan Production Party; and the assassinations of 1932 and the rebellion of February 26, 1936, would be rationalized in terms similar to the proposals enunciated by that party.[133]

These multiple forms of agitation against Inukai confirmed

[132] Maejima, *Nihon fuashizumu*, 297-298.
[133] The 1936 platform of the Seiyūkai is reprinted in *Japan Weekly Chronicle*, June 27, 1935, 825.

Prince Saionji's estimate that responsible party government was contingent on the political talents and the tenacity of the premier. With the smashing triumph of the Seiyūkai in the February election, the Senior Statesman could not possibly nominate another Minseitō cabinet; and, of the Seiyūkai leaders, only Inukai was committed to a cautious foreign policy and the primacy of the premier in cabinet decisions. Whether, given the political configuration produced by the Shanghai incident, the diplomacy of the powers involved, and the intrigues against the premier, Inukai could have remained in office for very long is uncertain. As it was, he was assassinated on May 15 by a group of army and naval officers seeking a Shōwa restoration.

THE ASSASSINS OF INUKAI

In the opening months of 1932, the Japanese political scene was marred by a series of bloody deeds. On February 9, the finance minister of the Wakatsuki cabinet, Inoue Junnosuke, was murdered during the election campaign; two weeks later, Baron Dan Takuma, the head of the Mitsui *zaibatsu* and a firm supporter of the Minseitō, was killed in downtown Tokyo; and, on May 15, a group of assassins slaughtered the premier in his official residence.[134] These flagrant attacks on responsible political figures seemed, in Hugh Byas' phrase, to usher in a period of "government by assassination." In order to identify and understand the motivations and consequences of the 1932 assassinations, it is vital that the behavior of the terrorists of 1932 not be linked with the concerns and policies prevalent in army central headquarters, or with the programs and attitudes which characterized the Cherry Society, the March incident, and the October incident. In a fundamental sense, the revolutionary behavior of the young officers in 1932 was a reaction against the policies of rationalization, economic planning,

[134] Hugh Byas, *Government by Assassination* (New York, 1943), 22-31; Storry, *Double Patriots*, 117-125; and Nakamura Kikuo, *Shōwa seijishi* (Tokyo, 1958), 42-47, are succinct accounts of these assassinations.

and state socialism; and, at best, it was only indirectly related to the Manchurian problem. Equally significant, the young officers were not, prior to the summer of 1935, a significant component of factionalism in army central headquarters. It would, therefore, be misleading to regard the assassinations of 1932 as part of one single phenomenon, the concerted efforts of the army authorities to impose their views on the government.[135]

The genesis of the 1932 assassinations was a composite of many influences, the most vital being the great depression, the writings of Gondō Seikyō, the establishment of the Land Loving School, and the organization of the National Principle movement. As recent graduates of the service academies, the young naval and army officers were imbued with the cult of *bushidō* and a reverence for the Imperial institution. Like most Japanese military personnel, they attributed the economic and social problems caused by the great depression to the selfish policies of the *zaibatsu* and professional politicians; and this latent hostility was fanned by literature of the major nationalistic societies of the late 1920's and early 1930's—the National Foundation Party (*Kokushonsha*), the Activist Society (*Gyōchisha*), and the State Foundation Society (*Kenkokukai*).[136] Although these organizations and their sophisticated leaders—Ōkawa Shūmei and Baron Hiranuma—were intimately associated with the staffs of army and naval headquarters, they did not win the loyalty of the young revolutionary officers involved in the 1932 assassinations. As noted previously, Ōkawa Shūmei and his friends in the Sakurakai talked about a Shōwa restoration in terms of the doctrines of Kita Ikki.[137] If Kita's *Outline of the Reconstruction of Japan* envisioned a reform of the economic, social,

---

[135] For a contrary view, Maruyama Masao, *Gendai seiji*, 40-46; and Hata, *Gun fuashizumu*, 46-60, which offers some vital reservations in regard to Professor Maruyama's explanation.

[136] Storry, *Double Patriots*, 96-101, is an admirable digest of these societies.

[137] Chapter II, 94-95.

and political privileges of the nobility, the financial magnates, and the political parties, it also accepted an industrialized Japan as being compatible with the true principles of the Japanese state. This last proposition, at least to the executors of the 1932 assassinations, constituted the fatal flaw in the policy of the leading nationalistic organizations.

The true prophet for contemporary Japan, in the eyes of the young revolutionaries, was Gondō Seikyō, whose writings castigated the capitalists in terms of an idealized version of pre-industrial Japan.[138] His *Handbook of Self-Government* (*Jichi mimpan*) extolled the spiritual qualities of the rural life, especially the familial pattern of social and economic organization. Anything which corrupted these values, in Gondō's judgment, was necessarily evil, including the impersonalized nature of big business and the political parties. In December 1930, Tachibana Kosaburo, with the economic backing of the Seiyūkai's most distinguished politician from Ibaragi, Kazami Akira, founded the Land Loving School (*Aikyō juku*). Located in Ibaragi, Tachibana's school was predicated on the teachings of Gondō's handbook; and it was designed to serve as a model colony which, by example, would demonstrate the superior way of life to be found in devotion to the practice of rational farming and a reverence for the Shintō religion.[139] This school attracted the attention of a few young naval officers stationed at the Ibaragi airbase; and, once convinced that Gondō's teachings offered a practical solution to the economic ills plaguing Japan, these officers, led by Ensign Mikami, organized, in August 1931, a group to promote their new cause.[140]

[138] Maruyama Masao, *Thought and Behavior in Modern Japanese Politics* (New York, 1963), 38-40.

[139] Storry, *Double Patriots*, 98-99.

[140] My understanding of the National Principle Group is based primarily on intelligence reports of the naval general staff, Gunreibu, *Gunkankei jōhō*, collected at the Zaidan shiryō chōsakai [Documentary Research Organization], Tokyo, Japan. I am indebted to Mr. Hata Ikuhito for calling my attention to these records and to Admiral Tomioka Sadatoshi for permission to use the resources of the Zaidan shiryō chōsakai.

Subsequently known as the National Principle group (*Kokutai genri-ha*), these officers added a new dimension to the Land Loving School: the systematic assassination of selected representatives of the groups responsible for the evil state of affairs in Japan. Their roster of death was impressively large— Inoue Junnosuke, Baron Dan Takuma, Inukai Ki, Suzuki Kisaburō, Count Makino, Prince Tokugawa, Count Itō Miyoji, and Prince Saionji.[141] Since this list included some individuals who had in fact defended the "right of supreme command" and the army's actions in Manchuria, it was patently inspired by a blind ideological commitment. Indeed, this indifference to the personal views of those slated for assassination clearly differentiates the proponents of the National Principle movement from those officers in central headquarters most prone to overt political conspiracies, the organizers of the Sakurakai and of the March and October incidents.

Fortunately, following the killing of Inukai, this small band of patriots was ferreted out by the military and naval police. This resulted in the prompt arrest and incarceration of the key figures in the National Principle group and it unquestionably saved the lives of the other candidates for assassination. Nevertheless, the revolutionary doctrines set forth by Ensign Mikami in 1932 would nurture another National Principle movement in army circles, one which culminated in the rebellion of February 26, 1936. This latter by-product of the 1932 assassination will be considered subsequently.[142] At the moment, it may be helpful to clarify the perverted definition of loyalty and patriotism which spawned the murder of Inukai in 1932 and which would inspire an even more dramatic program of violence in 1936.

To Ensign Mikami and his associates in the National

Also see Hata, *Gun fuashizumu*, 46-62; and Tateno, *Shōwa gunbatsu*, 138-147.

[141] *Ibid.* Also Nakamura, *Shōwa seijishi*, 44.

[142] Chapter v, 263-267.

Principle movement, Japan was a unique nation.[143] It was composed of a pure race (*shikishima minzoku*) which shared an ideal racial consciousness (*minzoku ishiki*). This purity of race was embodied in an imperishable national principle (*kokutai genri*). Since only Imperial Japan possessed this principle, the Japanese nation was inherently superior to any which existed in Europe or the Western hemisphere. Mikami understandably had difficulty in formulating precisely what would constitute a realization of the true national principle in contemporary Japan; and, in many respects, his ideas were inspired by an identification of the Imperial institution with a primitive form of communism. Japan, reasoned Mikami, was traditionally a familial state in which the Emperor symbolized the absolute unity of the Japanese people (*ue no zettai*). Within the polity of Imperial rule, all the people were equally related to the Throne. Given the premise of familial egalitarianism, Mikami indicted the existing inequalities of Japanese society as a profound distortion of the true national principle. In particular, he saw the parties, the *zaibatsu*, and the Emperor's advisors as the groups primarily responsible for the perversion of the Emperor's benevolent rule. It was his belief that these men had to be punished and converted to a program of renovating the nation in accordance with the true national principle. To this end, judged Mikami, the Throne would have to appoint an "Emperor-assembled and Emperor-speaking" Diet (*kami tsudori to kami katari gikai*). If the Throne were to abolish the decadent political parties and select representatives committed to the national principle, Japan could overcome the evils unleashed by the great depression. Since this political reform could be accomplished only if the Emperor's advisors allowed the Throne to exercise the Imperial will freely, it was necessary to pursue a program of direct

143 On the philosophy of this group, see Gunreibu, *Gunkankei jōhō,* "Kokka kakushin undō ni okeru nidai chōryū," a 1935 pamphlet of the National Principle Group. In Chapter v, 263-265, it is discussed more comprehensively.

violence. By systematic killings, maintained Mikami, the centers of evil—the *zaibatsu,* the parties, and the nobility—would be given cause to reflect on the errors of their past behavior and to rededicate themselves to the true national principle.

In articulating this program of reform through violence, Ensign Mikami carefully dissociated his motives and objectives from those of the leaders of the major ultra-nationalistic societies who piously talked about a Shōwa restoration. Regardless of their noble professions, insisted Mikami, such patriots were actually trying to deceive the people in order to acquire political power. "If the nation were to shun the 'true national principle' and dance to the flute of fascism," warned Mikami, "it will be a critical day for Imperial Japan."[144] Mikami and his followers wished no power for themselves, and this purity of motivation, they believed, would command the respect of all Japanese, including those marked for assassination.

It is not easy to comprehend the intensity of this ideology or the manner in which it rationalized a program of murder as a noble and selfless way to renovate the nation. Still, it would be unjust to the assassins of 1932 to depict their violence as an integral aspect of army factionalism or of the process by which the army augmented its power in the determination of national policies. The National Principle movement of 1932 was the manifestation of a profound political malaise among a small number of young army and navy officers. Moreover, although their murder of Inukai brought about the demise of party governments in Japan, it did not enhance the influence of the major political contenders for the premiership. In this ironic way, the assassins of 1932 contributed to one of their professed objectives—the muffling of those individuals who, in Mikami's words, wished the nation "to dance to the flute of fascism."

144 *Ibid.,* 4-5.

THE "WHOLE NATION" CABINET OF SAITŌ MAKOTO

Prior to and concurrent with the assassinations of 1932, the Inukai cabinet had been subject to political conspiracies and public indictments. These strands of discontent, as noted, were not woven into a clear pattern of opposition. The young officers in the National Principle movement were passionately and blindly lashing against what currently would be termed "the Establishment"; the army authorities were forging ahead with the creation of a Manchurian government; and the Seiyūkai leaders were working with Baron Hiranuma in support of a cabinet which would abrogate the restrictions imposed by the Washington and London Naval Treaties. This disparity of interests between the Seiyūkai leaders and the army authorities was also compounded by War Minister Araki's total disdain for the professional politician. Araki was no enthusiast of a "whole nation" cabinet which would be composed of such politicians, even if it publicly endorsed the army actions in Manchuria. Above all, in the climate of opinion produced by the recent assassinations, the war minister was determined to keep the army disassociated from ultra-nationalistic politicians. "It is absolutely not permissible," declared Araki on May 21, 1932, "for soldiers to act sectionally or like hired troops or to take orders from anyone like Hitler or Mussolini."[145] In one sense, the war minister was criticizing the recent assassins of Inukai; but his public statement also conveyed his desire to purge all politicians from the cabinet.

The war minister's opposition to a "whole nation" cabinet headed by Baron Hiranuma and Suzuki Kisaburō was not wholly representative of army thinking. Generals Tatekawa and Koiso, among others, supported this demand. Still, as war minister, Araki's sentiments were dominant; and his objections were endorsed by important naval leaders. Former Naval Minister Takarabe and Admiral Okada of the Supreme War Council lobbied against Baron Hiranuma, and in this con-

[145] *New York Times*, May 22, 1932, 3.

text no prominent political figure could command adequate support from both services.[146] Prince Saionji vainly set forth the candidacies of Admiral Takarabe and General Ugaki. However, the naval ministry vetoed Takarabe's appointment because of his role in the London Naval Treaty controversy; and War Minister Araki was adamantly against the general who had been the protégé of Tanaka Giichi and associated with the disarmament policies of the Minseitō cabinets. Finally, the Senior Statesman produced an arrangement suitable to all save the leaders of the Seiyūkai: the premiership would be entrusted to Admiral Saitō Makoto, the former governor general of Korea; and his "whole nation" cabinet would not include any minister of state who was actively enrolled in a political party.

The appointment of the moderate Saitō was a bitter blow to the Seiyūkai. As the majority party in the Diet, whose leaders called for a positive foreign policy via-à-vis the continent and the Anglo-American nations, it had every reason to anticipate the mandate to form a government. In the atmosphere surrounding the 1932 assassinations, however, the Emperor's advisors and the authorities of both services were not willing to admit Suzuki Kisaburō, Mori Kaku, and Baron Hiranuma into the highest positions of the government. This antipathy toward or distrust of "irresponsible" politicians, when combined with the competing and dissenting views set forth by the senior officers of both services, enabled Saionji to set aside the principle of parliamentary responsibility and party government. The immediate result may have yielded a government more moderate in composition than would have emerged from a Hiranuma-Suzuki cabinet. By nominating Saitō Makoto, however, the Senior Statesman also denied all political leaders access to the cabinet, thereby giving the government a totally bureaucratic cast. The Saitō cabinet, in effect, marked the appearance of a new form of political oligarchy in which the authority and influence of the political parties, the Emperor's

[146] On the selection of the Saitō cabinet in May 1932, see Aritake, *Okada keisuke*, 204-205.

advisors, and the premier would be appreciably altered—in some instances, almost eradicated.

Beginning in 1932, Japan witnessed a style of cabinet politics and policy-making in which the ministers of state were little more than spokesmen for their respective ministries. The premier became, in the process, an arbitrator between the competing demands of his ministers, especially among those advocated by the foreign, war, and naval ministers.[147] Parallel with this development, there appeared the embryonic forms of most of the administrative and policy-making agencies and procedures which eventually matured in the late 1930's. The role of Prince Saionji in the selection of the premier was replaced by the recommendation of the Elder Statesmen (*jūshin*), a group composed of all former premiers; the Inner Cabinet evolved as the key policy-making body in the form of the Five Ministers' Conference; and the drafting of legislative proposals passed from the Diet and the Privy Council to the Cabinet Research Bureau (*naikaku chōsakai*) and the Cabinet Consultative Council (*naikaku shingikai*). Essentially, with the "whole nation" cabinet of Admiral Saitō, there occurred a shift to a highly bureaucratic system which was characterized by a remarkable decentralization of power among the respective ministers of state. This pattern of policy-making, not the programs and actions of the ultra-nationalistic groups, the political parties, and army factionalism, would determine the foreign policies of the Japanese government after 1932. Before developing this theme, however, brief attention should be given to two other foreign policy developments: the conquest of Jehol province and Japan's withdrawal from the League of Nations.

WITHDRAWAL FROM THE LEAGUE OF NATIONS

The Council of the League of Nations, in February 1932, had formally interpreted the recent developments in Manchuria as being contrary to the principles of the Kellogg-Briand Pact

---

[147] The traits mentioned in this paragraph will be discussed in Chapter IV, 191-195; and Chapter V, 290-296.

and the Covenant of the League. Accordingly, it ruled that any political arrangement imposed unilaterally by the Japanese government in Manchuria would not be regarded as a legal or lawful entity. With this premise, the Council appointed a commission of inquiry—the Lytton Commission—charged with two main tasks: (1) the preparation of a comprehensive report on the origins and specifics of the 1931 Manchurian incident; and (2) the drafting of a series of proposals which, if respected by the Chinese and Japanese governments, would provide an equitable resolution of the Manchurian dilemma. In so doing, the Council claimed the right to intervene directly in the matter of Sino-Japanese relations. Regardless of its legal merits, this posture constituted a fundamental challenge to Japan's traditional China policy—namely, any dispute involving her continental interests had to be settled by direct Sino-Japanese negotiations. This axiom had been consistently articulated by Baron Shidehara throughout the fall of 1931; and the Inukai government was no less committed to it in the spring of 1932. The policy of opposing any scheme or proposal which would enable the Chinese government to "play barbarian against barbarian" also had been vindicated during Inukai's brief flirtation with the good offices of the American government in the opening days of the Shanghai incident. If the United States were unwilling to cooperate with Japan in an area in which the Occidental powers had extensive treaty rights and interests, the Japanese government could hardly permit the Western powers to participate in a settlement of the Manchurian problem. Consequently, when the Council adopted the non-recognition policy, this resolution only solidified support behind the army's Manchurian program. Hence, as part of its official decision to create an imperial Manchurian government under Pu Yi, the Inukai cabinet stipulated that this commitment would be honored "regardless of its international consequences."[148] In other words, the Council may have considered its new approach

[148] *Nihon gaikō nenpyō*, II, 206.

as an efficacious way to settle the Manchurian issue; but the Inukai cabinet understood immediately that its implementation would mean a fatal confrontation between the League and the Japanese nation.

The antithetical policies adopted by the Council and the Japanese government subsequently provoked Japan's withdrawal from the League of Nations. This fact, of course, in no sense implies that the Council was responsible for the creation of Manchukuo. With the demise of the Wakatsuki cabinet, the Supreme War Council and the Big Three had sanctioned the promotion of a Manchurian "independence" movement; and, without the official approval of the cabinet, the Kwantung army had organized local Manchurian administrative units, following the conquest of North Manchuria. Moreover, although Inukai's efforts to circumvent the army's policy had been finally crushed in the wake of the Shanghai crisis, they would not, in any event, have prevailed against the overbearing attitude of the army authorities. Still, after February 1932, the diplomatic issues posed by Japan's actions in Manchuria became a source of serious contention between the League and the Imperial government. From the Tokyo vantage point, Japan's commitment to Pu Yi's Manchukuo had displaced its earlier obligations imposed by the Kellogg-Briand Pact, the Nine Power Treaty, and the Covenant of the League of Nations. This fact was publicly confirmed on August 8, 1932, when the Saitō government formally recognized the new state of Manchukuo. Several days later, on the 28th of August, the Japanese foreign minister assured the Diet that Japan would never accept any recommendation offered by the League's commission of inquiry which "in one form or another" granted a modicum of Chinese authority over Manchuria. "It is my fervent hope," concluded Count Uchida, "that the day is not far distant when Japan, Manchukuo, and China, as three independent Powers closely linked together by a bond of cultural and racial affinities, will come to cooperate hand in hand for the maintenance and

advancement of the peace and prosperity of the Far East."[149]
That this vision of peace and prosperity would interest the
Lytton Committee was unlikely; but, by adopting a firm tone,
the Saitō cabinet hoped the League's inquiry commission would
be forced to recognize the futility of the non-recognition policy
and adjust its recommendations so as to concede the *de facto*
existence of Manchukuo.

Having organized and recognized the state of Manchukuo
and revealed its fixed intention to support the new government,
the Saitō cabinet was anxious to avoid a new incident which
would further antagonize the Western powers. The appropriateness of a quiescent continental policy, however, was not recognized by War Minister Araki. In December 1931, the army
authorities had urged the seizure of the Shanhaikuan pass; and
General Araki constantly badgered his colleagues in the Inukai
and Saitō cabinets with the claim that Manchuria would not
be secure until the army controlled Jehol province up to the
Great Wall. Since a new campaign in the fall of 1932 would
destroy whatever hope existed for a diplomatic accord with the
League of Nations, the foreign and naval ministers contested
Araki's recommendation. This concerted opposition prompted
the illusion that the army might be compelled to abandon the
projected Jehol operation. Yoshida Shigeru, in December 1932,
confidently estimated that the staffs of the foreign and naval
ministries unanimously agreed "the army should be restrained";
and Baron Hiranuma calculated that the desire to "suppress the
army" was so strong in naval circles that he could unite the
Katō and Takarabe factions in naval headquarters.[150]

These voices of resistance to the Jehol campaign were not
only inspired by a sensitivity to Japanese relations with the
League. The foreign and naval ministries were also fearful that
the projected conquest of Jehol would serve as the overture to
an incident involving the Soviet Union. This latter appre-

[149] USDS, Archives, *Japan: Political Affairs*, 894.00/434, is the official
English version of Uchida's speech before the Diet.
[150] Saionji-Harada, *Memoirs*, January 20, 1933.

hension stemmed from the activities of Major General Obata Tokushiro of the general staff. Obata was the protégé of General Mazaki, the vice-chief of the general staff, and of War Minister Araki; and, with the covert encouragement of these senior officers, Obata called for preparation for an immediate war against the Soviet Union. By securing the flank of Manchukuo —that is, by seizing Jehol—the Imperial army, in Obata's judgment, could risk a prompt confrontation with the Soviet army. This advocacy of a Soviet campaign did not mirror the sentiments of the majority of department heads in central headquarters, who regarded the rationalization of the army and the development of Manchukuo as essential prerequisites to waging any major war. Still, Obata's activities unleashed new factional strife which plagued central headquarters for several years and it provoked deep concern in the naval and foreign ministries about the real purpose of the Jehol campaign.[151]

Throughout 1932, the Saitō cabinet rejected the proposed conquest of Jehol on the basis of two main arguments. Since the League's commission of inquiry was in the process of drafting its evaluation and recommendations, the cabinet felt it would be senseless to alienate the Western nations by any aggressive action which would be interpreted as a deliberate insult to the League of Nations; and, secondly, there was some uncertainty as to the army's ultimate purpose in insisting on the seizure of Jehol. General Araki met the second reservation with an unqualified agreement that the Kwantung Army would not, in any circumstance, go beyond the Shanhaikuan pass or precipitate an untoward incident with the Soviet Union. The former objection lost its cogency by the middle of December 1932, when it became certain the Lytton Commission had prepared a report which denied the legitimacy of Manchukuo. Under these conditions, the Saitō cabinet, in late December, reluctantly sanctioned the Jehol campaign. True to his word,

---

[151] On Obata's views, see Satō Kenryō, *Tōjō Hideki to taiheiyō sensō* (Tokyo, 1960), 17. For a fuller discussion of army factions, see Chapter v, 246-279.

the war minister exercised meticulous control over the Kwantung Army; and General Mazaki, the vice-chief of the general staff, actually arranged to fly directly to Shanhaikuan in the event his physical presence were needed to assure absolute adherence to the directive not to advance beyond the Shanhaikuan pass.[152] Once Jehol province was occupied, the Kwantung Army, on May 31, negotiated the Tangku Truce with local Chinese officials.[153] Under the terms of this "local" agreement, the borders of Manchukuo were extended to the Great Wall; the Japanese army acquired control of the Shanhaikuan pass; and a zone north and east of the Peking-Tientsin district up to the Great Wall was demilitarized. In effect, with the Tangku Truce, the three main objectives postulated by the Supreme War Command and the Big Three in December 1931 were finally realized.

The pursuit of the army's policy—the seizure of North Manchuria, the creation of an "independent" Manchuria, and the acquisition of the Shanhaikuan pass—had, in conjunction with the diplomatic repercussions of the Shanghai incident, placed the Japanese government in basic contention with the policies of the League of Nations. Some seventeen months after the Mukden incident, on February 24, 1933, the assembly of the League convened to vote on the recommendations prepared by its commission of inquiry, the Lytton Report. In its official evaluation, the Lytton Commission stated that Japan's actions in Manchuria had not been "a simple case of the violation of the frontier of one country by the armed force of a neighboring country, because in Manchuria there are many features without an exact parallel in other parts of the world."[154] Nevertheless, while granting the complicated nature of Sino-Japanese relations, the commission recommended the formation of a new administrative arrangement for Manchuria that would adequately

[152] IMTFE, *Defense Document 2487*, 9.
[153] For the text of the Tangku settlement, IMTFE, *Exhibit 193*. Also *Nihon gaikō nenpyō*, II, 274.
[154] *Manchuria: Report of the Commission of Enquiry Appointed by the League of Nations* (Washington, 1932), 126.

protect Japan's special rights and interests and be consistent with the principle of Chinese sovereignty over Manchuria.

Immediately prior to the official vote on the Lytton Report, Matsuoka Yōsuke, the head of the Japanese delegation, addressed the assembly with a final justification of his country's support of the state of Manchukuo. His remarks had become commonplace by this time: Japan possessed special rights, interests, and responsibilities in East Asia; the Chinese central government was a legal fiction, since China was a bandit-ridden hopelessly disorganized country; Chinese violations of international treaties and conventions had become legendary, but Japan had always upheld the principles of international law; and the specter of communism had appeared in Asia. Surely, warned Matsuoka, the grave possibility of a Red China allied with the Soviet Union could not pass unheeded by the members of the League. "Gentlemen, our desire is to help China as far as is within our power. This is the duty we must assume. . . . I beg you to deal with us on our terms and give us your confidence. To deny us this appeal will be a mistake."[155] Specifically, Matsuoka asked the delegates to recognize the state of Manchukuo.

The appeal was without effect. With only Siam abstaining, the assembly unanimously endorsed the proposal of the Lytton Report. Following this action, Matsuoka returned to the rostrum and briefly noted the divergence of opinion between the League and Japan over the most appropriate way to promote peace and stability in Asia. In view of this contention, declared the Japanese spokesman, Japan would no longer cooperate with the League on the matter of Sino-Japanese relations. This announcement was received in silence and Matsuoka promptly approached the Japanese delegation. Ostentatiously motioning his associates to his side, Matsuoka then marched the delegation out of the assembly hall—a fitting gesture for a Japan now committed to a solitary and fateful diplomatic stance in East Asia.

[155] *New York Times,* February 25, 1933, 2.

CHAPTER IV

Quest for an Autonomous National Defense

"Most nations today are wandering in darkness. They struggle with each other, the strong preying upon the weak. This is the natural result of the individualistic civilization which Western nations have developed. No measure can save this situation except regeneration. . . . It is the mission of our nation to display the essence of our national polity, break down evil and injustice, and bring about the eternal peace of mankind."

War Ministry Pamphlet, 1935

THROUGHOUT the twentieth century, initially with the Anglo-Japanese alliances and later with the Washington Conference treaties, Japan's national security had been predicated on a policy of cooperation with the Anglo-American sea powers. This axiom was openly questioned during the London Naval Treaty dispute; and the Mukden incident demonstrated that the army's proprietary position in Manchuria was not to be moderated by the opinions of the Western powers. In fact, the intensity of the army's Manchurian policy pushed the Wakatsuki and Inukai cabinets into a defense of the seizure of South and North Manchuria. Despite this stance, the Japanese government, including the army authorities, remained hopeful that the major sea powers would not openly contest the changing state of affairs in Manchuria. With the Shanghai incident, though, the basic cleavage between the approach of the Western nations and Japan to the issue of special rights and interests in China was confirmed with greater clarity than had been evident in the opening months of the Manchurian affair. The actions and statements of the American government had provoked a minor "war scare" in Japan; and the Council of the League of Nations had subscribed to the non-recognition policy.

These developments alerted the Japanese government and

public opinion to a realization that the promotion of an "independent" Manchuria would signify the destruction of the Washington Treaty Order. "Although diplomacy is not a game of solitaire," observed one Japanese editorial in April 1932, it was evident that the problems of Asia must be settled without American or European intervention. "In a word," Japan must "advance with a policy of Asia for the Asiatics—an Asiatic Monroe Doctrine."[1] This appraisal was refined by Viscount Ishii in a candid address to the Council of Foreign Relations in the United States, in which the doyen of Japanese diplomats declared that Japan now sought two cardinal objectives, "equality and security."[2] To realize these national aspirations would, maintained Ishii, require a complete restructuring of the diplomacy of Asia, including a recognition that peace and stability would prevail in the Far East only if the Occidental nations gradually abrogated their treaty rights on the mainland. The presence of the Western powers in China, judged Ishii, "is not only derogatory to her integrity but it is also incompatible with our security."[3] Although he recognized that this conception of Asian affairs might cause some concern in the United States, Ishii assured his audience that Japan's foreign policy was "activated by the same principle incorporated in the Monroe Doctrine."[4]

Perhaps, if the diplomacy of the 1930's had been guided by the perspective of a George Canning, the enunciation of an Asiatic Monroe Doctrine would have been underwritten by the benevolent neutrality of the American fleets. In the age of the New Deal, however, the foreign policy of the United States remained committed to the principles set forth in the Nine Power Treaty, the Kellogg-Briand Pact, and Stimson's non-recognition doctrine, confident that a respect for the integrity of China, when coupled with armament limitation agreements and the

---

[1] United States Department of State [USDS], Archives, *Japan: Political Affairs*, 894.00/383.

[2] Viscount Kikujiro Ishii, "The Permanent Bases of Japanese Foreign Policy," *Foreign Affairs*, XI (1933), 220-229.

[3] *Ibid.*, 222.   [4] *Ibid.*

resolution of international disputes by pacific means, would promote stability in Asia more effectively than a Japanese version of a Monroe Doctrine.[5] Within Japan, any expectation that the Imperial government would conduct its continental policy in terms of the "territorial integrity of China" and the "outlawing" of force as an instrument of national policy appeared mischievous, ill-informed, and dangerous. Thus, the vice-foreign minister, Shigemitsu Mamoru, confessed that Japan's relations with the Anglo-American countries were, in 1933, complicated by the prevalence of "idealistic notions" about the problem of disarmaments in Western circles.[6] At the time of the Washington Conference, observed Shigemitsu, Japan, Britain, and the United States had linked together the major diplomatic, political, and strategic interests confronting the three nations. Unfortunately, he continued, the 1930 London Naval Conference had been confined to naval matters; and the Western powers were approaching the forthcoming 1936 conference on armament limitations as they had in 1930—that is, without an awareness of the peculiarities of the Asian scene, which, if only because of the activities of the Soviet Union, could not be handled in terms of disarmament. "Japan's position is that the international relations and political situation in Asia are quite different from those facing the powers in Europe. In Asia, the promotion of international peace by the abolition of war is impossible. It is too idealistic."[7] In order to rectify this misconception, Shigemitsu believed the Japanese government would have to undertake an extensive educational campaign designed to persuade "foreign governments and public opinion" that the vital issues of national security and

[5] The most thoughtful and detailed study of American policy is Dorothy Borg, *The United States and the Far Eastern Crisis of 1933-1938* (Cambridge, Mass., 1964).

[6] Japanese Ministry of Foreign Affairs, Archives, *Teikoku no taiShi seisaku kankei no ken* [Concerning the China Policy of the Imperial Government], III, "Gunshuku kaigi kankei" [Concerning the Naval Limitations Conference], September 9, 1933. [Hereafter cited as JMFA, *Teikoku no taiShi*.]

[7] *Ibid.*

international justice in Asia must "be divorced from the problem of disarmament."[8] Only if the Anglo-American nations recognized this fact, concluded the vice-foreign minister, could Japan and the Occidental countries cooperate in the quest for peace and stability in Asia.

Shigemitsu had identified a crucial, perhaps tragic, conflict between the guiding diplomatic axioms of the Japanese and American governments. Certainly, as several historians contend, the rhetoric of "disarmament" and the "outlawing" of war was somewhat irrelevant to the East Asian scene.[9] Whether this was primarily due to the actions of Imperial Japan between 1931 and 1933 or to the configurations produced by the conflicting concerns of the Soviet Union, the Western powers, Japan, and the Nationalist government of China is a subject which will continue to engage the attention of historians. One should therefore note that Shigemitsu's analysis was also governed by an assumption which eventually constituted a fatal flaw in Japan's national policy—namely, "Japan is in a position to bear the sole responsibility for maintaining order in the Far East. Consequently, it is imperative that we base our claim to this responsibility on the rationale of actual power."[10] The creation of Manchukuo and the withdrawal from the League had imposed a formidable obligation on the Japanese government. It would have to maintain a military establishment adequate for the attainment of three distinct and vital objectives: the ability to defeat the Soviet army, to enforce Japan's leadership on the Chinese government, and to guarantee the security of the home islands against the American fleet. These imperatives were slowly perceived in the fall of 1933 when the Saitō cabinet formulated the "Foreign Policy of Imperial Japan."

[8] *Ibid.*

[9] For example, George Kennan, *American Diplomacy, 1900-1950* (Chicago, 1951); and Nihon kokusai seiji gakkai [NKSG], *Nihon gaikōshi kenkyū: Shōwa jidai* (Tokyo, 1959).

[10] "Gunshuku kaigi . . . ," *op.cit.*

A Foreign Policy Consensus

The Inukai government, in April 1932, elected to organize Manchukuo, "regardless of its consequences"; and the Saitō cabinet, in August 1932, accepted as fact that one result might be Japan's withdrawal from the League. Although the implementation of both decisions would aggravate Japan's relations with the powers, the Saitō government still believed it could, in time, compromise the viability of the non-recognition doctrine. A firm Manchurian policy, reasoned Foreign Minister Uchida, when complemented by a meticulous respect for British interests in Central and South China, would eventually produce a *modus vivendi* with the British government. With this, Japan would once again solidify its naval security and the United States would abandon its objections to Manchukuo. The hope for a diplomatic accommodation with Great Britain lingered for many months; but, by the fall of 1933, it was clear the Anglo-American nations intended to support the non-recognition policy, a common purpose which implicitly suggested a détente against the Japanese empire. In this context, the foreign ministry drafted a comprehensive assessment of Japan's diplomacy; and, on October 20, the Saitō cabinet officially approved this "Foreign Policy of Imperial Japan" as the basic national policy.[11]

This cabinet decision articulated two simple propositions. The Japanese government must rely on diplomacy in the conduct of its relations with the Western countries; and the empire must, at the same time, acquire a national defense posture capable of overcoming any potential strategic threat. Within this framework, Japan would henceforth "promote peace in East Asia through the development of Manchuria," and continue to cultivate "friendly relations" with the Anglo-American nations in order to prevent an international crisis

11 JMFA, Archives, *Teikoku no taigai seisaku kankei no ken* [Concerning the Foreign Policy of the Imperial Government], I, "Teikoku no gaikō hōshin." [This is the complete text of the five ministers' decision. Hereafter cited as JMFA, *Teikoku no taigai*.]

at the 1936 conference on naval limitations.[12] In reference to China, the cabinet ruled that Japan should seek three objectives —namely, it should respect the "open door" policy, create a "viable relationship" between China and Manchukuo, and "eradicate" the Chinese boycotts of Japanese goods.[13] Since the Soviet Union posed an ideological as well as a strategic threat, the cabinet believed all diplomatic dealings with this power would have to be most circumspect. "Needless to say, Japan must not pursue any aggressive acts against Russia."[14] The American government, conceded the cabinet, was currently presenting some difficulties; but these were "due to the fact that the United States does not understand the historical context of Far Eastern problems. If the United States were to acquire a profound comprehension of our sincere wish to establish permanent peace in the Far East by means of our national power, the antithetical feelings between Japan and the United States would be dissipated."[15] To this end, Japan would have to educate the American people to an appreciation of the true situation in Asia. Finally, the cabinet judged that the empire would have to augment its naval security. Accordingly, concluded this policy statement, "we must demand an increase in our naval ratio" at the next international conference on naval limitations.[16]

This "Foreign Policy of Imperial Japan" was noteworthy in two basic respects. It marked the initial effort of the Japanese government to formulate a comprehensive national policy after Japan's withdrawal from the League of Nations; and it signified the emergence of the Five Ministers' Conference, or the Inner Cabinet, as the ultimate decision-making group in the government. On October 20, the resolutions and suggestions offered by the foreign ministry were considered by the premier and the foreign, war, naval, and finance ministers to be a reasonable and cogent analysis of Japan's national policy.

12 *Ibid.*, paragraph 1. [Since this document contains no pagination, reference is to specific paragraphs.]

13 *Ibid.*, paragraph 1.   14 *Ibid.*, paragraph 3.

15 *Ibid.*, paragraph 4.   16 *Ibid.*, paragraph 5.

Within a few weeks, however, War Minister Araki called the cabinet's attention to its ruling of October 20 that foreign policy was subsequently to be "decided by discussions among the state ministers."[17] Interpreting this as a mandate for a continuous dialogue among the five ministers, Araki presented an "Outline of an Inner Policy" as a necessary elaboration of the cabinet's foreign policy decision.[18] Here, the army's authorities equated the phrase "inner policy" with the development of Manchukuo. Beginning with this premise, the army's outline reasoned that Japan should "seek a settlement of the disarmament issue up to the point at which our security would be compromised. . . . We should seek defensive security in a manner that will avoid breaking up the next conference on naval limitations."[19] In addition to this directive on naval policy, the war minister insisted, "We must promote and control pro-Japanese movements in China" as one way to assure Japan's leadership in Asian affairs.[20] This "Outline of an Inner Policy" actually restructured the cabinet's earlier policy so as to emphasize three objectives: the development of Manchukuo, the promotion of political decentralization in China, and a policy of cooperation with the Western nations on the subject of naval limitations.

One of the ministries concerned with the army's stipulations, the naval department, greeted this inner policy somewhat critically. Countering with its "amendments" to the cabinet's "Foreign Policy of Imperial Japan," the naval ministry granted two propositions: "Japan's policy is based on the development of Manchukuo"; and Japan "must make every Chinese political faction follow the policy of the Japanese government."[21] Each

---

[17] JMFA, *Teikoku no taigai*, "Jugatsu nijūnichi goshōkaigi ni okeru rikugungawa teiji" [The Army's Presentation at the October 20th Five Ministers' Conference], paragraph 1.

[18] *Ibid.*, paragraphs 6-14.   [19] *Ibid.*, paragraph 14.

[20] *Ibid.*, paragraph 13.

[21] JMFA, *Teikoku no taigi*, 1, "Kaigun shūseian" [Naval amendments]. For the original naval viewpoint at the October 20th Five Ministers' Conference, see *ibid.*, "Godaijin kaigi no sekijō kaigun daijin no rōdoku

of these objectives, reasoned the naval authorities, would be contingent on the preclusion of any "alliance between the United States and China." Consequently, the naval ministry considered it unwise to predicate Japan's policy on the assumption that cooperation in the realm of naval limitations would assure the friendship of the American government. "Of course, Japan has no intention of going to war with the United States. Still, her policy is opposed to ours, and we must be prepared to be confronted by the United States. It is essential, therefore, that we make resolutions and preparations. At the next conference on naval disarmament, Japan must acquire sufficient defensive forces and become free of the disadvantageous restrictions imposed by the Washington and London treaties."[22] With this rejoinder to the army's inner policy, the Saitō cabinet had to restate its decision of October 20 according to the newly articulated dictates of both service ministries.

A new policy consensus was furnished on November 30 when the war ministry offered a final series of "amendments" to the "Foreign Policy of Imperial Japan."[23] The national purpose was now identified as the promotion of peace in Asia by means of "cooperative and friendly relations among China, Japan, and Manchukuo under the leadership of the Japanese empire."[24] The realization of this goal, declared the war ministry, would require the abrogation of the existing restrictions on naval armaments and this, in turn, would precipitate a grave "international crisis" at the 1936 conference on naval limitations. Since this development would cause a great deal of unrest within Japan, anticipated the army authorities, "we must guide public opinion in Japan to an awareness of the attitudes necessary to surmounting this crisis."[25] Apart from its domestic repercussions, the tensions to be provoked by the 1936 crisis would en-

---

seraretaru bun" [The Portion which the Naval Minister Read Aloud at the Five Ministers' Conference].

[22] *Ibid.*, "Kaigun shūseian," paragraphs 5 and 6.

[23] JMFA, *Teikoku no taigai*, "Rikugunshō shūseian," [Amendments of the War Ministry].

[24] *Ibid.*, Amendment #1.   [25] *Ibid.*, Amendment #4.

courage Chinese resistance to the policies of the Imperial government; and, to counter this trend effectively, Japan would have to "assist regional governments" on the mainland, while at the same time avoiding "overt extremes" in implementing this policy. "Naturally," the army's amendments concluded, "we must, unless the present national government offers some concrete proposal to strengthen friendly relations with Japan, prevent the Nationalist government, by the application of appropriate means, from advancing into North China."[26] These amendments, in effect, defined Japan's foreign policy to the mutual satisfaction of the war and naval ministries.

This amendment style of policy-making enabled each service to shape national policy according to its primary strategic concerns and estimates. In the process, the terminology of the cabinet's decision of October 20 had been radically altered, if not wholly emasculated. In lieu of educating the United States to a "profound comprehension" of the Asian scene was substituted a focus on the antithetical policies of the two countries and on the necessity to abrogate the Washington and London treaties; the emphasis on checking Chinese boycotts and a respect for the "open door" was replaced by a preoccupation with organizing local governments in and excluding the Kuomintang from North China; and the notion of cultivating friendly relations with the United States gave way to a projected campaign to inform the Japanese public about the "crisis of 1936." The Japanese government was by December 1933 committed to a policy which proposed to neutralize the influence of the Soviet Union, the Nationalist government of China, and the Anglo-American nations by a diplomacy rooted in the efficacy of Japan's military forces.

This policy was publicly affirmed by the claim of an Asiatic Monroe Doctrine; and, within the government, it was confirmed by the acceptance of the axiom, "The security of East Asia has come to depend entirely on the actual power of the empire."[27]

[26] *Ibid.*, Amendment #3.
[27] The phrase is from the naval amendments to the October 20th decision. "Kaigun shūseian," *op.cit.*

To postulate this need for an autonomous military capability was one thing; to implement it was another. In 1933, neither general staff believed Japan possessed sufficient power to risk a conflict with the Soviet Union or the Anglo-American nations. The story of Japan's foreign policy after 1933 would mirror the efforts to resolve the diplomatic and political problems posed by the discrepancy between the actual military capabilities of the Japanese empire and the quest for an Asiatic Monroe Doctrine which lacked the support of the Soviet Union, the United States, and Nationalist China.

IMPLEMENTATION OF THE NEW POLICY

For Japan to attain the foreign policy defined by the Inner Cabinet in late November 1933 would entail a major modification of the treaty system created at the Washington Conference, including the torpedoing of the 5:3 ratio and the imposition of a distinctively Japanese rendition of the phrase "respecting the territorial integrity of China." Obviously, this could not be done easily; but, since these new aspirations were designed to realize Japanese hegemony in Asia, they seemed estimable national goals. As Foreign Minister Hirota informed the Diet on February 22, 1934: "The path of a rising nation is always strewn with problems. . . . Japan, serving as the only cornerstone for the edifice of peace in East Asia, bears the entire burden of its responsibilities. Our diplomacy and national defense are rooted in this important position and its vast responsibilities."[28] The implication of Hirota's pronouncement eluded the attention of diplomats who did not read Japanese until April 17, when, for the benefit of Western news reporters, the official spokesman of the foreign ministry, Amau Eiji, casually paraphrased some recent dispatches in English. Amau was responding to a specific inquiry about Japan's attitude toward the efforts of the League to extend financial aid

[28] *Foreign Affairs*, III (1934), 13. I have rephrased the last sentence. The translation in the archives reads: "It is this important position and the vast responsibility in which foreign diplomacy and national defense are rooted."

to the Nationalist government of China.[29] The Imperial government was against this action, affirmed Amau, because it tended to support anti-Japanese movements on the mainland. Besides, remarked Amau, Japan, not the Occidental powers, was responsible for maintaining peace in Asia. Both comments were commonplace in Japanese circles and there was no anticipation that they would stimulate much concern. However, Amau's press interview was viewed in Washington with surprise and indignation. In an aide-mémoire of April 29, Secretary of State Cordell Hull dismissed the substance of Amau's statement: "In the opinion of the American people and the American government, no nation can, without the assent of the other nations concerned, rightfully endeavor to make conclusive its will in situations where there are involved the rights, obligations and legitimate interests of other sovereign states."[30] Confronted by this official protest, the Japanese foreign ministry finally abandoned the notion of including the Nine Power Treaty on the agenda of the 1936 conference on naval limitations.

Prior to Amau's *faux pas*, the foreign ministry had planned to seek an official reaffirmation of the Nine Power Treaty in a manner which would allow Japan to interpret the terms "equal opportunity" and the "territorial integrity of China" in the light of its responsibilities to maintain order in Asia.[31] With unconscious irony, the staff of the Asian Affairs Bureau noted that Japan would be able to diminish slowly the rights and interests of the Western nations in China, providing "the government does not again adopt such action as in the Twenty-one Demands."[32] This advice apparently was not appreciated

[29] International Military Tribunal Far East [IMTFE], *Exhibit 935*, is the text of the Amau statement. Also Gaimushō, *Nihon gaikō nenpyō narabini shuyō bunsho* (Tokyo, 1953), II, 286.
[30] *Ibid.*
[31] JMFA, *Teikoku no taiShi*, III, "Kafu kyūkoku jōyaku ni kitei to waga taiShi seisaku to no kankei" [Our China Policy and the Provisions of the Nine Power Treaty], undated. It was written, according to the archival staff of the foreign ministry, between April 13 and April 15, 1934.
[32] *Ibid.*

by the department's press officer; and, a few days after the uproar
generated by Amau's statement, the Asian Affairs Bureau advanced a set of ethical and imperial reasons why Japan should
not consider any formal discussion of the Nine Power Treaty:
(1) it would only encourage anti-Japanese sentiment in China;
(2) Japan should not, as in the 1931 Manchurian crisis, make
promises it could not fulfill; (3) it would contradict the
cabinet's policy calling for the promotion of an independent
North China; (4) any discussion of the China problem at the
conference on naval limitations would inspire the mistaken belief among the Occidental powers and China that Japan was
not the strongest nation in East Asia; (5) the government should
settle various political and economic matters as they arose
according to the "changing state of affairs" principle; and (7) in
place of a reconsideration of the Nine Power Treaty, Japan
should seek a joint communiqué with the United States that
would vaguely define the concepts of "equal opportunity" and
"territorial integrity."[33] This last suggestion was pursued one
month later when the foreign ministry offered to attempt to
reach a détente with the American government.

In mid-May, Ambassador Saito Hiroshi requested a confidential meeting with Secretary Hull in order to discuss a
matter of "momentous importance."[34] As outlined by Saito, his
government was prepared to participate in a mutual pledge
which would guarantee the equal opportunity of the two
countries in the Far East, as well as their Pacific territorial
possessions and interests.[35] In addition, Saito wished to designate
the United States as the stabilizing power in the Eastern Pacific,
with Japan to assume an identical role in the Western Pacific.
A delineation along these lines, volunteered the Japanese ambassador, would quash all warlike talk within Japan and it

[33] JMFA, *Teikoku no taiShi*, "Jikai gunshuku kaigi ni okeru kyūkoku
jōyaku o saikakunin suru koto no fuka nara riyu" [Reasons why it would
be inadvisable to reaffirm the Nine Power Treaty at the Next Conference
on Naval Limitations], April 18, 1934.

[34] Dorothy Borg, *Far Eastern Crisis of 1933-1938*, 92-95.

[35] United States Department of State, *Foreign Relations of the United
States* (Washington, 1952), III (1934), 654-659.

would compel the Chinese to abandon their wicked practice of playing one power against the other. This conception of Pacific affairs, however, failed to impress the secretary of state. Replying in a restrained voice, Cordell Hull dryly noted that the United States had "a special interest in preserving peace and order in China."[36] Since the American government could not accept the "clause or formula about Japan's claiming superior and special interests in the peace situation in Eastern Asia," the secretary hoped the Japanese government would respect the "sanctity of treaties."[37] By vigilantly preserving and observing its existing "legal and moral obligations," ventured Hull, the Japanese nation would best serve the cause of peace and justice in Asia. Although this advice was not unanticipated, it confirmed the estimate of the naval ministry that Japan could not possibly predicate its national policy on the premise of a rapprochement with the United States.

After the denunciations of the Amau statement and the dismissal of Ambassador Saito's request for a joint communiqué, the Okada cabinet, on July 14, 1934, officially decided to abrogate the Washington and London naval treaties.[38] During the following eight weeks, the staffs of the foreign and naval ministries went through the motions of drafting a number of conditions which were to be advanced in the preliminary discussions among the naval powers, including a demand for parity with the Anglo-American nations. These proposals were only gestures designed to prolong the discussions and to avoid provoking the United States into an enlarged program of naval construction. Thus, when Prince Saionji asked Foreign Minister Hirota whether Japan intended to terminate the existing treaties if the Western countries accepted every demand raised by the Japanese delegation, Hirota confessed, "We must abrogate them no matter how much the other powers agree to our proposals."[39] By the fall of 1934, the Japanese govern-

[36] *Ibid.*   [37] *Ibid.*
[38] Aritake Shuji, *Okada Keisuke denki* (Tokyo, 1957), 259.
[39] Saionji-Harada, *Memoirs,* September 7, 1934.

ment had calculated that any form of naval limitations would be contrary to its long-term national objective—the realization of an Asiatic Monroe Doctrine.

Parallel with the decision to enhance Japan's naval strength by terminating the armament limitation treaties, Vice-Foreign Minister Shigemitsu solicited support for a continental policy which would immediately reduce the influence of the Occidental powers in China and augment Japan's hegemony in East Asia.[40] These dual accomplishments could be attained, reasoned Shigemitsu, if Japan were to extend a "direct benefit to China ... [by] shattering all organizations which have been created in China by foreign nations."[41] In particular, Shigemitsu thought Japan should first undermine the maritime tariff system in China; and, secondly, issue a dramatic public appeal for the abolition of all extra-territorial rights in China. Shigemitsu developed these ideas by offering three practical steps which Japan could adopt: (1) appoint an ambassador who would reside in Nanking, rather than in the international settlement at Shanghai; (2) direct the consul general in North China to compromise the viability of the existing legation system in the Peking-Tientsin district; and (3) request the powers to abolish the legation districts which had been created in North China following the Boxer incident at the turn of the century. By posing as the protector of Chinese sovereignty, observed the vice-foreign minister, Japan would divert Chinese xenophobia against the Western nations; and, of necessity, this would make China more dependent on the political and economic assistance of the Japanese empire. Moreover, insisted Shigemitsu, the withdrawal of all foreign troops and naval forces from North China would greatly weaken the influence of the Western powers in this area, but "the withdrawal of Japanese forces from the northern provinces of China would not bring any serious disadvantages to Japan because the Imperial army would

[40] JMFA, *Teikoku no taiShi*, III, "TaiShi seisaku ni kansuru Shigemitsu jikan no kōju" [Instructions of Vice-Minister Shigemitsu Concerning Our China Policy], October 20, 1934.
[41] *Ibid.*, 3.

be stationed in the Great Wall district and in Manchuria."[42]

Although the recommendations of the vice-foreign minister were subtle and sagacious, the war ministry viewed them with a noticeable lack of enthusiasm. The official cabinet policy called for the promotion of regional governments in North China; and, as far as the army authorities were concerned, this policy would not be well served by the withdrawal of the Japanese army from North China. In addition, endorsement of Shigemitsu's plan would mean a policy of cooperation with the Kuomintang; and, in harmony with most Western observers in China, the army's China experts questioned the viability of the Nationalist government. Judging Chiang Kai-shek to be merely one more warlord, the intelligence division of the general staff branded the recommendations of the vice-foreign minister as based on an irresponsible and foolish conception of the Chinese political scene. The voice of the army authorities prevailed over that of the diplomat and, on December 7, 1934, the Inner Cabinet stipulated that "for the time being, it is desirable that Japan seek to reduce to a minimum degree the influence of the Chinese central government in North China."[43] In short, the cabinet was not willing to seek a rapprochement with the Nanking government on the basis of a *quid pro quo*— Japanese support for the Kuomintang in North China in exchange for Chinese recognition of Manchukuo and a comprehensive Sino-Japanese trade agreement.

RESIGNATION OF GENERAL ARAKI

The events and decisions of 1934 confirmed Japan's commitment to two aspects of the "Foreign Policy of Imperial Japan" which had been set forth by the Saitō cabinet in the fall of 1933. The Imperial government had decided, in the summer of 1934, to abrogate the Washington and London naval

---

[42] *Ibid.*, 7.

[43] JMFA, *Teikoku no taiShi*, III, "Shina mondai ni kan suru gunbu to no kyōgi no ken" [Conferences with the Military Concerning the China Problem], December 12, 1934. The cabinet decision of December 7 is an appendix to this document.

treaties; and, on the 7th of December, it had affirmed its resolution to foster regional governments in North China. The Saitō cabinet had also sanctioned a governmental educational campaign designed to alert public opinion to the nature and significance of the forthcoming "crisis of 1936." In pursuit of this directive, however, War Minister Araki provoked a number of controversies in central headquarters which eventually compelled his resignation and the scuttling of public emphasis on the "crisis of 1936."

Previously it was noted that, at the time of the Mukden incident, the staff officers in central headquarters had favored the outright conquest of Manchuria on the basis of three distinct considerations. The war ministry, especially Colonel Nagata's staff, was anxious to tap the economic resources of the three eastern provinces in order to strengthen Japan's "total war" capabilities; the operations division of the general staff stressed the strategic value of Manchuria vis-à-vis the Soviet Maritime Army; and the intelligence division of the general staff confidently estimated that control of Manchuria would enable the army to weaken the authority of the Kuomintang in the provinces of North China. These multiple considerations yielded a consensus in support of the Mukden incident; but they had not furnished a clear policy directive governing the army's subsequent activities on the mainland. Because of the dissension in central headquarters, particularly the contention between those officers who believed the army could immediately begin preparations for a Soviet conflict and those who insisted it would need several years before it could successfully wage a major war, the Supreme War Council wanted a war minister who commanded the respect of the war ministry and the general staff. This concern prompted the selection of Araki Sadao in December 1931; but, unfortunately, the new war minister failed to fulfill the expectations of the Supreme War Council.

During the opening months of his tenure as war minister, General Araki systematically removed every major departmental head in central headquarters. Included in this purge were the vice-war minister, Sugiyama Gen; the chief of the Bureau of Military Affairs, Koiso Kuniaki; and the vice-chief of the general staff, Ninomiya Harushige.[44] This sweeping personnel change unleashed some concern in army circles, particularly when the war minister designated General Yanagawa Heisuke as vice-war minister, General Yamaoka Jukō as the chief of the Bureau of Military Affairs, and General Mazaki Jinzaburō as the vice-chief of staff. These men were close friends of Araki's and, on the basis of their previous careers, the appointments of Yamagawa and Yamaoka could be attributed only to their personal ties with the war minister. In conjunction with his abusive treatment of the department heads, Araki promoted the members of the "German group" in central headquarters —namely, Nagata Tetsuzan, Tōjō Hideki, Umezu Yoshijirō, Suzuki Teiichi, Yamashita Tomoyuki, and Okamura Neiji.[45] In this fashion, Araki muffled the concern caused by his partiality to old friends and conveyed an impression of unqualified approval of the emphasis on economic planning and the rationalization of the army favored by the proponents of the "total war" doctrine.

This image was marred somewhat in the fall of 1932 by General Araki's public posture as a devotee of the spiritual basis of warfare. In addition to eulogizing Japan's *kokutai* (national principle) and *yamato damashii* (the soul of Japan), the war minister popularized the term *kōgun* (the Emperor's army). These phrases ascribed to the army an affinity for Japanese values and the Imperial institution which implied that it was superior to other governmental entities. The rhetoric of *kōgun, kokutai,* and *yamato damshii* kindled the imagination and spirit of most line officers and the military cadets, as well as drawing accolades from the leading ultra-nationalistic societies. To the extent that it improved the prestige and élan of the officer corps, the public stance of the war minister could not be faulted. Nevertheless, this revitalization of the mystique of

---

[44] Takamiya Tahei, *Gunkoku taiheiki* (Tokyo, 1951), 140-144, 157-158.
[45] *Ibid.*, 157-158.

bushidō tended to downgrade the importance of tanks, planes, means of communication, and a greatly improved industrial capacity. Consequently, the majority of staff officers in central offices became a little disenchanted with the war minister, an attitude which was intensified by the activities of Major General Obata Tokushiro.

Shortly after becoming war minister in December 1931, General Araki promoted Obata to colonel and placed him in charge of the operations section of the general staff. Within a hundred days, Obata became a major general and was placed in command of the third division of the general staff. As the protégé of War Minister Araki and the vice-chief of staff, General Mazaki, the army's newest major general was obviously being groomed for bigger things; and, in the closing months of 1932, Obata capitalized on his privileged status by launching a personal campaign for his favorite strategic idea—namely, that the general staff should base its planning on the premise of an immediate war with the Soviet Union. Since the approval of this recommendation would adversely affect the existing focus on the economic development of Manchuria and the refurbishment of the army with new equipment and new training programs, Obata's proposal provoked a great deal of anxiety in central headquarters. This concern was not lessened by an awareness that Obata would not be articulating his views so forcefully without the tacit encouragement of the war minister and the vice-chief of staff.

Despite the stature and authority of Obata's patrons, Generals Umezu, Tōjō, and Nagata leveled a caustic and devastating indictment of the doctrine of an immediate Soviet war, as well as ridiculing the possibility of any major operations in North China or Inner Mongolia. In their estimation, the army should adhere to a long-range program which gave priority to the development of a military-industrial complex, the cardinal prerequisite for waging "total war." Confronted by this opposition from the other departmental heads of the general staff, Obata's proposition was formally set aside in the spring of

1933. As General Minami confided to Baron Harada, the army authorities believed that Japan must not "send an expeditionary force to the Peking-Tientsin district or attack Russia. First of all, we must fully understand and give our full support to Manchukuo, and we must take steps to reestablish friendly relations with China."[46] Although Umezu, Tōjō, and Nagata were triumphant in May 1933, they were precipitately transferred from the general staff in August. Without discounting the humiliation suffered by Tōjō and Umezu, the treatment of Nagata, who was posted to an infantry regiment, was entirely scandalous. These August transfers shocked the staff in central headquarters, since they could only be regarded as a form of revenge engineered by Obata. Equally significantly, they strengthened doubts about the sincerity of the war minister's commitment to the full implications of "total war" planning.

This suspicion was not dissipated in the fall of 1933 when General Araki nurtured the concept of the "crisis of 1936." In the cabinet discussions leading up to the 1933 "Foreign Policy of Imperial Japan," the war minister had employed this theme in the context of a public crisis which would be stimulated by the termination of the Washington and London naval treaties. Publicly, however, Araki linked the "crisis of 1936" with the likelihood of a conflict with the Soviet Union; and one of Araki's intimates, retired Colonel Kobayashi Junichiro, organized the " '36 Club," which published a weekly magazine that dwelled monotonously on the inevitability of a Soviet conflict.[47] Moreover, in December 1933, the war minister publicly chastised the critics of the "crisis of '36" with a veiled warning:

> [Some] say that the crisis of 1936 is nothing but propaganda put out by the military authorities, or that those who died in past wars belonged exclusively to the lower ranks, and that no high officers died. Others are saying that the welfare of the farmers was sacrificed for the sake of the military budget. Such a movement—to separate the public mind from the military—

[46] Saionji-Harada, *Memoirs*, May 1, 1933.
[47] Richard Storry, *Double Patriots*, 167-168.

is an attempt to disturb the harmonious unity of the public mind, the essential basis of national defense; and the military authorities cannot overlook it. The two international movements for ruining a nation's power of self-defense are the anti-war movement based on the Third International and the movement to alienate the public mind from the military.[48]

This outburst, which labeled all opponents of the "1936 crisis" as Communists or pacifists, infuriated many officials, including Finance Minister Takahashi, who bluntly informed Araki: "The military must exercise prudence in speech and action. There will be no such crisis in 1935 and 1936."[49]

The personnel policies of the war minister, in conjunction with his public pronouncements, kept the staff of central headquarters in constant ferment and hindered the formulation and implementation of the desired long-range economic and refurbishment programs. By January 1934, only Araki's friends and protégés—Generals Mazaki, Yanagawa, and Yamaoka and Colonels Suzuki Teiichi, Yamashita Tomoyuki, and Okamura Neiji—remained loyal to the leadership of the war minister. As the intelligence experts of the Imperial navy phrased it: "While chanting effortlessly that he must promptly invest the Emperor's army with integrity and abolish all cliques from the army, War Minister Araki, in fact, built up his own large faction. The Imperial army is not so generous as to permit this deed."[50] Subject to the unrelenting pressure of the Supreme War Council, Araki, in late January, reluctantly resigned his portfolio in exchange for membership in the Supreme War Council.

POLICIES OF GENERAL HAYASHI

Prior to the personnel changes of August 1933, the new war minister, Hayashi Senjurō, had not been antagonistic to the

48 *Ibid.*, 142.

49 Saionji-Harada, *Memoirs*, December 13, 1933.

50 Gunreibu, *Gun kankei jōhō* [Intelligence Reports on the Military], "Seigun undō no jissei" [Real Conditions of the Purification Movement], February 8, 1934. [Hereafter cited as GKJ.]

policies of General Araki. Since he himself had been denied assignments in central headquarters throughout the heyday of General Ugaki, the complaints against Araki's treatment of Generals Sugiyama, Koiso, and Ninomiya had not impressed General Hayashi. Indeed, at the time of Inukai's assassination in May 1932, Hayashi had declined the post of war minister because he did not wish Araki to be tinged with responsibility for the violent deed of a group of young officers.[51] Between May 1932 and January 1934, however, Hayashi, along with most senior officers, became convinced that Araki's policies and pronouncements had generated serious factionalism in central headquarters. In order to completely disassociate himself from Araki, the new war minister shunned the ritual gesture of a personal conference with his predecessor.

Directly on assuming his post, Hayashi revealed his personal estimate of Araki's views by canceling the use of the term "crisis of 1936" in all army publications or speeches by officers on active duty; by dismissing the contention that preparations for a Soviet conflict should govern staff planning; and by expressing his approval of the foreign minister's desire to resume diplomatic negotiations with the Soviet Union in an effort to settle the North Manchurian Railway problem.[52] Moreover, Hayashi summarily transferred General Yamaoka to the Bureau of Equipment and Supplies in March 1934, designating Major General Nagata Tetsuzan as his new chief of the Bureau of Military Affairs. "In order to establish a fundamental army policy that could not be affected by a cabinet change," Hayashi directed Nagata "to prepare an encompassing program for the exploitation of Manchuria and Mongolia and for the general mobilization of agricultural districts during wartime."[53] With this mandate, Nagata assembled a new staff of

[51] Aritake, *Okada Keisuke*, 210. Also Fukuda Ippei, "Araki—The Man of the Crisis," *Contemporary Japan* (December 1932), 338.
[52] "Seigun undō no jissei," *op.cit.*, parts III and IV.
[53] *Ibid.*, part VI.

"economic experts" in his bureau, including Hashimoto Gun, Ikeda Junkyū, Katakura Chū, and Shimizu Moriaki.[54]

The new orientation imposed by the Hayashi-Nagata leadership in the war ministry was revealed in October 1934 in the official publication, *Basic Theory of National Defense and Suggestions for Its Realization*.[55] Opening with a Treitschke motif, "War is the father of creation and the mother of culture," this pamphlet, as one of its framers later confessed, purposely included "everything in the universe" under the concept of national defense.[56] This was not done carelessly. Prior to its publication, every bureau chief in central headquarters checked the original draft; and each pamphlet included a return postcard so that the public response could be accurately measured. By advocating the slogan "national defense," the war ministry deliberately sought to displace the "crisis of 1936" as a rallying point for public support of the army's economic policies. More affirmatively, the pamphlet was designed to marshal public opinion behind two propositions—the need for economic planning and for general mobilization in the event of a future war. Lest there be any misunderstanding of the purpose of the *Basic Theory of National Defense,* War Minister Hayashi informed a select group of political and economic figures:

Since the army bears the responsibility for national defense, it has a keen interest in the political and economic affairs of Japan. If some should say this constitutes political intervention by the army, we will reply that this view is an anachronism. . . . The fundamental direction indicated in the pamphlet must be carried out gradually, according to

[54] Takamiya, *Gunkoku*, 182. Also interview with General Katakura Chū.

[55] IMTFE, *Document 3089*. The Japanese title reads, *Kokubō no hongi to sono kyoka no teishō.*

[56] Ikeda Junkyū, "Seinen shōkō to kakushin shisō" [The Young Officers and Revolutionary Thinking], *Himerareta shōwashi* (Tokyo, 1956), 110.

legal procedures. Moreover, I shall personally do my best to realize this plan within legal means.[57]

Since the *Basic Theory of National Defense* marked the first public espousal of the terms "national defense" and "economic planning," it has been identified as the army's commitment to a program of Japanese fascism. In 1934, though, the distinguished Professor Minobe Tatsukichi was alarmed by the pamphlet's approach to international affairs.[58] After observing that the army's publication equated "militarism" with the Imperial system of government, Minobe predicted that this identification would stimulate a virulent form of nationalism in Japan, one which would establish an artificial dichotomy between national security and cooperation with the Western nations. The fundamental axiom of this pamphlet, declared Minobe, was the proposition that Japan must secure an "autonomous national defense" (*jishuteki kokubōken*); and this could only mean that Japan should scuttle the Washington and London naval treaties in favor of developing the South Seas and of revising the various treaties affecting the mainland. If this policy prevailed, warned the venerable professor of law, the Western countries would be obliged to adopt a similar approach to their own "national defense." The result would be a certain invitation to war with the Anglo-American nations, a prospect which Minobe did not believe would contribute to the ultimate security of the Japanese empire.

The fears and criticisms advanced by Professor Minobe did not seem very pertinent to the staffs of the foreign, war, and naval ministries. Parallel with the cabinet decisions of 1933 and 1934, which were, in fact, predicated on the necessity for an autonomous national defense, there appeared new administrative

[57] *GKJ,* " 'Rei no panfureto ni tsuki Hayashi Shō hikoshiki ni sono jitsugen o gemmei' to dai suru bunsho" [A Document on the Subject, 'An Informal Explanation of the Realization of the Pamphlet by War Minister Hayashi'], November 14, 1934.

[58] Minobe Tatsukichi, "Rikugunshō hatten no kokuboron o yomu," *Chūō kōron* (November 1954), 328-335. The article originally appeared in the November 1934 issue of *Chūō kōron.*

arrangements designed to coordinate the policies of the ministers of state under the mantle of a "national defense state." On July 14, 1934, the Okada cabinet established the Cabinet Consultative Council (*naikaku shingikai*), which included representatives from the major political parties, the leading industrial combines, and the House of Peers.[59] This council was directed by the finance minister; and it supervised another new agency, the Cabinet Research Bureau (*naikaku chōsa-kyoku*). The latter group was composed of representatives from the ministries of state and it was charged with the dual tasks of preparing legislative proposals to be submitted to the Diet and furnishing the cabinet with position papers on important economic problems. The Cabinet Research Bureau provided the first legal administrative liaison among the various ministries and, by 1935, it had devised a new administrative arrangement to govern Manchukuo. Subsequently, this body would formulate many of the laws which resulted in increasing governmental control over the political, economic, and intellectual activities of the Imperial subjects, a fact which led Premier Okada to label the Cabinet Research Bureau "a Frankenstein," the "single biggest mistake" of his premiership.[60] It may also be viewed as the bureaucratic manifestation of the government's quest for a "national defense state" which would endow the empire with an "autonomous national defense" capability.

THE PROBLEM OF SINO-JAPANESE RELATIONS

The Inner Cabinet of the Saitō and Okada governments had, in 1934 and 1935, sanctioned the development of Manchukuo, the abrogation of the Washington and London naval treaties, the strengthening of the Imperial army and navy, and the encouragement of regional governments in North China. Each of these facets of national policy was related to one pervasive objective, the imposition of Japanese hegemony on the continent. Paradoxically, the military potential of the Nation-

---

[59] Aritake, *Okada Keisuke*, 233-236 and 305-307.
[60] *Ibid.*, 303, 306.

alist government was not regarded as a basic impediment to the attainment of this aspiration. Since possible interventions by the combined Anglo-American fleets and/or the Soviet army were viewed with intense concern, it was assumed that, if Japan were to possess sufficient power to neutralize both of these threats, the Chinese government would be compelled to adopt a posture of deference toward the policies of the Imperial government. Ideally, this would be realized in a diplomatic fashion —namely, the Chinese government would recognize the futility of the time-honored technique of "playing barbarian against barbarian"; and it would recognize that a subordinate role under an Asiatic Monroe Doctrine would be a sensible and rewarding national policy. This vision did not, however, moderate the conviction of Japan's army authorities that the Kuomintang would accept Japanese hegemony only if it were subjected to constant pressure and the threat of force. In view of the Soviet threat, however, the Japanese army could implement this theory credibly only in the provinces of North China. On December 7, 1934, the Okada cabinet endorsed this approach when it confirmed the resolution to exclude the Kuomintang from North China. Shortly after this decision, however, the possibility of a simpler solution of the China problem was raised by the proffer of a *modus vivendi* by the Nanking government.

In January 1935, the Nationalist government despatched a semi-official good-will mission to Japan; and, on the 5th of February, Wang Ch'ung-hui, as the personal emissary of Chiang Kai-shek, conferred with Foreign Minister Hirota.[61] In the course of this conversation, Wang stated that the Nationalist government was prepared to negotiate a Sino-Japanese Friendship Treaty, providing it were based on three principles: (1) absolute equality between the two nations; (2) the abolition of all unequal treaties; and (3) the cessation of

---

[61] JMFA, *Teikoku no taiShi*, IV, "Hirota daijin O Chō-kei kaidan yōroku" [Digest of Foreign Minister Hirota's Talk with Wang Ch'ung-hui], February 26, 1935.

Japanese assistance to "local governments" in North China. After agreeing "in principle" to these conditions, Hirota indicated that "Japan is willing to ask the Powers to withdraw their troops from China. Still, the establishment of good Sino-Japanese relations is absolutely essential for any withdrawal of Japanese troops from the Tientsin region."[62] Wang interpreted this as a reasonable reply and suggested that the two countries should exchange ambassadors in order to initiate preliminary discussions of the projected treaty. The prospect of a Sino-Japanese Friendship Treaty understandably intrigued the Japanese foreign ministry, especially since each of the principles advanced by Wang Ch'ung-hui had been anticipated in the recent policy recommendation of Vice-Foreign Minister Shigemitsu. In effect, the Hirota-Wang conversation raised two fundamental questions: Was the Kuomintang actually prepared to accept Japanese economic, military, and political advice and assistance? Was the Okada cabinet willing to revise its current policy and permit the Kuomintang to consolidate its authority in North China? The answer to both questions proved negative, mainly because of the attitudes and actions of the Imperial army in the summer and fall of 1935.

The appointment of an ambassador to China was favored by the members of the Inner Cabinet, with the vital exception of the war minister. Although a decision of this sort would entail no specific commitment, General Hayashi was apprehensive lest such an appointment undermine the army's position in North China. Still, the views of his colleagues in the cabinet could not be ignored, and Hayashi ordered the general staff to reconsider the subject of North China in the light of the Hirota-Wang discussion. For several weeks, General Doihara conferred with the military attachés in North China, and the staffs of the Tientsin garrison and the Kwantung Army. These protracted consultations eventually yielded, on March 30, "The China Policy of the Kwantung Army."[63] Here, the army's China

[62] *Ibid.*

[63] *GKJ, Kahoku mondai shinsei jihen keii* [Particulars of the New Life

specialists recommended a Buddhistic stance of inaction: the government should neither support nor oppose the projected Sino-Japanese Treaty. Until the Kuomintang actually carried out some "pro-Japanese" deeds, ran the intelligence estimate, the Imperial army must insist on a rigid adherence to the terms of the Tangku Truce, as well as the continuation of its current policy, which was designed to foster local administrative units in North China. "The effects of the early anti-Japanese education of the Kuomintang will not evaporate in a day or two. On the contrary, if we were to reveal carelessly a cordial feeling toward China, this would inevitably encourage the Chinese to become more presumptuous. . . . We should not, therefore, render any financial aid or express a friendly attitude towards the Nationalist government."[64] Despite this opinion, War Minister Hayashi ruled that the army could endorse the proposal of the foreign ministry as long as the exchange of ambassadors would not connote any alteration in the cabinet's existing North China policy. With this crucial qualification, the foreign ministry, in early May, raised its Shanghai consulate to an embassy and entered into discreet conversation with Nationalist officials, ostensibly on the basis of Wang Ch'ung-hui's three principles.

This change in consular status irritated the army authorities in North China because, according to the Peking attaché, General Isogaya, it produced "echoes in China" which were most unfortunate.[65] In his content analysis of the Chinese press, Isogaya offered the following observations: on May 16, the China press regarded the exchange of ambassadors as "neither good or bad"; by the 16th of May, it was discussing the Manchurian problem in terms which implied that, if this issue were not settled to the satisfaction of China, the appointment of a Japanese ambassador would be a diplomatic farce; between

---

Incident and the Hopei Problem], "Kantogun taiShi seisaku" [China Policy of the Kwantung Army], March 30, 1935. [Hereafter, this volume of documents cited as *Kahoku mondai*.]

[64] *Ibid.*

[65] *Kahoku mondai*, "Shina jikyoku-hō dainijūkyū-gō" [Report #29. China Section], May 28, 1935.

May 17 and May 23, the press was contrasting the "aggression of the Japanese army" with the sensible "attitude of the Japanese foreign ministry"; and, after the 23rd, it was arguing the necessity to abolish all unequal treaties, as well as suggesting that the actions of the Imperial army in North China revealed a "lack of sincerity" in Japanese professions of friendship for China. General Isogaya concluded:

> In view of the above comments and criticisms, we find that the Chinese press, especially the organs of the Kuomintang and the Nanking government, beamed with joy when the change to an ambassador was announced. However, they soon treated this elevation as if it were a useless, empty gesture. Moreover, they soon advocated the recovery of Manchuria, the abolition of unequal treaties, and criticized the Japanese army. In effect, they displayed a typical Chinese trait: once they obtain A, they wish to secure a better A. . . . It seems the promotion of our diplomatic representative to an ambassador has only caused an anti-Japanese attitude of contempt for Japan.[66]

Whether this was a disinterested assessment is hard to judge; but, this sentiment, plus a rash of anti-Japanese demonstrations in Tientsin and Peking, furnished the Tientsin garrison with a convenient pretext for delivering some karate-like blows at the Kuomintang in North China.

NORTH CHINA CRISIS

During the absence of General Umezu, the commanding officer of the Japanese forces stationed in North China under the 1901 Boxer protocol, Colonels Takahashi Tan and Sakai Ryu, on May 29, paid an unannounced call on the Peking Military Council. After berating these Chinese officials about the recent "insults" to the Japanese empire, Sakai and Takahashi informed the council that it must abandon its Janus-headed policy by banishing all Nationalist military advisors

[66] *Ibid.*, part III.

and by abolishing the political organs of the Kuomintang in the Peking-Tientsin district. "We added," noted Sakai in his report to the general staff, "that we did not come to negotiate on these matters with you today. We came only to announce the decision of the Imperial army."[67] If Sakai and Takahashi anticipated unqualified support for their actions, they were temporarily disappointed. Sensing a major incident in the making, the naval general staff, on May 31, raised a vigorous objection to any type of diplomatic or military crisis in North China.

In "One View of the China Situation," the naval authorities invoked the gravest type of danger, the prospect of an Anglo-American intervention.[68] Pointing out that Britain and the United States had sufficient naval forces in the Pacific to act in defense of their treaty rights in North China, the naval staff warned that more than one-half of the major ships of the Imperial navy were either being overhauled or under construction. In this context, any serious incident in China would be the prelude to a diplomatic disaster. "If Japan were forced to concede to the Powers," declared the naval general staff, "just one such instance would produce great disorder in Japan and in the stability of the Far East. The situation could never be restored to its former position."[69] Besides, continued the naval warning, "even if the political and military circumstances were favorable to Japan, the actions of the Imperial army should be restricted to those steps which would not embarrass the Japanese state."[70] Although this evaluation was greatly overstated—a combined Anglo-American intervention in 1935 was hardly a viable possibility—the strong anxieties of the naval authorities conveyed a clear message: Japan could not risk another Mukden incident.

Shortly after the naval presentation, General Nagata, on June 5, drafted the war ministry's policy for the current situ-

[67] *Kahoku mondai*, "Hokuhei hosakan hatsu sambō jichō ate" [From Peking Attaché to Vice-Chief of the General Staff], #384, May 29, 1935.
[68] *Kahoku mondai*, "TaiShi shoken," May 31, 1935.
[69] *Ibid.*   [70] *Ibid.*

ation in North China.[71] Specifically, the Tientsin garrison was authorized to present the following demands: (1) the resignation of those Chinese officials who could be nominally held responsible for the recent anti-Japanese demonstrations; (2) the elimination of all Kuomintang military advisors from the Peking Military Council; (3) the withdrawal of all Nationalist troops from Hopei province to a point below the Paoting pass; and (4) the imposition of effective restrictions on all anti-Japanese organizations in the province of Hopei. These orders, in effect, endorsed the independent actions of Colonels Sakai and Takahashi; but the war ministry also ordered General Umezu to confine the subsequent actions of his garrison to reliance on economic pressure and support of the existing local governments. This veto of any additional political or military intrigues occasioned slight enthusiasm among the field officers who shared General Isogaya's opinion that "Now is a golden moment to realize what the army has desired for twenty years."[72] Still, the prudence and authority of the war ministry's plan were not openly challenged and the vice-war minister, advising the Kwantung Army, philosophically observed: "Let the Chinese, by means of this opportunity to negotiate, reflect on their anti-Japanese attitudes and dissolve those groups and movements which embody this sentiment. A transformation in their behavior and ideas would create the conditions which are necessary for a general solution of problems plaguing Sino-Japanese relations."[73] On June 10, General Umezu and General Ho Ying-ching of the Peking Military Council signed a "local" agreement which banished

[71] *Kahoku mondai,* "HokuShi kōshō mondai shori yōkō" [Outline for the Disposition of the Negotiations of the North China Problem], Jichō yori sambōchō ate [Vice-War Minister to the Chief of the General Staff], June 5, 1935. Also Gaimushō, *Nihon gaikō nenpyō narabini shuyō bunsho* (Tokyo, 1955), II, 293, but without indication of date or origin of document. In a personal interview, General Katakura Chū indicated that Nagata had written this China policy paper at the orders of the vice-war minister.

[72] *Ibid.,* Hokuhei hosokan, cable 689, June 9, 1935. This is a report of the naval attaché's conversation with General Isogaya.

[73] "HokuShi kōshō mondai . . . ," *op.cit.*

the Kuomintang party and the Nationalist army from the province of Hopei.[74]

The ease with which the Tientsin garrison had compromised the position of the Nationalist government in Hopei was not overlooked by the intelligence division of the general staff. General Doihara, on June 17, conducted a round-table meeting of the army's China specialists to consider what might be done along similar lines in the provinces of Chahar, Suiyuan, and Ninghsia.[75] After several alternative proposals had been advanced, these officers judged that the influence of the Nanking government could be judiciously compromised by the creation of one new "local" government for these provinces of North China. The army's self-styled "manipulators" of the Chinese warlords nominated General Sung Che-yuan of Chahar as their favorite candidate to head a new government; but, on June 18, Chiang Kai-shek precipitately summoned General Sung to Nanking, and placed General Ching of the Nationalist army in command of Chahar. This move stalled the main scheme of organizing a new government; but, by June 23, the night maneuvers and arrogant tone of the Tientsin forces and the Kwantung Army enabled General Doihara to cajole General Ching into another "local" agreement which expelled the Kuomintang and all Nationalist troops from Chahar. Together, the Ching-Doihara and Ho-Umezu accords erased all overt symbols of central government in the provinces of Hopei and Chahar.

NEW CHINA POLICY

The activities of the field armies in North China propelled the Nanking government into a renewed effort to open formal negotiations on the projected Sino-Japanese Treaty of Friendship. On June 17, the Chinese ambassador reviewed the principles outlined by Wang Ch'ung-hui and reiterated the willingness of the Nationalist government to sign a friendship

---

[74] *Nihon gaikō nenpyō,* II, 294.

[75] Hata Ikuhito, "Umezu Ka Ō-kin kyōtei keii" [Particulars of the Ho-Umezu Agreement], *Aziya kenkyū,* IV, 2 (1957), 65-114.

treaty which would incorporate his stipulations—namely, equality between the two nations, a pledge to support the abrogation of the unequal treaties, and a denial of any forms of assistance to "local" governments in North China.[76] Foreign Minister Hirota assured Ambassador Chiang that these proposals were being given careful consideration, but, of necessity, the Japanese government would need some time before it could reach an official decision. In order to devise an appropriate response to the Chinese offer of a treaty to be based on Wang's three principles, Vice-Foreign Minister Shigemitsu, on June 27, called a special staff meeting.[77] The conference opened on a sour note, Kuwashima Kazuo's complaint that the foreign ministry could not possibly formulate a China policy until it knew the specific intentions of the army authorities. After conceding the validity of this statement, Shigemitsu insisted, "Today, we must first decide the policy of the foreign ministry."[78] The vice-foreign minister then identified two axioms which should prevail in any policy towards the continent: (1) Sino-Japanese negotiations must always exclude the participation of any third major power; and (2) the responsibility for maintaining peace and stability in East Asia belonged exclusively to Japan, Manchukuo, and China.

Without directly quarreling with this professorial presentation, the head of the Asian Affairs Bureau, Kuwashima Kazuo, blandly asserted that, in the present context, the only type of treaty which the foreign ministry could honestly offer the Nanking government would require a *de jure* recognition of Manchukuo. Since this stipulation would be "asking too much" of Chiang Kai-shek, Tani Masayuki preferred some type of diplomatic accommodation which would confirm the *status quo* in North China, imply a *de facto* recognition of Man-

[76] JMFA, *Teikoku no taiShi*, IV, "TaiShi seisaku no unyō ni tsuki sashiatari torubeki sochi hi kansuru ken" [Measures for the Implementation of Japan's China Policy], June 24, 1935.

[77] JMFA, *Teikoku no taiShi*, IV, "TaiShi seisaku tōgikai yōroku" [Summary of a China Policy Meeting], June 29, 1935. Attending were Shigemitsu, Kuwashima, Morishima, Kamimura, Kuriyama, and Tani.

[78] *Ibid.*, 4.

chukuo, and include a public profession of the common cultural heritage shared by China and Japan, as well as the existence of a common strategic concern—the Soviet Union. A diplomatic agreement along these lines, Tani declared, would be acceptable to the war ministry because the army's latest actions in North China were inspired by a belief that "the government of Chiang Kai-shek would not be helpful in a future war with the Soviet Union."[79] Although the Kwantung army was planning to establish a strong military base in North China, judged Tani, "there is no ambition in the army to absorb North China."[80] After muffling the reservations of Kuwashima, the vice-minister seconded Tani's remarks; and the assembled group articulated a specific approach to the forthcoming negotiations with the Nationalist government. In particular, they list three guidelines—namely, (1) Japan should avoid a commitment to a comprehensive treaty, recommending, instead, that the Chinese government should be asked to prove its sincerity by settling specific issues one by one; (2) Japan should avoid listing the full extent of its demands in order to prevent problems comparable to those which had been provoked by the Twenty-one Demands; and (3) Japan should "scold" the Nationalist government into an acknowledgment of the preeminent position of the Imperial government in East Asia.[81]

After formulating what the foreign ministry believed to be the most judicious approach to the China problem, the diplomats directed their attention to a subject of equal concern, the strategy to govern their negotiations with the staff of the war ministry. The most effective ploy, reasoned Tani Masayuki, would be an emphasis on the army's long-range plans which marked the Soviet Union as the primary problem confronting the Imperial army. Pursuing this suggestion, Shigemitsu declared that the foreign ministry would inform the army authorities as follows:

> To step forward into Inner and Outer Mongolia through North China would only endanger the success of this ad-

[79] *Ibid.*, 11.   [80] *Ibid.*   [81] *Ibid.*, 12.

vance. Moreover, in view of the plans for future operations against the Soviet Union, it would be a mistake to slight the economic development of Japan's interests in Central and South China. Preparations for the Soviet operations would be achieved most effectively by concentrating on Inner Mongolia. The questions of North, Central, and South China and the Manchukuo-China problem should be given secondary emphasis.[82]

If Chiang Kai-shek would permit the Japanese army to construct airfields and wireless stations in North China and to improve the railway facilities in these provinces, concluded the vice-foreign minister, the cardinal desires of the army would be satisfied; and, in turn, the war ministry would not oppose a *modus vivendi* with the Nanking government.

The details of the inter-ministerial discussions of the China problem are still enveloped in a fog of uncertainty. Kuwashima Kazuo testified at the Tokyo International Military Tribunal that the war, foreign, and naval ministries reached a policy consensus as early as July 2, 1935, which approved the quest for a rapprochement with the Nationalist government.[83] In one sense, this testimony was correct, but it failed to clarify the qualified manner in which Shigemitsu's strategy had been approved by the army authorities. On July 20, for example, the "China Policy" advanced by General Nagata's staff maintained that peace and stability in East Asia could not be realized without friendly Sino-Japanese relations.[84] Nevertheless, insisted this presentation of the war ministry, friendly relations with China would be contingent on three developments: a willingness on the part of the Nationalist government (1) to exercise effective control over all anti-Japanese activities throughout China, (2) to sever its economic reliance on the Western powers, and (3) to integrate the Chinese

---

82 *Ibid.*, 9-10.   83 IMTFE, *Exhibit 3241.*

84 JMFA, *Teikoku no taiShi*, IV, "TaiShi seisaku ni kan suru ken" [Concerning Our China Policy], Gunmkyoku tai-an [Plan of the Bureau of Military Affairs], July 20, 1935, page 3.

economy with that of Japan and Manchukuo. Since these objectives could not be attained immediately, the war ministry's policy outlined three practical steps by which friendly Sino-Japanese relations could be promoted—namely, (1) some type of recognition of Manchukuo by the Nanking government; (2) the creation of a "special" economic and cultural relationship between North China and Manchukuo; and (3) a China-Japan-Manchukuo military pact to check Soviet penetration into Outer Mongolia. Above all, persisted the army's presentation, "until Chinese signs of friendship become more tangible, Japan must not negotiate a general treaty calling for Sino-Japanese cooperation, even if such an agreement were to be phrased in terms of 'a mutual respect of independence and cooperation.' "[85]

This adamant objection to any premature *modus vivendi* which might strengthen the position of the Kuomintang in North China was also voiced by the Tientsin garrison's "Plan for the Economic Exploitation of North China, in Conjunction with the Birth of a New Political Arrangement in North China."[86] Citing the May 14th decision of the Kwantung and Tientsin staffs to assemble as much capital as possible for investment in North China, this plan indicated that the army's capital accumulation and investment program would by-pass existing Japanese concerns in North China in favor of projects which would directly contribute to the "national defense" of the empire. In particular, the funds would be invested in the improvement of railroads, airports, harbor facilities, and coal mining. Although "other Japanese investors will be permitted to invest in whatever they like," the war and finance ministries would, in order to prevent "unreasonable" competition, control civilian investment in North China by means of the "Economic Exploitative Committee of North China."[87] Ideally, observed the field army, this economic developmental program

[85] *Ibid.*, 3.
[86] *Kahoku mondai*, "HokuShi shinseiken no hassei ni tomonau keizai keihatsu shidō-an," June 29, 1935.
[87] *Ibid.*

would be implemented by the creation of combined Japanese-Chinese-Manchurian business enterprises. If the Nationalist government were to oppose this pattern of investment, "we will work through local enterprises and wait for a better opportunity."[88] Naturally, concluded this economic policy, we will call for the "preservation of the open door policy," while, at the same time, systematically eliminating the influence of the foreign powers in North China.[89]

Subject to attainment of the economic objectives defined by the Tientsin garrison and the vital diplomatic reservations voiced by the war ministry's China policy, the army authorities were not opposed to a diplomacy which aspired to effect a *modus vivendi* with the Nanking government. In the closing weeks of July, the staffs of the foreign and war ministries met "in strict secrecy"; and, by August 4, they had devised a policy which would satisfy the army's interests in North China and the desires of the diplomats for formal negotiations with the Chinese government.[90] Specifically, this consensus held that the foreign ministry should try to promote friendly relations with China, but on the understanding that any treaty would have to be based on three principles— (1) the cessation of anti-Japanese movements in China, (2) a *de facto* recognition of Manchukuo, and (3) a military pact to combat the Bolshevik menace in Outer Mongolia. These three conditions, judged Foreign Minister Hirota, could be met by a series of specific agreements which would signify "the beginning of relations" between China and Manchukuo, commit the local governments "in the province of Chahar and the North China area" to a recognition of Manchukuo, and yield some declaration of joint military cooperation in "Chahar and the districts bordering on Outer Mongolia."[91] By August 4, the war and foreign ministries had

---

88 *Ibid.*   89 *Ibid.*

90 IMTFE, *Defense Document 2216*. This is a cable from Foreign Minister Hirota to his ambassador in China, advising him of these conversations.

91 *Ibid.*

formulated a China policy which superficially masked the contradictory approach and objectives of the two ministries.

It is noteworthy that the consensus reached on the 4th of August closely resembled a mediating proposal advanced by the naval authorities. On August 3, the naval ministry circulated its conception of Japan's "China Policy."[92] Postulating the stability of East Asia to be the main national objective, this estimate contained several dictums to guide the government's approach to the China tangle: (1) "Japan will not meddle in the domestic affairs of China, especially in terms of the centralization movement; but, if China relies on other countries, Japan will adopt actions to counter this trait"; (2) China should promote friendly relations "by making itself independent of the European countries and the United States, and by strengthening her police force against anti-Japanese movements"; (3) Japan should promote economic, cultural, and military ties with China; (4) Japan must compel China to abandon her negative attitude toward Manchukuo and to allow "close economic and cultural relationships" between North China and Manchukuo; (5) Japan must unite with China, at least in North China and Inner Mongolia, in order to halt Soviet aggression in Outer Mongolia; (6) after China has demonstrated its sincerity, Japan should negotiate a treaty based on the principle of "mutual independence and cooperation among Japan, Manchukuo, and China"; and (7) in trying to stabilize the East Asian scene, Japan must "carefully observe international conditions."[93] The reflections of the naval ministry were, in effect, a polite warning that the army should not be intractable in its approach to North China, if only because the major sea powers had extensive rights in North China which could not be flaunted.

Since the naval and foreign ministries wished to explore the possibility of a rapprochement with the Nationalist govern-

[92] JMFA, *Teikoku no taiShi*, "Shina seisaku," Kaigunshō gunmukyoku [Bureau of Naval Affairs], August 3, 1935.
[93] *Ibid.*

ment, the war ministry, on August 4, had deferred to this opinion, providing the *status quo* in North China would not be compromised in any way. This consensus, however, was soon dissolved by four developments: the murder of General Nagata Tetsuzan on August 12 and the subsequent resignation of War Minister Hayashi; the September 5th publication of the war ministry's *Japan and the Period of Change in the International Situation*; the September 7th proposals of Chiang Kaishek; and the September 24th press conference of General Tada Shun, the newly appointed commanding officer of the Tientsin garrison.

Commitment to an Autonomous North China

On August 14, Lt. Colonel Aizawa Saburo visited the war ministry and, after gaining admittance to General Nagata's office, literally hacked the chief of the Bureau of Military Affairs to death. This shocking murder of a superior officer understandably generated some concern in central headquarters, particularly when the Supreme War Council, at the insistence of Generals Araki and Mazaki, ruled that the war minister should atone for the embarrassment which Nagata's slaughter brought upon the Imperial army—that is, General Hayashi should be forced to resign his portfolio. The bloody deed of Colonel Aizawa and the ruling of the Supreme War Council were related to a bitter factional dispute in central headquarters, a subject which will be considered subsequently.[94] Here, it should be noted that, immediately prior to Nagata's assassination, the war ministry had sanctioned a China policy which approved the search for a *modus vivendi* based upon the *status quo* in North China. With the appointment of General Kuwashima as war minister in September 1935, however, the field armies and the new minister of war redefined the army's policy in North China in ways which eventually precluded any type of diplomatic accommodation with the Nationalist government.

Parallel with the uncertainties unleashed by the forced res-

[94] Chapter v, 266-267.

ignation of General Hayashi, the army published, on the 5th of September, its second major pamphlet designed to educate the Japanese public to the problems confronting the nation— *Japan and the Period of Change in the International Situation.*[95] Judging history to be nothing but the "rise and fall of nations," this pamphlet endorsed the views of Professor Simmond's *The Price of Peace*—namely, the world was bifurcated into two categories of nations, the "haves" and the "have-nots." Since Japan, with its limited natural resources, tiny islands, and a burgeoning population problem, was a "have-not" country, the European powers and the United States should, in the judgment of the army, either provide her with adequate land or at least permit Japanese immigration. Unfortunately, Japan was unable to rely on the help of the Occidental countries in its efforts to become a "have" nation. Furthermore, continued the pamphlet, as the distinguished American journalist Walter Lippmann had cogently indicated, since Great Britain no longer could assume responsibility for protecting the interests of the Western powers in the Far East, this task would have to be borne by the United States. In effect, this meant the United States would confront Japan, and, given the current American program of naval construction, thus posed a grave security threat to the empire. "By 1939, Japan's navy will be 63% [of the size] of the American fleet . . . [and] it is doubtful whether the United States will then remain silent regarding the Far Eastern situation. In this eventuality, China is very likely to start anti-Japanese agitations."[96] Apart from this worry, added the army version of the international situation, Japan faced the ideological and security menace of the Soviet Union. In order to prepare for the dangers raised by the American fleet and the Soviet army, Japan would, of course, have to increase its national defenses.

Turning its gaze toward China, the army's analysis adopted a

[95] USDS, Archives, *Japan: Military Affairs*, 894.20/147, is a translation of this publication.
[96] *Ibid.*, 14.

patronizing tone. Chiang Kai-shek controlled "only eight of twenty-four provinces"; and he was unable to crush the Chinese Communist movement or to prevent the Soviet Union from "taking over" Outer Mongolia and Tibet. This was indeed a sad and dangerous state of affairs, because "if the Communists should establish their headquarters in Szechuan province," the entire northwestern part of China would be Bolshevized.[97] This possibility threatened the "status of China," as well as the security of the Japanese empire. Consequently, Japan could not remain passive and allow the Nationalist government to continue its mistaken foreign policy of relying on the Western powers. If present trends continued, declared the army voice, "Japan will be obliged to beat her [China] into a realization of the situation."[98] This need not be necessary, concluded the army's presentation, if the foreign powers would only set aside "their mistaken idea of Asia as a colony and adopt a policy of recognizing Asia for the Asiatics."[99]

Two days after this public airing of the army's view of the changing world scene, the Chinese ambassador, Chiang Tso-ping, advised Foreign Minister Hirota that Chiang Kai-shek was personally prepared to negotiate a Sino-Japanese Friendship Treaty.[100] Such an accord, though, would have to reflect three principles: respect for the independence of China, willingness to sign a non-aggression pact, and a commitment to settle all disputes by peaceful means. Lest there be any mis-understanding of Chiang Kai-shek's position, the Chinese ambassador translated it into specific proposals—namely, the aboli-tion of all unequal treaties, support for the centralization of China under the Kuomintang, and the preclusion of any more "local" agreements between provincial Chinese officials and officers of the Japanese army. If Japan were to accept these rec-ommendations, continued Ambassador Chiang, there would be no need to continue the existing Shanghai and Tangku Truce

[97] *Ibid.*, 17.   [98] *Ibid.*, 22.   [99] *Ibid.*

[100] JMFA, *Teikoku no taiShi*, VI, "Hirota daijin Sho taishi Sho kairoku dai ni kai" [Minutes of the Second Conversation Between Foreign Minis-ter Hirota and Chiang's Ambassador Chiang], September 7, 1935.

agreements; and the two countries could restore the North China scene to the conditions which prevailed before September 18, 1931. In return for an acceptance of these proposals, the Chinese ambassador reported that Chiang Kai-shek would personally "conclude an economic treaty" with the Japanese government; and, once the desired changes in North China were consummated, Chiang would "even negotiate about military problems."[101] In effect, the Chinese government was suggesting a *quid pro quo*, a *de facto* recognition of Manchukuo in exchange for Japanese support of the Kuomintang in North China. Foreign Minister Hirota professed a sincere interest in the principles and proposals submitted by Chiang Kai-shek; and he terminated the interview with the observation that the Japanese government would consider them carefully before offering an official reply.

Eleven days later, on September 18, Hirota assured the Chinese ambassador that Japan "sympathized completely" with the principles enumerated by Chiang Kai-shek. Still, it would be unwise of Chiang, at this time, to make a desperate effort to restore Sino-Japanese relations to the *status quo ante* of the Mukden crisis."[102] Nevertheless, Hirota said that the Japanese government was anxious to promote amiable relations with China on the basis of Chiang's principles; and, he added somewhat prematurely, "Japan would be prepared to strive for the abolition of the truce agreements governing North China." The foreign minister concluded the conversation with the reflection: "The enforcement of Chiang's three principles and the abolition of the truce agreements are essential to the creation of friendly Sino-Japanese relations. In order to resolve these matters eventually, however, it is necessary to make some preliminary efforts to work out specific means by

101 *Ibid.*, 10-11.
102 JMFA, *Teikoku no taiShi*, VI, "Sho taishi dainiji kaidan ni tsuku suru daijin ōshū shin-an" [Summary of the Foreign Minister's Reply to the Second Conversation with Chiang's Ambassador], September 18, 1935, page 4.

which these issues can be settled."[103] For the benefit of his staff, Hirota translated this cryptic statement as follows: "Preliminary effort means determining our China policy in cooperation with the war and naval ministries."[104]

The difficulties in handling this inter-ministerial nettle were only increased by a public pronouncement by General Tada Shun. As part of its public service program, the war ministry had, in 1934, issued the *Basic Theory of National Defense*; and, a year later, it analyzed the changing state of international affairs. Since the North China issue also merited public attention, the newspaper section of the war ministry, in mid-September, offered a chosen number of reporters an opportunity to tour the Peking-Tientsin district. Through the courtesy of the army air corps, the press representatives were flown to Tientsin and General Tada Shun made the excursion eminently newsworthy with a flamboyant public statement. After echoing the recent pamphlet on Japan's position in the world, Tada focused his indictment of the Western powers and the Nanking government through the prism of the army's North China policy. The only real solution to the problems of Asia, declared Tada, would be a complete emancipation of all Oriental peoples from the "yoke of the white race."[105] Because the Kuomintang, and Chiang Kai-shek in particular, were currying the favor of the Occidental nations, "they were foreign lackeys, enemies of the Chinese race." On behalf of the Imperial army, Tada concluded his press statement with a personal appeal to "Chinese patriots" to cooperate with Japan in a sincere effort to create a "paradise in North China." This caricature of Chiang Kai-shek and invitation to the provincial Chinese authorities to launch an autonomous movement were, of course, prominently displayed in the Chinese and Japanese press, thereby rendering the recent diplomatic assurances of Foreign Minister Hirota meaningless.

It is difficult to determine whether this press conference was

103 *Ibid.*, 6.   104 *Ibid.*
105 Thomas A. Bisson, *Japan in China* (New York, 1941), 70.

deliberately arranged by the army authorities in order to structure the "preliminary efforts" of the war, foreign, and naval ministries to formulate an official response to Chiang Kai-shek's latest proposals according to the terms of the army's North China policy. Still, on September 20, the Inner Cabinet had ordered the bureau chiefs of the three ministries to draft a counterproposal to the principles articulated by Chiang; and four days later the Tada press conference was executed with care.[106] Moreover, when the Inner Cabinet met on the 28th of September, War Minister Kuwashima was unprecedentedly accompanied by the senior officers directly responsible for the army's North China policy—Generals Okamura and Nishio of the war ministry and the general staff and Generals Tada and Isogaya of the Tientsin garrison. Here, Kuwashima presented a policy guide which the foreign minister aptly termed "The Specific Contents of Japan's Basic China Policy: First of All, to Make the Five Provinces of North China Independent."[107] After listening to the policy of the war minister, the captive audience agreed "in principle" with the goal defined by General Kuwashima; and the cabinet indicated a willingness to approve preliminary efforts by the army to mobilize Chinese officials behind an autonomous movement. Despite the silent bodyguards of the war minister and the tone of the army's North China program, however, neither the foreign nor the naval minister would sanction the use of force in this undertaking, citing the implications this would have vis-à-vis the major sea powers. Nevertheless, a week later, on October 4, the Inner Cabinet officially approved two policies: (1) the encouragement of local governments in the provinces of North China; and (2) the conducting of the Sino-Japanese negotiations on the basis of the three principles adopted on August 5 by the staffs of the war,

[106] JMFA, *Teihoku no taiShi*, IV, Cable 687 (September 21, 1935), Foreign Minister Hirota to all consulates in China.

[107] JMFA, *Teikoku no taiShi*, IV, "TaiShi konpon seisaku no gutaiteki naiyō: mazu, hokuShi goshō no dokuritsu kosaku," undated. The substance of this document indicates it was written between October 8 and October 10, 1935.

naval and foreign ministries—namely, a cessation of anti-Japanese activities, a recognition of Manchukuo, and an anti-Comintern pact.[108]

Hirota's Three Principles

The staff of the foreign ministry was somewhat dismayed by this directive of the Inner Cabinet. Still, as Hirota reminded his subordinates, the decision to promote local governments in North China was only a reaffirmation of the cabinet's decision of December 7, 1934. In addition, the foreign minister suggested that his staff should view the cabinet's approval of the three principles and the army's approach to the North China problem as complementary decisions.

> In carrying out the present policy, we can capitalize on the political situation in China by playing the provincial and central governments against one another. Besides, it is not our aim to do this with the specific purpose of promoting or interfering with the process of unification or decentralization in China. Our objective is to negotiate a Sino-Japanese understanding based on the three principles adopted by the Imperial government.[109]

To this end, Hirota formally notified the Chinese ambassador, on October 4, that Japan was prepared to negotiate a Sino-Japanese Friendship Treaty. In lieu of the principles advanced by Wang Ch'ung-hui and Chiang Kai-shek, however, the foreign minister thought that the discussions should be predicated on three alternate principles— (1) the suppression of anti-Japanese movements; (2) some type of recognition of Manchukuo; and (3) a military agreement to combat the Soviet menace in Outer Mongolia.[110] Needless to say, Hirota made no allusions

---

[108] *Ibid.*, IV, "Kankei daijin ryōkai ni tai suru fuzoku bunsho" [Attached Document Indicating the Understanding of the Ministers], October 4, 1935. Also IMTFE, *Defense Document 2218* (Hirota cable of October 4, 1935).

[109] *Ibid.*

[110] *Nihon gaikō nenpyō*, 304. On the origins of these three principles, also see IMTFE, *Proceedings*, 29620-29629; *Exhibit 3241*; and *Defense Document 2023*.

to the other dimension of Japan's China policy, the intensification of the army's endeavors to promote "local" governments in North China.

Although the Japanese foreign minister had restricted his remarks to the desirability of a Sino-Japanese accord based upon Japan's three principles, the vivid language of General Tada and the Ho-Umezu and Ching-Doihara agreements had conveyed the gist of the army's ambitions in North China. The transparent discrepancy between the foreign minister's assurances that Japan really wished a rapprochement with the Nationalist government and the words and deeds of the field army created an impression of a "dual diplomacy." The belief that the army was pursuing an independent policy in North China at odds with the official national policy was shared by most foreign diplomats; and it has been incorporated into many historical appraisals of Japanese foreign policy. At best, this interpretation is a half-truth. The decision to promote "local" governments in North China had been officially formulated in the fall of 1933, confirmed in December 1934, and reaffirmed on October 4, 1935. Indeed, the term "dual diplomacy" distressed the army authorities almost as much as it did the Nationalist government. This sentiment was ventilated in mid-October when Morishima Morito of the foreign ministry, Captain Honda of the naval ministry, and General Okamura of the war ministry were despatched to Darien to brief the field officers on the proposed Sino-Japanese discussion.

At this Darien Conference of October 16-18, the spokesman for the three ministries explained why the government preferred to rely on Hirota's three principles in order to effect some type of formal diplomatic agreement with the Nanking government.[111] The assembled officers, however, complained that this policy failed to articulate the "unstated fourth prin-

111 JMFA, *Teikoku no taiShi*, IV, "Okamura shōshō raidan yōryō" [Gist of the Interview with Major General Okamura], October 18, 1935. The senior officers attending this conference were Generals Isogaya (the Peking attaché), Furushō (chief of staff, Kwantung Army), and Itagaki (vice-chief of staff, Kwantung Army).

ciple" of the cabinet's decision of October 4—namely, that the unification of China by the Kuomintang was neither desirable nor necessary. To prevent any misconceptions about this principle in the forthcoming diplomatic negotiations, the field officers wanted this "fourth principle" incorporated into the official cabinet decision, rather than remaining "a verbal understanding" among the war, naval, and foreign ministers. "After all," insisted General Okamura, "it is predictable that Chiang Kai-shek will persist in his negative attitude until he is driven to the wall. . . . Japan must, for the time being, maintain her policy based on the spirit of positive force."[112] Obviously, the army authorities had interpreted the October 4th decision from a different perspective than that of Foreign Minister Hirota. With "the spirit of positive force," the Tientsin garrison and the Kwantung Army intended to subvert the authority of the Nanking government in North China, while the foreign ministry was trying to commit Chiang Kai-shek to a Sino-Japanese Friendship Treaty.

The Darien Conference demonstrated that the dual aspects of the cabinet's decision of October 4 were not, as Hirota contended, complementary policies. After the Darien Conference, the field armies intensified their pressure on the provincial Chinese authorities, focusing their attention on Generals Yin Ju-keng and Sung Che-yuan. This covert organization of an "independence" movement apparently convinced Chiang Kai-shek that he would have to intervene directly in North China, lest the Japanese army impose another "local" agreement which might openly separate the provinces of North China from the central government. At least, on November 7, Consul General Suma reported that the activities of the army in North China were, in the Shanghai area, being blamed on the "pro-Japanese" members of the Kuomintang and "many prominent Chinese politicians who are in favor of negotiating with Japan are being

[112] *Ibid.*, 6.

forced to resign from important positions."[113] Chiang Kai-shek was not unreceptive to Japan's three principles, judged Suma; but popular resentment of the developments in North China would eventually compel Chiang to "oppose openly the Japanese policy."[114] This possibility was especially credible, added Suma, because Ambassador Chiang Tso-ping had informed Chiang Kai-shek on November 5 of the personal assurances by "War Minister Kuwashima and Finance Minister Takahashi that Japan would never resort to open aggression of North China."[115] The validity of this vital piece of information was communicated to Ambassador Ariyoshi on November 18 when Foreign Minister Hirota recapitulated the "new consensus" which had just been reached between the war and foreign ministries—namely, (1) although the field armies were not reluctant to risk a "showdown" with the Nationalist army, the war ministry appreciated the fact that Chiang would move his army into North China if an "independent North China movement" were organized; and (2) the war ministry would order the field armies to avoid the "actual use of force" in its handling of the North China scene.[116] Hirota added in a supplementary cable to Ariyoshi: "To stimulate an autonomous or independent North China hastily would [only] prevent the Nanking government from working out some proper measures. This view, not to mention that of the naval ministry, was accepted by the staff of the war ministry."[117]

A New Arrangement for North China

Concurrently with the imposition of the restraining hands of the foreign, war, and naval ministers on the actions and plans

[113] JMFA, *Teikoku no taiShi*, v, Consul General Suma (Nanking) Cable 1227 (four parts), November 7, 1935. Part II.
[114] *Ibid.*
[115] *Teikoku no taiShi*, v, Consul General Suma (Nanking), Cable 1222, November 7, 1935.
[116] *Ibid.*, Foreign Minister Hirota, Cables 302-304, November 18, 1935, to Ambassador Ariyoshi.
[117] *Ibid.*, Foreign Minister Hirota, Cable 306, November 18, 1935, to Ambassador Ariyoshi.

of the field armies, Chiang Kai-shek, on November 20, professed a willingness to continue the Sino-Japanese negotiations, as well as his admiration of the three principles enunciated by Foreign Minister Hirota. "Still," noted Chiang, "if any incident occurs in North China, it would raise a condition which would preclude any discussion of Hirota's three principles."[118] The generalissimo followed this carrot-and-stick statement with another attempt to reassert the fragile authority of the central government in North China.

The Chinese minister of war, General Ho Ying-ching, was despatched to Peking; and, on his arrival, Chiang Kai-shek notified Ambassador Ariyoshi that he was willing to begin formal discussions of a Sino-Japanese agreement to be based on Hirota's three principles, if the Japanese government would allow General Ho to stabilize the situation in North China by organizing a new administrative system for the provinces of Chahar and Hopei. Despite Ariyoshi's warm endorsement of Chiang's proposal, Foreign Minister Hirota, on November 22, responded, "In accord with the views of the war ministry, it is extremely doubtful whether Chiang Kai-shek honestly hopes to stabilize the political situation in the provinces of North China."[119] Consequently, Ambassador Ariyoshi was advised that, for the time being, Japan must "somehow or other" exercise its influence in North China, because any other approach would "result in making Chiang Kai-shek lazy in his efforts to work out proper measures for the handling of the North China situation."[120] Instead of a new arrangement headed by Ho Ying-ching, concluded Hirota, the war, naval, and foreign ministers believed "it will be best to let Sung Che-yuan issue a mild self-government declaration."[121]

[118] *Ibid.*, VI, "Shinagawa wa ware-ho sangensoku ni sani o arawashitari" [Indications of China's Approval of Our Three Principles], Memo dated January 20, 1936. It reviews the substance of Ambassador Ariyoshi's conference with Chiang Kai-shek on November 20, 1935.

[119] *Ibid.*, V, Foreign Minister Hirota, Cable 313, November 22, 1935, to Ambassador Ariyoshi.

[120] *Ibid.*   [121] *Ibid.*

After exploratory talks with the Chinese officials, Ariyoshi reported that a "mild" declaration by General Sung would not provoke any serious difficulties in Nanking.[122] The ambassador also stressed that if the Japanese army were to generate an autonomous movement by forceful means, "it is predictable" that this would preclude any peaceful solution of the North China situation. "Thus, before establishing any self-government," concluded Ariyoshi, "it is imperative that Chiang's current attitude be recognized; and it is vital that our war department avoid any steps involving the utilization of force."[123] Fortunately, the considered opinion of the Japanese ambassador in Nanking received a respectful hearing in the Inner Cabinet. On November 25, the Okada cabinet officially confirmed the policy which the war, naval, and foreign ministries had articulated three days earlier: Japan would discuss a Sino-Japanese accord on the basis of Hirota's three principles; and the crisis in North China would be settled by the creation of a "mild" autonomous government under General Sung Che-yuan.

Directly after this cabinet decision, Hirota advised Ariyoshi that the government had finally agreed to the recommendations of the foreign ministry. "At last," sighed Foreign Minister Hirota, the war ministry was officially committed to a policy which would enable the embassy in Nanking and the field army in North China "to cooperate and carry out our policy effectively."[124] The following morning, on November 26, when the substance of this accord was revealed, Hirota notified Ambassador Ariyoshi that he should, in his conversations with Chiang Kai-shek, "keep the discussion of the autonomy matter and the three principles separate because, generally speaking, the self-government matter is an internal Chinese problem."[125] At the moment, judged Hirota, it would be a serious mistake

[122] *Teikoku no taiShi*, v, Ambassador Ariyoshi, Cable 995, November 23, 1935, to Foreign Minister Hirota.
[123] *Ibid.*
[124] *Ibid.*, Foreign Minister Hirota, Cable 314, November 25, 1935, to Ambassador Ariyoshi.
[125] *Ibid.*, Foreign Minister Hirota, Cable 316, November 26, 1935, to Ambassador Ariyoshi.

for the Chinese government to send any Kuomintang political figures to North China.

> To establish new organizations, such as the Political Affairs Committee and the Military Department Committee proposed by Chiang Kai-shek, would only complicate the situation. It is preferable that the Nanking government trust the leading figures in North China. The subject of our three principles, on the other hand, is a matter which, by all means, should be negotiated between the two countries.[126]

Although he was unable to commit the Japanese government to any formal agreement governing North China, Chiang Kai-shek still insisted that any self-government declaration affecting Hopei and Chahar should, at least, be issued by the Nanking government. Overruling the dissenting voice of the war minister, the Okada cabinet conceded this point; and, on December 12, the Nationalist government issued a mandate which created the Hopei-Chahar Political Council under the chairmanship of General Sung Che-yuan. And the Chinese officials reassured the American ambassador that the new council "more or less" accorded with the wishes of the Kuomintang.[127] This tortuous rendition of the establishment of the Hopei-Chahar Political Council, however, could not mask the fact that the Japanese army had drastically curtailed the authority and prestige of the Nanking government in the provinces of North China.

The subversive accomplishments of the Tientsin garrison in Hope and Chahar were matched by those of the Kwantung Army in the province of Jehol. In 1933, under the terms of the Tangku Truce, a demilitarized zone had been formed in East Hopei. General Yin Ju-keng had served as the responsible Chinese administrator in this zone; and, subjected to the persuasive maneuvers of the Kwantung troops in Jehol and the bribes of the Special Service Agency of the general staff,

126 *Ibid.*
127 *Foreign Relations, 1935,* III, 486.

General Yin, on November 24, issued a proclamation establishing the East Hopei Anti-Communist Autonomous Council. In this, Yin charged that the disastrous foreign and fiscal policies of the Nanking government were subjecting China to the "terrors of communism"; and he declared that the new government in East Hopei would be "independent" of the Nanking regime.[128] In addition, General Yin heralded the East Hopei Anti-Communist Autonomous Council as the first step along the road to an eventual federation of the provinces of North China.

ANOTHER CONSENSUS ON JAPAN'S CHINA POLICY

The political intrigues of the field armies in North China in the fall of 1935 fatally compromised the efforts of the foreign ministry to commit Chiang Kai-shek to some type of *modus vivendi* with the Japanese government. The irreconcilable policies and aspirations underlying the diplomacy of the two governments did not, however, openly emerge in the negotiations of December 1935. When Ambassador Ariyoshi conferred with Chiang Kai-shek on the 20th of December, the generalissimo courteously avoided any discussion of the projected Sino-Japanese Friendship Treaty, referring Ariyoshi to newly appointed Chinese Foreign Minister Chang Chung.[129] The implication of this evasion was not lost on the Japanese ambassador, who reported, on December 26, that the East Hopei Anti-Communist Autonomous Council and the Hopei-Chahar Political Council had not quashed Chinese suspicions of the Imperial army. Although the army authorities might "in their hearts" sincerely wish to stabilize North China, complained Ariyoshi, "the Tientsin and Kwantung Armies oppose our talk with the central government with the contention that these talks will retard or check the autonomous organizations."[130]

[128] Borg, *Far Eastern Crisis of 1933-1938*, 160.

[129] JMFA, *Teikoku no taiShi*, VI, "Shinagawa wa ware-ho. . . ," *op.cit.* Also, *ibid.*, V, Ambassador Ariyoshi, Cable 1040, December 21, 1935, to Foreign Minister Hirota.

[130] *Ibid.*, V, Ambassador Ariyoshi, Cable 1064, December 26, 1935, to Foreign Minister Hirota.

Personally, Ariyoshi questioned the feasibility of "successfully creating any autonomous organization" for North China; and, after his brief conversation with Chiang on the 19th, he requested some new "instructions on this matter, because, in order to negotiate with Nanking, it is necessary to make some proper proposals."[131]

The suspicion that Chiang Kai-shek would elude any formal diplomatic accommodation was not abated by the conversation between the Chinese ambassador and Vice-Foreign Minister Shigemitsu on December 28, which did not diverge from a vague dialogue on the subject, "How good Sino-Japanese relations could be established under the present circumstances."[132] At this meeting, Ambassador Chiang professed a sincere wish to contribute to a new relationship between the two countries and he inquired whether Shigemitsu had any "specific proposals" to offer. "Japan has left the League of Nations," responded the vice-foreign minister, "and she is in a position to bring about a fine political situation in Asia. I wonder if China will try to stabilize the Asian political situation. . . . China need only accept the three principles advanced by Foreign Minister Hirota in order to contribute to the peace of Asia."[133] The dialogue went no further, as Ambassador Chiang simply expressed his appreciation of the candid reflections of the Japanese vice-foreign minister.

The official Chinese attitude toward Hirota's three principles was displayed on January 6, 1936, by Foreign Minister Chang Chung. In his interview with Ambassador Ariyoshi, the Chinese foreign minister stated that Chiang Kai-shek was completely opposed to any "impossible diplomatic negotiations."[134] In particular, he notified the Japanese ambassador that friendly

[131] *Ibid.*

[132] *Ibid.*, v, Memo 175 of the First Department of the Bureau of East Asian Affairs, December 28, 1935.

[133] *Ibid.*

[134] *Ibid.*, vi, Ambassador Ariyoshi, Cable 5, January 7, 1936, to Foreign Minister Hirota.

Sino-Japanese relations were contingent on a reasonable solution to the North China problem:

> The Nanking government cannot carry out its North China policy without the cooperation of Japan. Given the present circumstances in North China, every institution designed to link North China and the central government should be encouraged. There is no alternative to the establishment of special institutions which have the purpose of uniting North China and the central government. This policy will be implemented, taking into consideration the understanding of Japan.[135]

Confronted by this posture, the Japanese foreign ministry was obliged to reevaluate the China policy of the Imperial government.

On January 8, 1936, the department heads of the foreign ministry assembled in the office of the vice-foreign minister to clarify the issues posed by the latest statement of the Chinese foreign minister. The Nationalist government, estimated Shigemitsu Mamoru, obviously "hopes to check the activities of the Japanese army in North China through formal diplomatic negotiations which include a discussion of Chiang Kai-shek's principles."[136] Somehow or other, insisted Shigemitsu, the Japanese government would have to frustrate this policy and commit China to a diplomatic agreement based on the principles set forth by Foreign Minister Hirota. After wrestling with this problem for some time, the diplomat believed the following approach would constitute the most adroit strategy: (1) "As a way to avoid such discussions, Japan should state that acceptance and implementation of Japan's three principles would inherently include the aims of the Chinese principles."

---

[135] *Ibid.*

[136] JMFA, *Teikoku no taiShi*, VIII, "Shōwa ju-ichi-nen ichigatsu yōka gaimudaijin heya ni okeru tōgi no kekka ni motozuku taiShi gaikō shian" [Proposals for Our China Policy Based upon the Results of the Discussions Held in the Office of the Foreign Minister], January 8, 1936, 1. Attending were Hirota, Shigemitsu, Morishima, Ōta, Kamimura, and Suma.

(2) Since it would be difficult to spell out the substance of Japan's proposal before any formal negotiations, Japan should simply say that "the details of implementing Japan's three principles should be discussed after China has accepted our three principles." (3) Once China had agreed "in principle" to Japan's stipulations, it would be easy "to abolish the Chinese proposals during the conference discussions."[137] After the foreign ministry staff had outlined this ideal resolution, Vice-Foreign Minister Shigemitsu declared that any Sino-Japanese negotiations would have to be based on the premise that the Nationalist government would concede the validity of the following contention: "Since the frontiers of North China border on Manchukuo, the affairs of North China have a close relationship with those of Japan. Thus, . . . it is natural that Japan give guidance and advice in the settlement of the North China problem."[138]

The last observation forced the assembled diplomats to leave the realm of what was desirable and face the obvious fact that it would not be feasible to negotiate a treaty of friendship while the Japanese army was spreading its tentacles throughout North China. Somewhat belatedly, Shigemitsu stated that in the present circumstances, it was very unlikely that Chiang Kai-shek would accept Hirota's three principles as the basis for a Sino-Japanese conference. After a few comments, it was judged that Japan should, for the present, "avoid any discussion of the North China problem with the Nanking government." Whenever Chiang requested a consideration of the truce agreements affecting North China, Japan, said Shigemitsu, "should inquire whether China would be willing to grant a *de jure* recognition of Manchukuo and to conclude various agreements designed to promote friendly relations between China and Manchukuo."[139] If Chiang were to seek a specific clarification of Hirota's three principles, Shigemitsu thought Japan should confess that these principles were more a matter of tone than of substance:

[137] *Ibid.*, 2-3.   [138] *Ibid.*, 4.
[139] *Ibid.*, 4.

They are based on a spirit of respect for the promotion of friendly Sino-Japanese relations. In this spirit, Japan will discuss various problems between the two countries. . . . However, because it is difficult to resolve all problems at one time, any attempt to reach a comprehensive settlement would, after all, only delay the establishment of cordial relations between the two nations.[140]

In effect, the staff of the foreign ministry concluded that the Japanese government could not, as originally hoped, commit the Nationalist government to a Sino-Japanese treaty based on the principles of a cessation of all anti-Japanese activities in China, a *de facto* recognition of Manchukuo, and an anti-Comintern military pact. Instead, the diplomats proposed to "persuade" the Nationalist government that it should settle particular problems in the "spirit of Hirota's three principles."

The newly revised diplomatic estimate of Japan's China policy conceded the improbability of any official accommodation with the Nationalist government. While this occasioned some feelings of regret, it also inspired the hope that the foreign ministry would now be able to coordinate its diplomacy with the policies and actions of the army. To this end, Morishima Gōrō, the head of the Asian Affairs Bureau, submitted a "private plan" to Colonel Kita of the war ministry which indicated the foreign ministry would now concentrate on the North China problem.[141] In order to commit the Kuomintang to an agreement which granted the necessity for extensive Japanese economic ties between Manchukuo and the provinces of North China, reasoned Morishima, the Imperial army would have to confine its activities in North China to the realm of economic infiltration. A program of economic subversion,

140 *Ibid.*, 5.
141 On Morishima's views and activities, see JMFA, *Teikoku no taiShi*, VIII, "Shina chūton gunreikan ni tai suru shisi" [Indications of the China Policy of the North China Army], January 16, 1938; and "Nankin seiken no NiShi Nankin kaigi teian ni tai suru ken" [Concerning the Proposed Meeting in Nanking by the Nanking Political Authorities], Sambō dainibu [G-2, Army General Staff], February 2, 1936.

judged Morishima, would not precipitate a major political crisis which, in turn, would compromise the efficacy of Japan's diplomacy vis-à-vis Nanking. Indeed, if the army authorities would guarantee the preclusion of any new political or military incidents in North China, Morishima stated that the China policy of the foreign ministry would be based on four suppositions: that the Nationalist government would eventually (1) negotiate a Sino-Japanese treaty; (2) accept the current political *status quo* in North China; (3) reorganize and possibly dissolve the Kuomintang; and (4) adopt a foreign policy which would solicit the friendship of Japan, not of the Anglo-American nations.

This proposal for a coordinated China policy dovetailed with the cabinet's policy, which precluded the open use of force in North China and called for the exclusion of the Kuomintang from the provinces of North China. Morishima's "private plan," of course, viewed the Nationalist government as the responsible political authority in Central China, a premise which was not shared by many of the army's China experts. "China is not a country controlled by one sovereignty," insisted General Okamura. "A diplomacy which is based on negotiations with only the Nanking government is a castle built on sand."[142] Still, the Inner Cabinet had vetoed the overt use of force, and the Tientsin garrison had, temporarily at least, reached the limit of its political subversion in North China. In this context, the war ministry, on January 13, 1936, adopted "The Outline of a Policy to Deal with North China," which sanctioned the emphasis on economic subversion.[143] Japan would "give support and guidance" to the Hopei-Chahar Political Council and the East Hopei Anti-Communist Autonomous Council in order to permit the Chinese people "to enjoy their lives and jobs peacefully" in the provinces of North China. Although

[142] GKJ, "Gun no hokai suru taiMan kosaku no konpongi [Basic views of the army concerning the construction of Manchuria], October 10, 1935, 17.

[143] IMTFE, *Document 1634.* Also *Nihon gaikō nenpyō,* II, 222-223, is the Japanese text.

Japan should ultimately create an autonomous North China, the war ministry agreed that, for the present, it would be content with "a situation which would leave no room for the Nanking government in North China."[144] Since it would be prudent to avoid a premature effort to realize an autonomous North China, the army's outline ruled that the field armies should "take no measure which might be misunderstood by the powers as an indication that Japan was determined to organize an independent state like Manchukuo or that she intended to enlarge Manchukuo."[145] In harmony with this directive, the new outline recommended that the "smallest possible number" of Japanese advisors be appointed to the new political organizations in North China; and that the program of economic penetration be implemented by "private capital" on the principle of "live and let live."[146]

Once the war and foreign ministries agreed on this new China policy, it received the approval of the Inner Cabinet. By February 6, even the intelligence division of the general staff declared that its staff officers in China would seek "to guide the Nanking government according to the plan devised by the foreign ministry—namely, 'Morishima's private plan.' "[147] In effect, by early February, the Okada government had formulated a new China policy which presumably would coordinate the policies of the war and foreign ministries: the Tientsin garrison would avoid any political or military moves and promote a program of economic penetration in North China; the foreign ministry would seek a series of limited agreements with the Nationalist government which would eventually confirm the existence of a "special relationship" between North China and Manchukuo. The significance of this consensus was, however, blurred by the famous rebellion of February 26, 1936, and by subsequent interpretations of it.

[144] *Ibid., Document 1634,* 3.
[145] *Ibid.*   [146] *Ibid.,* 2.
[147] "Nankin seiken no NiShi," *op.cit.*

CHAPTER V

Factions, Rebellion, and National Policy

"Prior to the Russo-Japanese War, there was, as today, an insistence that the nation must decide on its course of action; and national policy had been unified by the agreement to ally with Great Britain and to thrash Russia. Today's arbitrary formulation of national objectives in various and divergent directions, however, resembles the situation which prevailed in Germany before the Great War. At that time, the German navy focused on England; the army stressed Russia as the object of national policy; and the politicians, shorn of power, were completely subdued. When England declared war, the German navy rejoiced, but the army was appalled; and ultimately the entire world became the enemy of Germany. In present-day Japan, even those who advocate the most uncompromising foreign policy probably would not claim that it is desirable to wage a war which gyrates enemies throughout the world. Nevertheless, public opinion remains divided and many confrontations exist, including those between villages and cities, the army and navy, and soldiers and diplomats. When I recall the situation in Germany before the Great War and examine contemporary Japan, I am unable to mask my grave anxiety."

Prince Konoe Fumimaro, July 1936

DURING the early hours of February 26, 1936, small groups of soldiers from the First Imperial Division quietly left their barracks and proceeded to the residences of prominent court, military, and governmental officials. By sunrise these youthful servants of the Throne had completed their missions with notable results: the Inspector General of Military Education, General Watanabe; the Lord Keeper of the Privy Seal, Admiral Saitō; and Finance Minister Takahashi were clain; Premier

Okada had been spared at the sacrifice of his brother-in-law, who had been mistakenly identified as the premier and promptly murdered; the Grand Chamberlain, Admiral Suzuki, lay grievously wounded; and Count Makino and Prince Saionji barely eluded their hunters, thanks to timely phone calls which enabled the venerable officials to flee their residences minutes before the arrival of their self-appointed executioners.[1] Simultaneously with these deeds, some fourteen hundred soldiers of the First Division, commanded by Captain Nonaka, bombed the printing presses of the leading Tokyo newspapers and occupied the main buildings in the Nagatachō section of Tokyo overlooking the Imperial Palace. Here, Captain Nonaka posted the "Manifesto of the Righteous Army of Restoration," which identified those groups most responsible for the betrayal of the national polity—the senior statesmen, financial magnates, court officials, and certain factions in the army—proclaiming:

> They have trespassed on the prerogatives of the Emperor's rights of supreme command—among other times, in the conclusion of the London Naval Treaty and in the removal of the Inspector General of Military Education. Moreover, they secretly conspired to steal the supreme command in the March Incident; and they united with disloyal professors in rebellious places. These are but a few of the most notable instances of their villainies. . . .

> In recent years, many individuals have also made the main purpose in life to be the amassment of wealth, regardless of the general welfare and prosperity of the people. The result has been the impairment of the glory of the Empire and the consequent suffering of the Japanese people. . . .

---

[1] Among the many publications on the February 26th incident, the following seem to be of greatest value: Hata Ikuhito, *Gun fuashizumu undōshi* (Tokyo, 1962), 112-166; Kōnō Tsukasa, *Ni-ni-roku* (Tokyo, 1958); Aritake Shuji, *Okada keisuke denki* (Tokyo, 1957), 309-337; Hugh Byas, *Government by Assassination* (New York, 1940) 119-129; and Robert J. C. Butow, *Tojo and the Coming of the War* (Princeton, 1961), 48-77.

Japan now confronts a grave internal and external danger. Therefore, it is our duty to take proper steps in order to safeguard the nation by killing those individuals responsible for this crisis. On the eve of our departure for Manchuria we have risen in revolt because of our acute anxiety over the evil conditions at home. We believe it is our duty, as subjects of His Majesty, to remove traitors and evil-doers surrounding the throne and to destroy their headquarters.

We, the children of our divine land of the gods, act with heartfelt sincerity.

May the spirit of our Imperial Ancestors assist us in our endeavors to save the nation.[2]

With this rhetoric, the Righteous Army had rationalized a program of assassination and rebellion as the appropriate way to renovate the nation.

APPRAISAL OF THE FEBRUARY 26TH INCIDENT

The pronouncements and violence unleashed by the rebellion of February 26 impressed many contemporary observers as a continuation of a calculated campaign of terror carried on by the army against the government. A decade later, the chief prosecutor at the Tokyo Military Tribunal restated this viewpoint when he officially leveled the indictment: "Militaristic cliques and ultra-nationalist secret societies resorted to rule by assassination and thereby exerted great influence in favor of military aggression."[3] Relying on the testimony of General Tanaka Ryūkichi, the prosecution located the genesis of the February 26th incident in the contentions between two factions of army officers—the Imperial Way group (*Kōdō-ha*) and the Control Faction (*Tōsei-ha*). As Tanaka described it: (1) the Imperial Way group was dominated by Generals Araki and

---

[2] United States Department of State [USDS], Archives, *Japan: Political Affairs*, 894.00/654, is a translation of this declaration. Also Butow, *Tojo*, 64.

[3] International Military Tribunal Far East [IMTFE], *Proceedings*, 442.

Mazaki, the Control Faction by Generals Nagata, Umezu, and Tōjō; (2) the Imperial Way adherents were dedicated to the unique spiritual and martial values of Japan, the Control officers to the ideology of fascism; (3) the irrational Kōdō doctrine inspired younger members of the Imperial Way to execute the 1932 assassinations, whereas the younger officers of the Control Faction preferred the *coup d'état* method employed in the March and October incidents of 1931; (4) the ascendency of the Control Faction under Generals Hayashi and Nagata provoked the rebellion of February 26, 1936; (5) this rebellion disgraced the senior kōdō generals, thereby forcing their resignations; and (6) the Control Faction then consolidated its power over the government and led Japan down the path of fascism.[4] The recollections of General Tanaka at the Tribunal obviously buttressed the prosecution's brief against Araki Sadao. They were belittled by the defense counsel, who noted, "Tanaka merely said that the younger radical officers looked up to Araki and Mazaki. . . . [This] means nothing more than that the younger radical officers respected them."[5] In the atmosphere of the war crime trials, it was understandable that the affirmations of the prosecution's witness, not the denial of a defendant, prevailed. General Araki was convicted as a Class A war criminal, a judgment which necessarily enhanced the credibility of Tanaka's version of the nature and significance of the factional strife between the two groups.

This division of the army into two main factions—the Imperial Way group and the Control Faction—was also described in the memoirs of Prince Konoe Fumimaro.[6] Writing in the final months of the Pacific War, the scion of the Fujiwara clan revealed that a Control Faction had been responsible for Japan's aggressive actions in China, as well as for the advance

[4] IMTFE, *Proceedings*, 1945-2177; 14288-14422; 15853-15951; 22713-22755; 22943-22968; 29030-29064; and 29406-29418. Also General Tanaka Ryūkichi, *Haiin o tsuku* (Tokyo, 1946).

[5] IMTFE, *Defense Document 3107*, 234.

[6] *Konoe Fumimaro no shuki: ushinuwareshi seiji* (Tokyo, 1946). Partial English translation, IMTFE, *Document 1467*.

into Southeast Asia. In the opinion of Prince Konoe, the triumph of the Control Faction after the February 26th incident marked the beginning of the Pacific War:

> The ideology of the Kōdō generals was exclusively concerned with the Soviet Union. They were, for example, completely opposed to Japan's interference in China or to the advance into Southeast Asia. . . . Consequently, when these officers were removed in the aftermath of the February rebellion, it furnished the Control Faction with an opportunity to alter Japan's foreign policy, a change which later caused the China Incident and the present war.[7]

Since this evaluation blamed Japan's military leaders for the tragic involvement in a war with the United States, it was well received by Japanese and Western historians in the postwar years. Indeed, the blending of the recollections of General Tanaka Ryūkichi and Prince Konoe Fumimaro inspired comprehensive analyses which have explained the terrorism of the 1930's, the increasing totalitarian nature of the Imperial government, and Japan's aggression after 1936 in terms of factional strife between the Imperial Way group and the Control Faction.[8]

From the point of view of the testimony of a prosecution witness and the memoir of a premier who was in office during the outbreak of the China war, the indictment of Japanese army factionalism as the primary cause of fascism at home and aggression in China cannot be faulted. In recent years, though, the subject of army factionalism has been reappraised in ways which compromise the usefulness of the Imperial Way-Control Faction dichotomy.[9] Still, the belief that the February 26th

[7] *Ibid.*

[8] E.g., Eguchi Bokuro, *et al.*, *Taiheiyō sensōshi* (Tokyo, 1953); Toyama Shigeki, *Shōwashi* (Tokyo, 1955); Maruyama Masao, *Gendai seiji no shisō to kōdō* (Tokyo, 1957); Iwabuchi Tatsuo, *Gunbatsu no keifu* (Tokyo, 1948); and Richard Storry, *The Double Patriots* (London, 1957).

[9] James Crowley, "Japanese Army Factionalism in the Early 1930's," *Journal of Asian Studies*, XXI, 3 (May 1962), 309-326. The "Control Faction" and "Imperial Way group" labels recently have been invested with

incident constitutes a seed-plot in modern Japanese history has been deeply woven into the fabric of postwar historiography. In particular, the assertion that Japan's thrust into China in 1937 was caused by the triumph of a Control Faction remains relatively unchallenged; and, regardless of the nuances or complexities of army factionalism, one is assured: "A clear strategic distinction between the two lay in the desire of the Imperial Way to move north against Russia, while the Control Faction urged penetration into China."[10] In view of the resiliency of this conviction, it seems necessary here to consider the formulation of Japan's new national policy in 1936 in terms of two distinct themes: (1) the origins and consequences of the February 26th incident; and (2) the adoption, on August 11, 1936, of the "Fundamental Principles of National Policy" by the Hirota cabinet. It is hoped that, in the process, the focus on the February 26th incident as a nodal point in Japan's foreign policy, and on the allegedly determining role of a Control Faction in the formulation of national policy, will be replaced by an awareness that Japan's foreign policy after February 26, 1936, was not, in substance or in policy-making procedures, noticeably dissimilar from that which had been evident in the 1933-1936 period.

FACTIONALISM UNDER GENERAL ARAKI

Amid the controversies engendered by the London Naval Treaty, as well as the anxieties produced by the fiscal, disarmament, and China policies associated with the diplomacy of Baron Shidehara, Japan witnessed a corrosion of the 1891 Imperial edict enjoining all officers to refrain from political activities. This process assumed visible form in the fall of 1930 with the organization of the Sakurakai. Some members of this

---

new connotations by Hata Ikuhito in "Tōsei-ha kōdō-ha," *Jiyū*, III, 5 (1961), 78-90, and his *Gun fuashizumu undōshi*; Fujiwara Akira, *Gunjishi* (Tokyo, 1961); Nezu Masashi, *Dai nihon teikoku no hōkai* (Tokyo, 1961); and Tateno Nobuyuki, *Shōwa gunbatsu* (Tokyo, 1963).

[10] Maruyama Maso, *Thought and Behavior in Modern Japanese Politics* (New York, 1953), 302-303.

group, including Lt. Colonels Hashimoto Kingorō and Nemoto Hiroshi, envisioned a *coup d'état* in March 1931 which would create a new government under General Ugaki Issei.[11] Although this conspiracy was aborted by Ugaki, the same group of officers, in October 1931, expressed their political ambitions in an ill-fated campaign to promote a cabinet headed by General Araki Sadao.[12] In both instances, Hashimoto and Nemoto had urged a senior officer to assume political leadership and, with the assistance of Ōkawa Shūmei, to renovate the country; in each instance, they were rebuffed by the senior officer who would presumably have benefited most from a political *coup d'état*. Although neither the March nor the October incident affected national policies, they were indicative of two traits characterizing some of the field-grade officers in central headquarters: a desire to correct the economic plight caused by the great depression by some form of state socialism; and a personal involvement with the leaders and programs of the prominent ultra-nationalistic societies.

Parallel with the aspirations and activities of the Cherry Society, other signs of resentment and opposition to the fiscal and foreign policies of the Minseitō cabinets were discernible in military and naval circles. The Supreme War Council, in July 1930, had memorialized the Throne, insisting that the government's disarmament policies should not overrule the minimal security requirements postulated by the general staffs, a dictate which implicitly censured Premier Hamaguchi's approach to the London Naval Conference. Moreover, the 1930 personnel changes in naval central headquarters had forced the resignations of those officers who deferred to the leadership of the premier and foreign minister in accepting the Reed-Matsudaira Compromise.[13] Beginning in the spring of 1931, War Minister Minami mobilized the Supreme War Council against additional efforts of the cabinet to reduce the budget of the army; and, in the summer of 1931, the war ministry decided to inform public opinion "abroad and in Japan" of the

[11] Chapter II, 97.   [12] Chapter III, 134.   [13] Chapter I, 79.

necessity to shelve the moderate diplomacy of Baron Shidehara in favor of a forceful resolution of the Manchurian problem.[14] These political indices of military policy were complemented by the operational planning of the general staff, both in Tokyo and in Port Arthur. The interaction of economic, diplomatic, and military attitudes and policies within the army, when fused with invocation of the "right of supreme command" and popular support for the Mukden incident, eventually shattered the Wakatsuki cabinet and reconstructed Japan's foreign policy in terms of the quest for an Asiatic Monroe Doctrine.

Without ignoring the implications of the March and October incidents, it seems clear that the main concerns of the army and naval authorities in 1930-1931 centered on the fiscal and foreign policies of the Minseitō governments. The prospect of comprehensive internal political and economic reforms undeniably captivated a small cluster of officers in the intelligence division of the general staff; but these officers failed to win the support of the senior army officers. In fact, the censure of their peers caused the dissolution of the Sakurakai. In other words, the advocacy of political coups and the overt threat of the use of military force against the legally constituted civilian authorities were effectively muffled in 1931, at least within central headquarters. This aversion to violence, however, was not characteristic of another group of army and naval officers, the National Principle group. In August 1931, Ensign Mikami Taku organized the *Kokutai genri-ha*; and, within a short time, the views of this group were hermetically sealed by a commitment to the agrarian communalism of Gondō Seikyō.[15] These young officers not only shunned the urban-based nationalistic societies but castigated the political activities of the Sakurakai. Mikami, for example, termed the October incident a "fascistic *coup d'état*" which revealed a profound misconception of the true national principle. In order to save the army and the nation from the evils of fascism, this group of young officers chose to dramatize their cause by the assassination of prominent court, political, and financial personalities.

The assassinations of 1932 attested the commitment of the National Principle group to this program of murder. It is also relevant to note that, when Ensign Mikami plotted the killing of Premier Inukai, he had also marked the distinguished ultra-nationalist, Nishida Zei, for assassination because of the belief that Nishida had participated in the "fascistic" October incident. This desire to kill Inukai and Nishida on May 15 was inspired by a conscious wish to disassociate the *Kokutai genri* movement from those individuals and organizations linked with the October incident. In this manner, reasoned Mikami, the selfless motivation behind the murder of the premier would be incontestable. In the testimony of one of Inukai's assassins:

> We thought about destruction first. We never considered taking on the duty of construction. We foresaw, however, that, once the destruction was accomplished, someone would take charge of the construction for us. . . . We believed that, if we could create a situation requiring martial law, a military government would be set up around Araki as war minister, and a start made upon the path of reconstruction.[16]

This sincerity of motivation was not overlooked by the leading spokesmen of the services. "When one considers what caused these pure-hearted young men to make this mistake," declared Naval Minister Osumi, "it demands the most serious reflection."[17] His counterpart, General Araki, sympathetically observed that the murders of 1932 had not been inspired by a desire for "fame, or personal gain, nor are they traitorous. They were performed in the sincere belief that they were for the benefit of Japan."[18] Despite this public benediction of the 1932 assassins, it would be unfair and misleading to assume that either Admiral Osumi or General Araki approved of political violence or of army and naval officers' overtly participating in political activities.

---

[16] As cited by Maruyama, *Thought and Behavior*, 53-54.
[17] *Ibid.*, 67.   [18] *Ibid.*

Aside from his friendship with Prince Konoe and General Mazaki, General Araki displayed no tolerance for political proclivities on the part of army officers, or for the efforts of politicians to align themselves with army officers for personal advantage. On May 21, 1932, as noted earlier, Araki pointedly reminded all divisional commanders that "It is absolutely not permissible for soldiers to act sectionally or like hired troops or to take orders from anyone like Hitler or Mussolini."[19] Of course, Araki occasionally criticized the deficiencies of contemporary Japan, where "capitalists are concerned only with their own interests and pay no attention to public life; politicians often forget the general situation in the country while absorbed in their party interests; [and] clerks and students forget their duty, giving themselves over to merriment and pleasure."[20] These indictments, though, were made in a context which stressed the "international crisis" confronting the nation and the need for public determination to overcome "whatever enemy opposes the spread of the Imperial Idea."[21] Araki's praise of Kōdō values was basically designed to augment the élan of the military establishment and to enlist public opinion behind the refurbishment and expansion of the army. It was not a covert invitation to political intrigues by military personnel, nor was it a clandestine appeal for a reformation of Japan's political and economic institutions. When, for example, his close friend Kobayashi Junichiro tried, in conjunction with the ardent nationalist Akao Bin, to organize discussion groups on the subject of national defense and armament control in army camps, Araki promptly ordered all divisional commanders to prevent this and similar activities.[22] This rigid censure of civilian patriots trying to infiltrate the world of the barracks was consistent with Araki's earlier treatment of Colonels

---

[19] Chapter III, 178.

[20] O. Tanin and E. Yohan, *Militarism and Fascism in Japan* (New York, 1934), 303.

[21] *Ibid., loc.cit.*

[22] Gunreibu, *Gun kankei jōhō* [*GKJ*], "Gunbunai hanAraki jitsujo" [True Circumstances of the Anti-Araki Movement in the Army], undated (written in late December 1933 or early January, 1934).

Hashimoto and Nemoto in October 1931, as well as with his pious praise of the motives underlying the 1932 assassinations.

This lack of sympathy for—perhaps aversion to—army officers' playing an overt role in domestic political and economic affairs was reflected in Araki's unwillingness to endorse the type of economic planning and educational campaign favored by the "total war" proponents in army central headquarters. The refusal of the war minister to pass beyond the "crisis of 1936" slogan and his tacit approval of General Obata's plea for an immediate conflict with the Soviet Union had precipitated a passionate controversy in army circles. As described earlier, Obata's argument was overruled; but, shortly afterward, the officers most responsible for this ruling—Generals Umezu, Tōjō, and Nagata—were transferred from the general staff.[23] This personnel shift accentuated the unrest regarding Araki's leadership, and the Supreme War Council soon decided to appoint a war minister more receptive to the "total war" philosophy.

Uneasiness about the personnel policies of General Araki had first appeared in 1932, in conjunction with his purge of every senior Chōshū general in central headquarters. Apart from this anti-Chōshū bias, Araki's original appointments also revealed a partiality for officers with a Tosa-Saga background —e.g., Generals Mazaki, Yanagawa, and Yamaoka and Colonels Yamashita, Obata, Okamura, Furushō, and Suzuki Teiichi. The selection of Yanagawa as vice-war minister and Yamaoka as chief of the Bureau of Military Affairs especially disturbed many staff officers, because neither had had previous experience in central headquarters. Araki's patronage of old friends and the Tosa-Saga orientation of his personnel policy fomented bitterness among the officers most immediately affected by the actions of the war minister. A number of these officers, headed by General Tatekawa and Colonel Hashimoto, soon clamored for the "purification" of all *han-batsu*, or regional cliques, from

23 Chapter III, 184.

central headquarters.[24] Accordingly this group was dubbed the *Seigun-ha*, the Purification Faction. Since it was largely composed of officers of a Chōshū origin who had recently been transferred by Araki, neither the Supreme War Council nor the staff in central headquarters was impressed by its criticism.

The accusation that the war minister was promoting a Tosa-Saga faction slowly acquired greater credibility in 1933, particularly when Araki executed a vendetta against Generals Tōjō, Umezu, and Nagata because of their adamant opposition to the views of Obata Tokushiro. As one informed police report observed in the fall of 1933:

> When Araki became war minister after the October incident, the personnel in army headquarters was reconstructed. Each time a cabinet changes, prefectural governors are fired; and, in a similar fashion, personnel changes were effected in the army. Anyone who was considered to have been in the Ugaki group was removed from central headquarters and officers of the general and colonel rank were shuffled about like policemen in a neighborhood precinct. Moreover, Obata, who is considered to be one of the most respected leaders of the Araki group, conspired to remove his rivals. . . . The Imperial army is not so generous as to permit this deed.[25]

Indeed, Generals Abe and Watanabe of the Supreme War Council quietly but effectively organized a Control Movement —the *Tōsei undō*—designed to quash the acrimonious feelings provoked by Araki's personnel policies. This movement was vigorously supported by the Seigun faction; but it would be misleading to identify the Control Movement with the earlier associates of General Ugaki. The Supreme War Council had selected Hayashi Senjurō as the replacement for General Araki for two main reasons: throughout Ugaki's tenure as war minister, Hayashi had been continuously assigned to field com-

[24] *GKJ*, "Rikugun fuashiyo undōshi gaikan" [A General View of the Fascistic Movement in the Army], February 21, 1934.

[25] *GKJ*, "Seigun undō no jissai" [Truth of the Purification Movement], part III.

mands; and, as noted previously, Hayashi had been one of Araki's strongest supporters in 1932.[26] Nevertheless, under Hayashi's leadership, Araki's most favored protégés were quickly replaced by a staff personally selected by Nagata Tetsuzan; and the war ministry pursued a concerted effort to draft an economic and manpower mobilization program that would enable the nation to wage a "total war."

REMOVAL OF GENERAL MAZAKI

Unlike the public posture of his predecessor which invoked the "crisis of 1936," General Hayashi favored the concept of "national defense" as the rationale for army and national policy. By cultivating the concepts of "general mobilization," "economic planning," and "national defense," the war ministry intended to nurture a viable political consensus in the Diet which would support the army's refurbishment and expansion plans. Since this policy placed priority on tanks, communications, and air power, most of the desired increased expenditures would be concentrated in the major armament industries. This fact did not imply a denial or downgrading of the traditional stress on the importance of the infantry or the worth of an aggressive combat spirit. Still, it posed a delicate moral problem. The peasantry had always been eulogized in military circles as the core of the army; and, in the 1930's, the rural sector of the economy was in desperate straits. As the 1932 assassinations revealed, the image of the peasant as the embodiment of the true national principle was especially revered by the younger officers. Any program which located the bulk of increased expenditures in the largest industrial combines could easily breed the suspicion that the new staff of the war ministry was willing, for political expediency, to sacrifice the welfare of the peasants and channel lucrative contracts to the *zaibatsu*. In order to obviate this potential resentment of the army's "national defense" policy, the war ministry's *Basic Theory of National Defense*

[26] Chapter IV, 207. The distinction between the "Control Faction" and the "Purification Group" is consistently drawn in contemporary naval intelligence reports.

compensated for the lack of a specific program of financial aid to the agrarian sector of the economy with a vigorous restatement of the paramount importance of the peasantry: "The most pressing problem of national welfare is to give relief to the farming, mountain, and fishing villages."[27]

This commitment to the primary importance of the agrarian problem had been deliberately proclaimed in order to allay the concern over this issue which prevailed throughout all ranks of the army, including the belief that the new emphasis on technology and economic planning would corrupt the army's combat spirit. This strategy only partially succeeded. Interpreting the *Basic Theory of National Defense* as an endorsement of their convictions, two leaders of the National Principle group —Captain Muranaka and Lieutenant Isobe—concluded in November 1934 that the army's obligation to the peasants would be best implemented by the assassination of the premier and the personal advisors of the Emperor.[28] This judgment echoed Ensign Mikami's program of 1932; but, unlike Mikami, Muranaka and Isobe discussed their plans with two responsible superior officers. Specifically, they disclosed their views and proposals to Captain Tsuji Masanobu, an instructor at the Military Academy, and Major Katakura Chū, a member of General Nagata's staff in the war ministry. After their efforts failed to dampen the ardor of Muranaka and Isobe, Tsuji and Katakura reported the incipient conspiracy to the military police. Muranaka and Isobe were promptly suspended from the academy and, after an official inquiry, they were compelled to resign their commissions.[29]

An episode of this sort ordinarily would have had slight ramifications within the army. However, Muranaka and Isobe were technically assigned to the Military Academy; and the inspector general of military education, General Mazaki Jinzaburō, was nominally responsible for the actions of all

[27] Maruyama, *Thought and Behavior*, 48.

[28] IMTFE, *Document 1417*; Hata, *Gun fuashizumu*, 99-107.

[29] In an interview, Katakura Chū remarked that he and Tsuji were formally reprimanded for their tardy notification of the military police.

soldiers at the academy. Because General Hayashi was in the process of reassigning virtually all senior officers from central headquarters who had been closely associated with General Araki, the exposure of the incident at the academy automatically jeopardized Mazaki's position. In order to prevent the war minister from utilizing the behavior of Muranaka and Isobe as a pretext for his reassignment, General Mazaki claimed that the chief of the Bureau of Military Affairs, General Nagata Tetsuzan, had contrived the incident at the academy for the specific purpose of embarrassing the inspector general of military education.[30] No doubt Mazaki advanced this interpretation as one way to divorce himself from the radical young officers; but his method of doing so inherently questioned the integrity of General Nagata, along with that of the war minister. Unfortunately, Mazaki did not confine his indictment of the Hayashi-Nagata hegemony in the war ministry to this partisan evaluation of the incident at the Military Academy. In an effort to overthrow the Okada cabinet, Mazaki vainly conspired with Kuhara Fusanosuke of the Seiyūkai in January 1935 to bring official charges of corruption against the ministries of war, finance, and railways.[31] Although this maneuver failed, another public controversy allowed Mazaki to abuse the government and augment his status throughout the ranks of the army.

On February 28, 1935, Baron Kikuchi Takeo delivered in the House of Peers a vitriolic censure of the legal philosophy of Japan's most distinguished professor of jurisprudence, Minobe Tatsukichi.[32] Overnight, Minobe's abstract theory of "the emperor as an organ of the state" was vilified by the Hiranuma element in the House of Peers, by the leading Seiyūkai representatives in the Diet, and by the phalanx of ultra-nationalistic organizations. In the midst of this uproar, the inspector general of military education issued a statement

[30] Storry, *Double Patriots*, 160-161, presents Mazaki's interpretation, without, of course, taking it at face value.

[31] Saionji-Harada, *Memoirs*, February 15, 1935.

[32] A concise summary of this crisis is Aritake, *Okada Keisuke*, 274-283. In English, Storry, *Double Patriots*, 163-166.

which also abused the writings of Professor Minobe. Although this type of comment was only one of many illustrations of the increasing political proclivity within army circles, it clashed with the official attitude of the Okada cabinet, including that of War Minister Hayashi. "Dr. Minobe's doctrine has been set forth for many years and," Hayashi assured the House of Peers, "there has been no instance when his doctrine has had an undesirable influence on the army."[33] Moreover, when the staff of the home ministry recommended the removal of Minobe from the faculty of Tokyo Imperial University, the home minister, Gotō Fumio, rebuked his subordinates with the rejoinder:

Personally, I am not averse to forcing Dr. Minobe to resign his public position, or to punishing other teachers who champion his theory. Still, the question is less a matter of removing him from Tokyo University than the pervasive influence which the concept of Kokutai exerts on the masses. Thus, it would be desirable first to prepare a clear theoretical exposition of the ideas of Kokutai among legal scholars. (And the securing of scholars capable of performing this task seems a baffling problem.) ... Since the cabinet is considering this point prudently, it is avoiding a clarification of the national polity.[34]

In view of the government's calculated defense of Professor Minobe, the "emperor as an organ" controversy was gradually reduced; and, on August 3, it was apparently resolved when the government issued a mild expression of concern about the unrest which had been inspired by Minobe's theory.[35]

Throughout the spring of 1935, General Mazaki had constantly irritated the government and the war ministry by his

[33] Maruyama, *Gendai seiji*, I, 62. A slightly different translation appears in Maruyama, *Thought and Behavior*, 61.

[34] *GKJ*, "Kikan setsu mondai, ni kan suru gunbu oyobi seifu no naibu jijo" [The State of Affairs in the Government and the Army Concerning the Emperor Organ Problem], April 9, 1935.

[35] Aritake, *Okada Keisuke*, 280.

distinctive evaluation of the November incident at the Military Academy, by his intrigues with Kuhara Fusanosuke, and by his role in the Minobe episode. Finally, War Minister Hayashi and the chief of staff, Prince Kanin, decided to force the resignation of the inspector general of military education.[36] This accord posed a ticklish personnel issue. Not only was Mazaki the senior Kōdō general in central headquarters, but it had been standard practice since 1924 to solicit the approval of the inspector general before officially posting the yearly August transfers. This custom had been introduced as one means of terminating the then existing Chōshū hegemony in central headquarters by giving the inspector general a limited form of veto power over the personnel policies of the war minister. In fact, no inspector general had ever challenged the authority of the war minister in personnel matters; and one need only recall the wholesale changes under Araki Sadao to illustrate the paramount authority of the war minister in assignments to central headquarters. Nevertheless, because Mazaki's removal would infuriate the Kōdō generals, General Hayashi and Prince Kanin tried to minimize the opposition by an informal discussion of the August transfer list.

In late June, Hayashi and Kanin flew to Korea and Manchuria, where they reviewed the reasons for Mazaki's impending transfer to the Supreme War Council with the senior field officers.[37] After this procedure, on July 12, Prince Kanin officially advised Mazaki of his new assignment. Hayashi originally had intended to place Mazaki on the inactive list; but, at the insistence of Prince Kanin, he sanctioned Mazaki's appointment to the Supreme War Council. This gesture was a calculated attempt to placate his personal pride and to minimize the resentment which his removal would provoke among the friends and associates of Generals Araki and Mazaki. Instead of receiving his elevation to the Supreme War Council

[36] Storry, *Double Patriots,* 170.
[37] Itō Masanori, *Gunbatsu kōbōshi* (Tokyo, 1957), II, 236.

in good grace, Mazaki challenged the legality of his removal.[38] The intensity of Mazaki's feelings prompted Kanin to agree to a three-day postponement of the official publication of the August transfers. During this respite, Mazaki and Araki naturally tried to marshal support for the reversal of Hayashi's proposed personnel changes. The cabinet, however, rallied to the side of the war minister. "The main objective," insisted Premier Okada, "is to remove Mazaki, who is at the root of all this mess."[39]

On July 15, the Big Three of the army—Generals Hayashi, Kanin, and Mazaki—formally reviewed the August transfer list, which had already been approved by the war minister and the chief of staff.[40] In this setting, Mazaki justified his own behavior in recent months and impugned the motives of his detractors. In particular, the inspector general contrasted his actions with those of Generals Tatekawa and Koiso in the March incident of 1931. Mazaki argued, with some merit, that if he were to be punished for political activities, those officers involved in the March incident should also be transferred to the inactive list. Having made this point, Mazaki unexpectedly claimed that General Nagata had been a key figure in the March incident. Thus, in Mazaki's opinion, it would be unpardonable of the war minister to permit Nagata to continue as chief of the Bureau of Military Affairs and, at the same time, demand that the inspector general retire because of political behavior. This allegation against Nagata caught Hayashi and Kanin unawares; and, after passing it off as an intemperate outburst, they reaffirmed the transfer of Mazaki to the Supreme War Council. At the end of this meeting, though, Mazaki intimated that he might still contest this ruling by means of audience with the Emperor. This threat impelled a hasty trip by the war minister to the Imperial summer residence where, on the evening of July 15, "the war minister unprecedentedly

[38] Takamiya Tahei, *Gunkoku taiheiki* (Tokyo, 1951), 209-210.
[39] Saionji-Harada, *Memoirs*, July 22, 1935.
[40] A convenient summary of this meeting is found in Takamiya, *Gunkoku*, 216-221.

informed the Emperor secretly about the impending personnel changes."[41]

Although the events of July 15 had sealed the fate of the inspector general, Mazaki and Araki raised another objection to the August transfers. When the Supreme War Council met on July 18, General Mazaki again introduced the matter of the March incident and pointed to Nagata Tetsuzan as one of its main instigators.[42] General Watanabe Jōtarō interpreted this charge as a scandalous attempt to embarrass the war minister and somewhat caustically observed that Nagata's involvement in the March incident had remained well concealed until the impending transfer of the inspector general. Mazaki's complaint against Nagata also distressed General Hishikari; and, although he was a close personal friend of Araki's, he too refrained from lending any support to Mazaki's evaluation of the March incident. Consequently, the latest diatribe of General Mazaki actually solidified the Supreme War Council behind the proposed transfers and the council endorsed the recommendations of the war minister. On August 1, Mazaki became a disgruntled member of the Supreme War Council and the Kōdō faction was, for awhile, banished from central headquarters.

THE ASSASSINATION OF NAGATA TETSUZAN

Prior to the animosities unleashed by Mazaki's transfer to the Supreme War Council, there were no viable personal links between the members of the Kōdō faction and the young officers of the National Principle group. Officers like Muranaka and Isobe had, before the Military Academy incident, considered the program outlined by the "Fundamental Principles of National Policy" to be in harmony with their idealized version of a renovated Japan. For example, one young naval officer,

---

[41] *GKJ*, "Hayashi rikushō no jinji shidanko ni niyo no kansoku" [Two Observations on the Decisive Action of War Minister Hayashi], July 17, 1935.

[42] Takamiya, *Gunkoku*, 223-228, is a good digest of this meeting. Storry, *Double Patriots*, 172-174, offers a recapitulation based on a memorandum of General Matsuura, a friend of Mazaki.

"deeply moved" by the army's publication, wrote a personal letter to the naval ministry in which he offered a series of suggestions as to how the Shōwa restoration could be attained:

> In the *Kokubō no hongi*, the army has unprecedentedly and openly cited the need for "a reformation of the economic system." The time for the Shōwa restoration is close at hand. . . . The army is truly a Caesar who has crossed a Rubicon. Unfortunately, however, since some parts of the pamphlet are imperfect and too abstract, the specific realization of its ideas depends upon our own efforts. Hence, we should subscribe 100 per cent to the views and opinions of the army; and we should expand and strengthen the *Kokubō no hongi*.[43]

This identification was comprehensible because the pamphlet of the war ministry had postulated two goals—a resolution of the agrarian problem, and the establishment of a comprehensive national defense plan. Still, as a contemporary observer recognized the pamphlet of October 1934 "regarded the National Defense Plan as the primary objective, the reformation of the nation as a secondary goal which would necessarily follow from a realization of the National Defense Plan."[44] After the incident at the Military Academy, this distinction was also understood by the leaders of the National Principle group.

In February 1935, the National Principle group published a catechism designed to convey the basic views of this movement. In it, the distinction between those groups which urged the renovation of the nation by giving priority to national defense planning and those which emphasized the national polity was starkly clarified—namely, the former individuals were described as "fascists," the latter as followers of the "national principle."[45] In the question-and-answer format of this catechism:

[43] *GKJ*, " 'Seinen shōkō' tegami no bunsho" [The Letter of a "Young Officer"], November 14, 1934.

[44] *GKJ*, "Rikugun no shisō teki kaisetsu" (An Exposition of Ideology Within the Army), November 14, 1934.

[45] *GKJ*, "Kokka kakushin undō ni okeru nidai chōryū: fuashizumu ha

QUESTION: What is the difference in viewpoints concerning "national defense"?

ANSWER: Both groups hold the same view that the present national defense is imperfect. However, politics, economics, thought, education, religion, etc., must be managed from one principle—reverence for the Emperor. In particular, the economic system must be reformed. It is not unreasonable to say that the fascists are National Socialists who wish to carry out a reformation under the slogan of the so-called national defense. The *Kokutai genri* group, however, believes that our national defense is inadequate because the nation as a whole is not under the control of the true national principle. If we wish to strengthen national defense, it is absolutely necessary to possess the excellent qualities of a large family body. In other words, the national principle must be regained. Speaking plainly, the uniqueness of *chūkō*—Emperor-parent obedience—must be regained in order to reform the national body. Consequently, politics, economics, thought, religion, literature, art, foreign policy, etc., must be managed by one principle, *kokutai*. This is the real strengthening of national defense. . . .

QUESTION: Do not fascists exist in the military?

ANSWER: Ensign Mikami Taku, who is considered to be the theoretician of the May 15th incident, is said to have attacked the October incident as a conspiracy by fascists in the army. He too stressed the importance of one national body.

QUESTION: But are there no fascists in the army today?

ANSWER: It is very natural to wonder; but, as has been said previously, the army itself is based on a foundation which cannot be the object of a reformation. Therefore, if fascists

to kokutai genri ha" [Two Basic Movements for the Renovation of the Nation: The Fascistic Group and the National Principle Group], February 5, 1935.

exist in the military, they will use fascistic groups in the civilian sphere as a symbol. They will make civilian fascistic groups step forward and control them from behind. Consequently, the self-consciousness of the people is very important. If the people close their eyes to the national principle and dance to the flute of fascism, there will be a critical day for Imperial Japan. This is what you must be most concerned about. However, the Japanese people should believe in the military. Officers and soldiers devote themselves to training and maneuvers. . . . The military is the Emperor's possession and all officers cannot be fascists. Let us trust the military.

Despite the last exhortation, the leaders of the National Principle group obviously did not believe the nation could be renovated by a planned economy which would be approved by financiers and politicians. As they viewed the contemporary scene, only fascists wanted "to compromise with political parties and the *zaibatsu* . . . and combine formal politics and the military."[46] Moreover, the young officers in the National Principle movement were not oblivious to the fact that the "national defense" program launched by Generals Hayashi and Nagata possessed all the attributes which they regarded as a perversion of the "true national principle."

This animosity acquired greater force in the summer of 1935, parallel with the Minobe controversy and the impending removal of the inspector general of military education. "In full knowledge of this dangerous atmosphere," noted the official police report on Mazaki's activities, the inspector general openly and repeatedly expressed to many officers his resentment over his impending dismissal.[47] Mazaki also linked his removal with his personal opposition to the "fascistic" policies of the war ministry. Stimulated by these statements, noted the military police, "Muranaka Kōji and Isobe Asaichi thus dis-

[46] *Ibid.*
[47] An English-language translation of the official report on the court-martial of Mazaki is reprinted in *Japan Advertiser*, September 23, 1937.

tributed seditious literature."[48] The reference is to the pamphlet, *Shukugun ni kansuru ikensho* ("Views on the Housecleaning of the Army") which appeared in early July 1935.[49] Writing from the viewpoint of "young officers," Muranaka and Isobe identified three main factions in central headquarters—the Control Faction, the Purification Group, and the Araki Group; and they judged the first two were, by virtue of their attacks on the Araki faction, obstructing the "national reconstruction." This political tract also depicted General Nagata as the leading conspirator in the March incident of 1931.[50] Whether this notion originated with Isobe and Muranaka or with General Mazaki is uncertain. Regardless of its source, it pinpointed Nagata as the "evil genius" responsible for the removal of General Mazaki and for the fascistic policies which were leading the army away from the true national principle.

This image of Nagata was, in the course of several conversations with General Mazaki, communicated to Lt. Colonel Aizawa Saburo.[51] On July 16, Aizawa stormed into the office of General Nagata and passionately articulated his objections to the transfer of Mazaki to the Supreme War Council. His reward for this unsolicited opinion was an assignment to Taiwan effective the middle of August. With further encouragement from Mazaki, Aizawa's hatred of this "evil genius" was intensified. Returning to the war ministry on August 12, Aizawa visited General Yamaoka, the chief of the Bureau of Military Affairs, and confided that "he came to kill Nagata and that he

[48] *Ibid.*

[49] This pamphlet appears as IMTFE, *Document 3166.* On microfilm, *Checklist of Archives in the Japanese Ministry of Foreign Affairs, 1868-1945* (Washington, 1954), entry IMT 598.

[50] To the best of my knowledge, this is the first written source claiming that Nagata was active in the March incident. Many postwar accounts repeated the charge, but the most careful appraisal of the incident—Hata Ikuhito, "Sakurakai shui-sho," *Rekishi kyōiku,* VI, 2 (1958), 81-89—offers no support for this opinion.

[51] In a postwar interview, Mazaki adamantly denied exerting any influence on Aizawa. Storry, *Double Patriots,* 176.

would also like to murder the war minister."[52] Yamaoka patiently listened to this revelation; and he allowed Aizawa to despatch a messenger to ascertain whether General Nagata was in his office. Upon receiving an affirmative reply, Aizawa left the passive Yamaoka and charged into the private office of the chief of the Bureau of Military Affairs. After plunging his sword into Nagata's back several times, Aizawa returned to Yamaoka's office, where he recapitulated his meritorious deed until his arrest by the military police interrupted the conversation.[53]

AIZAWA'S TRIAL AND THE FEBRUARY 26TH INCIDENT

The cold-blooded murder of a superior officer should have been handled by a simple and expeditious court-martial. Owing to the influence of the Kōdō generals, however, the trial of Aizawa was structured by a number of unusual circumstances. The Supreme War Council endorsed two stipulations advanced by Generals Araki and Mazaki: the murder of Nagata should be regarded as illustrating profound dissatisfaction with the leadership of War Minister Hayashi; and the Council should nominate a new war minister who was not identified with any one of the three main groups in central headquarters—that is, with the Seigun, Kōdō, or Tōsei factions. This resolution compelled the resignation of Hayashi and yielded the selection of General Kuwashima, who possessed the image of "neutrality" by virtue of his lack of any previous

[52] Yamaoka letter cited in Oki Osamuji, *Ninmen Yamashita Tomoyuki* (Tokyo, 1959), 112-113.

[53] Byas, *Government by Assassination*, 95-118, is a vivid account of Aizawa's behavior. One army analysis of November 1935 notes: "It seems there was a hidden motive in suddenly picking up the problem of the March incident after a few years. . . . Major General Nagata stood for the opposite side in the March incident but, in order to attack him, certain dramatists characterized him as the main actor in this incident. Moreover, they portrayed him as an important and reactionary personality and they agitated people with other motives. Consequently, the scandalous event of Nagata's assassination has happened. Colonel Aizawa is a miserable puppet dancing to false rumors." *GKJ*, "Kōgun ittai-ron" [General Essay on the Emperor's Army], November 9, 1935.

assignments in central headquarters.[54] The new war minister took over a nettle which he handled in a gingerly fashion. He ruled that Lt. Colonel Aizawa should receive a fair and public hearing; he approved the policy of launching an "autonomous" North China; and he revived the Minobe controversy in the cabinet. Each of these initial moves raised complex diplomatic and political issues. Since the North China problem has already been considered, one need only focus here on the domestic ramifications of the appointment of General Kuwashima, particularly as it contributed to the outbreak of the February 26th incident.[55]

With the concurrence of General Hayashi, the Okada cabinet had deliberately soft-pedaled the public indictments of the "emperor as an organ" theory. The new war minister, however, argued that Minobe's theory and the government's official censure of it had caused tremendous unrest within the army, as witnessed by the assassination of Nagata Tetsuzan.[56] In order to instill confidence in the army, Kuwashima insisted that the cabinet must adopt a more positive stance against the writings of Professor Minobe. Confronted by this demand, the cabinet formally announced that the law professor would be stripped of all public honors, including his faculty appointment at Tokyo University; and that the government believed the Emperor was the absolute repository of sovereignty, not an "organ of the state."[57] This public condemnation was implemented with the expectation that a forthright denunciation of Professor Minobe would allay the unrest described by War Minister Kuwashima. As it happened, the cabinet action only confirmed the conviction of the young members of the *Kokutai genri* movement as to the justness of their cause; and, in the drama produced by the trial of Aizawa, they resolved to

---

[54] A critical commentary on Kuwashima's role is *GKJ*, "Kuwashima rikushō haigeki no shinsō" [Truth of the Case Denouncing War Minister Hayashi], December 18, 1935.

[55] Chapter IV, 224-237.   [56] Aritake, *Okada Keisuke*, 282.

[57] *Ibid.*, 282-283.

destroy all the groups which were violating the true national principle, including the Okada cabinet.

Apart from the question of the nature of Aizawa's crime, the murder of General Nagata presented an apparently minor administrative problem. Should Aizawa be tried in Fukushima, where he was technically assigned; or should he be court-martialed in Tokyo, the scene of the assassination? With the approval of the war minister, jurisdiction was given to the First Division stationed in Tokyo.[58] This division was commanded by General Yanagawa, an intimate of Araki and Mazaki; and Yanagawa elected to sanction a public court-martial. Yanagawa also selected the procurator and judges and indicated that trial should be conducted in a manner that would enable the public to understand the complex motives underlying the assassination of General Nagata. To this end, the defense counsel, Colonel Matsui, was permitted to enlist the forensic talents of Dr. Uzawa, the president of Meiji University. Along with these arrangements, War Minister Kuwashima, in an unusual personnel change, appointed Colonel Murakami as chief of the military affairs section. Normally, an assignment of this importance would have been made in August; and it signified that Murakami was a friend of General Mazaki.[59] More crucially, according to the affidavit of Lieutenant Isobe, the organizers of the February 26th rebellion arranged, with the assistance of Colonel Murakami, a series of conferences with some senior Kōdō officers—namely, Generals Mazaki, Furushō, Okamura, and Yamashita.[60] These sessions included discussions of the need for a "national reconstruction" and, more specifically, how this reform could be promoted by a judicious use of the Aizawa trial and the assassination of Premier Okada. On December 20, Lieutenant Isobe and Captain Ogawa raised this possibility directly with General Mazaki:

[58] Byas, *Government by Assassination,* 119-128, remains the classic account of the public aspects of Aizawa's trial.
[59] *GKJ,* "Kuwashima rikushō," *op.cit.*
[60] Kōnō, *Ni-ni-roku,* 31-32.

Captain Ogawa declared that if the national polity clarification issue and the Aizawa trial did not progress to the satisfaction of those working for the Renovation of the State, he feared there would be bloodshed. General Mazaki told his two visitors that there was ample reason for such fear but that, if he said as much, he would be in the embarrassing position of one regarded as an instigator of junior officers.[61]

This Delphic response was less characteristic of General Yamashita Tomoyuki who, after reviewing the possibility of political assassinations with the youthful conspirators, sagaciously suggested that they "should not act without careful preparation."[62]

The melodramatic trial of Colonel Aizawa catharized the pathological convictions of the young leaders of the National Principle movement and the bitterness of the senior officers of the Imperial Way faction. Permitted by the presiding judge, General Satō, to present the motives which had inspired the murder of Nagata, the defense counsels, Dr. Uzawa and Colonel Matsui, transformed the court-martial into a public tirade against the responsible officials of the nation. Aizawa, according to Uzawa and Matsui, had executed Nagata because of the concerns and frustrations which had been produced by a sensitivity to the evil state of affairs in contemporary Japan. In particular, Aizawa realized that the Emperor was surrounded by men who were preventing a "national restoration," that the writings of Professor Minobe had rationalized the misuse of the Imperial prerogatives by the Okada cabinet and the plutocrats, and that a "military clique" which was closely allied with the bureaucrats and financial magnates had conspired to remove the noble General Mazaki from his post as inspector general of military education. "I marked out Nagata," testified Aizawa, "because he, together with the senior statesmen and financiers and members of the old army clique like General

---

[61] From the official report on Mazaki's court-martial, *Japan Advertiser*, September 23, 1937.
[62] Oki, *Ninmen Yamashita*, 112-113.

Minami and General Ugaki, was responsible for the corruption of the army. . . . He was the headquarters of all the evil."[63] In the process of the trial, the murder of Nagata was submerged in an ocean of polemics which indicted the existing pattern of government in terms of the mystique of *kokutai*, the national principle.

The pyrotechnics of the Aizawa trial were, in the judgment of an American military attaché, "perfect as a broadcasting station for the beliefs and accusations of the radical fringe of the nationalistic group."[64] The utilization of the court-martial as a nation-wide rostrum for the tenets of the National Principle movement was not fortuitous. As noted, the senior Kōdō generals and the organizers of the February 26th incident wanted to vindicate and popularize their conception of army factionalism and the deficiencies of Shōwa Japan through the trial of Colonel Aizawa. This harmony of interests invested the court-martial with unmistakably revolutionary objectives. Indeed, when the young officers on December 28 alerted General Mazaki to the need for a "clarification of the national polity," they were reprimanded by the Supreme War Councilor for their "lack of zeal."[65] Shortly afterward, Colonel Matsui and Dr. Uzawa notified Mazaki of the likelihood of a rebellion in the midst of the Aizawa trial.[66] In this context, the leaders of the National Principle group, according to the affidavit of Lieutenant Isobe, "received word of a conference among Generals Mazaki, Furushō, Yamashita, and Colonel Mura-kami"; and concluded that these senior officers would rally to the cause of a "national restoration" in the event of a great domestic crisis.[67] How much of this inference was the product of Isobe's imagination is difficult to judge. Certainly, the Kōdō generals knew about their revolutionary plans; and the generals had neither dissuaded the young officers with verbal

[63] Byas, *Government by Assassination*, 111.

[64] USDS, Archives, *Japan: Political Affairs*, 894.00/642. Embassy Report, March 20, 1936.

[65] *Japan Advertiser*, September 23, 1937.

[66] *Ibid.*   [67] Kōnō, *Ni-ni-roku*, 31-32.

admonitions nor bothered to inform the military police of the incipient rebellion. "In connection with this incident," observed General Terauchi shortly after the February uprising, "there are those not directly involved but who knew that such plans were afoot. Yet they kept silent."[68] This elliptical statement referred to Generals Mazaki, Furushō, Okamura, and Yamashita.

The expectation that the Kōdō generals would support the rebellion had not been completely misplaced. At 5:00 a.m. on February 26, General Mazaki arrived at the residence of the war minister, and with General Kuwashima he discussed the purpose of the rebellion with the young officers. After reviewing the proclamation of the Righteous Army, Mazaki assured Muranaka and Isobe, "As I understand very well the spirit in which you acted, I shall now go out to see what I can do."[69] With the departure of General Mazaki and Kuwashima, the rebellious troops barricaded themselves in the residence of the war minister and silently awaited word of the army's commitment to the national restoration. This posture was abandoned briefly in the morning of February 27 when the insurgents declared: "Men are lacking, but there is the valiant General Mazaki, in whose hands the Army of Justice should place everything."[70] Later that afternoon, however, Mazaki belatedly informed his admirers that he could not act of his "own accord, without taking advice in higher quarters. . . . It would be an outrageous proceeding if I were to accede to your request on my own authority, and I will not do it."[71] This ambivalent attitude fortunately did not mirror the sentiments of the other members of the Supreme War Council. Speaking for the

[68] Saionji-Harada, *Memoirs,* July 8, 1936.

[69] From the official report on Mazaki's court-martial, *Japan Advertiser,* September 23, 1937.

[70] *Ibid.*

[71] IMTFE, *Document 600,* 5. Although this document was not entered into the official records of the Tokyo Tribunal, an abstract of it is available, *Checklist of Archives, op.cit.,* Entry IMT 60. The document is the "Mimeographed Record of the Secret Operations of the February 26 Incident, Compiled by the Operations Division of the Headquarters for the Administration of Martial Law," April 1, 1936.

council, General Araki bluntly told War Minister Kuwashima, "We feel the revolting officers should commit suicide, and in our dealings with them we should let our attitude be apparent."[72]

This unqualified rejection by the Supreme War Council of the young officers' rationale for murder and rebellion was reinforced by other influential authorities. The Emperor personally castigated the so-called Righteous Army, indicating to the war minister that he regarded it as an "insurgent army."[73] The naval minister simply advised General Kuwashima that he had ordered a contingent of marines to Yokohama in case the army proved reluctant to move against the mutinous troops. Subjected to this pressure, War Minister Kuwashima surrounded the rebels with the Imperial Guard Division; and, on February 29, the rebels were confronted with a gentle ultimatum: "The Emperor himself has ordered you to return to your barracks. It is not yet too late. Cease your resistance and go home in order that your sins may be forgiven."[74] By late afternoon, only the abandoned barricades marked the perimeter of the rebellion. The troops, in small clusters, had marched to their barracks; the officers had surrendered to the military police. Of the leaders, only Captain Nonaka still remained behind the barricades; and he had imposed the appropriate penalty for ineffectual leadership—suicide by disembowelment.

AFTERMATH OF THE FEBRUARY 26TH INCIDENT

As the most momentous breach of discipline in the history of the Imperial army, the rebellion of the Righteous Army reverberated throughout the military establishment. The new war minister, General Terauchi Hisaichi, instituted a personnel directive designed to eradicate the Kōdō and Seigun factions. The leaders of these groups were either transferred to the

[72] *Ibid.*, 4.
[73] Saionji-Harada, *Memoirs*, March 14, 1936.
[74] Butow, *Tojo*, 68.

inactive reserve or barred from future assignments in central headquarters. Those affected by this ruling included Generals Koiso Kuniake and Tatekawa Yoshitsugu, Colonel Hashimoto Kingorō, and Major Tanaka Kiyoshi of the *Seigun-ha*; and Generals Obata Tokushiro, Okamura Neiji, Yamashita Tomoyuki, Yamaoka Shigeatsu, Yanagawa Heisuke, Colonel Suzuki Teiichi and Lt. Colonel Murakami Kisaku of the *Kōdō-ha*. In addition, five of the seven members of the Supreme War Council—Generals Araki, Mazaki, Abe, Hishikari, and Hishi—the army's ranking generals—Honjō, Minami, Matsui, and Hayashi—and War Minister Kuwashima were placed on the inactive list. In conjunction with these steps, Terauchi initiated two important administrative changes: the government revised the regulations governing the portfolio of war minister so as to restrict it to officers on the list of active generals; and the practice of submitting personnel changes to the formal approval of the Big Three was abandoned in favor of the earlier custom which invested this authority in the war minister.[75] These reactions to the February 26th incident were complemented in the realm of military justice, where the leaders of the rebellion and Colonel Aizawa were subjected to secret court-martials which invariably imposed the death penalty.

Although the new court-martials, transfers, and regulations effectively quashed the regional factions and the revolutionary movement of the young officers, they did not signify the demise of all factionalism. Within central headquarters, the criteria of the year of graduation from the Military Academy (*gakubatsu*), departmental affiliation (*heikabatsu*), and primary duty

[75] Interviews with Colonel Nishiura Susumu, General Katakura Chū, and General Satō Kenryō. On the active-duty regulation, Professor Yanaga has considered it "the most important single step that put the military on the road to supremacy." *Japan Since Perry*, 525. Hugh Byas, in 1936, judged: "The present change does not alter the power of the services over cabinets, but it restores control of army personnel to the War Minister." Hugh Byas Collection, Sterling Memorial Library, Yale University, Box 3, "Censorship, 1920-1941."

assignment (*shokumubatsu*) still flourished.[76] Unlike the Kōdō or Seigun groups, which were mainly regional cliques, this type of factionalism was dictated by the educational system and particular roles or assignments. Moreover, the prominent figures of the Kōdō and Seigun factions were not consigned to oblivion after the February 26th rebellion. Within a few years, Prince Konoe, as premier, would secure important cabinet and administrative posts for Generals Araki, Yanagawa, Yamaoka, and Suzuki Teiichi; and Generals Abe, Hayashi, and Koiso subsequently served as premiers. And there was the political dilemma posed by the behavior of General Mazaki.

Until his death, General Mazaki stoutly voiced the incredible argument that his enemies in the Control Faction had deliberately engineered the November incident at the Military Academy and the February 26th rebellion simply to disgrace him.[77] Although Mazaki was spared a court-martial, this was less the consequence of his innocence than of the influence of his friends and the delicate nature of army politics. Mazaki was actually held in custody for his part in the February uprising for over fifteen months. During this time Araki labored diligently on Mazaki's behalf, winning the powerful support of the president of the House of Peers, Prince Konoe Fumimaro.[78] Equally significantly, Mazaki threatened, in the event of a court-martial, to equate his role in the February 26th incident with those of Generals Ugaki, Tatekawa, and Koiso in the 1931 March incident. This would prove embarrassing to the army and it might even generate further turmoil in central headquarters. Thus, General Minami, who was no friend of Mazaki, declared, "If Mazaki is found guilty, then Ugaki and Mazaki are from some points of view equally guilty."[79] This attitude and Prince Konoe's influence were instrumental in the

---

[76] Crowley, "Japanese Army Factionalism," *op.cit.*, 326.

[77] Storry, *Double Patriots*, 191.

[78] "Somehow," Saionji remarked, "Konoe seems to defend Mazaki and Araki. . . . It is indeed regrettable for a man of such noble birth and character." Saionji-Harada, *Memoirs*, August 13, 1936.

[79] *Ibid.*, July 5, 1937.

army's failure to bring Mazaki to trial; and once the China incident began in 1937, the public memory of the February rebellion dimmed appreciably. In November 1937, Premier Konoe quietly secured the release of General Mazaki, marking the final act of the most tragic and bitter factional struggle in the history of the Imperial army.

FACTIONALISM AND NATIONAL POLICY

In terms of the preceding analysis, the appraisals of army factionalism and its relevance to national policy first offered by General Tanaka Ryūkichi and Prince Konoe Fumimaro would seem inadequate and grossly misleading. Factionalism was both more complex than that suggested by the Imperial Way-Control Faction dichotomy and of much less significance to the conduct and formulation of national policy. Between 1932 and 1934, army central headquarters had been vitally affected by the public posture and personnel practices of War Minister Araki, which (1) created a Kōdō clique of officers with a Tosa-Saga regional background; (2) precipitated a new Chōshū faction, the *Seigun-ha*; and (3) hampered, if not endangered, the efforts of the war ministry to devise and implement a long-term political and economic policy that would enhance the "total war" capabilities of the nation. These developments occasioned a general movement within the Supreme War Council and central headquarters designed to eliminate the discord engendered by the reappearance of regional cliques and to formulate a comprehensive policy which would guide the army's strategic, political, and economic plans and policies. In pursuit of these two goals, General Nagata assembled a new staff in the war ministry composed of the most distinguished graduates of the War College. In the process, however, Nagata by-passed or removed many talented staff officers simply because they had been associated with Araki's patronage of Tosa-Saga officers—e.g., Colonels Suzuki Teiichi and Yamashita Tomoyuki. This policy understandably sharpened the swords of resentment of the Kōdō generals;

and, following the ouster of Mazaki from the inspector generalate, some Kōdō officers brandished their sentiments before the leaders of the National Principle group. Considering the conviction of Araki as a Class A war criminal, it is worth noting that Araki had not been privy to any of the conspiratorial discussions or activities related to the outbreak of the February rebellion. Still, there is no denying that a hatred of Nagata and his policies was, for different reasons, rampant among the young officers of the *Kokutai genri-ha* and the Kōdō generals.

Two consequences of this harmony of hatred were the assassination of Nagata and the rebellion of February 26, 1936. Although each of these violent events affected domestic and foreign policy, it is difficult to regard the February 26th Incident as a seed-plot of modern Japanese history. The Control movement was not a unity, a faction comparable to the regional cliques of the *Kōdō-ha* and the *Seigun-ha*. Whatever consensus existed within the Control movement was furnished by a commitment to the doctrines of "total war" and the "national defense" state, and by a desire to eradicate regional cliques from central headquarters. Furthermore, there is more than a little irony in the image of Generals Hayashi and Nagata as the architects of a fascist movement and of a policy of expansion into China, both of which presumably were foisted on the government following the triumph of the Control Faction after February 26, 1936. Certainly, Hayashi and Nagata were not responsible for the 1933 cabinet decision which called for the exclusion of the Kuomintang from North China, as this had been adopted at the insistence of War Minister Araki; and, in the spring of 1935, Hayashi and Nagata had neither provoked nor encouraged the controversy over Professor Minobe's concept of the Imperial institution. Moreover, the war ministry had vetoed the promotion of an "autonomous" North China in July 1935; but with the death of Nagata and the resignation of Hayashi, this policy was sanctioned by War Minister Kuwashima. Finally, since it is generally believed the Imperial Way faction was opposed to any meddling in China, it is noteworthy that two Kōdō generals—Furushō and Okamura—had been prime movers in the creation of the Hopei-Chahar Political Council in the fall of 1935, an activity which complemented their mischievous encouragement of the leaders of the National Principle group.

In retrospect, three main observations on the anatomy of army factionalism should be noted before considering the formulation and adoption of a new national policy in the spring and summer of 1936. First, the rubric of an encompassing Control Faction-Imperial Way dispute cannot adequately or accurately explain the March incident of 1931, the assassinations of 1932, the murder of General Nagata in 1935, and the rebellion of February 26, 1936. Secondly, the increasingly authoritarian nature of the Japanese government and the extension of Japanese power in the provinces of North China were not caused by the machinations of a Control Faction. Throughout the 1933-1936 period, the Five Ministers' Conference and "The Foreign Policy of Imperial Japan," adopted by the Saitō cabinet, represented the prime policy-making group and the basic national policy of the Japanese government. Thirdly, army factionalism had little bearing on the commitment to exclude the Kuomintang from North China. In fact, the decision to promote regional governments in North China had been officially enunciated in 1933, under General Araki, confirmed in 1934 by General Hayashi, and vigorously championed in the fall of 1935 by General Kuwashima. In short, Japan's foreign and security policies were less the consequence of factional disputes than the product of three main considerations—namely, (1) Japan's changing diplomatic relations with the Western powers; (2) the competing versions of national defense articulated by the leaders of the army and navy; and (3) the interplay of disagreements within and among the foreign, war, and naval ministries over the most appropriate way to realize the objectives defined in "The Foreign Policy of Imperial Japan." This pattern was not visibly affected by army factionalism in the early 1930's; and, as the genesis of a new national policy in the summer of 1936 reveals, it was not altered by the rebellion of February 26, 1936.

SECURITY CONCEPTIONS IN 1936

The Saitō cabinet had, in the fall of 1933, defined Japan's national policy in terms of the dominant strategic concerns of both services.[80] This approach to national policy yielded a consensus in favor of three distinct objectives—the abrogation of the Washington and London naval treaties, the development of Manchukuo, and the promotion of regional governments in North China. Within the diplomatic context produced by the Mukden and Shanghai incidents, these goals seemed a reasonable and creditable way to realize an Asiatic Monroe Doctrine. By 1936, Japan had furnished Britain and the United States with the proper legal notifications of her intention to terminate the existing naval limitations agreements after December 1936; the Kuomintang had been effectively barred from the provinces of North China; and Manchukuo constituted the strongest magnet for governmental capital investment. Nevertheless, Japan's claim to a preeminent position in East Asia had not been recognized by the Occidental powers, nor was it confirmed by what Shigemitsu Mamoru called "the rationale of actual force." Japan's foreign and security policies were, in 1936, still plagued by several diplomatic and strategic problems, many of which had been aggravated by the army's blunt interpretation and implementation of the cabinet's North China policy. The Soviet Union was courting the Mongol tribes in Outer Mongolia with a Protocol of Mutual Assistance; the paradise of an "autonomous" North China had degenerated into precarious warlord regimes; the prospect of a Sino-Japanese Friendship Treaty based on Hirota's three principles appeared, more than ever, to be a wistful illusion; the Chinese Communists had relocated themselves in Shensi province, where they pleaded for a "united front" against

[80] Chapter IV, 190-195.

Japanese imperialism; the Anglo-American seapowers steadily affirmed their commitments to the Nine Power Treaty and the non-recognition of Manchukuo; and the Roosevelt administration had recently requested the enactment of the largest peacetime program of naval construction in American history. Solving the problems posed by these considerations formed the central task of the Hirota cabinet in the spring of 1936—namely, the reformulation of Japan's national policy in order to provide greater coordination between strategic planning and foreign policy, especially in reference to the conduct of Japan's China policy.[81]

Throughout the 1933-1936 period, Japan's continental policy had been marred by a fundamental inconsistency—the simultaneous desire for a Sino-Japanese rapprochement and for the exclusion of the Kuomintang from North China. When the foreign ministry proposed, in the spring of 1935, to negotiate a treaty with the Nanking government, the army authorities were concerned lest this buttress the unification movement in China and, more precisely, augment the power and prestige of the Kuomintang in North China. In order to preclude the latter possibility, the field armies had imposed the Ho-Umezu and the Ching-Doihara agreements in June 1935; and, in the fall, they launched the North China autonomous movement. These activities had been vindicated by the contentions that a fragmented North China under local warlords or an autonomous North China protected by Japan would be of greater utility than any détente with the Nanking government. In particular, the army authorities believed the decision to promote local governments in North China should take precedence over the projected Sino-Japanese accord because the former policy would (1) create a buffer zone between Manchukuo and Nationalist China; (2) permit the integration of the resources of North China with those in Manchukuo;

[81] My understanding of the Hirota cabinet was enriched by the reflections of Mr. Fujinuma Shōhei, chief cabinet secretary of the Hirota cabinet; and the Honorable Arita Hachirō, foreign minister of the Hirota cabinet.

and (3) increase the operational capabilities of the Kwantung Army in the provinces of Inner Mongolia. Permeating this army view of North China was both a distrust and resentment of the Kuomintang, sentiments which were not moderated by the relocation of the Chinese Communists in the province of Shensi. This insensitivity to the political aspects of the Communist movement was evident in the Darien Conference of mid-October; and, in September, General Isogaya had publicly notified the Chinese press representatives in Peking: "If Japan acts against the Communists, it will not be as a measure of assisting Chiang Kai-shek but in order to stamp out the Red regime, thereby protecting the areas bordering on Manchukuo."[82] This preoccupation with the defense of Manchukuo by systematically undermining the position of the Kuomintang in North China characterized the army actions in North China; and the autonomy campaign was pursued up to the brink of an open conflict with the Nanking government.

The threat of intervention by the Nationalist army and the loud complaints of the foreign and naval ministries forced the Japanese army authorities, in December 1935, to accept the East Hopei Anti-Communist Council and the Hopei-Chahar Political Council as the maximum political changes which could be effected in North China. This decision avoided the risk of war in 1935; but, in the process, the foreign ministry was compelled to abandon its quest for a Sino-Japanese Treaty based on Hirota's three principles. Once the new political organs were functioning in North China and there no longer appeared any possibility of a diplomatic détente with the Nanking government, the earlier basis of contention between the foreign and war ministries was largely resolved—that is, after December 1935, any Sino-Japanese diplomatic accord would have to be predicated on acceptance of the local governments in North China. As General Itagaki, the vice-chief of staff for the Kwantung Army, confessed to Foreign

[82] As quoted, *New York Times*, September 11, 1935.

Minister Arita in March 1936, the new political situation in North China was eminently satisfactory because it allowed the Kwantung Army to "concentrate on the northern and internal fortifications" of Manchukuo.[83] Obviously, the willingness of the war ministry and the general staff in January 1936 to anesthetize the "autonomous" movement in North China was related to the diminished prospects of any diplomatic accommodation with the Nanking government. It was also dictated by the fact that neither the cabinet nor the general staff believed Japan should court a war with the Nationalist government over the North China issue. Conflict with China contained the risk of a possible intervention by the powers which, given Japan's existing strength, could not be contested; and a premature involvement in protracted hostilities would impede the army's long-term economic policies. In order to comprehend the second obstacle to a forceful creation of an autonomous North China, it is necessary to review the basic strategic plans which crystallized in army central headquarters in the fall of 1935.

Beginning in 1930, the staff of the war ministry had been constantly perplexed by three tasks—the effective utilization of the resources of Manchuria, the rationalization of the army, and the coordination of Japan's industrial complex with the expanding and changing needs of the service. Despite the complementary relationships among these objectives, the seizure of Manchuria had not produced the necessary political and economic cooperation between the army and the Japanese business community. Confronted by the great depression, most business leaders subscribed to the classic axiom of reducing governmental expenditures as the most effective fiscal policy; and the army's paternalistic administration had succeeded in limiting private capital investment in Manchukuo. The alienation of the financial leaders and the army authorities was further aggravated by the assassinations of 1932, by the ide-

[83] IMTFE, *Defense Document 2487*, 26. Also Gaimushō, *Nihon gaikō nenpyō narabini shuyō bunsho* (Tokyo, 1955), II, 330-334.

ology of the Imperial Way, which branded capitalists as traitors, and by the slogan of a "national defense state," which threatened to invest military bureaucrats with the power to direct a planned economy. The lack of viable communications between the military and the *zaibatsu* was also compounded by the factional disputes in army circles and by the lack of a comprehensive military policy to guide the planning of the war ministry and the general staff. In an effort to resolve the last difficulty, General Nagata in August 1935 arranged the appointment of Colonel Machijiri Ryoki to his department, along with the selection of General Imai Kiyoshi as chief of the operations division and Colonel Ishiwara Kanji as head of the operations section of the general staff. These officers were rabid devotees of the "total war" doctrine; and Ishiwara and Machijiri had been personal friends since their student years at the Military Academy. In effect, just before his death, Nagata had marshaled a group of officers in the two key sections of central headquarters—the operations division of the general staff and the Bureau of Military Affairs of the war ministry—which shared the desire for a comprehensive national policy that would coordinate the army's strategic and administrative plans, along with the government's fiscal and foreign policies.

The consequences of this August personnel policy are suggested by the fact that, in the turmoil and difficulties generated by the murder of Nagata and the selection of General Kuwashima as war minister, the operations division and the Bureau of Military Affairs proceeded to formulate a new national defense policy. Postulating the need for an "autonomous national defense," Colonels Ishiwara and Machijiri concluded that Japan would have to abandon its "free economy" because it was not geared to the long-term requirements of the services.[84] Instead, the government would have to adopt two separate five-year plans which would

[84] Interviews with Generals Inada Seijun, Hashimoto Gun, and Satō Kenryō.

enable the army and navy gradually to enlarge their capabilities to the extent the empire would become strategically secure against the combined Anglo-American fleets and the Soviet army. To this end, Machijiri and Ishiwara judged that Japan should pursue a cautious foreign policy, including a renewal of the naval limitations treaties for a five-year period and the avoidance of any serious incidents in North China, lest this unite the Western sea powers in an effective coalition against the empire. During the initial five-year period, the army planners placed the highest priority on the rationalization of the army, the development of Manchukuo, and the adoption of a planned economy to direct capital investment within Japan. In particular, Colonels Ishiwara and Machijiri, with the economic expertise of Miyazaki Seiji of the South Manchurian Railway, drafted an economic plan to guide national military expenditures and economic development for the 1937-1942 fiscal years.[85] According to their estimates, the government should expend, in this five-year period, ten billion yen in order to double the production of iron ore and hydroelectric power and to effect a tenfold increase in the production of aircraft. Apart from this expenditure, the economic policy envisioned by Ishiwara and Machijiri called for the nation's entire foreign exchange in this five-year interval to be utilized for the purchase of machine tools from Germany and the United States. As defined by the operations division and the Bureau of Military Affairs, Japan's national policy should seek (1) some form of naval agreement which would forestall an openly competitive armament race; (2) a stabilization of the North China issue; (3) the economic development of Manchukuo and a directed domestic economy; and (4) the build-up of the army in the first five-year period, with priority

[85] My understanding of the army's economic planning described in this paragraph is primarily based upon the reflections of Generals Satō, Inada, and Katakura. In 1936, Inada was a member of Ishiwara's staff, Katakura and Satō were under Machijiri. In addition, see Nihon kokusai seiji gakkai [NKSG], *Taiheiyō sensō e no michi* (Tokyo, 1963), VIII, 222-226.

given to naval construction in the second five-year program. The advantages of this policy were twofold: it would allow the army to acquire a commanding superiority over Soviet forces in the maritime provinces; and it would alleviate, if not settle, the strategic problems posed by the Anglo-American fleets through a diplomacy which would reduce the tensions caused by an aggressive policy in North China and by the proposed abrogation of the Washington and London naval treaties.

The national defense policy articulated by the army authorities in the winter of 1935 was, except for the five-year economic plan, a restatement of the original proposals advanced by the war ministry in the fall of 1933. Understandably, it provoked objections in naval circles similar to those which had been raised in 1933 by Naval Minister Osumi. From the viewpoint of the naval general staff, Japan's continental policies, first in Manchuria and later in North China, had conflicted with the traditional interests and treaty rights of the Western powers. In this context, Japan could not rely on the friendly disposition of the Anglo-American nations. Rather, the navy would have to be expanded until it acquired a clear hegemony over the Western fleets and, until this was accomplished, Japan could not risk any conflict with the powers by a reckless China policy. "If the development of Manchuria is the key to the Soviet problem," noted the commanding officer of the home fleet in March 1936, "then this matter, along with the North China movement of the army, must be placed under the direction of one national policy."[86] Along with this wish to impose greater control over the army's approach to Manchuria and North China, the naval authorities devised their own version of economic development. In lieu of a focus on Northeast Asia—Manchuria, Inner Mongolia, and North China—the naval general staff substituted the

[86] NKSG, *Taiheiyō sensō*, VIII, 217.

hokushu nanshin doctrine, "Defend in the north, advance to the south."[87]

Japan was essentially an island empire, reasoned her naval strategists; and, as British history revealed, sea power and international trade constituted the essential bases of national security and economic prosperity for insular empires.[88] Since the acquisition of Manchukuo had not solved Japan's economic difficulties, it seemed prudent to defend Manchukuo by a moderate China policy and to concentrate on a peaceful expansion into the South Seas. A continuation of an openly aggressive policy in North China would, judged the naval general staff, only enhance the prospects of an Anglo-American alliance, whereas a cautious China policy would at least ensure the neutrality of Great Britain in all Sino-Japanese disputes. An advance into the South Seas, moreover, would provide the empire with an access to oil deposits, the prime natural resource. As defined by the naval authorities, the *hokushu nanshin* policy would permit the army to defend the northern area by the development of Manchukuo and the rationalization of the army; and this, in conjunction with a temperate China policy and an enlargement of the fleet, would enable the empire to expand into the South Seas.

Given the competing views of national defense underlying the planning of each service, it would be difficult indeed to formulate a single national policy. Still, by 1936, both general staffs shared one estimate, the necessity for a more moderate North China policy. This consensus enabled the foreign, war, and naval ministries in January 1936 to agree on the decisions to rely on economic subversion in North China and to seek limited diplomatic agreements in the realm of Sino-Japanese trade and commercial relations.[89] Following the February

[87] Fukudome Shigeru, *Shikan shinjuwan kōgeki* (Tokyo, 1955), 58-62.
[88] The recapitulation of naval policy in this paragraph is drawn mainly from an interview with Admiral Fukudome Shigeru, who, in 1936, was chief of the operations division of the naval general staff. Also Takagi Sōkichi, *RikuKai gunjin kishitsu no sōi* (Naval War College, 1944).
[89] Chapter IV, 237-243.

26th incident, this consensus also enabled the Hirota cabinet to seek an official national policy which would coordinate the diplomacy of the foreign ministry and the security plans of the two services. In fact, the naval ministry borrowed a page from the 1933 army manual on cabinet politics and, in mid-April, it confronted the inner cabinet with a proposed guide for national policy.

Although the attainment of an autonomous national defense represented the fundamental national objective, Naval Minister Nagano emphasized that this goal would have to be realized by peaceful means—thus signifying the paramount need for a carefully controlled and coordinated foreign policy.[90] To this end, the naval presentation noted that Manchukuo could become a viable state only if Japan pursued a program of extensive political and economic assistance, along with a military policy which was restricted to the development of the internal military fortifications of Manchukuo. Secondly, judged the naval recommendation, Japan could bring about a peaceful and stable East Asia only in a diplomatic context which confirmed and contributed to an alliance among China, Japan, and Manchukuo. In view of the recent attempts to negotiate a treaty based on Hirota's three principles, however, Japan would have to concentrate on limited trade agreements. Admittedly, conceded the naval authorities, North China represented a special problem because these provinces were essential to the security of Manchukuo; and, to handle this issue, Japan should rely on peaceful means in order to promote her economic interests in North China. Above all, insisted the naval voice, there must be no overt military aggression, since this would only act "as an excuse for a tripartite intervention" by the powers in defense of their treaty rights.[91] Furthermore, continued the naval outline, the tremendous social and economic unrest within Japan,

[90] On this naval guide for national policy, see NKSG, *Taiheiyō sensō*, VIII, 223.
[91] *Ibid.*

especially that symbolized by the Kōdō mentality of the February 26th incident, demonstrated that Manchukuo alone could not solve the problems raised by an immense population crowded on a handful of islands that were deficient in natural resources. The only solution to the nation's long-term economic problems would be an advance into the South Seas, where the oil resources and sparsely settled islands offered rich potentialities. The key to defense of Manchukuo and the advance southward, concluded the naval conception of national policy, was Japan's China policy. If Japan were to adhere to a reasonable policy in North China and make a courteous acknowledgment of British rights and privileges on the mainland, the changing European situation would induce the British government to recognize Manchukuo and support Japanese economic penetration into the South Seas. In turn, Japan could then meet any military or naval contingency posed by the American fleet or the Soviet army.

Within the world of probable potential enemies, the presentation of the naval ministry was based on a strategic axiom not easily contested—namely, Japan's military and naval capabilities in 1936 could assure victory in case of war with one Western power; they furnished the prospect of a stalemate in the event Japan were confronted by two major powers; but they could not prevent disaster if Japan were to become involved in a conflict with the Soviet Union, the United States, and Great Britain.[92] Given this premise, the focus on the China problem was merited, since China constituted the one subject of common concern to the three Occidental powers. Similarly, the argument that Japan could maximize its security by a moderate China policy and a simultaneous enlargement of the army and navy was equally compelling. Presumably, the Soviet military threat could be mastered by rationalizing the army and strengthening the internal fortifications of Manchukuo; and the American fleet would be neutralized by

[92] This axiom of naval planning was first called to my attention by Admirals Tomioka Sadatoshi and Takagi Sōkichi.

the fortification of the mandated islands and an Anglo-Japanese *modus vivendi*. In the whiplash of the February 26th incident, moreover, War Minister Terauchi was in no position to dispute the assertion that the abortive North China autonomy movement and the rebellion itself had demonstrated the necessity for a stringent control over the political activities of the army. Still, the army spokesman in the cabinet was not enthusiastic about the dimension in naval policy which had not been evident in 1933, when the Saitō cabinet had previously defined national policy. "It is likely," observed Admiral Takahashi, "that Japan's advance into 'Manchukuo' will soon reach its limit and, therefore, the empire's future commercial expansion must be directed to the Southern Seas. In such an event, the cruising radius of the Japanese Navy must be quickly expanded so as to reach New Guinea, Borneo, and the Celebes."[93] The plans and recommendations drafted by army central headquarters in the winter of 1935 had not designated the South Seas as the key to future economic development, nor had they conceded the necessity to build a fleet capable of dominating the South Seas. Recognizing the dissenting views of his service ministers, as well as an apparent accord on a new China policy, Premier Hirota, on April 17, 1936, requested General Terauchi and Admiral Nagano to draft one strategic policy guide for consideration by the Inner Cabinet; and, at the same time, Hirota appointed a Special Committee on the Current Situation to prepare a new policy vis-à-vis North China. The labors connected with both assignments resulted in a cluster of cabinet decisions in the summer of 1936 which culminated in the "Fundamental Principles of National Policy" of August 11, 1936.

A New National Policy Consensus

The war ministry in the fall of 1933 had seized the

[93] Royal Institute of International Affairs, *Survey of International Affairs, 1936* (London, 1937), 900. IMTFE, *Document 1618-A,* is a December 1935 statement of naval policy outlining a proposed program for the "guidance of public opinion" on the subject of naval armament.

initiative in the definition of Japan's national policy. Partly because of the political context produced by the reactions to the February 26th incident, the naval authorities managed, in the spring of 1936, to conduct the discussions of national policy in terms of its recommendations. After several weeks of negotiations between the war and naval ministries, Admiral Nagano, on June 30, presented the Inner Cabinet with an "Outline of State Policy."[94] According to this outline, the fundamental aim of national policy was the stabilization of Japan's national defense by the development of Manchukuo and by an advance into the South Seas. This could be accomplished, ventured Nagano, by a foreign policy based on "the Kōdō spirit and a consistent policy of overseas expansion."[95] More specifically, Japan could become the stabilizing power in Asia only by perfecting her naval and military armaments—that is, Japan would have to terminate the Soviet menace, neutralize the efficacy of the Anglo-American fleets, and impose a policy of collaboration among Japan, China, and, Manchukuo. Moreover, noted Nagano's outline, Japan was not endowed with natural resources and this presented serious obstacles to the "completion of national defense." In order to maximize the nation's economy, it would therefore be necessary to "reform our governmental system" for the purpose of unifying "political, financial, and economic policies both within and without the country."[96] In case the ministers of state were uncertain about the central objectives of national policy, Admiral Nagano succinctly listed the capabilities desired: the Imperial army "must be strengthened in order that we may be able to crush the Far Eastern forces of the Soviet Union with one decisive blow"; and the Imperial navy must be able "to maintain command of the Western Pacific against the American navy."[97] In effect, the "Outline of State Policy" was no more than a synthesis of the major ambitions prevalent in both general staffs.

[94] IMTFE, *Exhibit 977* (Japanese text).
[95] *Ibid.*, 1.   [96] *Ibid.*, 2.   [97] *Ibid.*, 2.

After Admiral Nagano had reviewed the gist of his proposal, Finance Minister Baba Eiichi agreed "in principle" with the aims postulated by the outline. However, the finance minister was uncertain about the ability of the government to underwrite a mammoth expansion of both services; and he requested greater precision in the reference to the "governmental reforms" and the manner in which the services thought the economy could be unified with the government's policies. Apart from these reservations, Baba hoped the Imperial government would not try "to correct the policies of foreign powers by a policy of militaristic aggression.[98] Foreign Minister Arita Hachirō assured the finance minister that the details of foreign policy were being worked out by the foreign, war, and naval ministries and that Japan's diplomacy would be confined to peaceful means.[99] Specifically, Arita identified North China as one region which would be prudently handled; and he observed that Japan's naval preparations against Britain and the United States were "purely defensive" in nature. Admiral Nagano seconded the explanatory remarks of the foreign minister; and, when no further questions were raised, Premier Hirota adjourned the Inner Cabinet with the request that Admiral Nagano should draft a series of specific recommendations "based upon the principles presented in the 'Outline of State Policy.' "[100]

Parallel with the joint defense policy prepared by the war and naval ministries in the spring of 1936, the Committee on the Current Situation was engaged in the formulation of a policy guide for North China. This committee was composed of representatives of the war, foreign, and naval ministries, under the chairmanship of Vice-Foreign Minister Horinouchi. Technically, the premier invested this group with the authority "to study, investigate, legislate, and report on our North China policy, . . . including policies which we will permit the governments in North China to adopt."[101] This mandate

[98] IMTFE, *Exhibit 978.*   [99] *Ibid.*
[100] *Ibid.*
[101] IMTFE, *Document 2446.* 9. My understanding of this committee was

was further enhanced by the ruling of the Inner Cabinet that "since the military was not experienced in matters of finance, economy, and transportation, . . . all economic and financial matters concerning North China would be decided by the committee."[102] Despite the power entrusted to the special committee and the vital importance of the North China problem, this new policy-making group was not legitimized by an Imperial ordinance. In fact, Premier Hirota failed to bring the committee "to the attention of the full cabinet" because, as Foreign Minister Arita explained in a note to his staff, "the decision to establish the committee was made among and between the prime minister and the concerned ministers of state."[103] In other words, the Inner Cabinet viewed Japan's China policy to be the prerogative of the war, foreign, and naval ministries; and the Committee on the Current Situation constituted an *ad hoc* administrative arrangement by which these ministries could coordinate their policies.

Underlying the appointment of this special committee was an informal consensus which granted the necessity to curb the army's highly individualistic style of interpreting and implementing the cabinet's China policy. This unanimity, though, did not signify a substantive modification of the army's influence on all matters pertaining to North China. If anything, the Committee on the Current Situation marked the cabinet's acceptance of the newly formed political organs in North China as accomplishments which were not to be amended by negotiations with the Nanking government. Indeed, the committee actually invested the army with complete administrative control over all economic and political policies affecting North China. This fact was obscured somewhat by the nominal position of leadership held by the vice-foreign minister in the new committee. Nevertheless, prior to the formal administrative enactment of the special committee, the

---

enhanced by interviews with Foreign Minister Arita and General Hashimoto Gun, the war ministry's representative on this committee.
    [102] *Ibid.*, 9-10.   [103] *Ibid.*, 11.

war and foreign ministers had reached an "understanding" according to which the army pledged that it would "not adopt any measures" which violated the intent of the policies devised by the Committee on the Current Situation; and, in return, the foreign ministry stipulated that the execution of policy would be placed "in the hands of the army authorities for some duration."[104] This inter-ministerial accord was pegged to a specific assurance that the field army in North China would never "dare to ignore the government's policy" by precipitating further incidents.[105] This pledge of good behavior was not casually given. In order to ensure a meticulous compliance with the decision to stabilize the North China situation, the field officers most prominently associated with the autonomous movement—Generals Tada and Doihara—were transferred from North China. More significantly, the Tientsin garrison was removed from the command jurisdiction of the Kwantung Army; and the newly created North China Army was staffed by officers who were both familiar and sympathetic with the strategic and economic policies governing the army's approach to North China.[106] These administrative changes in the spring of 1936 demonstrated the existence of a viable consensus between the foreign and war ministries which soon filtered into the official foreign policy of the Hirota cabinet.

After sixteen weeks of discussion, the Committee on the Current Situation finally drafted a position paper which satisfied the staffs of the war and foreign ministries. On August 7, 1936, Vice-Foreign Minister Horinouchi presented this estimate to the Inner Cabinet. Essentially, the committee listed five objectives to govern Japan's policy in North China: (1) the continuation of the political *status quo* for the immediate future; (2) the development of the economy of the

104 *Ibid.*, 12.

105 Japanese Ministry for Foreign Affairs [JMFA], *Teikoku no taiShi seisaku kankei*, VIII, "Suma soryoji Kita bukan kaigi" [Conversation Between General Kita and Consul General Suma], May 2, 1936.

106 *Foreign Relations of the United States*, III (1936), contains a number of reports indicating that these changes were perceived by American diplomats.

provinces in ways which would contribute to national defense capabilities of the empire; (3) the encouragement of a "Mongolia for Mongolians" movement in Suiyuan and Chahar; (4) the resumption of diplomatic negotiations with the Nationalist government on the basis of a "pro-Japanese, anti-Soviet" attitude; and (5) the ultimate realization of an independent North China.[107] Although this policy guide had been prepared in cooperation with the army authorities, War Minister Terauchi surprised his colleagues in the Inner Cabinet with a request for a more explicit statement of the government's approach to the Nanking government. In deference to the war minister, the Inner Cabinet appended two directives to the considered proposals of the committee. First, the ministers declared that the creation of a "special region in North China in which Japan, China, and Manchukuo could cooperatively defend themselves against the Bolshevik obtrusion of the Soviet Union" constituted the fundamental objective of the government's North China policy.[108] Secondly, the cabinet obtusely precluded the possibility of any support for the Kuomintang with the following ruling: "Concerning another provincial regime [in North China], Japan will not adopt any measure which might, as a result of its adoption, either hinder or help the unification or division of China. This decision is a basic principle of Japan's China policy which had been adopted on October 4, 1935."[109] Once the cabinet had settled the China policy to the satisfaction of the war minister, Premier Hirota requested the naval minister to review the security policies of the empire.

Six weeks earlier, on June 30, the Inner Cabinet had endorsed the "Outline of State Policy"; and the premier had asked Admiral Nagano to draft a more specific guide to national policy. This assignment, however, proved to be beyond the talents of the naval minister. When, for example,

[107] JMFA, *Teikoku no taiShi*, VIII, Cable 1387, from Foreign Minister Hirota to all consulates in China. Also IMTFE, *Exhibit 216*.
[108] IMTFE, *Document 1857 B*, 4.
[109] *Ibid.*

Foreign Minister Arita discreetly inquired about this matter on July 3, Nagano curtly replied that a specific security policy "was not exactly drafted; but his subordinates may possibly be studying it."[110] No doubt they were, but the ability of the naval authorities to formulate a more explicit set of recommendations was not noticeably apparent a month later when the naval minister, on August 7, placed the "Basic Principles of National Policy" before the Inner Cabinet.[111] In fact, the "Basic Principles" were more cryptic than those contained in the "Outline of State Policy." In this latest definition of national policy, Admiral Nagano postulated the "correction of the dominating policies" of the Occidental powers as the cardinal mission of the Imperial government in East Asia.[112] The desired rectification could be attained only if the diplomacy of Asia were conducted in "a spirit of co-existence and co-prosperity based upon the Imperial Way."[113] To effect this renovation, judged the spokesman for the two services, Japan would have to augment its military and naval strength so that it could act as the stabilizing power in East Asia. In brief, affirmed Nagano, Japan must strengthen Manchukuo and enlarge the fleet, thereby enabling the empire to neutralize the political and military influence of the Occidental powers in East Asia.

The terseness of Admiral Nagano's "Basic Principles of National Policy" patently stemmed from the competing policies advanced by each general staff. This fact was appreciated by the members of the Inner Cabinet; and, without discussion, the ministers of state endorsed Nagano's presentation. After this vote of acceptance, Foreign Minister Arita dryly suggested the need for a "clarification" of the principles which had just been sanctioned. With this prodding, the ministers engaged in a rather abstract and undirected discussion which led the Inner Cabinet to define the strategic objectives of Japan's national policy as follows: the "frustration of Soviet

[110] IMTFE, *Exhibit 978, 2.*
[112] *Ibid.*

[111] IMTFE, *Exhibit 216.*
[113] *Ibid.*

aggression in East Asia," and the "acquisition of naval power sufficient to secure command of the Western Pacific."[114] Since the latter objective would require access to the natural resources of the South Seas, the ministers also stipulated that "footsteps" into the South Seas were to be taken discreetly, lest they "stimulate the powers concerned and fail to efface their apprehension about our empire. We must make our progress gradually and peacefully."[115] After this profession of good intentions, no minister was prone to argue the necessity for a set of proposals that would delineate precisely how Japan could accomplish these aspirations simultaneously. Consequently, the decisions of August 7—the China policy offered by the Committee on the Current Situation, the principles drafted by Admiral Nagano, and the clarifying remarks of the cabinet—were fused into one comprehensive formulation. On August 11, 1936, this was presented to the Hirota cabinet and, without further comment, the ministers sanctioned the "Fundamental Principles of National Policy."[116]

According to the official judgment of the International Military Tribunal, this August 11th definition of national policy "set out in the utmost clarity the principles which were to guide Japan, both in her relationships with other nations and in completing her internal preparations for war."[117] Possibly, the term "utmost clarity" is somewhat of a misnomer. Still, the Hirota cabinet undeniably had enunciated an imposing list of diplomatic and military policies which would permit Japan to restructure the Asian scene in a "spirit of co-prosperity and co-existence based upon the Imperial Way." It is also manifest that this national policy had resolved dissimilar concepts of national defense by the affirmation of general aims and the avoidance of specific means. This latter device was essentially the result of the inability of the war and naval ministries to agree on a system of strategic priorities, and of the unwillingness

114 IMTFE, *Exhibit 704.*   115 *Ibid.,* 6.
116 IMTFE, *Exhibit 979.*   117 *Judgment,* 119.

or inability of the Inner Cabinet to formulate a list of strategic or diplomatic priorities.

In the absence of a reasonably precise cabinet policy, each ministry interpreted the "Fundamental Principles of National Policy" in the light of its paramount concerns and interests. The naval authorities, naturally, concentrated on the requisites for a program of "footsteps" into the South Seas. The naval ministry prepared a five-year building program calling for the construction of sixty-six new ships and fourteen new air units; and it organized a number of ostensibly private business organizations which were commissioned to promote Japanese investments in Southeast Asia. After some pressure by the naval ministry, the overseas minister also agreed that the mandated islands acquired after the First World War should be administered by "naval officers who are to be in charge of transportation and communication matters."[118] The army authorities decided to double the size of the Kwantung Army and to create a political entity in Manchuria based on the "spirit of building a Manchurian nation." In the opinion of the Kwantung Army, party politics and parliamentary government were most inappropriate means to "build a nation" in Manchuria.[119] Instead of emulating the constitutional system of Western countries, the staff of the Kwantung Army believed Japan should create a viable political system in Manchuria through a fusion of the principles of the Imperial Way with a cultivation of the racial pride of the Manchu tribes. And, on September 18, 1936, in conjunction with the promulgation of a Manchurian Imperial Constitution, the commanding officer of the Kwantung Army, General Ueda, announced: "The harmony of the races [in Manchuria] is to be realized through the attainment of the unique Imperial Way political system,

[118] IMTFE, *Document 794* (Japanese text). USDS, Archives, *Japan: Political Affairs*, 894.00/670; Tokyo Report 2019, "Japan's 'Southward Advance' Policy," September 2, 1936, is a succinct digest of the public manifestations of this policy.

[119] July 25, 1936, policy guide of the Kwantung Army, reprinted in *Odachi Shigeo denki* (Tokyo, 1958), 114-115.

which will mirror the true will of the [Manchu] people."[120]

Parallel with the adoption of these plans and policies by the army and naval authorities, the officials of the foreign ministry affixed their interpretation to the cabinet's national policy decision. The cardinal objective in North China, judged the diplomats, was the organization of a "special anti-Communist, pro-Japanese zone."[121] This zone was deemed essential to the fulfillment of the new principles of national policy because it would enhance the security of Manchukuo, as well as furnish the foundation for "a triple coalition and mutual assistance pact among Japan, Manchukuo, and China."[122] Ultimately, the zone would "include the five provinces of North China"; but, in view of the complex issues posed by the treaty rights of the Western powers in North China, the foreign ministry concluded that there was no need "to accomplish this in one stroke."[123] In lieu of direct force, the foreign ministry proposed to "take into account the 'face-saving' needs of the Nationalist government" and to rely on diplomatic pressure in order to induce "a formal recognition of a decentralized North China."[124] Apart from the question of North China, the foreign ministry defined two basic diplomatic objectives—the Kuomintang would have to cease its practice of "playing barbarian against barbarian"; and the Nanking government would have to recognize that stability and peace in East Asia could only be secured by a policy of sincere cooperation with the Japanese empire. Admittedly, it would be difficult to impose these policies on the Nationalist government; but the foreign ministry was confident that this could be done gradually, by negotiating a series of special pacts and agreements. Specifically, the diplomats envisioned a cluster of agreements which would yield (1) an anti-Comintern pact, (2) a Sino-Japanese military alliance, (3) the appointment of Japanese military advisors for the Nationalist army, (4) the opening of commercial air routes between the

120 *Ibid.*, 115.   121 IMTFE, *Document 1044.*
122 *Ibid.*, 2.   123 *Ibid.*   124 *Ibid.*

two countries, (5) a reciprocal tariff agreement, and (6) the designation of a Japanese political advisor who would "participate in the important internal administrative and foreign policy affairs of the Nationalist government."[125]

In retrospect, the Japanese cabinet had, in August 1936, as in October 1933, formulated national policy in terms of the strategic concerns and estimates of the Imperial army and navy. Both national policies, therefore, contained one identical maxim: peace and stability in East Asia could be realized only if the empire were to acquire naval supremacy in the Western Pacific, superiority over the Soviet army, and a political hegemony over China. The 1936 version of national policy, in effect, recommitted Japan to a quest for an "autonomous" national defense, appending, in the process, the need for economic resources which would permit the empire to wage a "total war" against its strategic enemies, i.e., the Soviet Union and the United States. To this end, Japan's army authorities had formulated a basic plan which stressed the rationalization of the army, the development of Manchukuo, and the adoption of some form of state economic planning; and her naval leaders had agreed on the need for extensive oil reserves and a fleet with operational capabilities extending into Southeast Asia, two requisites which were attainable only by fortifying the mandated islands and by acquiring colonies or special rights in Borneo and the Celebes. The establishment of Manchukuo and the withdrawal from the League of Nations had, in 1933, justified an autonomous foreign and security policy; and, within three years, this axiom had spawned two additional convictions—the need for some form of state economic planning and for access to the resources of the South Seas.

In the process of formulating the "fundamental principles" of the Japanese empire, the Hirota cabinet had also transformed the sense of mission underlying the objectives of national policy. In particular, the doctrine of an Asiatic Monroe

[125] *Ibid.*, 3.

Doctrine as the proper foundation for peace and stability in East Asia was replaced by the "principle of co-prosperity and co-existence based upon the Imperial Way." This new terminology signified a stronger identity with the mystique of Japan's unique role in the game of world politics than the earlier emulation of an American diplomatic doctrine; and, if it did not alter the policies of the Western powers, at least it inspired greater confidence in the propriety, the justness of Japan's new mission. Certainly, the intensity of this sentiment was conducive to the conclusion that an enlarged army and navy, careful economic planning, the development of Manchukuo and North China, and constant pressure on the Kuomintang would secure the requisites for an autonomous foreign and security policy. Still, similar expectations had been prevalent in 1933; and, eighteen months after the adoption of the 1936 "Fundamental Principles of National Policy," Japan found itself involved in a major war with China, committed to the dual objectives of "destroying the Kuomintang" and effecting the "rejuvenation of a new China." How the Japanese government became involved in this China conflict, as well as the ways in which these hostilities generated the decision to "rejuvenate" China by conquest, is the central concern of the following chapter.

CHAPTER VI

The China War

"Our external policy seeks peace based on justice, which is not the same thing as mere maintenance of the *status quo*. At home, our policies will be those the times require and where renovation is needed we will enforce it."

Prince Konoe, June 1937

"The China incident is a Far Eastern tragedy; but in order that such a tragedy may not be repeated Japan cannot hesitate to perform a major operation. In this sense, the fall of Nanking is merely the prelude to the general problem of China; and the real test of strength has only started."

Prince Konoe, December 1937

THE interministerial discussions and recommendations in the spring and summer of 1936, as well as the sessions of the Inner Cabinet, had been artfully regulated by Jeremiac warnings of distress and dismay about the foreign policies and armament expenditures of the Soviet Union and the United States. These alarms were not simply devices to validate the competing budget demands of the two services and to equalize the importance of two strategic concepts in the definition of national policy. In the spring of 1936, the American Congress was in the process of voting the largest peacetime naval budget in its history, one which Claude Swanson, the secretary of the navy, appropriately considered the inception of an "unparalleled renaissance" in naval construction;[1] and the Soviet Union was augmenting its military and political position in Outer Mongolia, as well as strengthening its Maritime Army with new equipment and added manpower. Each of Japan's strategic enemies, moreover, was an industrialized nation,

[1] As quoted by William Neumann, *America Encounters Japan* (Baltimore, 1963), 232.

richly endowed with natural resources; and each was able to concentrate its military expenditures in one direction, the Soviet Union in land forces and the United States in sea power. From the perspective of the Japanese general staffs, these nations already possessed the requisites for an "autonomous" national defense; and separately or together they posed grave challenges to the security and foreign policies of the empire. The magnitude of the problems confronting Japan in its quest for an autonomous national defense, along with the dynamics of an interservice rivalry, inspired the vocabulary of total war, economic planning, general mobilization, and southern expansion. It also engendered the tendency to regard all obstacles—political, diplomatic, economic, and strategic—to the attainment of an autonomous national defense as challenges or impediments to a morally sanctioned national mission. These sentiments and convictions were externalized in the 1936 "Fundamental Principles of National Policy," most vividly in the resolution to compel the acceptance of the "principle of co-prosperity and co-existence based upon the Imperial Way" as the standard by which the Occidental powers, Nationalist China, and Japan should conduct their national policies.

Permeating the discussions and decisions of the Hirota cabinet was a casual, almost naïve appraisal of the China scene. The ability of Nationalist China to resist the political hegemony of the empire was attributed solely to the international structure of Asian affairs, which encouraged the Kuomintang to depend on a policy of "playing barbarian against barbarian." This premise was buttressed by a contemptuous regard for the military prowess and political viability of the Kuomintang and the Nationalist army. This attitude, in turn, supported the assumption that the Kuomintang would always avoid a direct military confrontation with Japan. Two circumstances, in the opinion of the Hirota cabinet, accounted for Japan's current difficulties with Nationalist China. First, the military and naval power of the empire had not been augmented to such an extent as to dissipate Chinese confidence in the willingness and ability of the Western powers to restrain or restrict Japan's continental policy. Second, the behavior of the Japanese army in North China in the fall of 1935 had unwittingly revealed Japan's sensitivity to the treaty rights of the powers and its desire to avoid a direct confrontation with the Nationalist government. A faithful adherence to the newly articulated China policy—the enhancement of the economic, military, and naval power of the empire, the stabilization of the *status quo* in North China, and the negotiation of a series of treaties or agreements with the Nationalist government—would, in the considered judgment of the Hirota cabinet, gradually and peacefully remove the impediments to a satisfactory resolution of Japan's China problem.

The comforting notion that the Nationalist government did not, in itself, present any major strategic worries was reflected in the cabinet's confidence in the efficacy of the "coordinated" China policy drafted by the Committee on the Current Situation. From the Tokyo vantage point, North China was, by 1936, a buffer zone between Manchukuo and Nationalist China. The Tangku Truce agreement of 1933, and the Ching-Doihara and Ho-Umezu agreements of 1935, had compromised the authority of the central government in North China; and the East Hopei Autonomous Council and the Hopei-Chahar Political Council were not likely to offer effective resistance to a concerted program of Japanese economic penetration. The main problem confronting the foreign ministry centered on the negotiation of a diplomatic accord which would commit the Nationalist government to a recognition that the provinces of North China had a special relationship to the security of the Japanese empire.

Believing this to be the overriding issue and objective of Japan's China policy, the Hirota cabinet, in the fall of 1936, adopted a cluster of related decisions. Specifically, the cabinet sanctioned an anti-Comintern pact with Nazi Germany; it authorized the promotion of a "Mongolia for Mongolians" movement in Inner Mongolia; and, in lieu of Hirota's three principles, it favored the resumption of negotiations with the Nationalist government over the more limited subjects of tariff revision and a "joint" program of economic development in North China. The first two moves were considered as effective counterthrusts against Soviet penetration into Outer Mongolia and Comintern activities in China; the third step was regarded as the prelude to a more comprehensive Sino-Japanese treaty. Unfortunately for Japan, the anticipated returns of this coordinated policy were nullified within three months. The Mongolian autonomy movement was blocked by a victory of the Nationalist army over the Japanese-trained Mongolian forces; this military incident terminated the new Sino-Japanese discussions *sine-die*; and, in December 1936, the kidnapping of Chiang Kai-shek at Sian radically restructured the nature of Chinese domestic politics so as to intensify popular and governmental resistance to Japan's position in North China. Since these events were of some importance, it seems desirable to review them in greater detail.

IMPLEMENTATION OF THE FUNDAMENTAL PRINCIPLES

The clamor for a military alliance with Nazi Germany first became audible within the Inner Cabinet in September 1935, with the appointment of General Kuwashima as war minister.[2] A pact with Germany, insisted the army spokesman, would breach the diplomatic isolation of Japan that had been created by the non-recognition policy of the Western nations; and, more decisively, it would help restrain Soviet intrigues in China and Mongolia. Although General Kuwashima argued that a military pact with Nazi Germany would enhance the stability of Manchukuo and reduce the possibility of conflict with the Soviet Union, this contention was viewed skeptically by the naval and foreign ministers. They questioned, in particular, whether the postulated advantages of an anti-Comintern military pact would adequately compensate for the adverse

[2] Nihon kokusai seiji gakkai, *Taiheiyō senso e no michi* (Tokyo, 1963), V, 20. [Hereafter cited as NKSG, *Taiheiyō senso.*]

repercussions such a pact would generate among the major sea powers—namely, France, Great Britain, and the United States. As the policy of "southern advancement" gained currency in naval and diplomatic circles, however, the utility of a pact with Nazi Germany acquired additional dimensions. By the spring of 1936, the naval general staff was confident that Japan could arrive at a *modus vivendi* with Britain and France by the simple technique of aggravating the European diplomatic situation.

Once the two general staffs concurred on the wisdom of an agreement with Germany, the momentum for an anti-Comintern pact accelerated appreciably. In the process, though, the naval and foreign ministries emphasized the purely diplomatic advantages to be gained by a pact with Germany; and, despite the complaints of the army authorities, they insisted that the pact would have to be pruned of any military obligations. Since this viewpoint prevailed in the cabinet, the Anti-Comintern Pact which was officially negotiated in September 1936 was distinguished by a dearth of specific commitments. The treaty called only for the "exchange of information on the activities of the Communist International"; and it ruled that if either of the contracting parties were attacked by the Soviet Union, the other would "take no measures which would tend to ease the situation of the U.S.S.R."[3] As the cabinet advised the Privy Council on November 20, the treaty in no sense implied that Japan would act in concert with Germany or aggravate relations with the Soviet Union: "The fact that the conclusion of the Pact will further strengthen Japan's position ought to prove quite effective in making China decide her attitude. We are not without expectations, therefore, of being able to use this situation for promoting developments in the Sino-Japanese negotiations favorable to ourselves."[4] By confining the Anti-Comintern

[3] Ernst Presseisen, *Germany and Japan* (The Hague, 1958), 327-328, has an English translation of the pact.

[4] International Military Tribunal Far East [IMTFE], *Exhibit 479*; *Proceedings*, 5963.

Pact to vague professions, the Hirota cabinet intended to make it a tool which Japan could use in three diplomatic tasks— namely, (1) to alert the Kuomintang and the Western powers to the perils of relying on the Soviet Union as a deterrent to Japanese policies in North China; (2) to promote a *modus vivendi* with Great Britain; and (3) to moderate Soviet activities in China and Outer Mongolia. The Anti-Comintern Pact, in other words, was not intended as an overture to war with either the Soviet Union or Nationalist China, nor was it meant to ally Japan with Germany in the game of European diplomacy. Perhaps mistakenly, the pact was viewed by the Japanese government as a prudent and peaceful way to implement the "Fundamental Principles of National Policy"—that is, to promote the policy of southern expansion, the development of Manchukuo, and the stabilization of North China.

As part of its comprehensive reassessment of Japan's national policy, the Hirota cabinet had carefully circumscribed the discretionary authority entrusted to the newly created North China Army. Indeed, the cabinet decision of August 11 specifically directed the army to avoid "any independent military activities" and to assist "the diplomatic organs so they might be able to function properly."[5] Although the cabinet had officially banned any overt subversion in North China, its fundamental principles sanctioned the encouragement of a "Mongolia for Mongolians" movement by the Imperial army. The opening efforts of the Kwantung Army in this direction had been made in September 1935, simultaneously with General Tada's plea for an autonomous North China. At this time, the Kwantung Army began to organize and train an "independent" Mongolian army in Manchukuo; and, in January 1936, when the foreign, war, and naval ministries finally reached a policy consensus in favor of the political *status quo* in North China, the general staff authorized the continued development of this Mongolian army.[6] Under the direction of Colonel Imamura and Major Tanaka Ryūkichi,

[5] IMTFE, *Exhibit 9179*, 3.   [6] IMTFE, *Document 1634*.

prominent Mongol chiefs conducted a "State-Founding Conference" at Wu Chumuhsin from April 21 to April 26.[7] Here, Prince Teh agreed to head a military government in Inner Mongolia that would declare itself independent of Nationalist China; and, in return, the Kwantung Army promised to furnish Prince Teh's force with weapons and military advisors.

This program of military assistance conformed to the specific orders of the general staff; and, following the August 11th decision of the cabinet, it had acquired the sanction of official national policy. By mid-October, the staff of the Kwantung Army judged that its military protégé, Prince Teh, was ready to launch a military campaign in Inner Mongolia. This confidence, though, was not shared by the operations division of the general staff; and, in fact, Colonel Ishiwara Kanji tried to charm one of his colleagues in the Mukden incident, Colonel Imamura, into postponing, if not abandoning, the "Mongolia for Mongolians" movement. In view of the official cabinet policy, Ishiwara could not legally countermand this venture; and his personal pleas for postponement were rebuffed with the sally, "But we are only emulating what you did at Mukden in September 1931."[8] The retort, though not without some justification, proved to be only superficially correct. Prince Teh's army, even with Japanese weapons and advisors, was not the equivalent of the Kwantung Army. Instead of a series of easy military triumphs, the Mongolian troops of Prince Teh were routed by the Nationalist army after a week-long battle at Pailingmiao. Retreating to the sanctuary of East Hopei, Prince Teh's forces managed to escape complete annihilation. Still, this defeat proved fatal to the vision of an autonomous Inner Mongolia under the guidance of the Kwantung Army.

As the first clear-cut military victory of the Nationalist army in many years, the battle at Pailingmiao, noted the American

[7] IMTFE, *Document 724.*
[8] Interview with General Imamura Hitoshi.

ambassador to China, "evoked an angry manifestation of nationalism."[9] This surge of nationalism provided Chiang Kai-shek with a convenient excuse for temporarily ending his discussions with the Japanese ambassador; and it also buttressed the pleas for a policy of active resistance against Japanese aggression in North China. Moreover, the rhetoric of "national unity" and "resist Japanese imperialism" was employed by both the Kuomintang and the Chinese Communists in the aftermath of the military victory in Inner Mongolia. Still, Chiang Kai-shek had no desire to confront Japanese military power directly in North China; and he wanted to bring about national unity by crushing the Communist movement, not by allying with the Communist Party in a premature conflict with the Japanese empire. Hence, the generalissimo proposed to follow the triumph at Pailing-miao with a sixth and presumably final annihilation campaign against the Chinese Communists. When Chiang flew to Sian on December 7 to oversee the launching of this anti-Communist campaign, however, instead of compliance with his military directives, he found a political conspiracy.[10] The apparent willingness of the Mongol tribes to accept a Japanese army and Japanese advisors, as well as the implications inherent in the espousal of a Mongolian autonomous movement, had convinced many northern warlords that Chiang's anti-Communist policies were in error. On December 7, the spokesman for this group, Marshal Chang Hsueh-liang, dramatically placed Chiang Kai-shek under house arrest in Sian. Equally significantly, Chang publicly demanded that the sixth campaign against the Chinese Communists be abandoned in favor of a united front on the part of the Kuomintang and the Communist Party, an alliance with the Soviet Union, and an active program of military resistance to Japanese imperialism.

[9] Dorothy Borg, *The United States and the Far Eastern Crisis of 1933-1938* (Cambridge, Mass., 1964), 188.

[10] O. Edmund Clubb, *20th Century China* (New York, 1964), 206-212; and Charles McLane, *Soviet Policy and the Chinese Communists, 1937-1946* (New York, 1958), 79-91, offer fine summaries of the Sian incident.

The "kidnapping" of Chiang Kai-shek, as well as Marshal Chang's plea for a united front of the Nationalists and the Communists, produced consternation in Nanking and Moscow. The Chinese minister of war, General Ho Ying-chin, promptly recommended an aerial bombardment of the Sian rebels without, notes O. Edmund Clubb, "excessive solicitude for what might happen during the air bombardment to the generalissimo."[11] On December 17, *Pravda* shrilly accused Wang Ching-wei of having instigated the Sian incident on behalf of Japan's militarists.[12] Amid this initial confusion, the Chinese Red Army occupied Yenan in Shensi province and Chou En-lai flew to Sian in order to alleviate the tensions and uncertainties generated by Marshal Chang's actions. Precisely what transpired in the discussions among Chiang Kai-shek, Chou En-lai, and Chang Hsueh-liang remains uncertain. Retrospectively, Mao Tse-tung termed the Sian affair an "epic event . . . [which] established the indispensable premise for the formation of a united front"; and Chiang Kai-shek has maintained that no formal or specific agreement was reached with his captors or with the Communists at Sian.[13] Both estimates may well be correct. There is no evidence suggesting that Chiang actually agreed to the adoption of a united front against Japanese aggression; but, after returning to Nanking, Chiang dropped the sixth anti-Communist campaign—a decision which, in Mao's words, constituted the "indispensable premise" for a united front. The Sian incident, in other words, obliged Chiang to adopt a more forceful posture against Japanese activities in North China; and it compelled the Kuomintang to explore the possibility of a united front with the Chinese Communists.

The veil of uncertainty and confusion which shrouded the events at Sian perplexed the Japanese government as much as it did contemporary historians. Privately, on December 16, the intelligence division of the general staff wondered "whether

[11] Clubb, *20th Century China*, 208.
[12] McLane, *Soviet Policy*, 82.   [13] *Ibid.*, 91.

Chang Hsueh-liang plans to become the vanguard of the army to fight against Japan . . . or whether he desires to take the initiative in the anti-Chiang movement in order to recover his influence."[14] Ten days later, in an official press release, the Kwantung Army declared: "[If] the Chinese government should compromise with the Communist Party and kindred elements and accept communism and a policy of anti-Japanese resistance, the Kwantung Army will . . . devise whatever measures it deems necessary for the defense of Manchukuo and the preservation of peace throughout East Asia."[15] By early January 1937, the Asian Affairs Bureau of the foreign ministry concluded its analysis of the Sian incident: "Although the terms of the compromise [at Sian] were not made known, . . . we may not be too amiss in concluding that an agreement was reached at least on one point—namely, to resist Japan."[16] If true, this judgment rendered the tenets of Japan's current China policy somewhat suspect. Yet an awareness of the strident anti-Japanese mood prevalent in Nationalist political and military circles did not generate any compulsion to reconsider the guiding objectives of Japan's national policy. The Hirota cabinet remained confident that, by riding out the Sian incident with soft words and no military activities in North China, Japan could, in time, impose its wishes on the Nationalist government without recourse to open hostilities.

Hayashi Cabinet: A Cautious China Policy

Although the Hirota cabinet publicly minimized the significance of the Sian incident, the diplomatic and military implications of a viable united front in China were not discounted by the Japanese cabinet. On the contrary, the changing political context in China intensified the concerns of Japan's army leaders, especially their desire to implement a program of state economic planning. Beginning in January 1937, War

[14] IMTFE, *Defense Document 838*, 3.
[15] Clubb, *20th Century China*, 210.
[16] IMTFE, *Defense Document 844*, 24.

Minister Terauchi constantly badgered his cabinet peers with the demand that the government secure the enactment of a series of laws which would impose comprehensive governmental controls over business and labor organizations. Terauchi's strictures within the Inner Cabinet, though, did not alter the fact that only the Diet could legally institute the laws and regulations sought by the army authorities. As a "whole nation" cabinet, the Hirota government did not, mainly because of the dictates of Terauchi, include any prominent politicians from the Seiyūkai or the Minseitō; and the prospect of staff officers and financial bureaucrats directing a planned economy failed to intrigue the major centers of financial power, the *zaibatsu*.

The hostility between the major political parties and the army authorities flared into the open on January 21, 1937. Echoing the platform adopted by the Seiyūkai on the preceding day, Representative Hamada Kumitaro directed a torrent of verbal abuse at the war minister, charging that "the attitude of superiority and self-righteousness by the military and the bureaucracy and their meddling in the affairs of state were producing oligarchic tyranny, shutting out the popular will, and bringing about the negation of parliamentary government."[17] Instead of politely ignoring this interpellation, Terauchi construed Hamada's remarks as a calculated insult to the "honor" of the Imperial army; and he demanded that the representative formally apologize for his irresponsible statements. The spokesman for the Seiyūkai, however, ridiculed the parliamentary pretensions of the war minister with a rhetorical challenge, a game of harakiri. Hamada ostentatiously promised to atone for his speech by self-disembowelment, if the Diet ruled his address to be contemptuous of the Imperial army; but, if this accusation were not substantiated, Hamada thought the war minister should, in turn, convey his apology to the Diet by the same means. Though flushed with anger,

---

[17] Chitoshi Yanaga, *Japan Since Perry* (New York, 1949), 527.

Terauchi conceded the debate to the professional politician by remaining silent.

This political charade publicly embarrassed the war minister, but it hardly augmented the influence of the Seiyūkai in the cabinet. In fact, following his confrontation with Hamada, General Terauchi concluded the government could not obtain the type of legislation envisioned in the army's mobilization plans from the current Diet. After studying the domestic political scene, the staff of the war ministry came to believe the government should place its political and economic resources at the disposal of the Kokumin Dōmei party.[18] It was hoped that such covert assistance would enable this minority party to garner a majority of seats in the general elections scheduled for April; and, once this was effected, the government could then readily obtain the enactment of the desired legislation. As this political scheme crystallized in army central headquarters, the venerable Ozaki Yukio shed his customary soft-spoken role in the Diet with a withering blast at the increasing political proclivities of the army: "Nothing is easier and more pleasing to junior officers than to interfere in politics, while protected by the uniform, against a background of arms. So pleasing to them is this role that they are apt to run amuck and finally to ruin the state."[19] Once before, in 1913, Ozaki had abused a military oligarchy for its subversion of parliamentary government, a memorable indictment which is often viewed as the inception of a responsible parliamentary movement in Japan. By lending his prestige to the assault on the army's domestic plans and activities, Ozaki's speech automatically prompted recollections of the 1913 struggle between the Diet and the Katsura cabinet. To Terauchi and his staff, Ozaki's criticism signified the need for precipitate action on behalf of the political fortunes of the Kokumin Dōmei. Citing the recent parliamentary addresses of Ozaki and Hamada as

[18] Interviews with General Satō Kenryō and Katakura Chū.

[19] United States Department of State [USDS], Archives, *Japan: Political Affairs*, 894.00/712, Tokyo Report 2283, "Diet Interpellation, Mr. Yukio Ozaki," February 26, 1937.

being intolerable to the dignity and honor of the army, Terauchi, on February 23, resigned his portfolio, thereby bringing about the downfall of the Hirota cabinet.

This shattering of the Hirota cabinet by the army authorities signified a commitment to a radical political program and a rejection of violence or force as a means to attain this objective. Unlike the guiding lights of the Cherry Society, Terauchi's staff was not beguiled by the allure of a political *coup d'état*; and, in contrast to the proponents of the Imperial Way, they did not dismiss all political parties as betrayers of the true national principle. When the leaders of the army had, in 1934, articulated the realization of a "national defense state" by legal means as their cardinal political objective, Generals Hayashi and Nagata had believed this could be accomplished by an educational program which would popularize the necessity for economic planning and general mobilization. Although their postulate of a national defense state had been accepted by the Hirota cabinet in the summer of 1936, the political parties were, in 1937, still unwilling to support a legislative program which would grant the government enveloping controls over the economy. This recalcitrant attitude, moreover, was not moderated by the efforts of the war ministry to exclude the major parties from the determination and administration of the cabinet's economic policies. In order to subvert the political influence and power of the major parties, Terauchi's staff believed they could manipulate the general elections of April 1937 so as to transform the Kokumin Dōmei into a viable political party—an accomplishment which would, in effect, compel the Diet to enact whatever legislation was desired by the army authorities. The saboteurs of the Hirota cabinet, however, grossly misjudged the resiliency of the major parties and the sagacity of the Senior Statesman, Prince Saionji.

When General Terauchi forced the resignation of the Hirota cabinet, the war ministry confidently expected that it would be replaced by another "whole nation" government, one that would be more responsive to the army's wish to support the Kokumin Dōmei. This hope was rudely shaken when Prince Saionji nominated General Ugaki for the premiership. Given his personal rapport with the Senior Statesman, the leaders of the Minseitō, and the Imperial household, as well as his adroit and forceful direction of the army as war minister, Ugaki was not likely to pursue the brand of cabinet politics envisioned by General Terauchi and his key staff advisors. Consequently, the apprehension provoked in central headquarters by Saionji's nomination of Ugaki as premier impelled General Umezu, the vice-war minister, to summon an emergency meeting of all department heads in central headquarters at 1:00 a.m. on January 26 to review the implications of an Ugaki cabinet.[20] With remarkable alacrity, these officers concluded that the army should veto Ugaki's cabinet by refusing to provide a war minister. This resolution was defended on various grounds, including Ugaki's involvement in the March incident of 1931 and his past connection with the disarmament and foreign policies of Baron Shidehara. By citing these objections, ruled the army authorities, General Ugaki could be opposed on the grounds that his appointment would only reactivate a cancerous factional dispute in the army and unnecessarily jeopardize the economic and political policies approved by the government in the summer of 1936.

Although the army authorities had resolved to block Ugaki's appointment, they were anxious to avoid an open political controversy. Directly after the session in General Umezu's office, the chief of the military police, General Nakajima, ordered his staff to locate and detain General Ugaki. The military police spotted Ugaki's car en route to the Imperial palace and deliberately raised a temporary roadblock. After a brief delay, General Nakajima arrived and communicated the consensus of the war ministry.[21] In this fashion, the army

20 Katakura Chū, "Ugaki naikaku ryuzan su" [The Abortion of the Ugaki Cabinet], *Himerareta shōwashi* (Tokyo, 1956), 165.
21 Ugaki Issei, *Ugaki Issei denki* (Tokyo, 1954), 275-276.

authorities hoped to persuade Ugaki to decline the Imperial command to form a cabinet. Undeterred by the advice of Nakajima, however, Ugaki continued his trip to the palace and accepted the mandate to organize a government. During the following forty-eight hours, Ugaki discovered that Nakajima's words were not idle warnings. His closest associates during his days as war minister—Generals Koiso and Sugiyama—refused to serve as war ministers; and the Big Three of the army—Generals Sugiyama and Terauchi and Prince Kanin—formally ruled that the army would not supply any minister for a Ugaki cabinet. Since the revised regulations of March 1936 restricted the service portfolio to general officers on active duty, this was indeed an effective form of blackmail. Personally, Ugaki favored countermanding the decision of the Big Three with a direct order from the Throne; but Prince Saionji, recalling the ill-fated efforts of General Katsura in 1913 to organize a stable cabinet by invoking the assistance of the Throne in order to obtain a naval minister, turned Ugaki's advice aside. Without the concurrence of the army authorities, Saionji judged, no government could function effectively or for long. Ugaki had no alternative but to advise the Emperor of his inability to organize a cabinet.[22]

The precipitate manner in which the departmental chiefs of the war ministry and the general staff decided to abort the candidacy of General Ugaki revealed the main political purpose behind the resignation of War Minister Terauchi. It also placed the army authorities in a publicly embarrassing position. After preventing the formation of a Ugaki cabinet, Generals Terauchi and Sugiyama recognized that they could not nominate any general on active duty for the premiership and seriously expect the cooperation of the court advisors and of the other ministries of state. Still, the department heads in central headquarters wanted a premier who would firmly support the army's domestic economic plans and who had no apparent personal ties with the major financial and

[22] *Ibid.*, 277-278.

political leaders. These dictates necessarily restricted the list of potential premiers; and the Big Three of the army finally resolved the problem by advancing the candidacy of General Hayashi Senjurō. As war minister, Hayashi had espoused the type of programs which the army currently favored—a moderate China policy, a rationalization of the army, and the a-doption of a general mobilization plan—and, unlike Ugaki, he was not tainted by the stigma of excessive political ambition. Hayashi's candidacy, moreover, was received with favor by Prince Saionji. As war minister, Hayashi had waged a relentless battle against political intrigues by the staff of central head-quarters; and, during the Minobe controversy, he had demon-strated a responsible and conciliatory attitude. Once Hayashi received the mandate to form a government, he vindicated Saionji's confidence in his conservative political instincts. As premier, Hayashi refused to support a covert alliance between the cabinet and the Kokumin Dōmei; and, in contrast to Terauchi's behavior, he never publicly questioned the dignity or authority of the Diet.

The moderate tenor of the Hayashi cabinet became ap-parent on February 15 when the premier declared in his maiden parliamentary address, "I have no faith in a pugnacious foreign policy."[23] In place of a belligerent attitude toward China, Hayashi proposed to seek amiable solutions of particu-lar issues, especially in the area of tariff agreements. Basically, Hayashi affirmed, his government would seek five cardinal objectives: (1) a clarification of the national policy; (2) a faith-ful adherence to the Meiji constitution; (3) the promotion of political stability in East Asia; (4) an enhancement of the security of the empire; and (5) an increase in the nation's industrial capabilities. These objectives were, of course, stated in general terms; but they still indicated a more conciliatory attitude by the army leaders. On March 15, War Minister Sugiyama issued a belated reply to Ozaki Yukio's complaints

[23] For the English text of Hayashi's speech, see *Japan Advertiser*, Feb-ruary 17, 1937.

against the apparent tendency of staff officers to meddle in the affairs of the Diet: "My assistants have connections with other departments of the government for purposes of investigation and study, and it is necessary, from the broader viewpoint of national defense, that they express opinions. Junior officers must make inquiries but only the war minister translates the results into action."[24] Although these words defended the new political and economic overtones evident in the plans and activities of the war ministry, they were far less intransigent than the tone and posture displayed by General Terauchi.

The desire of the Hayashi cabinet to cultivate better relations with the Diet and the business community, as well as to soothe relations with the Western powers, was reflected in an unusual and remarkable cabinet appointment. Casting about for a diplomat with extensive experience in dealing with the Western nations, Hayashi chose the ambassador to Great Britain, Satō Naotake, as his foreign minister.[25] Satō was a strong advocate of friendly relations with the Anglo-American nations and his selection caught the Japanese press and foreign observers completely unawares. This initial surprise was not lessened when the new foreign minister, on March 13, delivered one of the most candid discussions of foreign policy in the history of the Diet. Point by point, Satō in effect criticized the basis and conduct of Japanese policies in Asia.[26] If the Japanese government were "to walk the open path straightforwardly," observed the foreign minister, there would be no major diplomatic problems with China or the Western powers. Japan could, allowed Satō, "avert a crisis at any time," if it were so inclined. The current difficulties with the United States stemmed from the latter's concern with China. If Japan would pursue a "fair policy" in China, the United States would have no cause for anxiety. Hence, ventured Satō, the empire should

[24] Cited by Alfred Vagts, *A History of Militarism* (New York, 1937), 319.
[25] The circumstances prompting Satō's appointment are best described in *Obata Toriyoshi denki* (Tokyo, 1957), 399-404.
[26] *Asahi shimbun*, March 14, 1937.

respect the "open door" policy in Central and North China, not only because it would promote friendly relations with the Anglo-American countries but because the idea of erecting a "bloc economy" among Japan, Manchukuo, and China was historically premature. Japan must, concluded the foreign minister, conduct its China policy from a different point of view—namely, it must negotiate with the Nationalist government on the basis of real equality.

Precisely why the new foreign minister delivered this public address is difficult to determine. Conceivably, Hayashi's assurances that his cabinet sincerely wanted to stabilize its relations with China along peaceful lines, to promote amicable relations with the Western sea powers, and to concentrate on domestic matters, particularly the development of the army and the navy, were misconstrued by Satō as an endorsement of his own approach to Japan's foreign policy. Inevitably, though, his speech provoked tremendous unrest in military, naval, and diplomatic circles, if only because it questioned the official rationale for the basic principles of national policy. That Satō was obviously out of touch with the main stream of cabinet policies was incontestable. And, within a week of his opening address to the Diet, Satō was subjected to an intense and hostile interrogation in the House of Peers. The foreign minister vainly strove to align his public statements with the actual principles of national policy. As reported in the press, Satō assured the members of the House of Peers:

> ... by saying that the Japanese nation can avert a crisis at any time it [is] so minded, he meant that Japan should avoid a positive challenge to another power, not that Japan should tolerate any provocation; (b) that in advocating a policy of conciliation and patience toward China he did not mean that Japan should be submissive if China trampled upon international justice or damaged the prestige of Japan; (c) that in stating economic blocs in the Far East were premature he did not mean to deny the "inseparable re-

lations" between Japan and Manchukuo: and (d) that by asking why Japan did not walk the open path straight-forwardly he did not mean to criticize the past actions of Japan.[27]

Despite these qualifying remarks, Satō's speech and his appointment as foreign minister signified the honest intent of the Hayashi cabinet to avoid any major domestic or foreign crisis which might hinder the development of a coordinated program of industrial expansion and the enlargement and rationalization of the Imperial army and navy.

The desire to stabilize Japan's relations with Nationalist China was completely compatible with the "Fundamental Principles of National Policy" adopted in 1936, and it indicated an appreciation of the repercussions of the Sian incident. Japan's past actions in North China and the Sian affair, judged the American ambassador to China in May 1937, had finally created a sense of unity among the Chinese people which "has grown so strong that it is rapidly becoming a part of the Chinese racial consciousness."[28] And the American counselor at Peking, after commenting on the growing nationalistic sentiments in General Sung's 29th Army, worried about the possibility of a major Sino-Japanese military incident in Hopei province, one that "might be precipitated by the Chinese military [being] imbued with a growing belief in their own prowess."[29] These political currents were not undetected in Tokyo. On April 16, the Inner Cabinet adopted its "Plans for Guiding North China,"[30] in which the ministers stipulated that the enlargement of the Tangku Truce zone and the formation of an independent North China, as well as the extension of the frontiers of Manchukuo into Inner Mongolia, would have to be postponed temporarily. Instead, the cabinet ruled, "It is vitally important to attend solely to the execution of

[27] USDS, *Foreign Relations of the United States, 1937*, IV, 43.
[28] *Ibid.*, 73.   [29] *Ibid.*, 87.
[30] *Nihon gaikō nenpyō narabini shuyō bunsho, 1840-1945* (Tokyo, 1955), II, 361-362. Also IMTFE, *Exhibit 219.*

cultural and economic measures" in North China.[31] In order
to impress this decision on the field armies, Colonel Shibayama
of the war ministry, Captain Fuji of the naval ministry, and
Mr. Morishima of the foreign ministry were despatched to
Tientsin and Port Arthur, where they reviewed the policy of
the Inner Cabinet in detail.[32] Lest there be any doubts about
the army's commitment to this emphasis on a quiescent North
China, the general staff, in June 1937, officially ordered the
field armies to avoid military incidents which might "occasion
any international trouble."[33]

This sensitivity to the China scene was also discernible in the
political party most attuned to the sentiments and convictions
prevailing in the war ministry. "Japan," noted a May 14th
statement of the Kokumin Dōmei, "will not selfishly fail to
appreciate that the Nanking government's power is gradually
expanding, as long as the special position of Japan in North
China is not infringed upon."[34] The qualifying clause constituted the nub of the problem. What precisely was Japan's
special position in North China? How important were the
provinces of North China to the economic and security plans
being devised in the ministries of state and the Cabinet
Planning Board? In January 1936, the field or "local" agreements imposed in the fall of 1935 were considered by the
Inner Cabinet as accomplished facts, not to be modified in any
formal talks with the Nationalist government; and the resources
of North China were, in the summer of 1936, regarded as
essential to ultimate realization of an autonomous military-
industrial complex. Although the legitimacy of the Ho-Umezu
and Ching-Doihara agreements, as well as of the Hopei-Chahar
Political Council and the East Hopei Autonomous Council,
were not being questioned within the Japanese government in
the spring of 1937, the army economic experts revised their

[31] *Ibid.*
[32] Morishima Morito, *Imbō ansatsu guntō* (Tokyo, 1950), 123.
[33] IMTFE, *Proceedings*, 21979.
[34] USDS, *Foreign Relations . . . , 1937*, III, 99.

earlier appraisals of the importance of the resources of North China.

On June 16, the chief of staff of the Kwantung Army, General Tōjō Hideki, notified the foreign ministry that "the resources for national defense will clearly be met with the resources of Manchuria and East Hopei."[35] In Tōjō's judgment, the Imperial army should, therefore, prepare for a successful conflict with the Soviet Union by refurbishing the army and by confining its continental investments to Manchuria and East Hopei. This revised estimate of the worth of North China, however, did not prompt any reconsideration of the existing political arrangements governing the provinces of North China. Rather than permit the Kuomintang to modify or set aside the existing political organs in North China, Tōjō, on June 7, remarked: "Judging the present situation in China from the point of view of military preparations against Russia, I am convinced that if [our] military power permits it, we should deliver a blow first of all upon the Nanking regime in order to remove this menace at our rear."[36] This advice, no doubt, expressed the prevailing sentiments of the Kwantung Army; but it did not conform to or modify the views of the Hasyashi cabinet and the army general staff. Even the Tokyo International Military Tribunal concluded that the policies of the Japanese government in the spring of 1937 were "not directed wholly or principally toward the conquest of China."[37] Preoccupied with implementing a comprehensive program of industrial and military expansion, the Hayashi cabinet was, in fact, anxious to avoid a serious conflict with the Nationalist government.

By meticulously controlling the behavior of the field armies

[35] Japanese Ministry of Foreign Affairs [JMFA], Archives, *Teikoku no taiShi seisaku kankei no ken*, VII, "Horinouchi jikan oyobi Ōa Tōakyokuchō to Tōjō kantogun sambōchō kaiwa yōryō" [The Gist of the Conversation Between Tōjō, Chief of Staff, Kwantung Army, and Vice-Minister Horinouchi and the Chief of the European and Asian Affairs Bureaus], June 16, 1937.

[36] IMTFE, *Document 1841*. [37] IMTFE, *Judgment*, 168.

and by confining its discussions with the Nanking government to minor matters, the Hayashi government tranquillized many of the diplomatic tensions caused by the military fiasco at Pailingmiao and the Sian incident. The cabinet also cultivated the support of the business community by its emphasis on constitutional principles and a cautious foreign policy. Hayashi's moderate tone in the Diet and his refusal to marshal the resources of the government behind the Kokumin Dōmei, however, did not induce the major parties to support the type of economic controls recommended by the Cabinet Planning Board. In effect, neither Terauchi's admonitions nor Hayashi's conciliatory gestures yielded the desired legislation. In the general elections of April, moreover, the major parties garnered an overwhelming number of Diet seats; and when Hayashi still refused to admit any party leaders into the cabinet, the contentions between the Diet and the government intensified. The cabinet submitted a series of economic programs and legislative drafts; and the Diet proved unwilling to enact any of them into law. Without resorting to dubious constitutional procedures, the Hayashi cabinet was, in effect, unable to fulfill the domestic economic programs sanctioned by the 1936 "Principles of National Policy." By mid-June, War Minister Sugiyama and Premier Hayashi conceded the desirability of a new cabinet; and, after several days of consultations with the ministers of state and the court advisors, a consensus was reached in favor of the scion of the Fujiwara clan, Prince Konoe Fumimaro.[38]

THE MARCO POLO BRIDGE INCIDENT

When Prince Konoe moved to stage center in the theater of cabinet politics, he apparently took on the role of premier with good intentions but dubious skill. To many Japanese historians, Konoe was a dangerous and unfortunate combination of a charismatic leader with a chameleon-like character, a political weather vane who yielded to the prevailing and

[38] Yabe Teiji, *Konoe Fumimaro* (Tokyo, 1952), I, 375-383.

fascistic winds blowing in Japan. In the trenchant words of Professor Maruyama:

> As the perfect case of "weak nerves" most readers will, of course, think of Prince Konoe. His political career certainly provides a wealth of examples of how fatally a weakness of character can operate at important moments. According to Marquis Kido's evidence, "Whenever any difficult questions arose he frequently said, 'I want to give up.' "[39]

Understandably, Konoe saw himself in a different perspective, as a man who vigilantly opposed the fascistic and imperialistic policies of the Japanese army, only to be overwhelmed by the Machiavellian intrigues of a Control Faction in the Imperial army. Declared Konoe:

> I felt it was my mission to control the army by every possible means without provoking it. It was because of this object that I tried to restore the Kōdō [Imperial Way] Faction people, but this effort was checked by some senior members of the army and some influence of the royal court. I, therefore, feel my responsibility in not having been able to control the army on account of my ineptness.[40]

Although one or the other of these portraits has governed postwar appraisals of Prince Konoe, neither does justice to the character of the man, or to his part in the process of events which propelled Japan into a major war on the continent.[41] As premier, Konoe was neither the spokesman for nor the puppet of Japan's "militaristic fascists"; and he was not a lonely counselor of moderation and caution in the highest echelons of the Japanese government. Konoe was selected as premier in June 1937 because of his political acumen and with the expec-

[39] Maruyma Masao, *Thought and Behavior in Modern Japanese Politics* (New York, 1963), 97.

[40] Konoe Fumimaro, *Ushinuwareshi seiji* (Tokyo, 1946); and IMTFE, *Defense Document 3107*, 248.

[41] A good critique of the various profiles of Prince Konoe is Okada Takeo, *Konoe Fumimaro: Tennō to gunbu to kokumin* (Tokyo, 1959).

tation that he could obtain the political support essential to the realization of the domestic economic legislation sanctioned by the 1936 principles of national policy. Ironically, this wish was to be consummated only after Japan became involved in a war with China, the one circumstance which both general staffs wanted to avoid at the time of Konoe's selection as premier.

In the process of organizing the Konoe cabinet, the ministries of state were anxious to commit the new premier to the policies which had already been formulated; and Konoe was naturally concerned with enhancing the scope of his authority in cabinet affairs. To this end, he tried to obtain the appointment of General Itagaki as war minister and Admiral Suetsugu as naval minister.[42] Since each of these officers was closely identified with extremist views and neither had been assigned to central headquarters for several years, their nomination for the service portfolios was vetoed, as Konoe remarked, "by some senior members of the army and some influence of the royal court." Reluctantly, the premier designate accepted the appointment of two officers who were intimately familiar with and proponents of the current views on security and foreign policies as his service ministers— namely, General Sugiyama Gen and Admiral Yonai Mitsumasa. Shortly after the formation of his cabinet, though, the outbreak of the Marco Polo Bridge incident on July 7, 1937, created a fluid political situation which gave the premier the type of latitude in cabinet politics he had tried to bring about through the appointment of General Itagaki and Admiral Suetsugu.

On the eve of the incident at the Marco Polo Bridge, the official policy of the Japanese government was identical with that which had been approved by the Hayashi cabinet— namely, to concentrate on the enhancement of the military and naval power of the empire and to avoid any serious incidents on the mainland. This policy had not, of course, altered the basic commitment to exclude the Kuomintang from North

42 Yabe, *Konoe,* I, 381.

China; and this was subject to modification only if the Nanking government were prepared to accept Japanese economic, political, and military advisors and assistance. By the terms imposed in the Tangku Truce and the Ho-Umezu and Ching-Doihara agreements, North China was placed beyond the direct political and military control of the Nanking government. Theoretically, since Japan's army authorities no longer deemed the resources of North China as vital to their economic plans, the Japanese government might have reached a *quid pro quo* settlement with the Nationalist government by admitting the Kuomintang into North China in return for a Sino-Japanese Friendship Treaty that would transform the Nanking regime into an Imperial satellite. Actually, the Chinese government had no intention of assuming a subservient position, nor was it prepared, as the events of 1935 had revealed, to endure supinely the imposition of another "local" military agreement which further compromised its sovereignty over the provinces of North China. This background of competing national policies—not the actions of a Japanese field army or of a Control Faction—would transform the incident at the Marco Polo Bridge into the prelude to a major war.[43]

Owing to the passions unleashed by the Sino-Japanese war and the lack of primary Chinese sources, the actual circumstances surrounding the outbreak of fighting in the vicinity of the Marco Polo Bridge remain obscure.[44] Both Chinese and Japanese officers testified at the Tokyo International Military Tribunal, however, that around midnight of

[43] For a different approach, see Yale Maxon, *Control of Japanese Foreign Policy* (Berkeley, 1957), 120-124; Richard Storry, *The Double Patriots* (London, 1957), 215-223.

[44] My understanding of the events between July 7 and August 20, 1937, is, in many respects, rooted in a series of interviews with the Honorable (s) Arita Hachirō, Hidaka Shinroku, and Kamimura Shinichi; Generals Hashimoto Gun, Wachi Takagi, Inada Seijun, Imai Takeo, and Satō Kenryō; Colonel Nishiura Susumu; Admirals Fukudome Shigeru, Hasegawa Kiyoshi, Tomioka Sadatoshi, and Takagi Sōkichi. Mr. Hata Ikuhito graciously shared his interview notes with Generals Kawabe Torashirō and Ikeda Junkyū.

July 7, Colonel Matsui of the Japanese army reported the occurrence of a brief skirmish to the Mayor of Peking, General Ching Teh-chin, and requested permission for a company of Japanese to search the town of Wanping for an allegedly missing soldier.[45] General Ching, instead, proposed sending a joint investigating commission and ordered the local Chinese commander at Wanping to resist any Japanese attempt to enter the town. Colonel Matsui accepted the Chinese proposal and appointed Lt. Colonel Morita as the Japanese representative on the joint commission. While this investigating body was being organized, Japanese troops forcibly tried to breach the Wanping defenses and were readily repulsed. Directly after this second skirmish, both sides rushed a battalion of men to the scene and, by the morning of July 8, a tense situation had arisen.

Although the town of Wanping was an important railway junction, there is no evidence indicating that the Japanese intended to seize or control it. On July 7, the entire infantry brigade stationed in North China, with the exception of fifty men in Peking and Major Ichiki's battalion at Fengtai, was engaged in field maneuvers.[46] The 1st Infantry Regiment was deployed at Tsingchow and the 2nd Infantry Regiment at Nantassu, south of Shanhaikwan. Because these exercises had been in progress since June 6, the bulk of the Japanese troops was not in a position suitable for operations in the vicinity of Wanping. The deployment of the main body of Japanese troops, plus the basic policy of army central headquarters, which specifically forbade any "incident," is strong evidence that the events of July 7 were not part of a prearranged plan of aggression. This is further substantiated by the behavior of the responsible field officers of the North China Army.

[45] IMTFE, *Documents 1750* (Deposition of General Ching Teh-chin), and *1790* (Deposition of General Wang Leu-ch'ai); also *Defense Document 973* (Deposition of General Hashimoto Gun).

[46] For a meticulous account of the deployment of the field army, see Hata Ikuhito and Shimizu Setsuro, "Ryōkōkō jiken" [The Marco Polo Bridge Incident], *Aziya kenkyū*, III, 2 (1956), 80-97.

Two weeks before the Marco Polo Bridge incident, General Tashiro, the senior Japanese officer in North China, suffered a serious heart attack. General Hashimoto Gun, chief of staff of the North China Army, was in *de facto* command of all Japanese troops. During the morning of July 8, General Hashimoto verbally ordered Major Ichiki, the commanding officer of the battalion which had been sent to Wanping, to avoid any operations pending an official investigation of the situation.[47] On the same morning, Hashimoto also informed General Kawabe Shōzō, the commanding officer of the North China Infantry Brigade, of the intention to effect a prompt settlement of the matter. However, when Kawabe arrived at Wanping at 3:00 p.m. that day, he significantly allowed Major Ichiki the convenient loophole of attacking if his company was fired upon by Chinese troops. During the early hours of the morning of July 9, Major Ichiki prepared to assault the Chinese position and, when Lt. Colonel Morita tried to intervene, Ichiki used Kawabe's verbal orders as sufficient justification for his decision to attack. He promptly led an unsuccessful charge against the Chinese defenders.

The situation in Peking was quite different. Colonel Matsui and Major Imai Takeo, the Peking attaché, conferred with responsible Chinese military officials in a sincere effort to dispose of the matter quickly. Concurrently with these negotiations, Hashimoto despatched Colonel Wachi to Tokyo for "consultations," and received orders from the general staff to effect a local settlement of the situation.[48] On the afternoon of July 9, Hashimoto flew from Tientsin to Peking, joined Matsui and Imai, and presented to General Ching the following terms (1) a Chinese apology for the incident; (2) punishment of the officers responsible for the difficulty; (3) replacement of the

[47] IMTFE, *Defense Document 973.* Also interview with General Hashimoto.

[48] Wachi was deliberately despatched to Tokyo because he was the one staff officer who did not sympathize with the directives of General Hashimoto. Interviews with Wachi, Imai, and Hashimoto. For a different interpretation of Wachi's trip, see Storry, *Double Patriots*, 221-222.

troops in the Wanping area by men of the Peace Preservation Corps; and (4) a rigid control of the Communist element in the region. Because these conditions did not raise a political issue, a point which had immediately concerned the Chinese, General Ching accepted the terms as the basis of a settlement. On July 11, at 11:00 a.m., representatives of both armies signed a local agreement which embodied the above-mentioned terms.[49]

With the single exception of Major Ichiki's attack on July 9, the North China Army, under the leadership of General Hashimoto, Colonel Matsui, Lt. Colonel Morita, and Major Imai, had followed the orders of the general staff. There were other currents, however, complicating the achievements of the field armies—developments much deeper than General Kawabe's attitude and powerful enough to transform the Marco Polo Bridge incident into the China War.

In Tokyo, the fracas in North China was not initially regarded with great concern. The chief of staff, Prince Kanin, cabled routine orders on July 8 to General Hashimoto, indicating that the incident should be settled quickly. After this, Kanin advised the Inner Cabinet that "Inasmuch as the government's policy of localizing the incident is thoroughly understood by the field commander, all necessary measures in connection with this matter will be left to the discretion of the commander stationed in China."[50] A few hours later, Mr. Ishii Itarō, the chief of the East Asian Bureau of the foreign ministry, General Ushiroku Jun, the chief of the Bureau of Military Affairs of the war ministry, and Admiral Toyoda Soemu, the chief of the Bureau of Naval Affairs of the naval ministry, reviewed the situation and drafted a recommendation which favored a policy of "non-expansion" and a "local settlement" that would not alter the political situation in Hopei province.[51] The Konoe cabinet, on the afternoon of

[49] The text of this accord is IMTFE, *Defense Document 1169.*

[50] Office Chief of Military History [OCMH], *Japanese Monograph 144,* "Political Strategy Prior to Outbreak of War." Appendix 3 is an English translation of Kanin's policy statement.

[51] Ishii Itarō, *Gaikōkan no isshō* (Tokyo, 1950), 271.

July 8, officially approved the position paper prepared by the war, foreign, and naval ministries; and the next morning General Kanin forwarded the four basic terms to be included in a "local" settlement of the incident.

From the Nanking perspective, the Marco Polo Bridge matter was not viewed as a local problem to be worked out by the field armies in North China. Parallel with the smooth negotiation going on in Peking, the Nanking government presented a formal note to Hidaka Shinroku, the Japanese consul, which requested that both armies withdraw to their original positions and which reserved the right to review any tentative settlement approved by the local military officers.[52] Along with this note, the Nationalist government despatched four army divisions to the Paoting valley in southern Hopei and it ordered General Sung Che-yuan, the chairman of the Hopei-Chahar Political Council, to proceed to Paoting pending a diplomatic settlement of the incident by the central government.[53] These actions were readily comprehensible; and, at the same time, they introduced some grave and complicating diplomatic and military problems. The Ho-Umezu accord had barred the Nationalist army from North China; the Japanese government still expected compliance with this agreement; and, in fact, the local settlement being worked out in Peking did not include any new political stipulations. Moreover, once the Nationalist forces started their march toward Paoting, the intelligence division of the general staff, under Colonel Nagatsu, alerted the Konoe cabinet to the dangers this would present to the North China Army.[54] On the basis of this intelligence report, Colonel Mutō Akira, the chief of the operations section of the general staff, and Colonel Tanaka Shinichi, the chief of the military affairs department of the war ministry, promptly called for an immediate mobi-

[52] IMTFE, *Defense Document 2148*.

[53] General Ching testified that "Repeated telegrams from our Supreme Commander [Chiang Kai-shek] ordered General Sung . . . to proceed to Paoting and to direct operations from there." IMTFE, *Document 1750*.

[54] Interviews with Generals Inada and Satō; also with Colonel Nishiura.

lization of five divisions within Japan. Since Mutō and Tanaka would be officially responsible for implementing any mobilization plan of the government, their advice is readily understandable. Confronted by the mobilization and despatch of Chinese troops and the diplomatic posture of the Nanking government, the chief of the operations division, General Ishiwara Kanji, reluctantly deferred to the opinion advanced by Colonels Mutō and Tanaka and, at 6:00 p.m. on July 10, Ishiwara officially advised the war minister of the need to mobilize five divisions in Japan.[55] Three hours later, War Minister Sugiyama phoned Premier Konoe and requested that an emergency meeting of the Inner Cabinet be called to consider the request of the army general staff. Prince Konoe not only concurred with the projected mobilization plan but thought the government should also issue a strong policy statement which would notify the Nanking government that it should refrain from trying to interfere with the local settlement being negotiated by the field armies.[56]

During the morning of July 11, the Inner Cabinet approved the mobilization plans submitted by General Sugiyama, as well as the premier's proposition that the government must adopt a public stance of firm support for the "localization" policy. Specifically, the joint army-naval agreement sanctioned by the cabinet called for the mobilization of five divisions, three to be assigned in North China, two in the Shanghai and Tsingtao regions; and it stipulated that the theater of operations would "be limited to the Peking-Tientsin area. As a matter of principle, force will not be resorted to in Central and South China."[57] In an official memorial to the Throne, the cabinet cogently summarized its approach to the incident:

(1) In despatching troops to North China, we aim, through demonstration of our power, to make the Chinese forces

[55] IMTFE, *Defense Document 971*, 10.

[56] Kazami Akira, *Konoe naikaku* (Tokyo, 1951), 30-31.

[57] OCMH, *Japanese Monograph 144*, Appendix 7, is a translation of the operational plans submitted to the cabinet.

apologize to us and to have them assume responsibility for future eventualities.

(2) Our attack against Chinese forces will commence only when it has become clear that they will not accept our demands.

(3) The principle of localizing the incident and settling it through negotiations by field commanders will be observed to the last.

(4) If it is proved that the newly mobilized troops need not be despatched, the projected despatch will be abandoned.[58]

Obviously, the cabinet, including the premier, believed the incident could be settled by a local agreement and a positive public stance, buttressed by the threat of a general mobilization.

In order to dramatize the emerging diplomatic crisis, Prince Konoe, directly after the cabinet session, conducted a public press conference. Here, the premier announced the projected mobilization of five divisions and he pleaded for a nation-wide approval of the government's decision. Insisted Konoe:

There is no room for doubt that the recent incident is entirely the result of anti-Japanese military action on the part of China. Needless to say, since security in North China is a matter of urgent necessity for peace in east Asia, the Chinese authorities must apologize to us for the illegal anti-Japanese actions and properly guarantee to refrain from repeating such action in the future.... As the maintenance of peace in East Asia is Japan's constant desire, the government will not relinquish the hope of peaceful negotiations on the basis of its localization policy.[59]

This press conference inevitably inspired the inference that the cabinet had definitely decided in favor of mobilization and a reinforcement of the North China Army. At the same time,

[58] *Ibid.*, Appendix 5, is a translation of the memorial.
[59] *Ibid.* Also the special edition of the *Asahi shimbun*, July 11, 1937.

it also obscured the fact that the field armies had already reached a settlement of the incident.

Each of these public impressions was misleading. During the afternoon of July 11, General Hashimoto notified the general staff of the local settlement; and General Ishihara promptly cancelled the mobilization plan sanctioned by the cabinet.[60] Instead of activating five divisions, Ishiwara authorized preparations for the despatch of two brigades from the Kwantung Army and one division from the Korean Army. This revised contingency plan was officially presented to the Emperor on July 14; and, in the course of this Imperial audience, General Sugiyama indicated that, in fact, nothing would be done prior to a firsthand report on the North China scene.[61] While this restraining hand was being placed on the proposed reinforcement of the North China Army, the popular press responded zealously to Konoe's plea for national unity. "Japan," claimed the *Hochi Shimbun*, "is destined to do something in the near future to demonstrate its mission."[62] The editors of *Chugai* intoned, "Japan will not allow conditions to shape themselves in this area as Nanking wishes."[63] This journalistic tone led the American ambassador, Joseph Grew, on July 13, to conclude that the cabinet, press, and business community were unanimously opposed to "any weakening of Japan's position in North China."[64] One exception to this consensus was articulated by the *Japan Weekly Chronicle*, an English-language publication, which observed on July 13: "Those who see dazzling visions of swift military success and the profits of subsequent exploitations are witless simpletons. . . . Statesmanship of the highest order

[60] IMTFE, *Defense Document 971*, 11-12.

[61] For a different interpretation, see Maxon, *Control of Japanese Foreign Policy*, 122.

[62] *Japan Weekly Chronicle*, July 22, 1937, 110. This issue contains an article, "The Press and the Crisis," which reviews the main editorials.

[63] *Ibid.*

[64] Joseph Grew, *Ten Years in Japan* (New York, 1944), 211.

is needed if the crisis is to be circumvented."[65] The only concrete steps taken in this direction, however, materialized within army central headquarters.

Despite its original request for mobilization, the general staff had no desire to escalate the incident in North China into a major crisis. In order to assist the field army to effect a local settlement and to appraise carefully the need for any reinforcements, Colonel Shibayama of the war ministry was ordered to fly to Tientsin and to prepare a firsthand evaluation of the situation. Arriving in Tientsin on the 15th, Shibayama conducted a three-day conference with the responsible field officers —General Hashimoto, Colonel Matsui, Lt. Colonel Ikeda Junkyū, and Major Imai Takeo. On the 18th, these officers agreed that the settlement of July 11 should be implemented at all costs and that reinforcements were not to be sent to North China.[66] Although this decision would be of immediate importance to the planning of the general staff, Shibayama did not cable his report directly to Tokyo. Perhaps because he feared the dire consequences of any distortion by a transmitting officer, he instead elected to fly back to central headquarters to deliver his evaluation in person. However, whether because of inclement weather or because of a side trip to the headquarters of the Korean Army, Shibayama did not arrive in Tokyo until July 20, a delay of more than forty-eight hours.

Originally, central headquarters had intended to wait for Shibayama's evaluation before issuing any new orders. However, the reports of the military attachés in China confirmed that Nanking had ordered the mobilization of all troops north of the Yangtze River and had not halted the northward movement of the four divisions that were heading toward Paoting. These warnings, plus aggressive advice from the Kwantung Army, supplied Colonels Mutō and Tanaka with sufficient ammunition to bombard the "lethargic" policy of General Ishi-

[65] *Japan Weekly Chronicle*, July 15, 1937, 177. This is a reprint of an editorial of July 13.

[66] Ikeda Junkyū, *Rikugun sōgii-in-chō* (Tokyo, 1953), 27-28. Also interviews with Hashimoto Gun and Imai Takeo.

wara. Around midnight of July 15, Ishiwara bowed to the attack of Mutō and Tanaka and informed the war minister that it was absolutely imperative for General Sung, the head of the Hopei-Chahar Council, to accept and implement the agreement of the 11th within seventy-two hours.[67]

General Sugiyama promptly requested another emergency cabinet meeting for the next morning and, at this session, emphasized that the Imperial army could not assume responsibility for the protection of Japanese lives and property in North China unless a final settlement were reached by the 19th. Foreign Minister Hirota thought that a firm statement to the Nanking government would be the best way to promote a quick settlement. The cabinet concurred, and, on July 17, Consul Hidaka presented an aide-mémoire to the Chinese government which insisted that Nanking put an immediate stop to all provocative actions and refrain from impeding the implementation of the accord reached by the local authorities.[68]

The Konoe cabinet's official demand that Nanking exclude itself from the settlement of the crisis coincided with an opposite resolution by the Chinese government. On July 16, Consul Hidaka received another note from the Nanking government reiterating the earlier demands that it must sanction any local settlement and that both sides withdraw their troops to their original positions.[69] After receiving the Japanese aide-mémoire of the 17th, which totally rejected these stipulations, the Chinese government appealed publicly to the signatories of the Nine Power Treaty for assistance in settling the Marco Polo Bridge incident.[70] The next morning, in the official reply to the Japanese aide-mémoire, the Chinese government stated that it must continue its military preparations because of the Japanese decision to mobilize and to reinforce the North

[67] IMTFE, *Defense Document 971*, 12.

[68] IMTFE, *Document 2143*, 3.

[69] IMTFE, *Defense Document 2148*.

[70] Royal Institute of International Affairs [RIIA], *Survey of International Affairs, 1937* (London, 1938), 186-187.

China Army.[71] In addition, it demanded again the right to approve formally any settlement negotiated by the field armies.

This rejection of the Japanese solution was implemented by Chiang Kai-shek's memorable address at Kuling, in which the generalissimo publicly listed four conditions for a peaceful solution of the incident: (1) no infringement of Chinese sovereignty; (2) no unlawful alteration of the Hopei-Chahar Council; (3) no removal of any official appointed by the Nanking government; (4) no restrictions on the stationing of the 29th Army of General Sung. He concluded, "If we allow one inch more of our territory to be lost, we shall be guilty of an unpardonable crime against our race."[72] Publicly, and in official communications, the Nanking government had vividly conveyed its determination to take part in any settlement of the Marco Polo Bridge incident.

Ten days after the outbreak of the incident, Nanking and Tokyo had adopted contradictory policies. The Nationalist government, fearing a new attempt to dismember part of China, proclaimed its determination to negotiate a solution which would not alter the *status quo* in North China; the Konoe cabinet, committed to the basic policy of reducing the influence of the Kuomintang in North China, demanded a "local" settlement and adopted a saber-rattling pose designed to frighten the Chinese government into passivity. Ironically, the policy of the Imperial army had been to negotiate a quick settlement which would avoid raising any political problems.

General Sung Che-yuan, the chairman of the Hopei-Chahar Committee, believed the attitude of the Japanese field officers was sincere and, on July 17, ignoring the repeated order of Chiang Kai-shek to withdraw to Paoting, attended the funeral of General Tashiro.[73] Sung's gesture was appreciated by the staff of the North China Army, and, after the funeral services, General Hashimoto and Lt. Colonel Ikeda Junkyū met in-

[71] Interview with Hidaka Shinroku.
[72] RIIA, *Survey* . . . , *1937*, 187.
[73] Ikeda, *Rikugun sōgii-in-chō*, 23.

formally with General Sung. During their conversation, General Hashimoto conveyed the necessity for a new settlement in order to prevent complicating moves by the Imperial army. The next morning, General Sung visited General Katsuki, the new Japanese commanding officer, and offered his personal apology for the Marco Polo Bridge incident.[74] In addition, Sung ordered the removal of all street barricades which had been erected in Peking and began the withdrawal of the Chinese troops which had been involved in the fighting at Wanping. At the very moment when the two governments had reached an impasse over the problem, the field armies had again managed to achieve an apparently successful solution.

The continued mobilization of Chinese troops north of the Yangtze could not be treated lightly by the army general staff. During the evening of July 18, Colonel Mutō again demanded the adoption of an operational plan of action for the North China crisis and the mobilization of three divisions. Ishiwara, ignorant of Sung's latest steps and without the evaluation of Colonel Shibayama, authorized Mutō's plan.[75] The following morning, before an emergency cabinet session, Mr. Ishii, General Ushiroku, and Admiral Toyoda, as was the custom, met to hammer out a joint policy recommendation for the cabinet.[76] However, Ishii and Toyoda refused to sanction Ushiroku's demand for mobilization. For the first time during the crises, an unresolved basic issue was referred to the cabinet for a decision.

Mr. Ishii was unusually persistent in his objections, and before the cabinet meeting he handed Foreign Minister Hirota a written memo declaring the absolute opposition of his bureau to any mobilization request.[77] Despite the dissension evident at the meeting of the bureau chiefs, the cabinet, according to Mr. Hirota, approved the army's plan "without any opposition."[78] But on July 20, Colonel Shibayama returned

[74] IMTFE, *Proceedings*, 20619.	[75] Interview with General Inada.
[76] Ishii, *Gaikōkan*, 277.	[77] *Ibid.*, 276.
[78] *Ibid.*

to Tokyo and presented a strong plea against reinforcing the North China Army.[79] Later that day, General Hashimoto cabled Ishiwara that reinforcements were neither necessary nor desired because the Chinese were carrying out the agreement originally signed on July 11.[80] Fortified by this information, the mobilization order was canceled again by Ishiwara on July 21.[81]

This policy could not be indefinitely shelved unless the Nanking government canceled the mobilization of its troops north of the Yangtze River and withdrew its divisions from the Paoting region. Some understanding with the central government was needed to realize these steps. General Ushiroku, the chief of the Bureau of Military Affairs, personally requested the staff of the foreign ministry on July 23 to open direct negotiations with the Chinese government.[82] Even the moderate Ishii, however, was not prepared to suggest a modification of the fundamental policy of the Konoe cabinet. A "local" settlement was the *sine qua non* of Japan's foreign policy. Hence, Chiang Kai-shek would have either to swallow his Kuling address and accept the settlement of July 11, or risk the grave consequences of undermining this settlement.

The stalemate between Tokyo and Nanking aggravated the North China situation and transferred the entire responsibility for avoiding hostilities to the field armies. Less prone to moderation than his staff, the new commanding officer, General Katsuki, on July 20 ordered the preparation of a plan of operations for the Wanping region and began to deploy his troops to advantageous positions.[83] On the Chinese side, General Hsiung Ping, the vice-chief of the Chinese Central Army, arrived in Peking on July 22, requested General Sung to retire to Paoting, and sought to instill a more positive policy in Sung's headquarters.[84]

[79] *Ibid.*, 277.
[80] *Ibid.* Also interview with Hashimoto Gun.
[81] IMTFE, *Defense Document 971*, 14.
[82] Ishii, *Gaikōkan*, 277.
[83] Interview with Generals Hashimoto and Imai.
[84] IMTFE, *Proceedings*, 20632.

The belligerent attitudes of Generals Katsuki and Ping had their effect on the troops of both armies. During the night of July 25 and the next morning, brief skirmishes occurred at Langfang and at the southwest gate of Peking. General Katsuki, with the approval of central headquarters, promptly forwarded a 24-hour ultimatum to General Sung, calling for the complete withdrawal of Chinese troops from the Wanping region and the retirement of Sung's 37th Division to the right bank of the Yungting river. On July 27, before the 24-hour deadline, the Chinese troops at Wanping launched an attack, and bitter fighting developed in the vicinity of the Marco Polo Bridge.[85]

Although the events in North China between July 25 and July 27 did not precipitate a major war, they altered the nature of the Marco Polo Bridge incident. This became manifest on July 27 when Prince Konoe publicly called for a "fundamental solution of Sino-Japanese relations"; and Foreign Minister Hirota added, "Japan wants Chinese cooperation, not Chinese territory."[86] The diplomatic *volte-face* meant that the Konoe government had cast aside its commitment to a "local" settlement in favor of opening direct negotiations with the Nationalist government. Given the public stances that the two governments had adopted in the opening week of the incident and the recent clash at Langfang, this alteration in policy may have been unavoidable. Still, in a belated move to break the diplomatic impasse between the two governments, the Chinese foreign minister, on July 25, had informed Consul Hidaka that Chiang Kai-shek was prepared to accept "a local settlement of the Marco Polo Bridge Incident. . . , along the lines of the three points covered by the settlement of July 11."[87] The renewal of hostilities in North

[85] General Wang testified: "Being so cornered and pressed, our authorities [were] ordered to attack." *Ibid., Exhibit 248,* 8.

[86] IMTFE, *Exhibit 617,* 17-18. This exhibit is the official report of the subcommittee appointed by the League of Nations to investigate the China incident.

[87] USDS, *Foreign Relations . . . , 1937,* III, 256. According to the "1937 Business Report" of the Japanese foreign ministry, Chiang indicated he

China and General Sung's withdrawal across the Yungting river, however, effectively nullified this overture. Conceivably, an earlier acceptance of the July 11th accord by Chiang might have avoided, at least for a while, a major Sino-Japanese conflict. As it was, the generalissimo quickly reverted to his previous diplomatic stance; and, on July 30, he affirmed, "The declaration I made at Kuling and the minimum four conditions laid down by me for the settlement of the Loukouchiao affair are unalterable.... The only course open to us now is to lead the masses of the nation, under a single national plan, to struggle to the last."[88]

Unfortunately, this declaration was discounted by the Konoe cabinet as pure rhetoric, words enunciated in order to smother the demands of the Communists and the ultra-nationalists for an immediate confrontation with Japan. This cynical estimate of Chiang's intentions was, of course, related to the premise that the Japanese army could, without difficulty, crush the Nationalist forces. The casual approach of the Konoe cabinet to a possible war with China was complemented by a Chinese article of faith. From the inception of the Marco Polo Bridge incident, Chiang had assumed, as he stated to the American ambassador, that the Japanese government "intended to use the Marco Polo Bridge Incident for the purpose of bringing about the complete separation of Hopei and Chahar provinces from the control of the Central government."[89] Given this conviction, the generalissimo anticipated that the Konoe government would demand the recognition of Manchukuo and the negotiation of an anti-Comintern pact as the price for a diplomatic settlement of the Marco Polo Bridge incident.

---

would approve the field settlement, providing the Imperial government issued a public statement which would "stipulate the incident had been resolved and announce spontaneously the withdrawal of the Japanese army to the positions held on July 7th." JFM, Archives, *Shina Jihen*, I, "Shōwa juninen tai shitumu hōkoku," 8.

[88] USDS, *Foreign Relations of the United States: Japan, 1931-1941* (Washington, 1946), I, 393.

[89] USDS, *Foreign Relations . . . , 1937*, III, 256-258.

In this eventuality, declared Chiang, "the Chinese government would not accept these demands and . . . war would therefore be inevitable."[90] To some extent, this proved to be a self-fulfilling analysis: neither the Imperial army nor the Konoe cabinet intended, on July 7, 1937, to separate Hopei province from the Nationalist government; but the public pronouncements of the generalissimo, as well as his veto of the local settlements, eventually yielded a major crisis which soon vindicated his prognosis of subsequent Japanese demands.

Without any discernible signs of consultation with prominent court, political, financial, or military leaders, Prince Konoe and Foreign Minister Hirota had, on July 27, committed the Japanese government to a policy which envisioned a "fundamental solution of Sino-Japanese relations." This stance was well received in Japan, judging by the popular press; and it drew appropriate accolades from those officers pleased by the prospect of a blitzkreig in North China. It also ignored the more cautious advice of the army general staff. To confront the Nationalist government with a list of encompassing political demands would, in the judgment of General Ishiwara's staff, lead to an unnecessary war and thus, in turn, impede the army's rationalization program.[91] In contention with this point of view, the vice-war minister, General Umezu, as well as the senior staff officers of the Kwantung Army—Generals Itagaki and Tōjō—were confident that the army could shatter the Kuomintang forces in North China with a blitzkreig, if Chiang were rash enough to challenge the power of the Imperial army.

After considering these dissenting views, the Konoe cabinet, on August 7, formulated its new approach to the China crisis. Meeting in a full cabinet session, the ministers of

[90] *Ibid.*

[91] Here, and subsequently, my characterization of the views within the officer corps is a synthesis from interviews with Generals Inada, Satō, Imamura, Imai, Hashimoto and Colonel Nishiura Susumu. Also from Hata Ikuhito's interviews with General Ikeda, Tanaka Shinichi, and Kawabe Torashirō.

state delineated three basic objectives to be obtained in the forthcoming negotiations—namely, that the Nationalist government should (1) create a demilitarized zone in the Peking-Tientsin district; (2) organize a new administrative arrangement for the provinces of North China, one that would be staffed by individuals "sympathetic" to a viable Sino-Japanese reconciliation; and (3) promise that it would negotiate a comprehensive Sino-Japanese treaty.[92] Lest there be any uncertainty about the specific objectives encompassed within these three propositions, the Inner Cabinet adopted a separate policy, the "Overall Adjustment of Sino-Japanese Relations."[93] Here, the aspirations of the Konoe government were articulated with much greater candor. Japan would expect a settlement which would include a *de facto* recognition of Manchukuo, an anti-Comintern pact, and the suppression of all anti-Japanese elements within China. These demands were, in effect, identical with Hirota's three principles—a fact which is not too surprising, since the foreign minister of the Konoe cabinet was Hirota Kōki. In 1935, Chiang had dismissed these principles as the basis of any Sino-Japanese détente; in 1936, the Hirota cabinet had set them aside as a workable China policy; and there was slight reason to believe that Chiang was prepared, in August 1937, to embrace Hirota's principles in order to settle the Marco Polo Bridge crisis. Still, the Japanese foreign minister, as well as the premier, believed these principles constituted the sole basis for a "fundamental solution" of the China problem. Only the operations division of the general staff apparently still remembered that Japan was not prepared to wage a "total war" in 1937, and that, therefore, it might be imprudent to press for a fundamental solution of all Sino-Japanese problems.

This note of uncertainty, though, was muffled by the misplaced sense of confidence in the cabinet. "The broad-minded policy of our government," Hirota assured Ambassador

[92] IMTFE, *Document 2146.*
[93] IMTFE, *Defense Document 2605.*

Kawagoe on August 8, "will probably be beyond the expectations of the Chinese themselves and [it] is worthy of winning the respect of the whole world for the fair and disinterested attitude of our empire."[94] The generous terms of the Konoe government, however, failed to elicit an official diplomatic reply from the Nanking government. Instead, on August 14, the Nationalist air force bombed the Japanese naval installation at Shanghai and, that evening, Nanking announced, "China is duty bound to defend her territory and her national existence."[95] The China war had begun.

A Policy of Chastisement

The sudden shift of the field of battle from Peking to Shanghai caught the Konoe cabinet, as well as both general staffs, completely by surprise. This glaring deficiency in contingency planning is difficult to explain, particularly since the 1932 Shanghai incident, not the events in Manchuria, had impelled the Anglo-American countries to reinforce their naval units and to exert direct diplomatic pressure on the Japanese government. In 1937, Japanese forces in Shanghai were obviously in a more precarious position than the North China Army; and the Western powers would certainly be more prone to interfere in order to pacify the Shanghai international settlement than to moderate a conflict centered in the Paoting valley and Inner Mongolia. Still, the possibility that Chiang might try to check Japanese penetration in North China with a major incident in Shanghai and an appeal for the diplomatic assistance of the Treaty Powers was never seriously entertained by the Konoe cabinet. This oversight placed the Japanese forces in Shanghai in a dangerous and embarrassing position, a context which prompted some shrill and indignant responses. On August 14, Admiral Hasegawa, the commanding officer in Shanghai, declared, "The Imperial navy, having borne the unbearable, is now compelled to take every possible

[94] IMTFE, *Defense Document 2030.*
[95] USDS, *Foreign Relations . . . , 1937*, III, 418.

and effective measure."[96] This announcement was most restrained, in comparison with the official statement of the Konoe cabinet:

> The Chinese, overconfident of their national strength, contemptuous of our own power, and also in league with the Communists, have assumed toward Japan an increasingly arrogant and insulting attitude. . . . [Japan] is now forced to resort to resolute action to bring sense to the Nanking government by punishing the atrocious Chinese army.[97]

Owing to the tardy manner in which the Konoe government had authorized reinforcements for Shanghai, however, the Imperial forces were in no position to deliver a prompt and disciplinary blow against the "atrocious Chinese army" in the Shanghai region.

Prior to the outbreak of hostilities in Shanghai, the behavior of Japanese naval and diplomatic officials in this treaty port had been most circumspect.[98] Following the killing of Naval Lt. Oyama, who died while presumably attempting to capture the Hunjao Airport singlehandedly on August 9, the Japanese consul general apologized for Oyama's bizarre activities; and Admiral Hasegawa promptly canceled all night patrols in the international settlement in order to prevent any untoward incidents. Western observers were impressed by these efforts to avoid a repetition of the circumstances which had caused the Shanghai incident of 1932; and they were visibly distressed by the arrival of Nationalist troops in the Shanghai area, especially in the "demilitarized zone" established in 1932.[99] In fact, the efforts of the Western diplomats to negotiate a local settlement of the Oyama affair were frustrated on August 12 when the mayor of Shanghai acknowledged that he could no longer speak for the Chinese government in the informal talks because this authority now resided with the Nationalist army.[100]

[96] OCMH, *Japanese Monograph 144*, 31.
[97] IMTFE, *Defense Document 1119*; and *Defense Document 986*.
[98] USDS, *Foreign Relations . . . , 1937*, III, 363-366.
[99] *Ibid.*, 385.   [100] *Ibid.*, 386.

These ominous developments in Shanghai did not modify the prevailing attitudes in Tokyo. The Konoe cabinet believed that the Nationalist government would prefer a diplomatic resolution of the crisis to a war with the empire; and the army authorities assumed that, in the unlikely event of hostilities, the Japanese army would quickly smash the Chinese forces in North China, thereby forcing Chiang to negotiate an armistice. Even Admiral Hasegawa, the officer directly responsible for the protection of the Japanese settlement in Shanghai, believed the Oyama matter would be handled expeditiously; but, as a precautionary measure, Hasegawa, on August 13, requested the despatch of three army regiments to Shanghai.[101] The naval general staff, however, regarded the events in Shanghai with greater concern; and it recommended that three divisions be sent to Shanghai.[102] Acting on the advice of the general staff, Naval Minister Yonai secured an emergency cabinet meeting to consider the problem. Here, Yonai pressed the request for three divisions, and War Minister Sugiyama discounted the need for such extensive reinforcements. "It seemed," remarked Baron Harada, "the army was not willing to send its troops. Foreign Minister Hirota avoided having the foreign ministry being drawn into the issue and he pushed the matter on to the army."[103] The emergency cabinet meeting, therefore, ended without any decision on Yonai's request. The following morning, however, Premier Konoe, Foreign Minister Hirota, and Finance Minister Kaya seconded the recommendation of Admiral Yonai and, although Sugiyama considered it a "foolish decision," he deferred to the judgment of the Inner Cabinet.[104] The army general staff then ordered the 3rd and 11th Divisions to Shanghai and the 14th Division to Tsingtao.

In view of the cluster of decisions which characterized the

[101] Naval General Staff, *Taiheiyō sensō kaigen-shi*, I, 15-16. This volume was part of the official operational history of the naval general staff and was written in 1942. Also interview with Admiral Hasegawa.

[102] *Ibid.*, 16.

[103] Saionji-Harada, *Memoirs*, August 13, 1937.

[104] Kazami, *Konoe naikaku*, 46.

policy of the Japanese government before the outbreak of the Shanghai fighting—the cabinet's China policy of August 6, the quarantine of the North China Army in the Peking environs, and the belated reinforcements of the Shanghai garrison—it seems reasonable to conclude that the hostilities in Shanghai were technically provoked by the Nanking government rather than by a willful act of the Japanese army or the Konoe cabinet. This of course does not imply that Nanking was responsible for the resultant war. Rather, it connotes a peculiar set of circumstances, especially the indignity and humiliations endured over a decade, plus the determination to resist any additional encroachment on Chinese soil, that led the Nationalist government to launch operations in Shanghai as a calculated but desperate gamble designed to thwart the relentless Japanese pressure in North China.

Until Chinese sources are available, it is difficult precisely to delineate the basic policy of the Nationalist government during this period. There is good reason to believe, however, that it had decided before July 7 to wage an all-out war if Japan again attempted to dismember North China by means of a military incident and a local settlement similar to those imposed in 1935. A crucial element in transforming the skirmish at the Marco Polo Bridge into a major crisis was the strong reaction of the Nationalist government in terms of its previous attitudes—e.g., the demand that General Sung implement a previously agreed-upon plan of operations calling for the withdrawal of his army from Peking to the Paoting area; the prompt demand that it approve any local settlement; the immediate general mobilization and the despatch of Nationalist troops into North China; the Kuling address of Chiang Kai-shek; and the influence of General Ping of the Nationalist army on the local Chinese army in Peking during late July. No doubt these responses were promoted by the belief that the Japanese army was, in reality, about to establish an "autonomous" North China. It is also conceivable that the Nationalist government had sufficient confidence in its new German-trained divisions to rely upon a field of battle in Shanghai as one way to check Japan's imperial policy.

If the logic underlying the decision of the Nationalist government to provoke a major military incident in Shanghai eludes precise identification, there is ample evidence suggesting that it was based on unwarranted estimates of the diplomacy of the Western powers and of the capabilities of its German-trained divisions.[105] By mobilizing all Nationalist troops north of the Yangtze on July 9, Chiang deliberately conveyed the impression that he was planning to concentrate his forces in the Paoting pass. This image had noticeable effects in Japanese governmental and military circles, not the least of which was the conclusion that the elite Chinese divisions—the 30th, 87th, and 88th—were moving northward toward Paoting. In fact, these "crack" divisions, trained and advised by German military advisors, were being grouped in the mountains between Nanking and Shanghai. Consequently, when the Shanghai incident broke out in mid-August, the Nationalist army seemed to command an overwhelming superiority. Between August 14 and August 23, noted the American consul in Shanghai, the "Chinese probably had about 80,000 men in the field, [the] Japanese naval landing party not more than 12,000."[106] Despite this initial advantage, the Chinese were unable to penetrate the Japanese sector of the international settlement; and, with the arrival of Japanese reinforcements, the initiative slowly passed to the Imperial army.[107] During the month of September, General Iwane Matsui, the commanding officer of the Shanghai Expeditionary Army, systematically pushed the Chinese forces beyond a twenty-mile radius of the international port, after which Matsui began to clamor for additional troops and operational orders that would sanction an advance to Nanking.

[105] Borg, *Far Eastern Crisis of 1933-1938*, 308-317.

[106] USDS, *Foreign Relations . . . , 1937*, III, 493.

[107] For a careful account of the Shanghai crisis, see Aoki Tokuzō, *Taiheiyō sensō zenshi* (Tokyo, 1963), II, 53-56; and NKSG, *Taiheiyō sensō e no michi*, IV, 20-23.

In conjunction with the disappointing performance of his elite divisions, Chiang's difficulties were compounded by the responses of the Western powers. When the Shanghai fighting began, Chiang probably calculated that his initial tactical advantages in Shanghai, and the desire of the powers to protect their treaty rights and nationals in Shanghai, would force the Japanese to negotiate an armistice on the basis of the *status quo ante* of July 7. At least, on August 23, Chiang confessed his keen disappointment over the fact "that the United States did not cooperate with England in an attempt to avert the present crisis, which could have been averted by [a] joint representation to Japan and China."[108] Confronted by the passive diplomacy of the Anglo-American nations, Chiang, on August 21, signed a non-aggression pact with the Soviet Union.[109] This maneuver, though, failed to deter the advance of the Kwantung Army into Inner Mongolia. In this context, the Nationalist government advised the League of Nations that the current hostilities in China marked a continuation of Japan's "aggressive program [which] started in Manchuria in September 1931"; and, on September 13, the Chinese government formally appealed to the League for assistance against "a case of aggression, pure and simple."[110]

The Nanking government patently wanted the League to condemn Japan under the terms of the Kellogg-Briand Pact and to impose a comprehensive economic boycott on the Japanese empire. The Council, however, appointed a special subcommittee to examine the China incident; and on October 6 the advisory committee ruled that "the military operations carried on by Japan against China by land, sea, and air are out of all proportion to the incident that occasioned the conflict."[111] Unfortunately, from the Nationalist viewpoint, neither the committee nor the assembly of the League recommended the adoption of any specific steps against the Japanese

[108] USDS, *Foreign Relations . . . , 1937*, III, 460.
[109] Borg, *Far Eastern Crisis of 1933-1938*, 416.
[110] USDS, *Foreign Relations . . . , 1937*, IV, 18.
[111] USDS, *Foreign Relations . . . , Japan*, 394.

empire, preferring, instead, the convening of a conference of the Nine Power Treaty nations to consider the China problem. The Konoe cabinet, however, had no intention of participating in a conference at which the Western powers would try to arbitrate the Sino-Japanese dispute. In the opinion of War Minister Sugiyama, any form of intervention, mediation, or arbitration by the Western nations before the Imperial army had obtained a crushing defeat of all Nationalist forces would "never make China feel contrition" for her arrogant behavior.[112] Certain that the Nationalist government would never effect a "fundamental solution" of Sino-Japanese relations until it was obliged to abandon the practice of "playing barbarian against barbarian," the Konoe cabinet boycotted the Nine Power Conference held in Brussels. Without the cooperation of Japan, the Brussels Conference yielded no tangible benefits for the Nationalist government, although the official resolution of the League of Nations offered a vacuous profession of sympathy which confirmed "its moral support of China" and urged all member nations to consider how "they can individually extend aid to China."[113] In the absence of any collective diplomatic and economic sanctions against Japan, Chiang Kai-shek was faced with two dismal alternatives: to negotiate an armistice without the face-saving and restraining influence of an international conference; or to continue the struggle against the Japanese empire.

The diplomatic and military plight confronting the Nationalist government by mid-October was, to some extent, self-imposed. Its handling of the Marco Polo Bridge incident and the launching of hostilities in Shanghai had unleashed a major war, even if they cannot be regarded as the basic cause of the conflagration. The gradual escalation of the fighting after the Shanghai clash into a general or total war, however, flowed mainly from the basic policies and aspirations sanctioned by the Konoe cabinet. Throughout the summer and fall of 1937, with the exception of the army general staff, the

[112] IMTFE, *Exhibit 3268.*   [113] IMTFE, *Exhibit 617 A*, 1.

political and military leaders of the Japanese government assumed that the Nationalist government could be beaten into
a posture of complete submission. To some extent, this attitude was understandable. In August, the North China Army
easily subdued Hopei province; and General Terauchi created
a Peace Maintenance Commission in Peking charged with
the task of keeping civil order. The apparent success of this
new agency had, by early September, inspired the hope that
the Japanese army could create a new government for North
China patterned after Manchukuo; and under his discretionary authority as field commander, General Terauchi ordered
his staff to assemble a group of cooperative Chinese politicians as the prelude to the creation of a puppet government in
North China. These activities were complemented by the
Kwantung Army, which moved into Chahar and Suiyuan
provinces and organized the Federated Autonomous Government of Inner Mongolia headed by Prince Teh.

The military victories and political intrigues in North China
and Inner Mongolia, in conjunction with the resolution to
boycott the Brussels Conference, kindled the belief that
Chiang Kai-shek would, of necessity, be compelled to negotiate
a settlement on the basis of the conditions contained in the
August 7th decision of the Konoe cabinet. Thus, on September 5, Foreign Minister Hirota informed the Diet, "In
accordance with the right of self-defense as well as with the
cause of righteousness . . . our country is determined to deal a
decisive blow, so that it [China] may reflect on the error of its
ways."[114] Premier Konoe added in his parliamentary address of
the same day, "[If] China fails to realize its mistakes and per-
sists in its stubborn resistance, our Empire is fully prepared for
protracted hostilities."[115] Whether the words of the premier
and foreign minister mirrored their honest opinions or were
uttered in order to marshal public confidence behind the
government's policy and to impress on the Nationalist govern-

[114] USDS, *Foreign Relations . . . , Japan*, 392-393.
[115] *Ibid.*, 368.

ment the futility of its current stance is not certain. Regardless of the intent, the Japanese government had, in effect, committed itself to a policy of chastisement, one which presumably would not be set aside until the Nationalist government accepted an armistice and a treaty based upon Hirota's three principles.

By portraying the hostilities on the mainland as a moral crusade which would be pursued until the Chinese government abandoned its wicked practices, the Konoe cabinet, at least publicly, embraced the prospect of "protracted hostilities" with no concern. The sternly paternalistic tenor of its China policy, moreover, proved most gratifying to the cabinet, the armed forces, and public opinion. Apparently only the army general staff remained committed to the premise which had permeated the 1936 "Fundamental Principles of National Policy"—namely, that Japan was not yet able to effect a fundamental solution of the China problem by force. To regard the China incident as a purely military problem would, in the judgment of the operations division, inevitably lead to major campaigns which would draw the army deeper and deeper into the mainland. Rather than dissipate men and material in such a China war, these officers preferred a quick diplomatic resolution of the conflict so that the government could concentrate on the economic development of Manchukuo and Japan, as well as on the rationalization of the army. Throughout the fall and winter of 1937, the army general staff tried to impose its approach to the China incident, only to be frustrated in its concerted bid for political control over the conduct of the war against China.

Initially, the general staff displayed its lack of interest in an all-out military campaign by a series of negative decisions. It repeatedly rejected General Matsui's request for an advance to Nanking; it refused to sanction a pincer movement which would link the North China Army and the Shanghai Expeditionary Army and bring the coastal provinces of China between Tientsin and Shanghai under the control of the Imperial army; and it precluded the formal establishment of a North China government by General Terauchi. Along with these steps, the general staff recommended that the government seek the assistance of Nazi Germany in effecting an armistice. When the foreign ministry failed to act on this proposal, the army authorities tried to force this issue in a more direct fashion. At the direct insistence of General Ishiwara, the commanding officer of the operations divison, and General Tada, the vice-chief of the general staff, General Sugiyama on September 11 notified the Throne that the general staff favored a prompt settlement of the China incident. "The army," stressed Sugiyama, "did not possess any territorial ambitions in China . . . [and] it desired some action through diplomatic channels."[116] When this declaration produced no inclination on the part of the cabinet to solicit the help of the German government to settle the incident, General Tada retaliated with a proposal designed to place all aspects of the China incident under the authority of the general staff—namely, the creation of a Supreme Command (*Daihon'ei*) to be composed of the staff officers of both general staffs.

This proposal for a Supreme Command was phrased in terms of the necessity "to coordinate" the political and military aspects of the China incident. Although this seemed to be a reasonable recommendation, in fact, as Naval Minister Yonai warned, it was a "conspiracy" by which the general staff sought to displace the cabinet's control over national policy. If a Supreme Command were instituted, observed Yonai, "the army general staff would make unreasonable proposals and would press them upon . . . the war and naval ministers by saying that they were decided at the Supreme Command."[117] Since this rather crude bid for political power was viewed with suspicion by all the cabinet ministers, including General Sugiyama, the premier was able to table the recommendation. In doing so, however, the cabinet and the naval authorities indicated that,

[116] Saionji-Harada, *Memoirs*, September 10, 1937.
[117] *Ibid.*, September 10, 1937.

if the army general staff believed it was essential to coordinate the political and military aspects of the China incident to a greater degree, they would support the creation of a Supreme Command on two conditions: (1) that the Supreme Command, like those which were instituted in the Sino- and Russo-Japanese wars, included the ministers of state; and (2) that the determination of basic military policies would remain "under the command of the war and naval ministers."[118] In effect, the cabinet's alternative plan would have placed the control of operations under its direction; and, because the purpose of the original proposal had been to impress the strategic views of the general staff on the cabinet, the general staff belatedly declared that greater coordination between the cabinet and the general staff was not an immediate problem.

Although the general staff was unable to marshal sufficient political support for the creation of a Supreme Command, its demand that the government give serious consideration to the means by which the incident could be terminated compelled a reconsideration of the cabinet's China policy. After ten days of inter-ministerial discussion, the foreign ministry drafted the "Essential Points of Policy Toward the China Incident"; and, on October 1, it was approved by the Inner Cabinet.[119] In view of the accomplishments of the field armies in August and September, this cabinet division affirmed that the Nanking government would have to meet six basic stipulations in any diplomatic resolution of the hostilities: (1) a *de facto* recognition of Manchukuo; (2) an anti-Comintern pact; (3) the suppression of anti-Japanese movements; (4) an enlargement of the demilitarized zone in Shanghai; (5) a recognition of Prince Teh's new regime in Inner Mongolia; and (6) the payment of an indemnity. In the act of reformulating the objectives of the hostilities in China, the cabinet had, in effect, disregarded the advice of the general staff; and, in lieu of moderating its political demands, it proposed to confront the

118 *Ibid.*, October 4, 1937.
119 IMTFE, *Defense Document 1362.*

Nationalist government with terms far more demanding than those advanced in August. Only in one respect had the "essential points" deferred to the views of the general staff—namely, the cabinet stipulated that any political organs created by the field armies in the course of the hostilities would "have no influence on the arrangement of diplomatic relations after the advent of peace."[120]

The revised China policy of the government, especially the call for an indemnity, understandably disturbed those army officers who favored a prompt armistice agreement. Still, in order to maximize the opportunities for diplomatic negotiations, the general staff curtailed the operations and the political programs of both field armies. Each of these actions was assailed by many influential officers—e.g., by Vice-War Minister Umezu; General Homma, the chief of the intelligence division; General Ueda, the commanding officer of the Kwantung Army; and by the field commanders, Generals Matsui and Terauchi—who challenged the propriety and wisdom of the cautious military and political plans sanctioned by Generals Tada and Ishiwara. In their judgment, one apparently shared by the premier and the foreign minister, the most expeditious way to terminate the China war was to wage an aggressive and coordinated series of campaigns in North and Central China. This attitude was rooted in the strategic principle that the enemy's forces should be constantly sought out and engaged until he surrendered or requested an armistice. Moreover, since the official policy or objective of the fighting was to effect a "fundamental solution" of the China problem, the demand for an intensified program of operations was hardly incompatible with the policy directives of the cabinet. Generals Tada and Ishiwara, however, bitterly resented the diplomatic stance of the foreign minister, as well as the public utterances of the premier which described the government's objectives in terms of crushing the will of the Chinese people to fight and of erecting "a permanent structure of peace in the Orient in

120 *Ibid.*, 4.

collaboration with all the constructive forces in China which will be liberated by our present action."[121]

The unwillingness of the Konoe cabinet to solicit diplomatic help in order to initiate some conversations with the Nanking government was prompted by several considerations. Traditionally, Japan's China policy had been predicated on the axiom that all Sino-Japanese disputes were to be settled by direct negotiations without the intervention or assistance of the Western powers; the Anglo-American nations were already committed to a policy which denied the legitimacy of Manchukuo; the foreign policy of the Nationalists seemed to be based on the expectation that the Nine Power Treaty countries would be able to coerce Japan into an armistice agreement; and the triumphs of the field armies in August and September apparently confirmed the empire's ability to impose a "victor's" peace on the Nanking regime. This configuration of beliefs impelled the decision to veto any form of cooperation with the League or the Brussels Conference, as well as to rebuff the overtures of the British government, which suggested that its "good offices" be utilized in terminating the China incident.[122] Two suppositions distinguished the foreign policy of the Konoe government: Japan could not effect a satisfactory resolution of the China incident by seeking the assistance of the Anglo-American nations; and Japan could, if necessary, crush the military and political foundations of the Nationalist government. Neither of these suppositions was directly challenged by the general staff. Instead, Generals Tada and Ishiwara argued that it would be better to negotiate with Chiang Kai-shek than to destroy the Nationalist government; and they insisted that the cabinet could invoke the help of the German government without raising serious diplomatic risks.

Subjected to the constant prodding of the general staff, the cabinet, on October 22, decided to solicit the aid of the

[121] As cited by Hugh Borton, *Japan Since 1931* (New York, 1940), 116.
[122] IMTFE, *Document 820.*

German government in order to begin negotiations with Chiang Kai-shek. Within forty-eight hours, Chiang indicated his willingness to consider any Japanese proposals; and Ambassador Dirksen indicated that his government would play the role of "letter carrier" between Nanking and Tokyo.[123] The problem confronting the cabinet now was the formulation of the precise terms to be offered the Nationalist government. After a week of discussion, the foreign ministry drafted a seven-point program which satisfied the Inner Cabinet; and, on November 3, Foreign Minister Hirota informed the German ambassador of Japan's basic terms: (1) an autonomous government in Inner Mongolia; (2) a new demilitarized zone in North China "along the Manchukuo border to a point south of the Peking-Tientsin line"; (3) an enlarged demilitarized zone in Shanghai; (4) the cessation of anti-Japanese activities in China; (5) a "common fight against Bolshevism"; (6) a reduction in customs duties on Japanese goods; and (7) a guarantee of political and economic rights for Japanese nationals in China.[124] These terms, Hirota emphasized, were not subject to modification; and, if the Nationalist government was unwilling to accept them, the foreign minister assured Ambassador Dirksen that Japan "would carry the war to the point of the total defeat of China and exact far more difficult terms."[125]

Despite the warning of the Japanese foreign minister, Chiang Kai-shek, on November 5, stipulated he would "not accept any Japanese demands so long as the Japanese were not prepared to restore the *status quo ante*" of July 7, 1937.[126] This response tended to confirm the impression that Chiang would never negotiate a satisfactory agreement until his position became more precarious. Accordingly, the field commanders urged a dual program of action—namely, to press the attack in Central China and occupy Nanking; and to create

---

[123] USDS, *Documents on German Foreign Policy, 1918-1945*, Series D (Washington, 1949), 776. [Hereafter cited as *D. Ger. F.P.*]
[124] *Ibid.*, 778.   [125] *Ibid.*   [126] *Ibid.*

new political governments in North China and Shanghai. In harmony with this advice, the Inner Cabinet concluded that the only sensible solution to the China incident would be the attainment of "a truly bright North China."[127] In this context, the general staff was subjected to tremendous political pressure to sanction the recommendations of the field commanders. As the Lord Keeper of the Privy Seal sadly observed, "The difference of opinion between the army men in China, men without political authority, and those who hold responsible positions in the government is very great . . . [and] Premier Konoe doesn't seem to be trying to take any measures to lessen these differences."[128] In fact, only the general staff felt constrained to resist the demand for an enlargement of hostilities and the creation of puppet Chinese governments.

In the opening weeks of November, General Tada, the vice-chief of the general staff, moved to strengthen his authority over the field armies in two ways. First, he removed General Ishiwara from command of the operations division. As one of the main architects of the Mukden conspiracy and the creation of Manchukuo, Ishiwara was constantly plagued by the tendency of his subordinates in the general staff, especially Colonel Mutō Akira, and of the field commanders to challenge his operational orders on the grounds that they conflicted with his outlook and activities during the Mukden incident. In the process of transferring Ishiwara to the Kwantung Army, however, General Tada also removed Colonel Mutō from the operations division, replacing these officers with General Hashimoto Gun and Colonel Kawabe Torashirō. This shuffle of personnel created greater harmony within the general staff; and, in order to augment his authority over Generals Terauchi and Matsui, Tada revived the request for the creation of a Supreme Command. In particular, Tada claimed the general staff could not sanction further campaigns in China, unless it had more complete control over the field commanders; and he

---

[127] IMTFE, *Defense Document 2507.*
[128] Saionji-Harada, *Memoirs,* November 18, 1937.

argued that the ministers of state could not share the responsibilities of the Supreme Command. Premier Konoe agreed to the views of General Tada, with the crucial reservation that the general staff "would exist purely as the highest command section of the Supreme Command."[129] Unlike the Supreme Command of the Russo-Japanese War, it would not include ministers of state and it would not be responsible for the determination of basic policies. Consequently, as implemented by the Imperial ordinance of November 20, the Supreme Command was composed of the operations divisions of both general staffs and its authority was confined to directing all operations on the mainland.

General Tada had enhanced his position in the general staff by important legal and personnel changes. He was also opposed to any "war of annihilation" because, in the word of General Satō Kenryō, extensive hostilities in China would "cause the breakdown of our Armament Expansion Plan and the Five-Year Production Expansion Plan."[130] Even so, Tada was unable to quash the arguments in favor of a campaign to seize Nanking. Foreign Minister Hirota and General Matsui both contended that the capture of Nanking would irreparably damage the political viability of the Nationalist government; and prominent business leaders endorsed the viewpoint of the Japan-China Business and Industrial Association—namely, considering the heavy cost in lives and materials incurred in the China incident, "a military government should be set up not only in North China, but in all China."[131] This sentiment was also echoed by Prince Konoe, who publicly observed that it was "too late" to approach the Chinese government with moderate words. "There is no choice," insisted the premier, "but to deal a blow in a determined manner...."[132] And, on November 28, Konoe cryptically indicated that a prolongation of the fighting in China would eventually lead to the ap-

---

[129] *Ibid.*, November 10, 1937.   [130] IMTFE, *Judgment*, 206.
[131] Saionji-Harada, *Memoirs*, November 19, 1937.
[132] IMTFE, *Document 2603-13*, 3.

pearance of new local governments which the Japanese government might recognize in order to realize a political settlement of the incident.[133] In this context, the general staff still managed to exert a restraining influence. On December 1, it authorized the advance to Nanking, but with the clear understanding that the seizure of this city would not affect the government's willingness to negotiate a settlement with Chiang Kai-shek; and it approved the creation of a new political government in North China with the reservation that this should not be allowed to "prejudice any settlement to be reached with the Nationalist government."[134] Despite these qualifications, the Nanking campaign and the new North China government inherently broadened the political and military nature of the China incident.

A POLICY OF ANNIHILATION

Once General Matsui launched the advance on Nanking, Chiang Kai-shek reconsidered his original response to the Japanese peace terms. On December 3, he notified the German ambassador that he was now prepared to negotiate a settlement of the incident on the basis of the conditions outlined by Hirota on the 3rd of November.[135] The German foreign office elatedly called for "a cessation of hostilities," and the Japanese general staff promptly endorsed the recommendation of the government's "letter carrier." Although the cabinet was not formally convened to discuss this proposal, on December 7 Foreign Minister Hirota informed the German ambassador, Herbert von Dirksen, that the peace terms of November were no longer appropriate. In particular, Hirota noted that with the fall of Nanking so imminent, "the field armies" were becoming more exacting in their demands.[136] No doubt they were, but this hardly explains why the Konoe cabinet refused to abide by its earlier commitment to negotiate a settlement on

---

[133] RIIA, *Survey . . . , 1937*, 244.

[134] JFM, Archives, *Matsumoto kiroku: Shina jihen*, I, "NiShi jihen shori keika" [A Review of the Unfolding China Incident], June 6, 1938, 53-55.

[135] *D. Ger. F.P.*, 787-789.   [136] *Ibid.*, 799.

the basis of the conditions established in early November. Indeed, although the foreign minister indicated the need for "more exacting" terms on December 3, the cabinet was unable to formulate its new terms until December 19. During this interval, the general staff desperately tried to commit the government to a settlement of the incident in harmony with the conditions set forth on November 3, only to be frustrated by the political skill and policies of the premier.

When Chiang Kai-shek revealed a willingness to come to terms, General Tada stipulated that the general staff preferred an immediate cessation of hostilities and the opening of formal armistice talks. Recalling the policies of the great Bismarck during the Franco-Prussian War, Tada advocated a policy similar to that which Prussia had followed after the battle of Sadowa—namely, offering generous terms to a defeated adversary. Only in this fashion, reasoned the spokesman for the general staff, could Japan effect a viable diplomatic resolution of the China incident that would permit the government to concentrate its energies on the main strategic threat to the empire, the Soviet Union. This conception of diplomacy, though, was less appealing to Prince Konoe, who discounted the political and military strength of the Nationalist government. "When recognition is withdrawn from Chiang's government," predicted Konoe in early December, "that is, after Nanking falls, Chiang Kai-shek's government is going to collapse. And Japan is going to issue a statement withdrawing recognition from Chiang's government."[137] The presumption that the fall of Nanking would spell the demise of the military and political power of the Nationalist government was not

---

[137] Saionji-Harada, *Memoirs*, December 11, 1937. This sentiment was not confined to the private world of the premier. On December 14, Konoe publicly stated: "By abandoning Peiping, Tientsin, Nanking, and Shanghai, the National Government has become but a shadow of its former self. . . . In the circumstances, if a new regime should arise in the wake of the collapse of the National Government, Japan would have no choice but to consider concrete measures for co-existence and co-prosperity with it, provided it is a regime headed in the right direction." *International Gleanings* (January 15, 1938), 3.

shared by the general staff. On the contrary, General Tada
argued that the China incident should be regarded as a
political problem which could be settled only with the cooperation of Chiang Kai-shek. To ignore the Nationalist government, in Tada's estimation, would saddle the army with two
Herculean tasks: Japan would have to extend the war into
South China in order to shatter all Nationalist forces, and it
would have to create a new Chinese government. In order to
prevent the undertaking of any "war of annihilation," General
Tada, with the support of the service ministries and the naval
general staff, demanded that the premier summon a Liaison
Conference between the Inner Cabinet and the Supreme
Command. Only in this fashion, insisted Tada, could the
government systematically consider the strategic and political
issues involved in Chiang's latest overtures for a negotiated
peace.

Although Tada's urgent request for a Liaison Conference
could not be set aside, it was apparent that the general staff
wished to use such a conference as a political mechanism by
which to impose its Bismarckian approach to the China incident on the cabinet. Reluctantly, Premier Konoe scheduled
a Liaison Conference for December 14 to review and formulate
the government's basic policies vis-à-vis the China incident. In
preparation for it, General Tada drafted a presentation of the
strategic considerations underlying the views of the general
staff; and Premier Konoe devised a political strategy which
would enable the cabinet to retain control over the determination of national policy. Twenty-four hours before the convening of the Liaison Conference, the premier announced the
appointment of Admiral Suetsugu as his new home minister.
This change in the cabinet flabbergasted Prince Saionji and
the members of the Imperial household; and it incensed the
officials of the naval ministry.[138] Suetsugu had been vice-
admiral, senior in rank to Naval Minister Yonai; and he had
been forced into retirement because of his excessive political

[138] *Ibid.*, December 18, 1937.

zeal during the London Naval Treaty controversy. Moreover, the Emperor's advisors and the naval authorities had, in June 1937, indicated their lack of confidence in Suetsugu by blocking his candidacy for the post of naval minister. The startling nature of Konoe's action was appreciated even by the American ambassador, who noted that, following the February 26th incident, cabinet ministers "had not been chosen from those groups . . . out of which developed the political assassinations and attempted coups of the last half dozen years. Now, with the appointment of Admiral Suetsugu, that principle of avoidance is abandoned."[139] If the court and naval officials were, with good reason, distressed by the inclusion of Suetsugu in the Konoe cabinet, it is reasonable to suggest that the articulate admiral had been precipitately brought into the government because the premier was vexed by the attitudes of the army general staff.

The first clue to the purpose of Suetsugu's appointment was provided by the admiral on December 14. Directly after the announcement of his selection as home minister, Suetsugu was interviewed by the press; and he courteously outlined his evaluation of the China war. With the fall of Nanking, reasoned Suetsugu, the government would have to devise a new political and military strategy because Chiang Kai-shek would become "one of those old warlords." In this context, North China would need a "special regime" and eventually two more regimes would be required in Central and South China. Actually, claimed the new home minister, Japan must now embark on a program which would bring "perpetual peace" to East Asia.

Whether or not this will mean the ejection of the white people from East Asia is a very serious problem that must mark a great turn in world history. From the standpoint of world peace, unless the colored races are liberated so that they can receive the benefits of heaven's equality with the

[139] USDS, *Foreign Relations . . . , 1938*, IV, 587.

white peoples, and unless white domination of the world is reconstructed, the so-called justice and humanity so often voiced by the white peoples will remain but empty invocations.[140]

However gratifying this vision of Japan's role in China and Asia may have been, it was radically different from that being advanced by the Supreme Command. If Premier Konoe had adhered to the normal cabinet procedures of policy-making, the sentiments of his home minister might have had only tangential consequences in the formulation of Japan's China policy. As it was, the new cabinet minister was showered with special privileges by his patron, Prince Konoe.

In the fall of 1933, the Inner Cabinet had become the official policy-making group of the Japanese government; and throughout the 1933-1937 period, no home minister had participated in the deliberations and decisions of the Inner Cabinet. At the request of Premier Konoe, though, the new home minister was invited to the December 14th Liaison Conference.[141] Since the avowed purpose of the conference was the preparation of a coordinated diplomatic and military policy for the China incident, Prince Konoe opened the meeting with a brief comment on Chiang Kai-shek's apparent willingness to negotiate a peace settlement.[142] Konoe then asked the spokesman for the Supreme Command, General Tada, to review the military situation. Instead of focusing on operational matters, Tada briefly summarized the peace terms sanctioned by the cabinet in November and observed that, since Chiang accepted these conditions, the general staff favored an armistice and diplomatic negotiations. Following this terse presentation, Foreign Minister Hirota alluded to the change in the military situation between early November and mid-December and recommended that the conference reconsider the nature of the

---

[140] USDS, Archives, *Japan: Political Affairs*, 894.002/350.

[141] Kazami, *Konoe naikaku*, 88.

[142] *Ibid.*, 77-93; Ishii, *Gaikōkan*, 299-300; and JFM, Archives, *Shina jihen*: I, "NiShi jihen," 104-109, review this Liaison Conference.

peace terms. Hirota, however, made no specific suggestions; and Konoe then solicited the opinion of the home minister. Responding to his cue, Admiral Suetsugu delivered a scathing operational critique of the China incident in which he gratuitously offered several suggestions on ways to coordinate the operations in North and Central China. Such matters, retorted Tada, were no concern of a home minister. With this acrimonious exchange, the premier intervened and suggested a brief recess, after which the conference would reconsider the November peace terms.

When the Liaison Conference reconvened, the premier precluded further discussion of military operations by asking Ishii Itarō, the head of the Bureau of Asian Affairs, to recapitulate the cabinet decision of October 1. Following Ishii's summary of the cabinet's peace terms, both service ministers— General Sugiyama and Admiral Yonai—expressed their willingness to adhere to these conditions in the projected negotiations with the Nanking government. The home minister however, immediately challenged this view by posing a rhetorical question: "After the heavy loss of lives incurred in the Nanking campaign, would the Japanese people be satisfied with such terms?"[143] The personal secretary of Prince Konoe and a major figure in the Seiyūkai, Kazami Akira, seconded Suetsugu's query. This led General Tada to ask sarcastically whether the government intended to determine national policy on the basis of public opinion or the long-term security interests of the empire. Before Admiral Suetsugu could reply, the premier ruled that it was apparent no policy consensus could be reached in the Liaison Conference; and, after observing that the conference had failed to formulate a policy to govern the China incident, Konoe adjourned the meeting.

The presence of Admiral Suetsugu at the Liaison Conference had produced a negative but crucial accomplishment. It had prevented a reaffirmation of the October 1 peace terms as the guiding China policy of the government. Interpreting this

---

[143] Kazami, *Konoe naikaku*, 95-96.

outcome as indicative of the need for a new policy, the premier summoned a full meeting of the cabinet on December 17 to consider the subject of the peace terms to be offered in the negotiations with the Nationalist government.[144] In effect, the premier was pursuing the same tactics he had employed at the Liaison Conference—that is, he circumscribed the authority of the Inner Cabinet by adding new voices to the policy discussions of the government. At the cabinet meeting, Konoe first indicated the need for a new China policy and then asked the home minister to outline a suggested policy. In lieu of a cluster of specific conditions, Admiral Suetsugu urged the cabinet to sanction four basic demands—namely, the Nationalist government must agree (1) to sign an anti-Comintern pact; (2) to create special regions and demilitarized zones "in areas desired by the two governments"; (3) to guarantee close economic cooperation with Japan; and (4) to pay an indemnity. According to the postwar recollections of the education minister of the Konoe cabinet, Marquis Kido, "The plan for epitomizing the peace terms under four points was drafted by Home Minister Suetsugu himself."[145] If this is true, it is difficult to believe they were articulated without prior discussion with and approval of the premier and the foreign minister. Moreover, the assembled ministers realized it would be very difficult for Chiang Kai-shek to commit himself to these vague terms as the prelude to an armistice; and they knew the army general staff wanted to end the war on the basis of moderate political demands. Nevertheless, since the premier, the home minister, the foreign minister, and the education minister strongly endorsed "Suetsugu's" peace terms, the full cabinet, without a dissenting voice, approved these four conditions as the official China policy.

Many years later, during the Tokyo Military Tribunal, the purpose of this cabinet decision eluded the memory of Marquis Kido. "I failed [in December 1937] to fully understand . . . that

144 *D. Ger. F.P.*, 803.
145 IMTFE, *Defense Document 2502*, 64.

the army had made a firm determination to bring about peace at any cost. . . . What I heard from Konoe was that he could not grasp the army's real intentions."[146] At that time, though, Kido considered the attitude of the general staff most inappropriate. In fact, he preferred to confront Chiang with abstract peace terms so they could be used "to cover everything" in the formal peace negotiations.[147] Although Kido may have anticipated a settlement of the China incident on the basis of the cabinet's four propositions, there is good reason to assume that the premier, home minister, and foreign minister had already written off the possibility of an accommodation with the Nanking government. Stated bluntly, the subsequent overtures to the Nanking government were gestures designed to overcome the adamant opposition of the general staff to a political and military program which aspired to replace the Nationalist government with new political organs patterned after those in Manchukuo. Certainly General Tada viewed the diplomacy of the government in this light and the process of events in December and January would seem to confirm the suspicions of the army general staff.

Throughout the brief cabinet meeting of December 17, neither War Minister Sugiyama nor Naval Minister Yonai expressed a word of approval or disapproval of the plan submitted by Admiral Suetsugu. And, three days later, at the December 20th meeting of the Liaison Conference, Sugiyama and Yonai remained silent, neither supporting nor challenging General Tada's vehement objections to the cabinet's decision. Since the spokesman for the general staff was a solitary dissenter, the premier properly ruled that the Liaison Conference also approved the transmission of the four terms as the basis for a negotiated settlement of the China incident.[148] On December 23, Hirota revealed the new terms to Ambassador Dirksen; and he asked that they be communicated to Chiang

146 *Ibid.*, 64.
147 Saionji-Harada, *Memoirs*, December 27, 1937.
148 IMTFE, *Defense Document 2146*, 7.

as the only basis for a termination of the hostilities. The German ambassador was somewhat dismayed by the tenuous nature of the conditions and pressed for greater clarification. On the understanding that his remarks were for Dirksen's personal information and that "under no circumstances" were they to be passed along to Chiang Kai-shek, the Japanese foreign minister indicated Japan would, in fact, require the following: (1) a recognition of Manchukuo; (2) a recognition of Prince Teh's government in Inner Mongolia; and (3) the continuation of the existing "demilitarized zone" in North China, plus an enlarged demilitarized zone in the Yangtze region.[149] Whether Hirota also discussed the political configurations behind the new peace terms is uncertain. Still Dirksen advised his foreign office that "a considerable part of the cabinet, under the pressure of the field army and industry, considers the terms too mild and hopes they will be rejected by China in order to make it possible to carry through the war of annihilation against Chiang Kai-shek."[150] In hopes of reducing this possibility, Dirksen repeatedly reminded Hirota that Chiang could hardly accept the four terms without some form of clarification. Finally, on December 30, the Japanese foreign minister allowed Dirksen to transmit his previous explanation of the demands as impressions "gained from conversations with leading Japanese personalities."[151]

The Liaison Conference on December 20 had approved the decision to settle the incident on the basis of the cabinet's four general stipulations. Despite the terminology of this decision, the army general staff doubted whether the premier intended to effect an accommodation with the Nanking government. This suspicion was not lessened when the full cabinet, on December 24, adopted an "Outline of Measures for the China Incident."[152] Here, the government proposed to organize a new regime in North China "capable of winning confidence not only in North China but also in Central and South China."

[149] *D. Ger. F.P.*, 803.   [150] *Ibid.*   [151] *Ibid.*, 812.
[152] JFM, Archives, *Shina jihen*, I, "NiShi jihen," 56-57.

In addition, the cabinet affirmed its intention to consider "the establishment, at a good opportunity, of a new government in areas occupied by our troops in Shanghai which will have connections with the new regime in North China." If implemented, these proposals would violate the peace terms affirmed by the cabinet one week earlier. The cabinet's outline resolved this discrepancy with the stipulation that, in the event of a settlement with the Nationalist government, the "new regimes will be adjusted according to the peace conditions." Despite the semantics, the cabinet's "Outline" did not anticipate any accommodation with Chiang Kai-shek; and, judging by Hirota's half-hearted use of the facilities of the German foreign office, it was not even inclined to test the willingness of the Nationalist government to accept the peace terms advanced by the cabinet on the 17th of December.

The lethargic diplomacy of the Japanese foreign ministry, as well as the cabinet's "Outline" for the disposition of the China incident, enabled the field commanders to organize new political units in North and Central China; and it allowed Foreign Minister Hirota to cite the "pressure of the field armies" as the cause of Japan's new China policy. In order to break the circular nature of the cabinet's policy, General Tada demanded that the government hold an Imperial Conference. The Liaison Conference of December 20 had technically committed the government to seeking a negotiated settlement with Chiang Kai-shek; and, Tada argued, if this decision were confirmed in the presence of the Throne, no field commander would suggest withdrawing recognition from the Nanking government.[153] That is, by holding an Imperial Conference, Tada stressed, the general staff could effectively quash the "strong opinions" of Generals Matsui and Terauchi and the cabinet need not be concerned about the political proposals or activities of the field armies in its efforts to negotiate a peace agreement with Chiang Kai-shek. In effect, Tada's recommendations struck at the rationale which blamed the field armies

[153] Saionji-Harada, *Memoirs*, January 8, 1938.

as the obstacle to a negotiated settlement of the China incident; and it is easy to understand why the premier considered the demand for an Imperial Conference as a scandalous proposal. "Tada is such an unreasonable fellow," complained Konoe. "Sometimes I wonder how he ever got as far as he did."[154] Regardless of his personal feelings, the premier could not easily shunt aside the considered opinions of the Supreme Command.

On January 10, the premier summoned a third session of the Liaison Conference for the specific purpose of deciding the basic question: "Should negotiation with the Nationalist government be continued, or should the Japanese government cease to recognize the Chinese government?"[155] By posing the central issue in this form, the premier foreclosed the possibility of the general staff's questioning the wisdom of the peace terms enunciated by the cabinet and the Liaison Conference in December. And, instead of arguing the need for more moderate peace terms, the spokesman for the general staff was obliged to question the viability of the new political institutions created by the field armies and to discount the apparent unwillingness of the Nationalist government to accept an armistice on the basis of the terms formulated by the Japanese government. Tada's efforts in these directions were belittled by Home Minister Suetsugu, who dismissed the argument in favor of further conversations with the Nationalist government as purely academic. Chiang, insisted Suetsugu, would not negotiate a peace settlement; and the field armies were in the process of obviating the need for a Nationalist government. In rebuttal, Tada replied that the army general staff could dissolve the political arrangements instituted by the field armies, if the decision to negotiate with Chiang were made in the presence of the Emperor. Moreover, added Tada, the Supreme Command unanimously favored negotiations with

154 *Ibid.*

155 IMTFE, *Document 3090* (Japanese text); and JFM, Archives, *Shina jihen,* I, "NiShi jihen," 421-426 and 439-441, are the best sources on this.

the Nationalist government. At this point, Admiral (Prince) Fushimi, the chief of the naval general staff, endorsed the sentiments of General Tada; and Fushimi added that the Emperor should be permitted to ask questions in the Imperial Conference, because otherwise no member of the Supreme Command could openly express his views on the grave political issues involved in the China incident. For the first time since the appointment of Admiral Suetsugu, a naval voice other than that of the home minister had become audible in the Liaison Conference; and, when confronted by the joint request of both general staffs, the premier ruled that an Imperial Conference would be convened for the purpose of deciding the most appropriate way to resolve the China incident.

The request for an Imperial Conference at which the Emperor would solicit the views of the Supreme Command on the diplomatic and political aspects of the China incident presented a delightful political paradox: the army general staff was, in effect, seeking the support of the Throne for its approach to the China situation. Since the cabinet blamed the "pressure of the field armies" for the diplomatic impasse with the Nationalist government, Tada intended to use the Imperial Conference as a way to commit the army, through the Supreme Command, to a policy which would enable and force the cabinet to intensify its efforts for a negotiated settlement with Chiang Kai-shek. By seeking the political help of the Throne, however, Tada's activities provoked some concern in court circles. Neither the Senior Statesman, Prince Saionji, nor the officials of the Imperial household wanted the Emperor to be placed in a situation in which the Throne would be responsible for the determination of national policy. After considering the purport of Tada's request, however, the Emperor's advisors agreed to an Imperial Conference on the understanding that the Emperor would only help to clarify the issues under discussion and that his inquiries were not to be construed as directives for the cabinet or the Supreme Command. These elaborate precautions eventually proved unnecessary. Despite the consensus reached at the January 10th Liaison Conference, Premier Konoe, in his formal petition to the Throne, indicated that it "would be best to let the premier manage the procedure of the conference because the purpose of the conference was one of deciding our national policy."[156] In addition, Konoe notified the court officials that the Emperor should not make any inquiries at the conference because the premier would present a policy "which had been decided by the government."[157] In effect, Konoe had restricted the nature of the proposed Imperial Conference. The Imperial presence would not provide a means for the Supreme Command to press its approach and views on the cabinet. Rather it would be used to silence the general staff's opposition to the China policy of the cabinet.

In the process of amending the format and intent of the Imperial Conference proposed at the January 10th session of the Liaison Conference, Premier Konoe also requested the presence of Baron Hiranuma at the Imperial Conference. Although the premier phrased this request in terms of the need for Hiranuma's "experience in diplomatic affairs," the president of the Privy Council was an intimate of Admiral Suetsugu and an articulate advocate of terminating all negotiations with the Nationalist government. Hiranuma's presence was desired as a pointed reminder for the general staff that the cabinet's policy was based on a consensus of the responsible political leaders of the country. At 2:00 p.m. on January 11, the Inner Cabinet, the chiefs and vice-chiefs of both general staffs, Admiral Suetsugu, and Baron Hiranuma assembled in the East Room of the palace. As soon as the Emperor entered and was seated in his elevated chair, the premier convened the Imperial Conference and announced the cabinet had that morning adopted a "Fundamental Policy for the Disposition of the China Incident."[158] Konoe then asked Foreign Minister Hirota to read the entire decision of the cabinet.

[156] IMTFE, *Document 3090.*   [157] *Ibid.*

[158] The most complete source on this conference is JFM, Archives, *Shina jihen: Matsumoto kiroku,* I, 131-162, which includes the cabinet's

The "ultimate aim" of the Japanese empire was, intoned the foreign minister, the reorganization of Sino-Japanese relations in order "to bring about perfect harmony between the two countries." To this end, the cabinet believed it would be absolutely essential for China, Japan, and Manchukuo to cooperate in the pursuit of three tasks: (1) to promote the joint economic welfare of the three countries; (2) to unite in an anti-Communist military alliance; and (3) to eradicate all issues which might "soil their mutual friendship." These objectives, continued the cabinet's spokesman, would be realized if the Nationalist government negotiated a settlement of the China incident on the basis of the following conditions:

(1) A formal recognition of Manchukuo.

(2) A formal renunciation of its anti-Japanese and anti-Manchukuo policies.

(3) The creation of neutral zones in North China and Inner Mongolia.

(4) The establishment of new political organs in North China which would confirm the sovereignty of the Nationalist government and would be "suitable to the realization of the co-prosperity of Japan, Manchukuo, and China."

(5) The formation of an "anti-Communist and autonomous government in Inner Mongolia" which would possess the same status under international law as Outer Mongolia.

(6) A promise to cooperate with Japan in an anti-Soviet policy in East Asia.

(7) An agreement by which Japan and China would, in the zones occupied by the Japanese army in Central China, "cooperate in order to maintain public order and to develop the economies of these zones."

(8) A pledge that Japan, Manchukuo, and China would

---

policy, as well as the formal presentations of the chiefs of staff and Baron Hiranuma. The cabinet's "fundamental policy" is reprinted in Aoki, *Taiheiyō sensō zenshi*, II, 174-177. Also see IMTFE, *Document 3090*, Appendix 2.

conclude "necessary" agreements in the matter of customs, trade, aviation, and transportation.

(9) The payment of reparations to the Japanese Empire.

If the Nationalist government were to seek a reconciliation in harmony with these stipulations, Hirota added, the Japanese government was prepared to "cooperate sincerely with China in the reconstruction and development of China." If the Nationalist government failed to request a settlement of the incident within seventy-two hours, concluded Hirota, the empire would proceed "to annihilate the Chinese central government" and "to rejuvenate a new China" by promoting new governments on the mainland.

Following Hirota's reading of the cabinet's China policy, the assembled officials remained silent and motionless for many seconds. Finally His Imperial Highness, Prince (General) Kanin, the chief of the army general staff, cautiously voiced a mild reservation about the prudence of a policy which regarded the Nationalist government as a totally defeated regime; and then, speaking for the Supreme Command, Kanin indicated his concurrence with the policy adopted by the cabinet. Since there was nothing more to say, the Emperor, at 2:55 p.m. retired from the East Room of the palace without uttering a single word in the first Imperial Conference since the Russo-Japanese War.

Although the army general staff had been brilliantly outmaneuvered at the Imperial Conference, General Tada's obstinate advocacy of a Bismarckian diplomacy had, at least, forced the cabinet to reveal openly the aspirations and attitudes which prevailed in its discussion of the China incident. No longer could the premier and foreign minister cite the "pressures of the field armies" as the primary cause of the increasing scope of the hostilities; and there was no longer any ambiguity about the cabinet's commitment to a "war of annihilation." Still, the "Fundamental Policy for the Disposition of the China Incident" sanctioned by the Imperial

Conference had spelled out an imposing list of demands; and it had allowed Chiang Kai-shek a period of seventy-two hours in which to accede to the Japanese demands. Perhaps because these stipulations offered no real chance of a negotiated settlement, Foreign Minister Hirota never bothered to convey the substance of the cabinet's policy to the Nationalist government. On January 12, Hirota simply notified the German ambassador that Chiang must approve the four general terms advanced on the 23rd of December within seventy-two hours or the Japanese government would adopt a "totally different" approach to the China incident.[159] The following day, the Chinese foreign minister requested a clarification of the Japanese terms; but Hirota dismissed the inquiry as a typical subterfuge of the Kuomintang.[160] Ambassador Dirksen, though, reminded the Japanese foreign minister that only four very vague conditions had been officially communicated to the Nationalist government. Under these circumstances, Dirksen suggested that Hirota explicitly indicate the substance of the Japanese terms or, failing this, that he permit Dirksen to cite Hirota's earlier clarifying remarks as the official statement of the Konoe government. Pleading the necessity to consult with the premier first, Hirota instead promised to provide a prompt reply to the ambassador's recommendations.

The next morning, January 14, the Liaison Conference met to review the current stage of negotiations with the Nationalist government. Here the foreign minister blandly reported that the Chinese government had indicated no disposition to settle the incident according to the conditions established in the Imperial Conference. "Therefore," Hirota declared, "there is nothing else we can do except to launch our alternate plan —namely, to transform the present hostilities into a long-term war."[161] This conclusion of the foreign minister, however, was ridiculed by General Tada, who commented on the folly of a

---

[159] *D. Ger. F.P.*, 814.   [160] *Ibid.*, 816.
[161] Saionji-Harada, *Memoirs,* January 19, 1938. Ishii, *Gaikōkan,* 302, claims the Inner Cabinet, on January 13, formally decided to sever the negotiations with Chiang Kai-shek.

policy designed to "annihilate" the government of China. In words, declared the spokesman for the general staff, this could be easily done; but, in fact, a long-term conflict on the mainland would entail huge expenditures of personnel, material, and money, expenditures which could not be implemented without gravely weakening Japan's military posture vis-à-vis the Soviet Union. These vehement and caustic comments were interpreted by Prince Konoe as signifying a wish for "the cessation of hostilities in China . . . and of preparing against the Soviets."[162] Such an attitude, judged the premier, was most inappropriate for "a country which has seen consecutive victories."[163] Ignoring this rebuke, Tada still pressed for a negotiated settlement with Chiang and, in desperation, he indicated that he would be willing to fly to Chiang's headquarters in order to facilitate a negotiated settlement of the incident. At this point, Naval Minister Yonai broke his hitherto complete silence in the Liaison Conference meetings and reminded Tada that the decision to terminate all relations with the Nationalist government had been made in the presence of the Emperor. If Tada persisted in his demands, remarked Yonai, "either the army general staff or the cabinet must resign *en masse*."[164] When Tada responded with a silent glare at the naval minister, the premier called a two-hour recess, so that the general staff could reconsider its approach to the China incident.

During this interval, the general staff vainly tried to circumvent the decision of the Imperial Conference. Utilizing his position as an Imperial prince, General Kanin went directly to the palace and requested an audience with the Emperor. However, as the Emperor later informed Baron Harada, "I calculated that this might definitely be a scheme to overturn what had already been determined; and I refused his request."[165] In this context, the general staff conceded its defeat at the afternoon session of the Liaison Conference: "To have a

---

[162] *Ibid.*, January 19, 1938.   [163] *Ibid.*
[164] *Ibid.*   [165] *Ibid.*

change in the government at the present time," admitted General Tada, "is not wise. The general staff has confidence in the government and it will concur with the decision of the government."[166] With this profession, the conference quickly decided to "annihilate" the Nationalist government; and, later that afternoon, Hirota terminated the good offices of the German foreign ministry, indicating that Japan no longer sought an accommodation with Chiang Kai-shek.[167] Ambassador Dirksen was visibly dismayed by this step and he warned the Japanese foreign minister that a protracted war against China would ultimately yield three unhappy consequences. It would, predicted Dirksen, alienate the Anglo-American countries, lead to the Bolshevization of China, and weaken Japan vis-à-vis the Soviet Union.[168] This prognosis was not unfamiliar to the foreign minister, as General Tada had been articulating identical warnings for several months, and Hirota reassured Ambassador Dirksen that such fears would prove ill-founded.

On January 16, the Konoe cabinet held a formal press conference, at which the premier read the following announcement:

> The Chinese government, without appreciating the true intention of Japan, blindly persists in its opposition to Japan, with no consideration either internally for the Chinese people in their miserable plight or externally for the peace and tranquillity of all East Asia.

> Accordingly, the Japanese government will cease henceforth to deal with that government and it looks forward to the establishment and growth of a new Chinese regime. . . . With this regime, the Japanese government will cooperate fully for the adjustment of Sino-Japanese relations and the building of a rejuvenated China.[169]

This démarche rendered the formation of puppet governments

166 *Ibid.*   167 *D. Ger. F.P.*, 819-820.
168 *Ibid.*, 821.
169 See *New York Times*, January 16, 1938, 33, for a good English text.

on the mainland inevitable; and it committed the empire to the total destruction of the Nationalist government.

Within the "total war" milieu created by this new vision of the China incident, the Diet would, within ninety days, enact the type of governmental controls over industry and labor postulated in the 1936 principles of national policy; and, in less than a year, the mission of the empire would be redefined by Prince Konoe as the building of a New Order in Asia. As these subsequent developments are beyond the purview of this study, they are mentioned only to signify the importance of the decisions to "annihilate" the Nationalist government and to "rejuvenate" the Chinese people with the spirit of the Imperial Way. In effect, the démarche of January 16 altered and intensified the domestic, diplomatic, and security policies sanctioned by the 1936 definition of national policy in ways that nurtured by 1940 the authoritarianism of a "national defense state" and, by 1941, the policy of southern advancement which brought on the Pacific War. Nevertheless, although the dynamics of the China incident propelled the Japanese government into an ambitious imperialistic venture which was compatible with the foreign and security policies first adopted by the Saitō cabinet in 1933 and revised by the Hirota government in the summer of 1936, these earlier policies—the quest for absolute security vis-à-vis the Soviet Union and the United States and for a political hegemony over China—had not dictated or compelled the adoption of the policy developed by the démarche of January 16, 1938. Precisely why the Konoe cabinet elected to wage a "war of annihilation" must, at least on the basis of the available sources, remain conjectural. It is clear, however, that the fracas at the Marco Polo Bridge did not mushroom into a total war because of the machinations of a Control Faction of army officers or because of the reckless and independent actions of the field armies. Nor would it be fair to explain the rationale behind the policies of the Konoe cabinet in terms of the strategic plans of the Imperial army which had structured Japan's foreign policy so decisively in the 1931-1937 period. One suspects that several members of the cabinet—Premier Konoe, Foreign Minister Hirota, Home Minister Suetsugu, and Education Minister Kido—believed that Japan could and should realize the "principles of co-prosperity and co-existence based upon the Imperial Way" by the subjugation of China. To this extent, the China war may be viewed as a continuation of the objectives sanctioned by the 1936 principles of national policy.

During the closing months of the Pacific War, Konoe Fumimaro affirmed somewhat bitterly, "The announcement of January 16, 1938, brought about no favorable results, a fact of which I am well aware without having anyone point it out to me. I, myself, confess it was an utter blunder."[170] The cogency of this retrospective evaluation, however, was marred by its failure to reveal the motivations and aspirations which underlay the decisions adopted by the Konoe cabinet in the opening months of the China conflict, as well as by its nomination of a Control Faction as the culprit responsible for the China venture of the Imperial government. This self-flagellation also ignored the immediate domestic consequences of the dual charge to "annihilate" the Nationalist regime and to "rejuvenate" the Central Kingdom with the benevolent guidance of the Imperial Way. At the very least, the January démarche induced desperate political, economic, bureaucratic, and military groups to subscribe to this definition of the China war. This was no mean achievement, as it transformed the hostilities into a Great Patriotic Endeavor. The moral tone of Japan's non-recognition policy did not, of course, resolve the strategic problems which had plagued the empire in its quest for an autonomous national defense. On the contrary, the concerns dictated by the Anglo-American sea powers and by the Soviet Union were now entangled with those posed by the rejuvenation of China.

The tragic dimensions of this new configuration of security policies did not pass unnoticed by the Japanese Emperor. On

170 IMTFE, *Defense Document 2104*, 1.

January 11, the Emperor had silently witnessed the articulation and adoption of a Herculean continental adventure in an Imperial Conference. A month later, when the Liaison Conference was still floundering in its inability to reach a consensus on the most appropriate way to conduct the hostilities in China, the Emperor gently inquired, "Is it possible to put into effect a simultaneous plan for long-term hostilities in China, military preparations against the Soviet Union, and the expansion of the navy?"[171] No one responded, though General Sugiyama promised to look into the matter. Henceforth, the Emperor would not receive another invitation to participate in the policy deliberations of the Liaison Conference. More than words, the silence of the ministers of state signified the degree to which the rhetoric of the China conflict had launched the empire on a perilous mission, one inspired by an imperial ideology which was not circumscribed by careful or even credible strategic calculations.

[171] Saionji-Harada *Memoirs*, February 1938.

Epilogue

BETWEEN the convocation of the London Naval Conference and the proclamation of the Konoe non-recognition démarche of the China war, the scale and intensity of change in Japan's foreign policy were of dramatic proportions. They may be gauged by the key phrases evident in official policy pronouncements. In 1930, the preservation of Japan's "treaty rights and interests" in Manchuria by a policy of friendship and cooperation with the Anglo-American sea powers pervaded cabinet decisions; by 1933, this vocabulary had been displaced by a compulsion "to maintain the peace of East Asia" through the realization of an Asiatic Monroe Doctrine; by 1936, the vision of infusing the diplomacy of East Asia with "the spirit of co-prosperity and co-existence based upon the Imperial Way" defined the national objective; and, by 1938, this goal was restated in terms of the "rejuvenation of China," to be effected by wielding the Kusunosuki sword in a just war. Although the changing and increasingly ideological objectives of national policy mark significant transformations, they do not explain the process by which the Japanese government became committed to a style of diplomacy which precluded cooperation with any land or sea power with strong Asian interests. Perhaps only the most sanguine historian would offer any one thesis to explain the nature and direction of change in Japan's foreign policy. The following reflections, therefore, are not statements of certitude. At best, they voice some personal impressions which are designed to clarify the thematic structure of this presentation and to convey additional nuances of familiar sets of facts.

The outbreak of a major diplomatic or military crisis unavoidably affects the foreign and security policies of a country. Japan was no exception to this rule and the clashes at Mukden and the Marco Polo Bridge thrust the empire in bold new directions of foreign policy. To affirm this truism, however, is not to claim that, in both incidents, one witnessed a common pattern of decision-making in which the field armies, in conjunction with the assistance of the general staff, exercised ultimate control over the determination of national policy. In fact, common denominators are difficult to locate in these diplomatic, military, and political crises. In 1931, the Kwantung Army willfully provoked an incident at Mukden; but, in 1937, the North China Army neither sought nor organized the confrontation at the Marco Polo Bridge. In September 1931, the general staff sanctioned the seizure of South Manchuria by its interpretation of the "supreme command" prerogative; but, in July 1937, the general staff forestalled operations in North China. In the fall of 1931, the inability of the Wakatsuki cabinet to effect a diplomatic settlement satisfactory to the demands of the chief of staff caused the formation of a new government; but, in the fall of 1937, the lack of a diplomatic accord in harmony with the dictates of the general staff yielded no change of cabinets.

Granting these divergent patterns, there were still two traits common to both crises: (1) the operational orders of the general staff were not technically flaunted by the field armies; and (2) basic policies were formulated in the cabinet. During the Wakatsuki cabinet, for example, although the commands of General Kanaya precluded the conquest of North Manchuria, his orders were reluctantly obeyed by the Kwantung Army; and, during the fall of 1937, the field armies of Generals Matsui and Terauchi disdainfully complied with the commands of General Tada. In the winter of 1931-1932, the seizure of North Manchuria and the establishment of a new Manchurian regime were sanctioned by the Inukai cabinet; and, in 1937-1938, the organization of new regimes in North and Central China were authorized by the Konoe cabinet. In both crises, moreover, the cabinet was subjected to powerful political currents which pushed the government into programs of expansion and imperialism; and, in both crises, one of these currents was the pervasive domestic endorsement of the endeavors proposed by the field armies. Even so, the peculiar cluster of circumstances in 1931 and 1937 which produced major alterations in foreign policy cannot be compressed into one maxim, to the effect that the control and determination of national policy were exercised by field armies who manipulated army headquarters and the cabinet.

In denying that this maxim constitutes a reliable guide to an understanding of policy formulation in the Imperial government, there is no intent to minimize the significance of military incidents, or to ignore the importance of staff officers in the determination of national policy. The caveat is much less comprehensive. Policy in both crises was affected by the views and recommendations of staff personnel. In fact, all ministers of state, as well as both chiefs of staffs, were responsive to the advice of their subordinates. If this is undeniable, there is still no reason to divest the responsible officers of personal responsibility, to consider them as *bunraku* puppets manipulated by subordinate officers. Generals Minami and Kanaya were ardently censured by their staff officers because of their deference to the advice of Premier Wakatsuki and Foreign Minister Shidehara; but their orders prevailed. Generals Araki and Mazaki proposed the advance to Chinchow and to the Shanhaikuan pass, but hardly because of their passive personalities, or obsequiousness to the views of subordinate officers. Generals Tada and Ishiwara were not disposed to endorse the recommendations of the field commanders, even though both had previously espoused a Sino-Japanese accord based upon the Imperial Way. To state the matter briefly, instead of labeling the occupants of the highest positions of command as weak personalities or lifeless puppets, the historian should consider these men as major actors in the drama of cabinet and army politics, especially in moments of crisis and in the act of formulating national policies.

Throughout the 1930's, the threat and actual occurrence of military clashes on the China mainland accentuated the authority of military personnel in matters of foreign policy. A less vivid but almost equally decisive manifestation of political influence by army and naval officers centered on the utilization of the communications media in order to assail, alter, or propound national policies. Several instances of this form of behavior were considered in this presentation. Of these, the following seem most significant: (1) Admiral Suetsugu's interviews with the press launched the controversy over the Reed-Matsudaira Compromise and the "right of supreme command"; (2) General Araki's fiery addresses on the "crisis of 1936" and the Imperial Way generated a belligerent climate of opinion, one that he employed against his critics in the cabinet and in central headquarters; (3) the newspaper sections of the war and naval ministries vulgarized the terms "total war," "the national defense state," "parity with sea powers," and "advance to the South Seas" as a technique to marshal public opinion behind their security concepts; and (4) General Tada's incantation of a North China Paradise aborted a potential *modus vivendi* with the Nationalist government. If the purpose and consequences of these activities were multiple and diverse, they still signified one political development. By utilizing the press in this fashion, the Imperial injunction against overt involvement in domestic politics on the part of military personnel—an injunction which had governed the behavior of officers throughout Meiji and Taishō Japan—was gradually compromised.

As early as 1934, the official spokesman for the two services had publicly asserted the propriety of this type of political behavior. By this time, General Araki had informed the members of the Diet that since national defense was a complex problem, "there should not be any difference of opinion between the government and the Supreme Command. There must be confidence that governmental decisions have passed through the agencies of Central Headquarters."[1] And Naval Minister Osumi had declared, "Naval officers and men are forbidden to submit petitions, hold meetings, or make public their views of the administration." "Still," he added, "they

[1] Matsushita Yoshio, *Meiji gunsei shiron* (Tokyo, 1956), II, 301.

could discuss matters relating to national defense."[2] This blanket endorsement of political activity in matters of national defense policies encouraged the merchandising of policies sanctioned by the service ministries. Whether the educational campaigns of the army authorities in support of the "basic principles of national defense" and of their naval counterparts on behalf of a program of "southern advancement" would have yielded an effective political consensus remains uncertain. As it happened, the Great Patriotic War against China catalyzed a national commitment which promoted the advance into the South Seas, as well as the attainment of a national defense state.

This inclination to condone and encourage open discussion of national defense policy by military and naval personnel was tantamount to opening Pandora's box. Among the more unsavory results, of course, was the rebellion of February 26, 1936. Setting aside its effects on the members of the National Principle group, it is noteworthy that the public rhetoric and publications of the two service ministries were mainly linked with responsible and official policies. For this reason, the evolving political and economic programs of both services were far more influential than the political opinions and deeds of staff officers who conspired to alter or promote policies by means of political schemes or *coups d'état*. Throughout this presentation, attention has been given to the tendency of several clusters of staff officers to countenance and urge various forms of political conspiracy. In this regard, the behavior of the activist members of the Cherry Society and of the Purification Group may have posed serious command problems. Nevertheless, it would seem improper to credit these officers with major influence, if only because the Sakurukai was dissolved following the October incident in 1931 and the leaders of the *Seigun-ha* were cashiered or consigned to field duty in the wake of the February 26th incident.

This distinction between staff officers who, as part of their assigned duties, drafted economic and political plans and those

[2] *Japan Weekly Chronicle*, February 1, 1934.

who conspired with professional politicians and the leaders of prominent nationalistic organizations in order to effect a Shōwa reformation is not casually drawn. The members of the so-called Control Faction in central headquarters did not consciously or willfully encourage acts of political terrorism as a Machiavellian move in behalf of the attainment of a "national defense state." If the fear of assassination or army coups influenced policy-making in the cabinet—and it remains to be shown how it did—the conspiratorial whispers and abortive escapades of the field-grade officers in army headquarters did not determine the perspectives governing basic army policies. More crucially, the activities of these officers, as well as the assassinations of 1932 and 1936, did not occasion a recruitment of staff officers who were partial toward radical political behavior. There is no compelling reason to consider the March and October incidents, the 1932 murders, and the February 26th rebellion as a sequence of events which a Control Faction adroitly engineered in order to acquire a position of leadership and to impose a policy of war with China. Actually, rather than regard army central headquarters as a hothouse which nurtured a brand of political radicalism, it would seem more pertinent to concentrate on the process by which every staff officer who articulated a program of domestic violence or military coups found his professional career seriously, often fatally, jeopardized. The imperial army was not a praetorian institution; its leadership did not aspire to garner political power via mutinies, coups, or threats of army rebellion. To obscure this fact is to ignore a more complex topic —namely, how the enveloping power of the two service ministers in the formulation of policies proceeded through customary and legally recognized channels of administrative authority.

There is no single explanation of the process by which the authority of the service ministers and of the strategic plans of both services became more pronounced in the formulation of national policies. There were, for example, at least three main styles of cabinet politics in the 1930's, each of which was distinguished by a different pattern of decision-making. Between 1930 and 1932, party cabinets prevailed and, in this era, the preeminent position of the premier was sanctioned by a brand of parliamentary responsibility; between 1933 and 1937, the "whole nation" cabinet flourished and the Inner Cabinet emerged as the institutional mechanism for the formulation of official state policies; and, in 1937, the Supreme Command, the Liaison Conference, and the Imperial Conference became relevant to the determination of national policy. The manner in which the general staffs, service ministries, and strategic axioms affected the foreign policies of the government varied in each of these styles of cabinet politics. Common to each, however, were two traditions sanctioned by past political practice and by the Meiji Constitution: a remarkable degree of cabinet autonomy in matters of foreign and security policies, and authority invested in both services by the "right of supreme command." One is tempted to venture that these two traditions—cabinet autonomy and the right of supreme command—yielded a configuration in which cabinet decisions on issues of "national defense" were consistently circumscribed by one political necessity. No decision would be politically viable, if it were adopted without the active concurrence of the service ministers. In many respects, the demise of party cabinets and of a policy of cooperation with the Anglo-American powers was the consequence of this lack of concurrence; and, similarly, the quest of an "autonomous national defense" was occasioned by a nebulous form of concurrence between the service ministries.

By the late 1920's, the cabinet, the services, and the political parties were clearly plagued by tensions and conflict engendered by open discussions of Japan's security problems. This situation, in part, was precipitated by immediate and potential challenges to Japan's position in Manchuria—most noticeably, by the Soviet Union and the Chinese nationalistic movement. The terms "Shidehara and Tanaka diplomacy" served as a public mask for these tensions and disagreements over foreign policy. Parallel with this open controversy, the doctrine of "total war" gained momentum within army circles. Inherently, this style of strategic planning embraced economic, educational, and diplomatic factors as legitimate facets of staff concern. Regardless of the passionate quarrels being waged over the Manchurian problem and the encompassing scope of the "total war" philosophy, there was no apparent tendency in army central headquarters to regard the "right of supreme command" as a political vehicle by which the army could overturn "Shidehara diplomacy" or impress its economic and political plans on cabinet policies. Historically, the "right of supreme command" had invested each service with complete control over all its internal administrative affairs; and it had confirmed complete control of the conduct of military operations in time of hostilities. It had not, however, been viewed as empowering the service ministers or general staffs with the right to set national policy, as witness the conduct and determination of policy during the Sino and Russo-Japanese Wars, World War I, and the Siberian intervention. The proposition that the "right of supreme command" invested the general staffs and/or the service ministers with a veto power in cabinet decisions on national defense was first articulated during the London Naval Treaty controversy.

During this episode, the distinctive and original interpretation of the "right of supreme command" articulated first by Admiral Katō, later by the Seiyūkai leaders and Baron Hiranuma's group in the Privy Council, was set aside by the cabinet and the Supreme War Council. Nevertheless, throughout the controversy, the premier never claimed the legal authority to overrule the naval minister in matters affecting national security; and those naval officers who failed to endorse the sentiments of the general staff were systematically retired. Hence, although the principle of cabinet autonomy in policy-making was confirmed, the premier and foreign minister, as well as the service ministers, became painfully conscious of the practical necessity to authorize decisions which did not dramatically or generally flaunt the considered opinions of the general staffs.

The "right of supreme command" controversy of 1930 had been provoked by the disarmament policies of the Hamaguchi government. And, as the government prepared for the 1932 Geneva Conference on Armament Limitations, the war and foreign ministers, along with the premier, sought to preclude a repetition of the London Naval Treaty dispute by working out, in advance, a set of political rules to govern the formulation of Japan's policies and the conduct of the negotiations at the Geneva Conference. Although they were anticipating the repetition of a past crisis, the "right of supreme command" created an unprecedented situation in September 1931 when it was utilized to sanction the seizure of South Manchuria. Once the Kwantung Army had acted in this fashion, the cabinet avoided a formal constitutional ruling on this act. In the process, it was obligated to seek a diplomatic settlement of the Manchurian crisis which would confirm and strengthen Japan's position in Manchuria. Once this policy was decided upon, the Wakatsuki cabinet reasserted its control over policy-making. To be sure, many senior staff officers in the general staff, as well as the Kwantung Army, urged an outright seizure of North Manchuria. Yet, the "right of supreme command" could not be invoked in this fashion without political chaos; and General Kanaya, the chief of staff, successfully precluded any advance into North Manchuria throughout the existence of the Wakatsuki cabinet. Whether a different style of diplomacy by the Council of the League or the Nationalist government would have yielded a settlement which would have forestalled further operations in Manchuria is highly uncertain. At best, one can observe the following: (1) The Wakatsuki cabinet believed it could prevent the seizure of Manchuria, if the Nationalist government would negotiate a new treaty; (2) War Minister Minami and General Kanaya adhered to this decision even though they were subjected to tremendous pressure to flaunt the premier's policy;

(3) the Kwantung Army was not permitted to carry out the occupation of North Manchuria by a tortuous interpretation of the "right of supreme command"; and (4) during the tenure of the Inukai cabinet, the advance to Chinchow, as well as the creation of Manchukuo, were technically sanctioned by official cabinet decisions. These latter decisions, especially the formation of Manchukuo, may have been personally distasteful to Inukai; but, when he assumed office, the Big Three of the army and the Supreme War Council had already formulated a comprehensive Manchurian policy and General Araki, as war minister, proved to be an effective advocate of army policy in the cabinet.

During the 1930-1932 period, the "right of supreme command" had been invoked in two different ways. The consequences in each instance, however, had abridged the authority of the premier and foreign minister in matters of foreign affairs; and they had noticeably enforced the premise that strategic estimates by military and naval personnel should be given priority in the process of policy-making by the cabinet. Related to this development was a subtle but basic change in the outlook and position of the service ministers. In 1930, Admirals Takarabe and Yamanashi accepted, without any evident tension, the leadership of the premier and foreign minister. They were, however, replaced by officers who had passionately criticized the policy of the premier and the deference to him displayed by Takarabe and Yamanashi. In 1931, General Minami, with noticeable misgivings, deferred to the premier in the opening moments of the Mukden crisis, but General Kanaya, with equal signs of distress, sabotaged the premier's policy by authorizing the seizure of South Manchuria. Neither Kanaya nor Minami, though, was prepared to shatter the government by approving operations in North Manchuria. Their rectitude in this matter was bitterly resented by many army officers, as was the behavior of Yamanashi and Takarabe in most naval circles during the preceding year; and they too were replaced by officers less inhibited by a deference to the political authority of the premier. This corrosion of the premier's authority within the cabinet was also related to a critical and questioning regard for the principle of cabinet responsibility to the Diet. No premier, not even Hamaguchi, had conceded or affirmed that matters of national defense or foreign policy should be ultimately decided by the Diet. Once the service ministers had compromised the authority of the premier in the cabinet, it was an easy step to deny the need for a "party" government.

With the formation of the Saitō "whole nation" cabinet, the hallmarks of Taishō democracy—cabinets based upon parliamentary responsibility and a diplomacy based upon armament controls and cooperation with the Anglo-American countries —were obliterated. These developments admit no simple explanation; but it is reasonable to link them with the disintegration of the security system provided by the Washington Conference. In part, this was the consequence of the diplomacy of the Western powers, especially American naval policy and the non-recognition doctrine adopted by the League of Nations and the United States. Perhaps in greater part, it was the product of Japanese actions in Manchuria. Whichever one wishes to stress, by August 1932, the Japanese government had resolved to settle the Manchurian problem "from the unique standpoint of the Imperial government." The commitment yielded Manchukuo and Japan's withdrawal from the League of Nations; and it meant a new diplomatic context in which "the security of East Asia has come to depend entirely on the actual power of the empire." Given this axiom—and it was undeniably viable as of 1933—the cabinet understandably assigned the highest priority to strategic concerns in the formulation of national policy. In this context, the increasing authority of the service ministers and the priority given strategic policies were not viewed by the major actors of the government as illegal or unwarranted. On the contrary, the complexity of Japan's security problems tended to reinforce doubts about the legitimacy of party leaders as active participants in policy-making and to intensify a reliance on the judgment of the ministers of state as the sole criterion in the determination of national policy.

This bureaucratization of the policy-making process was symbolized by the appearance of the Inner Cabinet as the final voice of authority in matters of national policy. Henceforth, as General Araki informed his cabinet colleagues in November 1933, policy was to be "decided by discussions among the state ministers." The meaning of his words was manifest: the views of the service ministers should govern the deliberations of the cabinet. But discussions foundered owing to a fundamental cleavage between the advice of the naval and the army authorities. Should the government seek naval supremacy, superiority over the Soviet army, or a political hegemony over China? In the fall of 1933, the Inner Cabinet sanctioned all three objectives, but with no determination of priorities and no agreement on the style of diplomacy which would realize the basic aspirations of the service ministers. Without recapitulating the story of competing service doctrines in the formulation and conduct of foreign policy in the 1933-1937 period, two facets of this interservice conflict merit brief attention. First, the illusive search for an "autonomous national defense" intensified and broadened the economic and political aspects of strategic planning. In naval circles, the demand for a 10:7 ratio with the American fleet was dropped in favor of "parity" with the Anglo-American fleets; and the preoccupation with defending the existing empire and Manchukuo was supplemented by the "Defend the north—advance to the south" axiom which postulated access to the resources of the South Seas as the paramount requisite for naval security. In army circles, the development of Manchukuo and the rationalization of the army as the cardinal objectives of military policy induced the preparation of comprehensive programs for the domestic economy as an integral part of "total war" planning. Secondly, these innovations also intensified the reliance on staff planning, which further augmented the bureaucratization of policy-making. Under the Inner Cabinet, the state ministers were less deferential to the senior statesmen, the Privy Council, the Supreme War Council, the advisors to the Throne, or prominent industrial and political personalities in the act of discussing, formulating, or deciding basic policies. Rather, one saw an increasing reliance on formal or *ad hoc* committees run by senior staff personnel—e.g., the Cabinet Consultative Committee and the Committee on the Current Situation.

The encompassing power acquired by the ministries of state, as well as the policies they espoused, provoked all sorts of political tensions. Within some army circles, those charged with devising economic policies were dubbed "fascists," men who were perverting the army's traditional compassion for the peasantry and disdain for financiers. Within political circles, the preclusion of politicians from the cabinet, as well as from the new administrative committees, was castigated as a wanton violation of the Imperial injunction to refrain from domestic politics. However justified these critics may have been, they were unable, either by use of violence or parliamentary debate, to alter this direction of change. The major restraint on the ministers of state was twofold in nature: internal dissension provoked by competing views of national defense, and the unwillingness of the Diet to write into law the type of economic legislation desired by the ministers of state. By the spring of 1937, the competing views of the service ministries vis-à-vis foreign policy had been harmonized, at least temporarily. The anti-Soviet preoccupation of all strategic planning had marked the strengthening of Manchukuo and the army, in conjunction with the maintenance of the North China *status quo*, as the most efficacious way to master the Soviet menace; and the oceanic preoccupation of naval planning had labeled the resources of Southeast Asia as basic to the attainment of naval security. Both axioms viewed the resources of Manchukuo and the South Seas as the requisites for a viable industrial state, one capable of waging "total war" against either the Soviet Union or the United States. The compulsion

to enlarge and rationalize the two services and the domestic
economy also produced a 1937 cabinet consensus in support
of a five-year program of economic development. Since the
belligerent tactics of General Terauchi in the Hirota cabinet
and the mollifying words of Premier Hayashi had failed to win
sufficient political support for this type of planned economy in
the Diet, the ministers of state solicited the political talents of
Prince Konoe on behalf of their domestic policies.

The selection of Prince Konoe seemed a prudent choice.
Certainly his credentials were impressive. Scion of the Fujiwara clan, one of the nation's most venerable aristocratic
families, Konoe had, in past years, been the protégé of Prince
Saionji and the ministers of the Imperial household. The
prestige of his birth and of his early patrons were augmented by
wide-ranging social contacts with prominent military, naval,
and political personalities. In some respects, however, many of
his associates and friends were distinguished by a flair for
provoking serious controversies—e.g., Generals Araki and
Mazaki, Admiral Suetsugu, and Kazami Akira of the Seiyūkai.
They were, moreover, for different reasons, vociferous critics
of the personnel and policies prevailing in the ministries of
state. To what extent Konoe shared this attitude remains uncertain. Still, there was a style to Konoe's politics as premier
which reflected a desire to curtail the entrenched bureaucratic
control over national policy. When, in June 1937, he vainly
lobbied for the appointment of Admiral Suetsugu and General Itagaki as his service ministers, Konoe could not have been
insensitive to the discord these appointments would have
provoked in the ministries and the Inner Cabinet. Nor, one
suspects, was he oblivious to the fact that this discord would
have inherently enhanced the ability of the premier to influence policy.

Konoe failed in his initial maneuver; but, as the China
crisis unfolded, his political strategy was executed to better
advantage. By capitalizing on the evident discord within army
circles and between the two general staffs, Konoe, in effect,

compromised the authority of the Inner Cabinet and the general staffs in policy-making. The government's China policy was ultimately decided by the full cabinet, and, in this act, the voices of Home Minister Suetsugu and Educational Minister Kido were both articulate and influential. Perhaps, in retrospect, the non-recognition doctrine of the Konoe cabinet seems less sagacious than the Bismarckian advice of the army general staff. It is difficult, however, to fault the premier for retaining effective cabinet control over national policy; and there is no denying that Konoe's policies mirrored the aspirations of his friends—Araki, Mazaki, Suetsugu, Kido, and Kazami—as well as the views of field commanders, captains of industry, and his political rival, Baron Hiranuma, the president of the Privy Council. Konoe had marshaled a strong political consensus behind the resolution to effect a rejuvenation of China. Only the army general staff dissented, vigorously but to slight avail.

In his postwar memoirs, Prince Konoe portrayed the China war as the work of a Control Faction of army officers; and he recalled his valiant struggle against the political and military views of this group of officers. By transferring responsibility for the China war to a clique of militarists, Konoe misled his contemporaries and historians. He also did himself a grave disservice—namely, he masked his adroit political leadership, he obscured his political objectives and aspirations, and he distorted the type of political problems he encountered as premier. The quality of the man as premier, if not the consequences of his actions, may be intimated by a single observation: Konoe was the first premier since Hamaguchi to exercise the authority of the premier actively and successfully in order to implement a basic policy decision over the adamant opposition of the general staff. Whether his leadership should be condemned because it thrust Japan into an ill-fated political adventure is beyond the purview of this study and, in fact, it may be the province of Japanese historians. It would be unfortunate, however, to canonize the views and recommendations set forth by the army general staff in 1937, and, in particular, those of General Ishiwara Kanji. To regret wistfully the general staff's inability to dictate national policy in 1937 would deny the legitimacy of the power of the cabinet and premier to decide official policy. If this power had been denied in 1937, or in 1931, one can only speculate what the domestic and international consequences might have been. As it was, national policy was, throughout the 1930's, technically and legally formulated by the cabinet; and throughout these years, notions of national security and appraisals of the diplomatic scene were basic to the types of decisions reached.

Whatever faults or consequences one attributes to the security and foreign policies of the Imperial government during the 1930's, they were formulated by responsible political and military leaders. It seems equally evident that an inordinate emphasis on the subject of "national defense" served to rationalize aggression and authoritarianism as the best ways to overcome the challenges posed by the demands of total war and two strategic enemies endowed with plentiful natural resources. It is not easy to dismiss this obsession with national security, this compulsion to acquire a status of military and economic parity with the United States and the Soviet Union. Neither of these powers was prepared to support firmly Japan's treaty rights in Manchuria, let alone to encourage additional economic privileges in China or new rights in the South Seas. Perhaps it is not amiss to view the diplomatic, economic, and military circumstances prevailing in Japan in the age of the great depression as reminiscent of a Greek tragedy. The element of hubris—a burning desire for full equality which, in effect, meant naval and military superiority in East Asia—had, in the past, been a commendable virtue. This, combined with the good fortune of past decades—the regionalization of sea power, the impotence of Ch'ing and Republican China, and the weakness of Tsarist and Communist Russia—had yielded an empire and the status of a world power. Subsequent developments—the China and naval policies of the American government, the surging tide of Chinese nationalism, the maturing power of the Soviet Union, and the demands of total war—were less auspicious. Without an intense racial and national pride, perhaps these new issues would not have been viewed as they were. Still, this racial and national pride had been crucial in the notable achievements of Meiji and Taishō Japan; and, judging by the painful manner in which European powers have been compelled to adjust to the phenomenon of nationalism in colonial areas and to the overwhelming might of the Soviet Union and the United States, it is difficult to castigate Japan's leaders for their unwillingness to abandon the quest for parity with their strategic enemies, or to moderate their special claims in Manchuria.

Confronted by a formidable cluster of diplomatic, economic, and military problems, the Imperial government resorted to a series of potential solutions: Manchukuo, a Japanese Monroe Doctrine, Hirota's three principles, an advance to the South Seas, a national defense state, and the rejuvenation of China. If there is a sort of immanent logic in these aspirations, it would be reckless to view them as predetermined. It would seem hazardous, as well, to condemn these policies as immoral. Is the historian of modern Japan, especially a Western historian, to label the garnering, defense, and extension of an empire as an illegitimate form of state action? Is he to consider a commitment to the preservation of treaty rights as more moral than an attempt to propagate the qualities of the Imperial Way, first in Manchuria, second in North China, and third throughout the entire republic of China? Rather than wrestle with this historiographical nettle, it seems more prudent to invoke the standard of *raison d'état* as a measuring rod for a concluding reflection on the policies and leaders of the Imperial government.

Although the rules of statecraft remain ill-defined, the pursuit of national policies which are beyond the acknowledged military capabilities of a nation is a perilous game. Japan, in

1931, could, as her professional officers advised, seize Manchuria. The consequences of this act became extremely complex, once the powers had espoused the non-recognition doctrine. According to the considered opinions of both general staffs, Japan could not risk a confrontation with either the Soviet Union or the Anglo-American sea powers. This awkward situation was eased by an awareness that none of the Occidental powers was prepared to contest openly the creation of Manchukuo. In anticipation of a future crisis with these nations, the language of "economic planning," "the South Seas," and the Imperial Way gained currency as practical and creditable means to promote an autonomous national defense. By 1937, three distinctive views on national defense had materialized: the oceanic orientation of naval planning, which considered sea power and the South Seas as the basis of national security; the Soviet orientation of army planning, which designated the security of Manchukuo and a rationalized army as essential to national defense; and the cabinet's policy, which concluded that each of these goals would necessitate the "total mobilization" of the economic and manpower resources of the empire. The interaction of these security concepts during the China incident contributed to two fateful results. It tended to preclude the adoption of any one strategic policy to guide either the conduct or termination of the conflict; and it helped inspire the notion of shattering the Nationalist government by a war of annihilation.

This willingness to embark on the most ambitious of national enterprises—a war of political annihilation and the imposition of a national ideology, the Imperial Way, on an alien state—would have fateful consequences for Japan, China, the Western powers, and the colonies of Southeast Asia. Why the Konoe cabinet pursued this policy remains shrouded in obscurity, mainly because of the flurry of postwar memoirs and the dearth of primary sources. If uncertainty still precludes a firm assessment of this decision, at least it is not to be attributed to the nefarious influence of the general staffs, a clique of militarists, or the irresponsible deeds of field armies. The paradox and the irony of the decisions to conduct a war of chastisement and a war of annihilation reside in the exercise of effective control over the general staffs by the cabinet. In retrospect, the obstinate disregard of the strategic advice offered by the general staff may well be regarded as the fatal flaw in the diplomacy of the Konoe government. Before affirming this judgment, however, it seems appropriate to remark that Prince Konoe was not responsible for the postulate of an autonomous national defense, or of its corollary, a new style of imperial hegemony in East Asia. To the extent that these postulates helped to define and rationalize the China war, the historian cannot casually demean or censure the leadership of the Fujiwara nobleman.

As were his immediate predecessors in the office of premier, Konoe too was ensnared in a painful tangle of geographical, technological, diplomatic, and military circumstances. None of the major actors in East Asia—Nationalist China, the Soviet Union, the United States, and Japan—had been disposed to perpetuate the *status quo* embodied in the Washington Conference treaties; and, after 1931, none of the other powers were prepared to endorse Japan's continental policies, first in Manchuria, later in North China and Inner Mongolia. Throughout the twentieth century, Japan's hegemony in Northeast Asia had been confirmed by her military strength and by alliances with the maritime powers. When they were confronted by a formidable group of critics in the 1930's, it is not surprising that Japan's political and military leaders steadfastly adhered to the traditional aspiration of the empire, hegemony in Northeast Asia, or that this gave rise to a quest for political and military autonomy.

The dimensions of the problems posed by this commitment to autonomy were not undetected in Japan. On the contrary, the determination to effect a new basis for Japanese hegemony in East Asia gave a tragic consistency to Japan's foreign and security policies in the 1930's. If, for several years, every premier had subscribed to the desirability and necessity of an autonomous national defense, Premiers Saitō Makato, Okada Keisuke, Hirota Kōki, and Hayashi Senjurō also had tempered this sentiment with an awareness of the hazardous nature of this policy. They neither discounted the risks of a major war with China, nor were they insensitive to the dangers inherent in any major program of domestic economic and political reforms. These conservative instincts, however, were less evident in the behavior and statements of Prince Konoe. His conception of political leadership was more ambitious, more optimistic, and more confident. On assuming the premiership in June 1937, Konoe affirmed:

> Evolutionary reforms and progress within the Constitution must be our watchdogs; but the country demands national reform, and the government, while neither Socialist nor Fascist, must listen to its call. The impetus of the great [Meiji] Restoration has carried us thus far with honor and success; but now it is for the young men to take up the task and carry the country forward into a new age.[3]

This was, unhappily, no rhetorical manifesto; and the youth of Japan soon learned that the country was to be carried forward into a new age by a war of political annihilation against the Nationalist government of China.

[3] Hugh Byas Collection, Sterling Memorial Library, Yale University, "Scrapbook" (June 1937).

the Imperial Government], 8 vols. on the 1933-1937 period.

Zaidan hojin shiryō chōsakai [Documentary Research organization]; Gunreibu kiroku [Records of the Naval General Staff].

PARTICULARLY

Gun kankei jōhō [Intelligence Reports on Army Matters], 1933-1936;

Kahoku mondai shinsei jiken keii [Particulars of the New Life Incident], 1935;

Taiheiyō sensō kaigun senshi [Naval History of the Pacific War], 1942.

UNPUBLISHED SOURCES, ENGLISH-LANGUAGE

United States Department of State, Archives.

PARTICULARLY

Japan: Military Affairs;

Japan: Political Affairs;

Record Group 43: London Naval Conference.

Hugh Byas Collection, Sterling Memorial Library, Yale University, New Haven, Connecticut.

Henry L. Stimson Collection, Sterling Memorial Library, Yale University, New Haven, Connecticut.

PUBLISHED SOURCES, JAPANESE-LANGUAGE

Checklist of Archives in the Japanese Ministry of Foreign Affairs, Tokyo, Japan, 1868-1945 (Washington, D.C., 1954).

Gaimushō [Japan's Ministry of Foreign Affairs], *Nihon gaikō nenpyō narabini shuyō bunsho, 1840-1945* [A Chronological Table of Japanese Foreign Policy and Important Documents], 2 vols. (Tokyo, 1955).

Nihon kokusai seiji gakkai, Taiheiyō sensō genin kenkyūbu [Japan Association of International Relations, Research Group on the Origins of the Pacific War], *Taiheiyō sensō e no michi* [Road to the Pacific War], Vol. VIII: *Betsukan*

Bibliography

A SHORT NOTE

As THIS is a selected bibliography, in no sense does it attem
to cover the extensive secondary literature on the diploma
and military history of Imperial Japan. With a few
ceptions, English-language publications have been confined
items directly cited in the presentation. Although this
striction is less evident in terms of Japanese publications, h
too the selection is limited to those items which, in
opinion, seem most pertinent to the main concerns of
study. Japanese specialists desiring a more complete indica
of the scale of publications on Japan's prewar diplomacy sho
consult the bibliographies included in the following: N
Kyōzō, *Kyokutō kokusai gunji saiban kiroku: moku*
oyobi sakuin [Catalogue and Index of the Internati
Military Tribunal Far East] (Tokyo, 1953); and the N
kokusai seiji gakkai [Japan Association of International
tions] series on diplomatic history—namely, *Nihon gai*
kenkyū: Meiji jidai [Studies in Japan's Diplomatic Hi
The Meiji Era] (Tokyo, 1957); *Taishō jidai* [The Taishō
(Tokyo, 1958); and *Shōwa jidai* [The Shōwa Era] (T
1959). The most convenient guide to publications on mi
affairs is Fujiwara Akira, *Gunjishi* [History of the Mi
(Tokyo, 1961).

UNPUBLISHED SOURCES, JAPANESE-LANGUAGE

Gaimushō [Japan's Ministry of Foreign Affairs], Ar
  PARTICULARLY
  Shina jihen [China Incident];
  Shina jihen: Matsumoto kiroku [China Incident: Ma
    to Papers];
  Teikoku no taigai seisaku kankei no ken [Concern
    Foreign Policy of the Imperial Government],
    covering the 1933-1936 period;
  Teikoku no taiShi seisaku kankei no ken [China P

shiryōhen [Special Volume: Collection of Documents] (Tokyo, 1963).

Harada Kumao, *Saionji kō to seikyoku* [Prince Saionji and the Political Situation], 8 vols. (Tokyo, 1952). A rough English translation—*Saionji-Harada Memoirs*—was prepared for the Tokyo Tribunal and is available on microfilm at the Library of Congress.

Hara Kei Nikki [Diary of Hara Kei], 9 vols. (Tokyo, 1950-1951).

Kido Kōichi Nikki [Diary of Marquis Kido Kōichi] (Tokyo, 1947).

Kita Ikki, *Nihon kaizō hōan taikō* [Outline for the Reconstruction of Japan] (Tokyo, 1933 edition).

Kōno Tsukasa, *Ni-ni-roku* [The February 26, 1936, Incident] (Tokyo, 1957).

Koyama Kango, *Koyama Kango nikki* [Diary of Koyama Kango] (Tokyo, 1955).

Muranaka Kōji and Isobe Tokuichi, *Shukugun ni kansuru ikensho* [Views on the Housecleaning of the Army] (Tokyo, 1935).

Nakano Masao, ed., *Hashimoto taisa no shuki* [The Memo of Colonel Hashimoto Kingoro] (Tokyo, 1963).

Rikugunshō [War Ministry], *Kokubō no hongi to sono kyōka no teishō* [Basic Principles of National Defense and Ways of Strengthening It] (Tokyo, 1934).

Ugaki Issei (Kazushige), Nikki [Diary of General Ugaki Issei] (Tokyo, 1954).

PUBLISHED SOURCES, ENGLISH-LANGUAGE

Rowan Butler, ed., *Documents on British Foreign Policy, 1919-1930*, Second Series (London, 1956—), Vols. I and VIII.

Conference on the Limitations of Armaments (Washington, D.C., 1922).

International Military Tribunal for the Far East, *Record of the Proceedings, Documents, Exhibits, Judgment, Dissent-*

ing Judgments, Preliminary Interrogations, Miscellaneous Documents (mimeographed, Tokyo, 1946-1949).

London Naval Treaty of 1930: Hearings Before the Committee on Naval Affairs, United States Senate (Washington, D.C., 1930).

Manchuria: Report of the Commission of Enquiry Appointed by the League of Nations (Washington, D.C., 1932).

Office of the Chief of Military History has a series of monographs written by Japanese army and naval officers under the aegis of Japanese Research Division, Office of the Military History Officer, United States Army Forces, Far East and the Eighth United States Army. Particularly, "Political Strategy Prior to Outbreak of War," *Japanese Monograph Nos. 144, 146, 147, 150,* and *152.*

Report of the American Delegation on the Conference on the Limitation of Armament (Washington, D.C., 1922).

Ryusaka Tsunoda, *et al., Sources of Japanese Tradition* (New York, 1958).

The Sino-Japanese Negotiations of 1915 (Washington, D.C., 1921).

United States Department of State, *Foreign Relations of the United States* (Washington, D.C., 1948-1956), Vols. III and IV of the 1932-1938 years.

——, *Peace and War, United States Foreign Policy, 1931-1941* (Washington, D.C., 1943).

——, *Documents on German Foreign Policy, 1918-1945,* from the Archives of the German Foreign Ministry, Series D, 1937-1945 (Washington, D.C., 1949).

MEMOIRS, JAPANESE-LANGUAGE

Arita Hachirō, *Hito no me no chiri o miru* [Seeing the Mote in the Eye of Someone Else] (Tokyo, 1955).

——, *Bakuhachi to hito wa yū* [Some People Call Me a Fool] (Tokyo, 1959) .

Fukai Eigo, *Sumitsuin jūjō gigiroku oboegaki* [Notes on the Minutes of the Privy Council] (Tokyo, 1953).

——, *Kaiko shichijūnen* [Recollections of Seventy Years] (Tokyo, 1946).

Hiranuma Kiichirō, *Kaikoroku* [Memoirs] (Tokyo, 1955).

Horinouchi Kanjō, *Chūgoku no arashi no nake de* [In the Midst of the China Storm] (Tokyo, 1950).

Ikeda Junkyū (Sumihisa), *Rikugun sōgi iinchō* [Head of the Funeral Commission of the Army] (Tokyo, 1953).

Ikeda Seihin, *Zaikai kaiko* [Reminiscences of the Financial World] (Tokyo, 1957).

Imamura Hitoshi, *Kaisōroku* [Memoirs], 4 vols. (Tokyo, 1960).

Ishii Itarō, *Gaikōkan no isshō* [Life of a Diplomat] (Tokyo, 1950).

Kamimura Shinichi, *Gaikō gojūnen* [Fifty Years of Diplomacy] (Tokyo, 1960).

Kawabe Torashirō, *Ichigaya dai kara ichigaya dai e: saigo no sanbōjichō no kaisōroku* [From the Heights of Ichigaya to the Heights of Ichigaya: Memoirs of the Last Vice-Chief of the Army General Staff] (Tokyo, 1962).

Kazami Akira, *Konoe naikaku* [The Konoe Cabinet] (Tokyo, 1946).

Konoe Fumimaro no shuki: *ushinuwareshi seiji* [Memorandum of Prince Konoe Fumimaro: Failed Politics] (Tokyo, 1946).

Morishima Morito, *Imbō, ansatsu guntō*: *ichi gaikōkan no kaisō* [Conspiracies, Assassinations, and Sabers: The Recollections of a Diplomat] (Tokyo, 1950).

Okada Keisuke, *Kaisōroku* [Memoirs of Okada Keisuke] (Tokyo, 1950).

Shidehara Kijūrō, *Gaikō gojūnen* [Fifty Years of Diplomacy] (Tokyo, 1951).

Shigemitsu Mamoru, *Shōwa no dōran* [Upheavals of Shōwa Japan] (Tokyo, 1952), 2 vols. An abridged English translation has appeared, *Japan and Her Destiny* (New York, 1958).

——, *Gaikō kaisō roku* [Diplomatic Reminiscences] (Tokyo, 1953).

Tanaka Ryūkichi, *Hai-in o tsuku* [Affixing Responsibility for the Defeat of Japan] (Tokyo, 1946).

Tōgō Shigenori, *Jidai no ichimen* [One Aspect of an Era] (Tokyo, 1952). An abridged English translation, *The Cause of Japan* (New York, 1957), is available.

Tsukui Tatsuo, *Watakushi no shōwashi* [My History of Shōwa Japan] (Tokyo, 1958).

Wakatsuki Reijirō, *Kofūan kaikoroku* [Recollections of Kofuan] (Tokyo, 1950).

Yoshizawa Kenkichi, *Gaikō rokujūnen* [Sixty Years of Diplomacy] (Tokyo, 1958).

MEMOIRS, ENGLISH-LANGUAGE

Hallet Abend, *My Life in China* (New York, 1945).

Chiang Kai-shek, *Soviet Russia in China: A Summing Up at Seventy* (New York, 1957).

Sir Robert Craigie, *Behind the Japanese Mask* (London, 1946).

Joseph C. Grew, *Ten Years in Japan* (New York, 1944).

Sir John Pratt, *War and Politics in China* (London, 1945).

Henry L. Stimson, *The Far Eastern Crisis* (New York, 1936).

Henry L. Stimson and McGeorge Bundy, *On Active Service in Peace and War* (New York, 1947).

Herbert von Dirksen, *Moscow, Tokyo, London: Twenty Years of German Foreign Policy* (London, 1951).

BIOGRAPHICAL STUDIES, JAPANESE-LANGUAGE

Aoki Tokuzō, *Wakatsuki Reijirō: Hamaguchi Yukō* [Biography of Wakatsuki Reijirō and Hamaguchi Yukō] Tokyo, 1958).

Arai Tatsuo, *Katō Tomosaburō* [Biography of Admiral Katō Tomosaburō] (Tokyo, 1958).

Aritake Shuji, *Okada Keisuke* [Biography of Admiral Okada Keisuke] (Tokyo, 1956).

————, *Saitō Makoto* [Biography of Admiral Saitō Makoto] (Tokyo, 1958).

Isa Hidea, *Ozaki Yukio den* [Biography of Ozaki Yukio] (Tokyo, 1951).

Itō Masanori, *Katō Kōmei (Takaaki) den* [Biography of Katō Kōmei] (Tokyo, 1929).

Iwabuchi Tatsuo, *Inukai Ki* [Biography of Inukai Ki] (Tokyo, 1958).

Kawahara Jikichiro, *Katsura Tarō* [Biography of General Katsura Tarō (Tokyo, 1958).

Kono Isao, *Katō Kōmei (Takaaki)* [Biography of Katō Kōmei] (Tokyo, 1958).

Mitarai Tatsuo, *Minami Jirō* [Biography of General Minami Jirō] (Tokyo, 1957).

Obata Toriyoshi denki [Biography of Obata Toriyoshi] (Tokyo, 1957).

Odachi Shigeo denki [Biography of Odachi Shigeo] (Tokyo, 1958).

Ogata Taketora, *Ichigun gunjin no shōgai: kaisō no Yonai Mitsumasa* [Life of One Naval Officer: Recollections of Admiral Yonai Mitsumasa] (Tokyo, 1951).

Oka Yoshitake, *Yamagata Aritomo* [Life of Prince Yamagata Aritomo] (Tokyo, 1958).

Okada Takeo, *Konoe Fumimaro: Tennō to gunbu to kokumin* [Konoe Fumimaro: The Emperor, the Military, and the People] (Tokyo, 1959).

Oki Osamuji, *Ninmen Yamashita Tomoyuki* (Hōbun) [General Yamashita Tomoyuki] (Tokyo, 1959).

Satō Kenryō, *Tōjō Hideki to taiheiyō sensō* [General Tōjō and the Pacific War] (Tokyo, 1960).

Sorimachi Eiichi, *Ningen Yamamoto Isoroku* [Biography of Admiral Yamamoto Isoroku] (Tokyo, 1964).

Takagi Sōkichi, *Yamamoto Isoroku to Yonai Mitsumasa* [Biography of Admirals Yamamoto Isoroko and Yonai Mitsumasa] (Tokyo, 1958).

Tanaka Giichi denki kankokai, *Tanaka Giichi denki* [Biography of General Tanaka Giichi], 2 vols. (Tokyo, 1960).

Tanaka Sōgorō, *Nihon fuashizuma no genryū: Kita Ikki no shisō to shogai* [The Source of Japanese Fascism: The Life and Thought of Kita Ikki] (Tokyo, 1954).

Ujita Naogi, *Shidehara Kijūrō* [Biography of Baron Shidehara Kijūrō] (Tokyo, 1958).

Watanabe Ikujiro, *Ōkuma Shigenobu* [Biography of Ōkuma Shigenobu] (Tokyo, 1952).

Yabe Teiji, *Konoe Fumimaro* [Biography of Prince Konoe Fumimaro], 2 vols. (Tokyo, 1952).

Yamaguchi Jūji, *Higenki no shōgun: Ishiwara Kanji* [Ishiwara Kanji, The Tragic General] (Tokyo, 1952).

BIOGRAPHICAL STUDIES, ENGLISH-LANGUAGE

Burton Beers, *Vain Endeavor: Robert Lansing's Attempts to End the American-Japanese Rivalry* (Durham, 1962).

Robert Butow, *Tojo and the Coming of the War* (Princeton, 1961).

L. Ethan Ellis, *Frank B. Kellogg and American Foreign Relations, 1925-1929* (New Brunswick, N.J., 1962).

Elting Morrison, *Turmoil and Tradition: A Study of the Life and Times of Henry L. Stimson* (Boston, 1960).

Armin Rappaport, *Henry L. Stimson and Japan, 1931-1933* (Chicago, 1963).

A. Frank Reel, *The Case of General Yamashita* (Chicago, 1949).

Earl A. Selle, *Donald of China* (New York, 1948).

DIPLOMATIC HISTORY, JAPANESE-LANGUAGE

Aoki Tokuzō, *Taiheiyō sensō zenshi* [History of the Period Prior to the Pacific War], 3 vols. (Tokyo, 1952).

Ashida Hitoshi, *Dainiji sekai taisen gaikōshi* [Diplomatic History of the Second World War] (Tokyo, 1960).

Eguchi Bokuro, *et al., Taiheiyō sensōshi* [History of the Pacific War], 6 vols. (Tokyo, 1952).

Hattori Shiso, *Nihon kindai gaikōshi* [Diplomatic History of Modern Japan] (Tokyo, 1954).

Hosoya Chihiro, *Shiberiya suppei no shiteki kenkyū* [Historical Investigation of the Siberian Intervention] (Tokyo, 1955).

Kiyozawa Kiyoshi, *Nihon gaikōshi* [History of Japanese Diplomacy], 2 vols. (Tokyo, 1941).

Kurihara Ken, *Tennō: shōwashi oboegaki* [The Emperor: Notes on Shōwa History] (Tokyo, 1955).

Nihon kokusai seiji gakkai [Japan Association of International Relations], *Taiheiyō sensō e no michi* [Road to the Pacific War], 8 vols. (Tokyo, 1963).

    Vol. I: *Manshū jihen zen'ya* [Eve of the Manchurian Incident].

    Vol. II: *Manshū jihen* [Manchurian Incident].

    Vol. III: *NiChū sensō* (jo) [Sino-Japanese War—Part I].

    Vol. IV: *NiChū sensō* (ge) [Sino-Japanese War—Part II].

    Vol. V: *Sankoku dōmei: NichiSō chūritsu jōyaku* [Tripartite Alliance: Soviet Japanese Neutrality Pact].

    Vol. VIII: *Betsukan shiryōhen* [Special Volume: Collection of Documents].

Royama Masamichi, *Tōa ni kansuru jōyaku to gaikō* [Diplomacy and Treaties in Greater East Asia] (Tokyo, 1942).

Shinobu Seizaburo, *Kindai nihon gaikōshi* [Diplomatic History of Modern Japan] (Tokyo, 1948).

——, *Nihon no gaikō* [Japanese Diplomacy] (Tokyo, 1961).

Togawa Isamu, *Shōwa gaikōshi* [Shōwa Diplomatic History] (Tokyo, 1962).

Toyama Shigeki, *et al.*, *Shōwashi* [History of the Shōwa Period] (Tokyo, 1955; revised ed., 1959).

Ueda Toshio, ed., *Taiheiyō sensō genin ron* [Essays on the Origins of the Pacific War] (Tokyo, 1952).

DIPLOMATIC HISTORY, ENGLISH-LANGUAGE

Reginald Bassett, *Democracy and Foreign Policy* (London, 1952).

Thomas A. Bisson, *Japan in China* (New York, 1938).

Dorothy Borg, *Far Eastern Crisis of 1933-1938* (Cambridge, Mass., 1964).

Raymond L. Buell, *The Washington Conference* (New York, 1922).

Council on Foreign Relations, *Survey of American Foreign Relations, 1931* (New Haven, 1931).

Alexander de Conde, ed., *Isolation and Security* (Durham, 1957).

Robert A. Devine, *The Illusion of Neutrality* (Chicago, 1962).

Robert H. Ferrell, *American Diplomacy in the Great Depression* (New Haven, 1957).

——, *Peace in Their Time: The Origins of the Kellogg-Briand Pact* (New Haven, 1952).

Russell H. Fifield, *Woodrow Wilson and the Far East: The Diplomacy of the Shantung Question* (New York, 1952).

A. Whitney Griswold, *The Far Eastern Policy of the United States* (New York, 1938).

Francis C. Jones, *Japan's New Order in East Asia* (London, 1954).

George Kennan, *American Diplomacy, 1900-1950* (Chicago, 1951).

Walter Lippmann, *Interpretations, 1931-1932* (New York, 1932).

Charles B. McLane, *Soviet Policy and the Chinese Communists* (New York, 1958).

James Morley, *Japanese Thrust into Siberia* (New York, 1957).

Shigenobu Okuma (comp.), *Fifty Years of New Japan* (London, 1909), 2 vols.

Ernst L. Presseisen, *Germany and Japan: A Study in Totalitarian Diplomacy, 1933-1941* (The Hague, 1958).

Royal Institute of International Affairs, *Survey of International Affairs, 1936* (London, 1937); *1937* (London, 1938).

Masamichi Royama, *Foreign Policy of Japan, 1914-1939* (Tokyo, 1941).

Tatsuji Takeuchi, *War and Diplomacy in the Japanese Empire* (New York, 1935).

George E. Taylor, *The Struggle for North China* (New York, 1940).

Eleanor Tupper and George McReynolds, *Japan in American Public Opinion* (New York, 1937).

Gerald E. Wheeler, *Prelude to Pearl Harbor* (Columbia, Mo., 1963).

Westel W. Willoughby, *The Sino-Japanese Controversy and the League of Nations* (Baltimore, 1935).

Chitoshi Yanaga, *Japan Since Perry* (New York, 1949).

MILITARY AND MILITARISM, JAPANESE-LANGUAGE

Fujiwara Akira, *Gunjishi* [History of the Military] (Tokyo, 1961).

Fukudome Shigeru, *Shikan shinjuwan kōgeki* [A Historical View of the Attack on Pearl Harbor] (Tokyo, 1955).

Gunreibu (Naval General Staff), *Taiheiyō sensō kaigun senshi* [Naval History of the Pacific War], undated but written in the winter of 1942.

Hata Ikuhito, *Gun fuashizumu undōshi* [History of the Movement of Military Fascism] (Tokyo, 1962).

——, *NiChū sensōshi* [History of the Sino-Japanese War] (Tokyo, 1961).

Hayashi Saburo, *Taiheiyō sensō rikusen gaishi* [General Military History of the Pacific War] (Tokyo, 1950).

Horiba Kazuo, *Shina jihen sensō shidōshi* [Operational History of the Chinese Incident], 2 vols. (Tokyo, 1962).

Inoue Kiyoshi, *Nihon no gunkokushugi* [Japanese Militarism] (Tokyo, 1953).

Itō Masanori, *Gunbatsu kōbōshi* [Rise and Fall of Army Cliques], 3 vols. (Tokyo, 1958).

Iwabuchi Tatsuo, *Gunbatsu no keifu* [Genealogy of Military Cliques] (Tokyo, 1948).

Maeda Haruyoshi, *Shōwa hanranshi* [History of the Shōwa Rebellions] (Tokyo, 1964).

Maejima Ken, *Gunbatsu antō hishi* [Secret History of the Feuds Within the Army Cliques] (Tokyo, 1946).

Maruyama Masao, *Gendai seiji no shisō to kōdō* [Thought and Movement of Modern Politics] (Tokyo, 1957). In particular, the essay, "Nihon fuashizumu no shisō to undō" [Ideological Movement of Japanese Politics].

———, *Thought and Behavior in Modern Japanese Politics*, ed. by Ivan Morris (New York, 1963), is an excellent translation of Maruyama's main essays.

Matsushita Yoshio, *Nihon gunji hattatsushi* [History of the Development of the Japanese Military] (Tokyo, 1937).

———, *Meiji gunsei shiron* [Historical Essays on the Meiji Military Organization], 2 vols. (Tokyo, 1955).

———, *Nihon gunsei to seiji* [Politics and the Japanese Military System] (Tokyo, 1960).

Otani Keijiro, *Rakujitsu no jōshō: shōwa rikugunshi* [Prelude to Sunset: A History of the Shōwa Army] (Tokyo, 1959).

Suzuki Teiichi, *Kokubō kokka no kōryō* [Essential Points of the National Defense State] (Tokyo, 1941).

Takagi Sōkichi, *RikuKai gunjin kishitsu no sōi* [Character Differences between Army and Naval Officers] (Naval War College, 1944).

Tateno Nobuyuki, *Shōwa gunbatsu* [Shōwa Military Cliques] (Tokyo, 1963).

MILITARY AND MILITARISM, ENGLISH-LANGUAGE

E. E. N. Causton, *Militarism and Foreign Policy in Japan* (London, 1936).

Outten Clinard, *Japan's Influence on American Naval Power* (Berkeley, 1947).

Kenneth W. Colegrove, *Militarism in Japan* (Boston, 1936).

John Maki, *Japanese Militarism* (New York, 1945).

Yale Maxon, *Control of Japanese Foreign Policy* (Berkeley, 1957).

Sadako N. Ogata, *Defiance in Manchuria: The Making of Japanese Foreign Policy, 1931-1932* (Berkeley, 1964).

Harold and Margaret Sprout, *Toward a New Order of Sea Power* (Princeton, 1943).

O. Tanin and E. Yohan, *Militarism and Fascism in Japan* (New York, 1934).

Alfred Vagts, *A History of Militarism* (New York, 1936).

POLITICAL HISTORY, JAPANESE-LANGUAGE

Baba Tsunego, *Konoe naikakushi ron* [Essay on the Konoe Cabinet] (Tokyo, 1946).

Eguchi Bokuro, *Teikoku shugi to minzoku* [Imperialism and the Japanese People] (Tokyo, 1949).

Hosokawa Morisada, *Jōhō Tennō ni tassezu* [Information Does Not Reach the Emperor], 2 vols. (Tokyo, 1953).

Iwabuchi Tatsuo, *Yaburu hi made* [Until the Day of Defeat] (Tokyo, 1946).

Kinoshita Hanji, *Nihon fuashizumushi* [History of Japanese Fascism], 3 vols. (Tokyo, 1951-1952).

——, *Nihon kokka-shugi undōshi* [History of the Movement of Japanese Nationalism] (Tokyo, 1952).

Maejima Shōzō, *Nihon fuashizumu to gikai* [The Diet and Japanese Fascism] (Tokyo, 1956).

Mita Takeo, *Sensō to kyōsan-shugi: shōwa seiji hishi* [Communism and the War: A Secret History of Shōwa Politics] (Tokyo, 1950).

Nakamura Kikuo, *Shōwa seijishi* [Political History of the Shōwa Period] (Tokyo, 1958).

Nezu Masashi, *Dai nihon teikoku no hōkai* [The Collapse of Imperial Japan] (Tokyo, 1961).

Sakuta Kotaro, *Tennō to Kido* [The Emperor and Marquis Kido] (Tokyo, 1948).

Takamiya Tahei, *Tennō Heika* [Emperor Hirohito] (Tokyo, 1951).

Yamazaki Tansho, *Naikaku seido no kenkyū* [Study of the Cabinet System] (Tokyo, 1951).

POLITICAL HISTORY, ENGLISH-LANGUAGE

Hugh Borton, *Japan Since 1931: Its Political and Social Development* (New York, 1940).

Hugh Byas, *Government by Assassination* (New York, 1942).

Maruyama Masao, *Thought and Behavior in Modern Japanese Politics* (New York, 1963), edited by Ivan Morris.

Robert A. Scalapino, *Democracy and the Party Movement in Prewar Japan* (Berkeley, 1953).

Richard Storry, *The Double Patriots* (London, 1957).

A. Morgan Young, *Imperial Japan, 1926-1938* (New York, 1938).

ARTICLES, JAPANESE-LANGUAGE

Chūō kōron (November 1954) has a supplement which includes famous articles from past issues.

PARTICULARLY

Inomata Tsunao, "Nōmin to fuashizumu" [The Peasant and Fascism], 339-351, which appeared in July 1935.

Minobe Tatsukichi, "Rikugunshō hatten no kokubōron o yomu" [A Reading of the Essay on National Defense Published by the War Ministry], 328-335, which appeared in November 1935.

Hata Ikuhito, "Sakurakai shuisho" [Document on the Purpose of the Cherry Society], *Rekishi kyōiku* [Teaching of History], VI, 2 (1958), 81-89.

——, "Umezu Ka Ō-kin kyōtei keii" [Particulars of the Ho-Umezu Agreement], *Aziya kenkyū* [Asian Studies], IV, 2 (1957), 65-114.

——, "Rikugun no hanbatsu 'sakurakai' " [Regional Cliques of the Army, the Sakurakai], *Jiyū* [Freedom], III, 3 (1960), 88-101.

——, "Gō ichi gō jiken" [May 15th Incident], *Jiyū*, III, 4 (1960), 82-137

——, "Tōseiha—kōdōha" [The Control and Imperial Way Factions], *Jiyū*, III, 5 (1960), 78-90.

——, "Ni-ni-roku jiken" [February 26th Incident], *Jiyū*, III, 6 (1960), 96-108.

Hata Ikuhito and Shimizu Setsuro, "Ryōkōko jiken" [Marco Polo Bridge Incident], *Aziya kenkyū*, III, 2 (1956), 80-97.

Himerareta shōwashi [Secret History of Shōwa Japan] (Tokyo, 1956). This is a special issue of *Chisei* and it includes the personal recollections of Generals Suzuki Teiichi, Araki Sadao, Ikeda Junkyū, Imamura Hitoshi, Katakura Chū, Tanaka Shinichi, Imai Takeo, and Tanaka Ryūkichi.

Ikeda Junkyū, "Tōseiha to kōdōha" [The Control Faction and the Imperial Way Faction], *Bungei shunjū* [Literary Criticism], XXXIV, 2 (1956), 92-108.

Ishii Kinichiro, "Kita Ikki to seinen shōkō" [Kita Ikki and the Young Officers], *Shisō* [Thought], 404 (February 1958), 59-74.

Kawamura Zenjiro, "Hara Kei naikaku" [The Hara Kei Cabinet], *Rekishi kyōiku* [Teaching of History], VIII 2 (February 1960), 35-40.

Kurihara Ken, "Daichiji dainiji ManMō dokuritsu undō" [First and Second Manchurian-Mongolian Independence Movement], *Nihon gaikōshi kenkyū: Taishō jidai* [Studies of Japan's Diplomatic History: Taishō Era] (Tokyo, 1958), 52-64.

Oyama Adzusa, "Yamagata Aritomo 'Teikoku kokubō hoshin-an'" [Yamagata Aritomo's Proposal for the National Defense Policy of the Empire], *Nihon gaikōshi kenkyū: Meiji jidai* [Studies in Japan's Diplomatic History: The Meiji Era] (Tokyo, 1967), 170-177.

Shimada Toshiko, "Umezu Ka Ō-kin kyōtei no seiritsu" [Conclusion of the Ho-Umezu Agreement], *Nihon gaikōshi kenkyū: Shōwa jidai* [Studies in Japan's Diplomatic History: Shōwa Era] (Tokyo, 1959), 50-70.

Shisō [Thought], 399 (September 1957), is a special issue on "Nihon no gunkokushugi" [Japanese Militarism]. Of particular interest,

Imai Seiichi, "Taishōgo ni okeru gunbu no seijiteki

chii" [Political Position of the Military in the Taishō Period], 3-21. Second part of this article appears in *Shisō*, 402 (December 1957), 106-122.

Fujiwara Akira, "Sōryokusen dankai ni okeru nihon guntai no mujun" [Contradictions of the Total War Movement in the Japanese Army], 22-32.

Usui Katsumi, "Tanaka gaikō ni tsuite no oboegaki" [Memorandum on Tanaka Diplomacy], *Nihon gaikōshi kenkyū: Shōwa jidai*, 26-35.

——, "Cho Sakurin bakushi no shinso" [True Story of the Explosion which killed Chang Tso-lin], *Himerareta shōwashi* (Tokyo, 1956), 26-39.

——, "Shidehara gaikō oboegaki" [Memorandum on Shidehara Diplomacy], *Nihon rekishi* [Japanese History], 126 (December 1958), 62-68.

——, "Chūgoku no taisen sanku to nihon no tachiba" [China's Participation in the First World War: From a Japanese Viewpoint], *Rekishi kyōiku* [Teaching of History], VIII, 2 (1960), 22-28.

ARTICLES, ENGLISH-LANGUAGE

James B. Crowley, "Japanese Army Factionalism in the Early 1930's," *Journal of Asian Studies*, XXI, 3 (May 1962) 309-326.

——, "A Reconsideration of the Marco Polo Bridge Incident," *ibid.*, XXII, 3 (May 1963), 277-291.

Richard N. Current, "The Stimson Doctrine and the Hoover Doctrine," *American Historical Review*, 59 (1953-1954), 513-542.

Robert H. Ferrell, "The Mukden Incident, September 18-19, 1931," *Journal of Modern History*, XXVII, 1 (March 1955), 66-72.

Fukuda Ippei, "Araki—the Man of the Crisis," *Contemporary Japan*, I, 3 (December 1932), 385-394.

Akira Iriye, "Chang Hseuh-liang and the Japanese," *Journal of Asian Studies*, XX, (November 1960), 37-41.

Viscount Kikujiro Ishii, "The Permanent Bases of Japanese

Foreign Policy," *Foreign Affairs*, xi, 2 (January 1930), 220-229.

Walter Lippmann, "The London Naval Conference: An American View," *Foreign Affairs*, viii, 4 (July 1930), 499-532.

Richard Storry, "The Mukden Incident of September 18-19, 1931," *Far Eastern Affairs*: *Number One* (St. Antony's Papers, No. 2), 1-12.

———, "Konoye Fumimaro, 'The Last of the Fujiwara,'" *Far Eastern Affairs*: *Number Two* (St. Antony's Papers, No. 7), 9-23.

Payson Treat, "Shanghai, January 28, 1932," *Pacific Historical Review*, ix, 3 (September 1940), 337-343.

INDEX

Abe, General, 275
Adachi, Kenzō, 137, 149, 169
Adams, Brooks, 3
Aikyō juku (Land Loving School), 174
Aizawa, Lt. Colonel Saburo, 224, 274; assassinates Nagata, 266-67; trial of, 267-71
Akamatsu, Katsumaro, 138
Akao, Bin, 253
Amau statement, 196-97
American Naval Board, 36, 37, 44, 55, 65
Anglo-Japanese Alliance, 5, 11, 27, 30
Anti-Comintern Pact, 303-06
Araki, General Sadao, 85, 91, 111, 116, 125, 152, 159, 207, 246-47, 252-53, 274-78, 382, 392; anti-Choshū bias, 254-55; becomes war minister, 153; condemns February 26 rebels, 273; crisis of 1936, 202, 205-06, 253-54; criticizes assassins of Inukai, 178; Kōdō rhetoric, 203-04; opposes Inukai, 170; opposes removal of Mazaki, 261-62; partiality toward Tosa-Saga officers, 254-55; patronage of Obata, 203-04; purges Nagata, Tōjō, Umezu, 204-05, 254; purges senior staff officers, 202-03; rebukes Akao Bin, 253; resignation of, 201-06; urges seizure of Jehol, 183-84. *See also* Imperial Way faction
Arita, Hachirō, 291-92, 295
Ariyoshi, Ambassador, 233-38
army: 1907 defense policy, 5-6, 10; 1936 defense policy, 282-85; *à l'outrance* philosophy, 86; Diet criticism of, 14, 311-12; economic planning, 282-85; evaluates 1913 Chinese revolution, 17-18; forces dissolution of Second Saionji cabinet, 12-13; four-division reduction of, 30, 87-88; general traits of officer corps, 83-84; military incidents, 83, 93-102, 114-26, 173-80, 244-79, 324-38; total war philoso-

phy, 88-90, 142; two division expansion problem, 152. *See also* army factionalism; army general staff; Big Three of army; China incident; Manchurian incident; North China "autonomy movement"; Shanghai incident; (Supreme War Council) war ministry; [war ministers] Araki, Sadao; Hayashi, Senjurō; Mazaki, Jinzaburō; Minami, Jirō; Nagata, Tetsuzan; Ugaki, Issei
army factionalism: Aizawa trial, 262-72; appraisals of, 246-49, 276-79, 323; Araki's policies as minister, 202-06; assassination of Nagata, 266; China group, 96-97; control faction (Tōsei-ha), 245-49, 266; control movement (tōsei-undō), 255-56, 277-78, 383-84; hanbatsu, 85-86, 96; Hayashi's policies as minister, 206-07; Imperial Way Faction (Kōdō-ha), 99, 203, 206, 246-47, 249-62, 269-70, 271-72, 392-93; National Principle Group (*Kokutai genri-ha*), 173-77, 251-52, 263-65; officer career patterns, 83-85; Purification Group (*Seigun-ha*), 254-55, 266, 273-74, 383; young officers, 172-73, 265-66. *See also* Araki, Sadao; Hayashi, Senjurō; March incident; May 15 incident; Mazaki, Jinzaburō; Military Academy incident; Nagata, Tetsuzan; October incident; Ugaki, Issei; Yanagawa, Heisuke
army general staff: authorizes Nanking attack, 358; complicity in Mukden incident, 116-17, 119-21, 122-25, 127-28, 136, 148; 1931 view of Manchuria, 111; 1936 North China policy, 243; prevents seizure of North Manchuria, 128-29, 133, 141, 144; urges settlement of China war, 351-54, 356-57, 359-62, 365, 367-69, 373-75. *See also* Araki, Sadao; Imamura,